A Host at Last

Also by Abram L. Sachar

A HISTORY OF THE JEWS

SUFFERANCE IS THE BADGE

THE COURSE OF OUR TIMES

A Host at Last

by ABRAM L. SACHAR
Chancellor of Brandeis University

An Atlantic Monthly Press Book

LITTLE, BROWN AND COMPANY • BOSTON • TORONTO

FIRST EDITION

T 11/76

LIBRARY OF CONGRESS CATALOGING IN PUBLICATION DATA

Sachar, Abram Leon, 1899–
   A host at last.

   "An Atlantic Monthly Press book."
   Includes index.
   1. Brandeis University, Waltham, Mass. – History.
I. Title.
LD571.B42S22   378.744'4   76–20452
ISBN 0–316–76590–2

ATLANTIC–LITTLE, BROWN BOOKS
ARE PUBLISHED BY
LITTLE, BROWN AND COMPANY
IN ASSOCIATION WITH
THE ATLANTIC MONTHLY PRESS

Published simultaneously in Canada
by Little, Brown & Company (Canada) Limited

PRINTED IN THE UNITED STATES OF AMERICA

To the students of the first twenty years, who helped give Brandeis
its image of intellectual vitality and passionate concern
for the underprivileged and disinherited

Foreword

Launching a privately sponsored university in the mid-twentieth century, without an initial capital endowment and without hope of alumni support for at least a generation, presented many problems that earlier universities did not have to face. I have attempted here, after a twenty-year incumbency as the first president, to select the highlights in the story of the unusual means that were attempted to fulfill the high hopes of the founders. Of course, not every contribution in academic planning and in crucial resources could be detailed. The narrative is highly selective, but I hope enough is included to explain how this little Benjamin in the clan won its place in the fellowship of quality universities and is likely to retain it.

I am beholden to many good friends, loyal staff, and faculty colleagues for their help with the manuscript that improved its accuracy and perspective. There is room here only for general thanks to them, no less sincere, however, when it is not individually identified. But there is a very special debt to Natalie Greenberg, my editor at the Atlantic Monthly Press; to my former research assistant, Marylou Buckley, now with Boston College; and to my son Howard, professor of history at George Washington University, all of whom scrutinized the entire text and were affectionately ruthless in modifying judgments that were inevitably subjective when they were offered by one who had the responsibility for two decades of day-by-day activities. Above all, there is an inexpressible debt to my wife. In the preparation of my other volumes I could count on her sacrificial patience and good critical judgment. Here I was writing the story of a university in whose building she was an invaluable collaborator: it is her story as much as mine.

Brandeis University
Waltham, Massachusetts
March 1976

Contents

A Host at Last

I

The American Tradition
of Privately Sponsored Colleges

FROM the earliest days of American history, higher education was considered the special province and responsibility of the denominational groups. The founding fathers looked to the clergy and their parishioners to teach the young, guide their elders, and to convert the Indians. In 1636, a tubercular young Puritan minister, John Harvard, who had been educated at Emmanuel College in Cambridge, England, bequeathed his little library and a few hundred pounds to establish a college on the Charles River in the Massachusetts Bay Colony, hoping that it would help to train "a learned clergy and a lettered people." The General Court was so overwhelmed by the magnitude of the gift that it ordered the new Cambridge school to be henceforth called "Harvard Colledge." Unfortunately, John Harvard's munificence was not enough to ensure the school's survival. It quickly fell upon hard times and had to suspend operations. Studies were not resumed until Henry Dunster, an English curate, became president in 1640. He was the sole faculty member and four students were enrolled in his classes. Dunster proved to be a good administrator and promoter, but in 1653 he horrified the colony by turning Baptist. He was fired as president, publicly admonished, and was placed under bond "to keep the peace." Lack of funds continued to plague the college until a group of Congregationalist ministers, the Harvard Corporation of the time, hesitantly petitioned the General Court to use some of the principal of the college's first substantial money gift, the one hundred pounds sterling that Ann Radcliffe, Lady Mowlson, had contributed to form the nucleus of a scholarship fund. The court, aghast at the suggestion of encroaching upon a trust, refused, and instead assigned the tolls and the rentals from the Charlestown ferry to tide Harvard over its difficulties. Of course, since nothing is as permanent as what is enacted as temporary, the tolls continued to be paid to Harvard for two hundred years. During this same period, the towns and villages of the colony assessed themselves voluntarily — so many bushels of grain, cords of wood, and like provender — to keep the college alive. This forerunner of annual giving, known as "the colledge corn," kept Harvard functioning precariously until hard cash became more common in the new world.

The base of Harvard's support ultimately came from those who were urged by the clergy to protect a beleaguered faith from the erosion of the irresponsibles. The Commencement speaker of 1677 observed sadly, "Mad nobodies, haranguers at street corners, have more influence with the populace than reverent men, filled with the singular gifts of the divine spirit." Solicitation for contributions remained primary in the tasks of the president and the Corporation, to save the faith as well as to make sure that a little bit of England was preserved and sustained on the banks of the Charles; and many of Harvard's early gifts came, like those of Ann Radcliffe, from the mother country.

William and Mary, founded in 1693, and named for the reigning British sovereigns, was linked from the outset with the Episcopal tradition dominant in Virginia. Its charter obligated the college to educate youth piously "in good letters and manners" and to "propagate the Episcopal faith among the Indians." A duty on exports of tobacco was assigned to supplement its perpetually insecure budget. It took strenuous debate to enact the tax; the attorney general was not overly impressed by the claim that the college would help save souls. He interrupted the initial debates with the shout: "Souls! Damn your souls! Raise tobacco!" Financial problems continued to threaten the existence of the college, and it was necessary to persuade the legislature to preempt the taxes on peddlers and export duties on skins and furs. Financial problems were never shaken off and the college closed twice, for years at a time, during both the Revolution and the Civil War. Ultimately it had to become a unit of the Virginia public educational system.

In 1701, Yale was launched by Congregationalist clergy, themselves Harvardians, who were especially concerned to counteract the softening of the Puritan tradition at Harvard, which was beginning to earn the label of "godless." One group of frustrated hard-liners among the pioneering trustees pleaded their case with a metaphor. "The affair of our school," they wrote, "hath been in a Condition of Pregnancy: Painfull with a witness have been the Throwes thereof in this General Assembly; But we just now hear, that after the violent pangs threatening the very life of the babe, divine providence as a kind of obstetrix hath mercifully brought the babe into the world, and behold a man-child is born, whereat we all rejoice." Perhaps it was the uniqueness of the metaphor that helped to win the support of an American-born English merchant, Elihu Yale, who had amassed a fortune as a director of the East India Company. The appeal by Cotton Mather, who became president of Yale, offered a brand of immortality that proved irresistible. "Sir, though you may have your felicities in your family . . . yet certainly if what is forming at New Haven might bear the name of Yale College, it would be better than an Egyptian Pyramid." Elihu's contribution took the form of nine bales of merchandise, mainly dry goods, valued at about $550. The gift was considered critical enough to redeem Cotton Mather's promise. Old Elihu protested that what he was doing was little enough and did not deserve such acclaim, but he accepted the honor and was proud of it.

Disciples of the "new light," in the revival of Presbyterianism, broke away from Yale to found Princeton in 1746, Timothy Dwight and the senior Aaron Burr being among its first presidents. Princeton had to cope with physical as well as fiscal problems in its early years; its presidents almost invariably succumbed to fever soon after they assumed office. It became necessary for its representatives to travel to Scotland, preaching and begging funds from Scottish Presbyterian congregations, themselves very much down at the heel too. Not until a sturdier Scotsman, John Witherspoon, was induced to migrate to New Jersey in 1768 did Princeton begin to enjoy relative stability. The practice of raiding congregations to acquire presidents never ceased, and every head of Princeton, including Woodrow Wilson, was a Presbyterian minister or the son of one. As the college so often deprived congregations of their ministers to serve as faculty, it tried to make up for its pure-hearted pilferage through consolation payments to the bereft churches, a kind of academic alimony.

Columbia, founded as King's College in 1754, was funded by the contributions of Episcopalians supplemented by the proceeds of a lottery. When an outcry was raised, the college yielded half of the revenue so that New York could build a jail and a pesthouse. Having yielded for such a purpose, there was little problem when the campus was moved in 1897 from its original site to the grounds of an insane asylum on Morningside Heights. The president was invariably a communicant of the faith, and far into the twentieth century it required a special change in the bylaws of Columbia to name Dwight Eisenhower president, since he belonged to a small Kansas sect, the Church of the Brethren.

In truth very few of the newly established colleges of New England and the East could escape the hazards of precarious support. Pioneering a college was rarely related to peace of mind. But neither was insecurity a deterrent. Ingenious methods were often devised to supplement resources. In the 1820s, a network of Kenyon Circles of Industry was organized, local sewing clubs whose members undertook the support of Kenyon College as their project. Ministers rounded out starvation salaries by soliciting subscriptions, taking a percentage so that they and their families could survive. If all such strenuous efforts still left the colleges financially vulnerable, this was to be expected. After all, the faculty and administrators were doing God's work and they had no right to expect assured security. As late as 1869, when Charles Eliot was inaugurated as president of Harvard, he hailed the impecunious status of the faculty as an inspiring example of self-sacrifice in a materialist society. He noted: "The poor scholars and preachers of duty defend the modern community against its own material prosperity. Luxury and learning are ill bed-fellows."

Brown University was founded in 1764 as a Baptist bailiwick under the name Rhode Island College. It was a continuous struggle to keep its doors open, and the word went out that "the corporation at their last meeting passed a resolution that if any person would, previous to the next Commencement, give to the college six thousand dollars, he would have the right to name it." Similar philanthropic bargains were offered by other struggling colleges, and as they received the stipulated sum they accepted the names of their benefactors — James Bowdoin, William Denison, Henry Rutgers, William Carleton. Nicholas Brown got an even better deal: Rhode Island became Brown at a discount, with only a five-thousand-dollar contribution. But he soon found that he was on a treadmill and his initial down payment ultimately expanded to $160,000. In his instance there was no regret. Brown was genuinely interested in the university, and his gifts, especially for an endowed chair in belles lettres and the humanities, came from a whole heart.

None of the Protestant-founded institutions could escape financial anxieties, for virtually none had endowments. Between 1850 and 1866 twenty-five colleges were abandoned when those who had the means to be helpful remained uninterested. The pioneering enthusiasts turned to the poor, and the colleges that survived made do with their humble offerings and the services of their underpaid ministers.

In the thirteen colonies, Catholics were few in number and as little welcome as Jews and Quakers. In the infant republic the Catholic stronghold, such as it was, centered around Baltimore and Washington. Maryland had been founded by wealthy English Catholics as a refuge and, although the Acts of Toleration of 1649 had long since been legally rescinded, they were by and large observed in practice. Meanwhile, descendants of the founding families welcomed a thin trickle of Catholic immigrants. Among these were Roman Catholic priests who had been members of the Society of Jesus until the order was suppressed throughout the world in 1773 by Pope Clement XIV, himself under pressure from various governments that felt threatened.

By 1789 Bishop John Carroll of Baltimore, a relative of the more famous Charles, one of the signers of the Declaration of Independence, was anxious to found a Catholic college. Without it there would be few opportunities for Catholics to obtain a higher education in their own country and an even gloomier prospect for a native-born clergy. Carroll, himself Jesuit-educated, obtained a charter for a college at Georgetown and requested the doubly exiled Jesuits to serve as its faculty. They were reluctant. The reestablishment of their order depended upon keeping a low profile, and besides, many of them feared they had been too long away from teaching and scholarship. Even after 1806, when permission was granted to restore the Society of Jesus in the United States and Georgetown became an acknowledged Jesuit institution, the faculty continued to refer to itself simply as "the Gentlemen of Maryland," so tenuous was their hope of complete acceptance. Georgetown was no wealthier than any other young denominational college, but it possessed, as would other Catholic colleges and universities, a "living endowment" in the unpaid services of celibate members of their religious orders.

The growth of Catholic-founded colleges and universities in the United States in the nineteenth century to more than two hundred by 1900 was made possible by two providential developments. First came the acquisition, through the Louisiana Purchase, of former French and Spanish territories, where French Jesuits had laid the foundations for what would become St. Louis University and other colleges. Then came the tidal wave of immigration in the later 1840s, set off by the famines and crop failures that swept northern Europe from westernmost Ireland to East Poland. Catholics gravitated in large numbers to the big cities, and it was primarily in such centers that the Catholic-sponsored colleges were established and grew to impressive influence; Georgetown and St. Louis were followed by Fordham, Boston College, Loyola, and many others.

The Quakers fostered a constellation of colleges that began in Pennsylvania and then fanned out to many parts of the country. A highly unpopular sect, the Quakers had a special interest in the founding of such colleges. As pacifists, they had opposed fighting in the American Revolution and had been equated with the Loyalists, most of whom had fled to Canada in the bitter quarrels of the War for Independence. They were model citizens, demonstrating a rare talent for becoming prosperous without resorting to "sinful" but lucrative trading in slaves and rum. In 1836, they founded the oldest publishing house in North America, J. B. Lippincott and Company. Their philanthropy, often unidentified publicly, worked its beneficence quietly and modestly. Yet nothing that they did — or did not do — helped to restore an image of trust and favor. They could not live down the opprobrium that had been generated when the colonies were fighting for survival. In the mid-nineteenth century some of their leaders expressed the conviction that the establishment of colleges and preparatory schools, dedicated to the highest standards, would be a much more practical way to establish a new image. Every religious denomination had been making superb contributions to American higher education. Why not the Quakers? Such an approach might very well remove the blemishing misconception of disloyalty. The counsel was followed, and soon a network of choice colleges came into being — Haverford, Swarthmore, Bryn Mawr, Earlham, and others. Within a generation, the Quaker name had been completely rehabilitated.

As Americans moved west, church and college moved with them and were among the earliest concerns of the pioneers. The need to preserve religious loyalty remained as vital in the colleges of the Middle West and the West as in the East and the South. New England Congregationalists opened up the Northwest Territory, and such colleges as Oberlin in Ohio almost immediately came into being. The founding principal of Oberlin, John H. Shepherd, took it as his mission to the Northwest, in 1833, to save its people from "rum, brandy, gin, whiskey" and the church from "Romanists, Atheists, Deists, Universalists, and all classes of God's enemies." Yet within a short period the objectives of Oberlin had been sufficiently liberalized for the college to become the first institution in the country to admit women students on an even footing with men. From the outset it had placed no bar on the basis of color, and it played a heroic role in the antislavery movement by sacrificial cooperation with the Underground Railroad. In addition, Oberlin had a special welcome for "wayward girls from New York City who were to be rehabilitated."

It was clear then, before the explosive expansion of land-grant colleges in the nineteenth century and the establishment of state universities and municipal colleges supported by taxation, that the denominationally founded college was the norm in American life. Of the approximately two hundred colleges and universities founded before Horace Mann began his crusade for public education in the nineteenth century, all but twenty-five had a denominational base. This was understandable. It was a response to the unique pragmatism of the American spirit. Religious loyalty to a denominational group was increasingly linked to practical social effort.

By the time of World War II, the residuum of denominational origins had all but disappeared in most of the better institutions. The swaddling clothes of the pioneering days had been laid away. The curriculum was militantly secular, the courses unrelated to theological orthodoxy. It was rare to have even compulsory attendance at religious services. Yet there was the pride of paternity, the comfort of playing host, the satisfaction of fulfilling a religious mission in modern, practical terms of service to the common good. Every denominational group could point to colleges it had founded and sustained — the Catholics, the Baptists, the Methodists, the Lutherans — all with scores of institutions to their credit, down to the Quakers, the smallest of all, with eight or ten nationally respected colleges.

Astonishingly enough, only the Jews — the people of the Book, whose sons and daughters sought opportunities in higher education in greater proportion than did any other group — had never pioneered a college for which they were responsible and where they could play host. The phenomenon bears exploration and understanding.

While there were Jewish settlements in the United States well before the Revolution, they were not large enough in numbers, affluent enough, or concentrated substantially enough in one locality for cohesive community action. Major Mordecai Noah, a visionary of the early nineteenth century, was apparently the first American Jew who is known to have broached the suggestion that the Jews establish a college or university in the tradition of the other sectarian groups. Noah was a colorful character who had dabbled in newspaper ventures as a publisher and editor; he had written popular plays and had been a theatrical impresario. He was an early young hawk who advocated defiance of Britain before the War of 1812. He was constantly arguing and fought several duels, in one of which he killed his opponent. He became sheriff of New York and encountered some of the prejudice that made it difficult for Jews, even when insignificant in numbers, to advance on their merits. "What a pity," an outraged citizen wrote, "that Christians are to be hung by a Jew." Noah responded, "What a pity that Christians should have to be hung."

In 1825 Noah announced a bizarre scheme to organize a Jewish training settlement from which Jews could go to Palestine to reestablish a homeland there. Of course Palestine would first have to be wrested from the Turks, but the irrepressible Noah was quite sanguine that this could be accomplished. Meanwhile, he purchased several thousand acres of land in Grand Island, northwest of Buffalo, and named it Ararat to recall the spot where another Noah landed his Ark after the great flood. Among those who participated in the flamboyant ceremonies were a number of leading Indian chieftains in full regalia, for Noah believed ardently that the Indians were descended from the lost ten tribes of Israel.

This was the restless character, labeled "Major Bombastes Furioso" by the *New York Post*, from whose fertile imagination came the proposal that the Jews of America establish a college in the tradition of other sectarian groups. In 1843 and 1844, with understandable anxiety that Jewish young people, including his own children, could not observe their religious traditions in the colleges founded by his Christian neighbors, Noah sponsored the establishment of a college where, "while obtaining a classical education, they could acquire a liberal knowledge of the principles of their religion." He was echoing the clarion to action that had brought into being Harvard, Yale, Princeton, and the other institutions which Christian zeal had fathered. Noah's concern was so compelling that he was ready to found the college himself and share substantially in its financial burdens. But the call fell on ears that were as skeptical as they had been when they heard of the proposed utopia on Grand Island. Like so many similar attempts to found a university in the century that followed, fulfillment required much more than grandiloquent announcements or even the acquisition of site and charter.

It should be noted that though overwhelming obstacles stood in the way of establishing a Jewish-sponsored college, Jewish families were not remiss in their support of higher education. Major private gifts to already existing universities had been of crucial importance. Julius Rosenwald, Lucius Littauer, and Jacob Schiff represented scores of Jewish philanthropists who were exemplary benefactors. But a family gift to a college that had already gone through the travail of pioneering could not be compared with the corporate contribution of a denominational group that was ready to assume responsibility for the ongoing life of a major university.

The basic problem for the Jewish community was not financial, though it loomed large, as it did for all denominational groups involved in the sponsorship of universities. The primary difficulty was that the time never seemed propitious to move ahead with such proposals. American Jews, with intimate ancestral ties abroad, constantly had to respond to emergency situations that demanded priority. As immigrants poured in during the final decades of the nineteenth century — first hundreds of thousands, then millions — prodded by persecutions and restrictions in Eastern European countries, the major resources of the Jewish community were preempted to adjust the newcomers to American life. World War I brought misery to the millions who remained encysted in the war-torn areas, and massive relief programs had to be mounted that were unparalleled in the history of philanthropy. The rise of Hitler, the expulsion of Jews from Nazi-dominated lands, the Holocaust with its incredible toll, the displaced persons' camps, the daring expedients to salvage the flotsam and jetsam of the survivors, the desperate plans to smuggle a fraction of them into Palestine — all these tragic needs placed enormous burdens on the American Jewish community, responsibilities no other denominational group had ever been called upon to assume. When the claims upon Jewish compassion were so compelling, how could one press for support to launch a university, however strong the moral obligation had become?

To compound the problem, the necessary investment resources were now discouragingly oppressive. The hundreds of institutions that were launched before the twentieth century could begin modestly and grow slowly. But a university born in the postwar world necessitated millions for launching and additional millions for survival. The curriculum now covered a vast academic range; facilities, especially for modern science, required a fortune in commitments. Unless adequate resources were assured, only such faculty would be attracted as could not get positions elsewhere. So the concept of a Jewish-founded university, appealing as it was to a proud and sensitive Jewish community, had to be given a very low priority.

Yet the proposals continued to be advanced, stimulated primarily because of the restrictions that kept the denominationally founded colleges limited largely to white Christian enrollment. Even when these exclusive policies eased somewhat after World War I, only a small number of Jews found it possible to gain admission. A brilliant Louis Brandeis, claiming a background that seemed to fit the gentleman's lineage, could pass muster at Harvard and could achieve a record in the law school that remained unmatched for decades. But a Jewish applicant had to be gold to pass for silver, and with the increase in numbers of native-born American Jews and the inevitable increased desire for college opportunities, the discrimination became a galling outrage. President Abbott Lawrence Lowell of Harvard, who was troubled by the increase of applications for admission from Jewish students, stated that a quota would have to be imposed, although a rather generous one. In the professional schools, the admissions difficulties for Jews were even more serious. Medical schools drew the line sharply. For those who survived the battle to achieve a degree in medicine, one of the most favored fields of endeavor among Jews since long before Maimonides, there were heartbreaking disappointments ahead, since the denominationally sponsored hospitals offered few internships and even fewer places for Jewish physicians on their staffs.

Of course, there was very little expectation that the establishment of a college under Jewish auspices could have more than the slightest influence upon the problems of discriminatory practices. What could one or two or even ten Jewish-founded colleges do to open up college opportunities for Jewish students who sought them? Most Jewish leaders, too, realized that quotas must be fought where they existed, and that it would be abandoning principle to establish a university as a refuge. Nevertheless, the discriminatory practices of many of the most desirable colleges kept alive the issue of a Jewish-sponsored university. In the early 1940s, Henry Monsky, president of B'nai B'rith, the largest mass organization in Jewish life, revived the project and appointed a national committee, on which I served, to seek a campus in the Middle West. But all the eloquent arguments that were marshaled in support could not counteract the anxieties of the Nazi terror and the disasters that engulfed Jewish life abroad.

Then, in 1946, there was a totally unexpected turn. A New England medical and veterinary campus, on the brink of bankruptcy, suddenly became available. With virtually no initial investment the dreams of a century could be freed of "vain fantasy, more inconstant than the wind."

II

Birth Pangs: "Tetchy and Wayward Was Thy Infancy"

MIDDLESEX University in Waltham, Massachusetts, a suburb of Boston, was a small, privately owned and supported institution which was primarily a medical and veterinary school, though it was also empowered to give degrees in the liberal arts. It had been founded in 1926 by a Boston surgeon, Dr. John Hall Smith, who had committed his personal resources to the venture — several millions that had been earned, not in medical practice but through fortunate investments in real estate. Though he was part of the Protestant elite of Massachusetts, Dr. Smith had heretical convictions about medical school admissions. He steadfastly refused to set up restrictions on the basis of race or creed, and Middlesex increasingly became a refuge for Jews who were barred elsewhere and for whom Middlesex was almost a last, desperate measure. The university was in endless trouble with the medical association, which questioned its standards and withheld accreditation, and the state constantly threatened to revoke its charter. Dr. Smith insisted that such problems arose because the association was determined to prevent Middlesex from graduating large numbers of Jewish doctors and veterinarians into a tightly held Protestant monopoly.

Dr. Smith died in 1944, fighting to the end, and, in the process, exhausting virtually all of his life's savings. His son, C. Ruggles Smith, an alumnus of Harvard and of the Harvard Law School, abandoned his practice and took over the university presidency. For two years after his father's death he struggled to keep Middlesex open. Parts of the campus were sold off to meet faculty salaries and other current bills. Maintenance was curtailed and the plant began to fall apart. The Massachusetts legislature then suspended the first three years of the medical program, permitting a year of grace for the senior class to graduate. Only the veterinary school remained, but with very little hope that it could be salvaged.

As bankruptcy and collapse loomed, a most unlikely intermediary emerged, Dr. Joseph Cheskis, who had been serving as the dean of liberal arts. Cheskis was a Jewish immigrant from Lithuania who had come to the United States by way of a number of teaching posts in France. He had developed an uncanny linguistic skill, although it was a quaint experience to hear his French and Spanish spoken with a Litvak accent. He had joined the Middlesex faculty as the underpaid head of its humanities division and had become its dean. One of his most heart-warming duties was to recruit professors who were in flight from Hitler-dominated Europe. They were a harried lot, low-salaried, unprotected, but grateful for an academic berth when no others had been available. Now Middlesex too was about to go under. Cheskis had lived with adversity too long to be overwhelmed by it. He had established valuable relationships with national Jewish organizations during his negotiations to relocate refugee academicians. He determined to revive these relationships in the hope that, through them, something might still be salvaged from the impending wreckage. After all, Middlesex had been a friend in need to Jewish students and faculty: some of its problems could be traced directly to an admissions policy that permitted no compromise with decency and humaneness. Were there not some resources in the Jewish community that might now be marshaled?

Cheskis's inquiries vindicated his intuition. He learned that a committee of public-spirited Jews in New York were seeking a campus for a Jewish-founded university. The committee was headed by Dr. Israel Goldstein, the rabbi of one of the country's most influential Conservative congregations. Dr. Goldstein, unlike so many of the men who had dreamed of such a venture, was no visionary. He had had long experience in organizing projects — in his own synagogue, in the councils of Conservative Judaism, in the Zionist movement, and in such communal agencies as the Board of Conciliation, which he founded. In the mid-1940s, outraged by the unfair practices of many of the medical schools, he began exploring, with the cooperation of a small group of New Yorkers, the possibility of developing a Jewish-sponsored college that could cope with the problem of discrimination as well as offer a climate hospitable to positive Jewish values.

Dr. Cheskis strongly urged Ruggles Smith to negotiate for the pooling of resources — Middlesex to offer its campus and existing facilities, the New York committee to assume the responsibility for the survival and the ongoing support of the medical and veterinary school. Smith acted promptly and on January 7, 1946, dispatched a letter to Dr. Goldstein, suggesting that Middlesex University might offer a practical possibility for his committee's objectives. He described the campus in rather enthusiastic terms. "It represents an investment of more than a million dollars," with "a plant admirably designed for its needs," with a "good library." Unfortunately, Smith added, the university had been locked in

a hopeless struggle with the anti-Semitic authorities in the medical establishment, and it could not survive without an assured constituency and
an endowment. Smith said he would recommend the transfer of the
campus and its charter if Goldstein's group demonstrated it had the
capacity to "re-establish the School of Medicine." The condition was
added, apparently as a salute to Dr. John Hall Smith's long battle for
principle, that when the university passed to its new sponsors there
would never be discrimination on the basis of creed or ethnic origin.

Dr. Goldstein responded cordially and visited Middlesex soon afterward. Even allowing for the ravages of a severe New England winter, it
was disappointingly clear that Smith had vastly exaggerated the Middlesex assets. The buildings were in deplorable condition; the grounds
were unkempt and needed complete rehabilitation. But Goldstein and his
committee were not discouraged. The ninety acres of the Middlesex
campus were favorably located on the Charles River, close to Boston and
yet far enough away to offer a pastoral atmosphere. With adequate
funding, Goldstein hoped the landscaping could be brought to its potential, and the buildings, however neglected and dilapidated, could be
reconstructed and expanded. But over and above the physical factors was
the undoubted psychological stimulus the acquisition of an actual campus would create.

With both parties eager for the transfer, negotiations began at once to
convert Middlesex into the as yet unnamed Jewish-sponsored university.
Within a few weeks the deal was completed; the campus and the charter
passed to the Jewish committee with no purchase investment — a better
bargain therefore than the acquisition of Manhattan from the Indians
for twenty-four dollars in beads.

But the committee had no money, no constituency, and no educational
objectives except the conviction that the school represented a corporate
gift of the Jews to American higher education. Dr. Goldstein therefore
first sought a letterhead committee of outstanding public figures whose
names would give prestige to the undertaking. He secured the cooperation of Dr. Albert Einstein, who, having fled Germany, was then living
in Princeton at the Institute for Advanced Studies. With the Einstein
name on the masthead of the foundation, Dr. Goldstein quickly obtained the endorsement of scores of other nationally prominent personalities — Jewish community leaders, churchmen, political figures, college presidents, educators, publishers.

When the negotiations were completed to transfer title, it was
deemed important to shed quickly the identification with Middlesex.
Initially there was some sentiment to adopt the name of Albert Einstein,
but the idea evoked little enthusiasm. It was argued that an American
university should bear the name of a native American who symbolized
the best traditions of American life. The discussion was academic, however, since Dr. Einstein himself neither sought the identification nor

encouraged it. Dr. Goldstein then canvassed the list of those who had endorsed the project, and there was an almost unanimous judgment that the university be named for Louis Dembitz Brandeis, the late justice of the United States Supreme Court.

The name was an inspiration. Brandeis had died in October 1941 after one of the most influential careers in American history. He had earned the reputation of "the people's lawyer" because of his long years of gallant fighting for social causes before World War I. He had become an ardent Zionist and had considerable influence on President Wilson in persuading him to endorse the Balfour Declaration in 1917, which validated the right of the Jews to establish a homeland in Palestine. He was the first Jew to sit on the Supreme Court of the United States. With Oliver Wendell Holmes, he had consistently supported the liberal position in a Court dominated by conservatives. The name Brandeis, therefore, seemed to combine most felicitously the prophetic ideal of moral principle and the American tradition of political and economic liberalism. The choice of name was universally applauded, but it carried with it a sobering responsibility. The new university would have to live up to the symbol it represented. Einstein wrote: "Brandeis is a name that cannot be merely adopted. It is one that must be achieved."

Unfortunately, before the venture could prove its viability, there were already internal dissensions that threatened disaster. The Einstein name was an enormous asset, but the old man had rather austere views of what such a university should be and there were temperamental clashes with Dr. Goldstein almost from the outset. When he had been approached to lend his name as a sponsor of the University, Dr. Einstein took it for granted that he was to be more than a public relations embellishment. He went on the assumption that matters of academic policy and important organizational steps would be discussed with him and that he would have a role in the decision-making. He was especially concerned that Goldstein might take it upon himself to structure the University and begin making commitments which would influence the academic orientation in ways he could not countenance. His old friend Dr. Stephen Wise, a dominant force in American Jewish life who knew Dr. Goldstein well and was critical of his flair for press releases, cautioned Dr. Einstein to insist upon safeguards to hold him in check. In a letter of June 28, 1946, Dr. Wise said: "You write to me in confidence. I answer you in the same spirit. As a friend, I say to you, you ought not tie yourself up with the Foundation bearing your name, and the Jewish University, unless there be some completely trustworthy person, like our friend Otto Nathan, standing at the side of Dr. Israel Goldstein, to give him the benefit of his own wise judgment and your judgment, and thus ensure for him at once a place in relation to the proposed university. . . . You must have someone at the side of Dr. Goldstein whom you can trust."

Unfortunately, disagreements and misunderstandings mounted and made Dr. Wise's caution quite prescient. Dr. Einstein began to regret his decision to participate, and after only a few months he resigned, saying that his confidence had been so severely breached he refused to accept any further responsibility for a university "where Goldstein would continue to play an important part." He cited two climactic actions which had forced his decision: Dr. Goldstein's alleged negotiations without prior consultation with him "for submission of Dr. Sachar's name as President of the University," and his invitation to Cardinal Spellman of New York to participate in a major interpretive function that was scheduled for November.

Dr. Goldstein realized he had no alternative but to forestall Dr. Einstein's resignation by stepping out himself. But he denied that he "had made any commitment to Dr. Sachar about the Presidency of Brandeis," and expressed bewilderment that Dr. Einstein would make an issue of the invitation to Cardinal Spellman.

In his denial of any commitment to me about the presidency Dr. Goldstein was entirely accurate. Dr. Einstein had apparently been the victim of irresponsible gossip. There had indeed been a conference in Miami with me several months before in which Dr. Goldstein had sounded out my interest in a Jewish-founded university, and he had asked if I would be willing to join the panel of national sponsors he was recruiting. I expressed warm approbation of the project and indicated my willingness to serve on a national council of about a hundred public figures. But no word of presidency was sounded or even intimated, and later, when Dr. Einstein again withdrew and Dr. Goldstein offered to return, he suggested no names for the presidency except his own.

The other "breach of confidence" referred to by Dr. Einstein related to the invitation extended by Dr. Goldstein to Cardinal Spellman. In a short volume on the origins of Brandeis University, published a few years later, Dr. Goldstein dismisses the serious import of his action and refers to the invitee, without naming him, only as "an eminent Christian Churchman." Dr. Einstein is made out to be capriciously sensitive. What Dr. Goldstein omits is the fact that Cardinal Spellman had only recently returned from a visit to Spain, where he had publicly expressed extravagant admiration for Generalissimo Franco. The Holocaust was too immediate for Dr. Einstein to condone this salute to the collaborator of Hitler, and the episode must have been especially painful for one whose dearest associates had been victims of Fascist fury. One of our trustees, Adele Rosenwald Deutsch, who lived in Princeton and enjoyed Dr. Einstein's friendship, repeated to me a conversation in which he had said bitterly, "How was it to be expected that I could have any further confidence in the sensitive discretion of Dr. Goldstein, who recognized no outrage nor even indignity in an invitation to the cardinal at the public launching of the Jewish-founded university?"

When the resignation arrived, Dr. Goldstein realized at once that the hostile withdrawal of a man of Dr. Einstein's prestige would be ruinous to the entire venture. His own association had been a matter of great pride: he had obtained title to a potentially valuable campus and a charter that protected its degree-granting power. It was heartbreaking for him to leave at such a juncture. But the decisive tasks that would bring a functioning university into being still lay ahead — to win the substantial support such an enterprise demanded, and to induce the participation and enrollment of a quality faculty and student body. He was convinced he could not accomplish this if it became known that Dr. Einstein withdrew after a quarrel with him. He considered that he was the more expendable at this stage, and for this reason he eliminated himself, with no strictures and no recriminations. Dr. Einstein promptly withdrew his resignation and appealed to a number of close friends to help him in the tasks of reorganization, naming Dr. Otto Nathan as his liaison. Leadership then passed to a New England committee headed by a well-known Boston attorney, George Alpert, who had early identified himself with the project and who had served most resourcefully as legal counsel in the negotiations transferring the Middlesex campus and charter to the Jewish committee.

During the next nine months, until June 1947, when another disastrous internal crisis erupted, the conviction gradually emerged that the University would have to be a totally new venture. The Massachusetts medical establishment had, indeed, been thwarted in its attempt to get the Middlesex charter revoked, but it had become clear that, even with more encouraging results in funding, the medical and veterinary programs could never be more than third rate. Would it not be tragic if, after so many decades of aspiration and hope, the contribution of the proud and sensitive American Jewish community was identified merely as a precariously sustained institution that functioned ineffectually and without dignity? Would it not be wiser and more courageous to cut loose from the past and concentrate on the creation of a liberal arts college, born of confidence, uninhibited by any legacy of frustration?

Hence, disregarding the pledges that had been made in all good faith to Ruggles Smith and the Middlesex trustees, that the transfer of campus and charter to the new group would save Middlesex as a medical school, the judgment to start anew prevailed. The official announcement to suspend the medical school operation was released immediately after the small group of seniors were awarded their degrees at the 1947 Commencement. A face-saving effort was halfheartedly made to continue the veterinary school, but the accreditation authorities intervened and permitted only a preveterinary enrollment for one year, a final probationary period. Yet here too it was considered irresponsible to struggle on, when there was so little expectation that promises to entering students could be fulfilled. Hence, despite indignant and well-publicized protests and demonstrations by the disappointed students and their parents, the veterinary school also terminated operations in June 1947. It was announced that Brandeis University, retaining only the physical campus of Middlesex, would be launched as a liberal arts university. The target date for its opening was postponed for another year, until the fall of 1948. All efforts were now turned to the overriding task of creating the support which was indispensable to transform plans and dreams into reality. At this stage, the fund-raising affairs were mainly limited to New York and Boston and their environs.

Meantime Dr. Einstein was becoming as uneasy with the procedures of the Boston leadership as he had been with Dr. Goldstein's. A high-powered public relations and development staff had been employed, which operated on the theory that frequent announcements of imposing goals would create an aura of success and increase confidence in the viability of the project. Hence there were constant references, in interviews and press conferences, to totals obtained that equated hopes with confirmed pledges, and a figure over two million dollars crept into the releases. The three or four larger commitments were reannounced at each affair, though the largest of them, $100,000, had to be quietly canceled when the donor's wife threatened to have him committed for an act that she labeled insane! Undiscouraged, the staff steadily escalated the goals; by the end of 1946 it became $5 million, by March of 1947 the Boston press was referring to it as $15 million.

It was a brave ploy at a time when the payment of minor bills kept being postponed and when the attenuated monthly payroll of the dying medical school was a continuous frustration. Dr. Einstein became increasingly alarmed by the fund-raising strategy. It would have been difficult for any responsible businessman to remain comfortable in such a promotional climate. For Dr. Einstein, the world's most meticulous scientist, it became intolerable. The storm signals were clear, but the trustees were too deeply involved with the problems of the University's survival to note their serious import. Suddenly, in June 1947, the gathering crisis exploded when Dr. Einstein announced that he was again withdrawing from the Brandeis sponsorship, this time with finality, and he prohibited any further use of his name.

In his statement Dr. Einstein offered no reason for the irretrievable break. But Alpert explained publicly that Dr. Einstein had wished to offer the presidency of Brandeis to Harold J. Laski, a British intellectual who had played a major role in fashioning the ideology of the Labour party. He had been a visiting professor at Harvard, where he had been continuously identified with left-wing movements. After a visit to Russia he had written most sympathetically of the Communist revolution. When he had been accused by a British newspaper of following the Communist line, he had sued for libel and lost! Alpert claimed he had to resist Einstein where the future of the University effort was at stake. "I had no intention of identifying Laski with communism," he said, "but, having filed suit and having a British court throw out his suit, Laski projected an image that would hopelessly complicate the problem of a university that was seeking to establish itself. . . . I can compromise upon any subject but one," he added. "That one is Americanism. So far as I am concerned, there cannot be now, nor can there ever be, the slightest compromise concerning that."

The charges and countercharges in the public press continued for a full week, during which Dr. Einstein remained silent. Then, on June 28, he issued a statement which explained his withdrawal. He accused Alpert of lying about the whole issue. He had indeed, with the board's authorization, felt out Laski about his interest in the University and had been told at once that he, Laski, was not temperamentally fitted for such an executive post and that he did not wish to leave England. Dr. Einstein had then gone on the assumption that the issue was closed and he was astonished when Alpert suddenly reopened the whole matter. Several years later I met with Einstein's close friend and the trustee of his estate, Dr. Otto Nathan of New York University, who offered his own version of the dispute. Nathan said that the quarrels between Einstein and Alpert had been constant, especially over publicity. Alpert, Nathan averred, knowing full well that in any controversy with Einstein he would have very little credibility with the public, seized upon the Laski issue, months after it was moot, and released the lurid story about his unwillingness to compromise his Americanism. "It was this cheap demagoguery," said Nathan, "that had so alienated Dr. Einstein."

Einstein's withdrawal carried with it not only the resignation of the New York trustees but the cancellation of most of the support that had been pledged at the fund-raising meetings. The financial loss was negligible, since the response to all the frenetic campaigning in New York had been less than indifferent. It was the outraged reaction to the public recriminations and name-calling that was even more devastating. Alpert had to build afresh and, at this point, he was limited to whatever he could salvage in the Boston area. The Jewish Brahmins resisted his appeals for cooperation, some because they had no confidence in him and his reputation as a difficult collaborator; some because they feared that the venture would become an exclusive Boston responsibility that would threaten the financial resources of the established institutions, especially the Beth Israel Hospital. Above all, as in New York, Alpert had to contend with the heavy undercurrent of resentment against him for having demeaned a man whom many regarded as the greatest living Jew, besmirching his name by identifying him with Communist fellow travelers.

Rebuffed by the first- and even the second-line leadership, Alpert turned now to men who were not as well known but who were attracted to the University's concept and who had already pledged financial support. I do not suppose any university ever had a more unlikely group of founding fathers. With Alpert they were eight, although Dudley Kimball, the eighth, had come over from the Middlesex board and can perhaps be described more as a founding uncle than a founding father. He liked to jest that he was the nonsectarian member of the board. Alpert, Kimball, and Norman Rabb, the youngest of the founders, were college-educated. Of the others, only James Axelrod had been born in the United States, and none of the remaining four possessed a full high school education among them or spoke English without a pronounced East European accent. Morris Shapiro and Meyer Jaffe had emigrated from Russia in their teens, had learned their not always certain English in night classes, and had gone on through Horatio Alger methods — hard work and no play — to make modest fortunes.

It was the two remaining members of the founding group who continue to fascinate those who explore the origins of Brandeis. Of the group, perhaps Abraham Shapiro provided the widest contrast to the Nicholas Boylstons, the Lady Ann Radcliffes, and the royal or would-be royal patrons of other American universities. He was born in Lithuania and had reached the United States by way of South Africa. Like the others, he had come to affluence through unremitting toil and had built a small shoe manufacturing business in Worcester. Along the way he had acquired considerable Boston real estate of great value. Among his many philanthropies, he created an emergency fund for those in the shoe business who fell upon hard times. It was Shapiro who subscribed the first fifty thousand dollars for Brandeis as soon as the Boston group assumed responsibility for the concept. His Catholic friends, who were legion, never forgot the experience of some Boston pilgrims who wished to climax their visit to Rome by receiving a papal blessing, but they could not break through the overcrowded Vatican schedule. Shapiro happened to be staying in their hotel and learned of their disappointment. He immediately called one of the American dignitaries on the papal staff whose college education he had financed, and the pilgrims, to their astonishment, were in the presence of His Holiness early the next day. Among my deep regrets is that Abraham Shapiro died in the first year of the University and thus did not share in some of our later achievements.

Finally there was Joseph Ford, "Uncle Joe" even to those who knew him slightly. He had hoped as a boy in Russia to become an engineer, but the obstacles for a Jew in search of a university education were too formidable. He migrated before he was twenty and first worked as a cutter of women's nightgowns. He attended evening school for a time, mainly to learn some serviceable English. Like Abe Shapiro's, Ford's philanthropies were legion, but because of his own early denial of opportunity he had a particular, if quiet, passion for giving to schools and colleges. Not that he left out hospitals, temples, homes for the elderly, and the whole network of Jewish and civic causes. Every stray dog or cat could be sure of shelter in the Ford menagerie. Who but Joe would spend the interval between the trustees' breakfast and the trustees' meeting by scooping up a handful of Danish pastries and feeding whatever campus dog was in mooching attendance?

Such homely kindliness did not fit the stereotype of the successful soft-goods manufacturer. What surprised the educational consultants even more were Uncle Joe's remarkably austere expectations for the University. When plans were discussed for the Brandeis faculty and the curriculum, he startled his fellow trustees by insisting on standards that seemed unattainable. When he was cautioned that such standards would inevitably discourage applications for enrollment, he suggested gently that "if they cannot make the grade at Brandeis, then let them go to Harvard!"

These were the men who joined Alpert to help create a modern university in the heart of the world's most distinguished center of learning. They were modestly successful in business and their professions, but they had almost no experience in the management of educational institutions. As they turned to tasks whose risks they probably never realized, there was no cheering from the sidelines, but there were plenty of boos.

Beset on every side, Alpert received a telephone call from Dr. Goldstein, who indicated that he was now ready to return to the leadership of the project. The Boston group went in a body to New York, and in a conference at the Waldorf-Astoria they explored with Dr. Goldstein the meaning of his proffered availability. He indicated that he was ready to take over the presidency of the University, but that he would have to impose some conditions. He was unwilling at this time to bring in as members of the Board of Trustees any of the Boston group except George Alpert and Norman Rabb. He wished to use the next few months to seek out "men and women of eminence in academic and cultural fields." He assured the men who had refused to give up after he and Dr. Einstein had resigned that he would be glad to have them remain with the fund-raising foundation. But, as trustees of the University, they would have to wait until the character of the board had been set by other appointees; then, "in due course and in due proportion, the members of the Boston group would be added."

Alpert and his colleagues were deeply affronted. They felt that Dr. Goldstein had not earned the right to set conditions that excluded the men who had become the sole beachhead of support for the University. Virtually all the fancy letterhead supporters had vanished. The main pledges made during Dr. Goldstein's brief incumbency had evaporated after his resignation. In the months that followed, until Dr. Einstein, too, had resigned, it was the loyalty and tenacity of Alpert and the Boston group that had kept the project breathing. Yet here was Dr. Goldstein snubbing these men, telling them that they were not of sufficient caliber to serve on the board. They were the first to realize that informed judgment was indispensable in creating a university of quality, and they were prepared to welcome counselors, as trustees, from the academic world. But such new recruits, they said, must be invited as collaborators and not as substitutes.

In a second conference the next day with just Alpert and Axelrod in his synagogue study, Dr. Goldstein insisted upon his conditions. The Boston group caucused briefly in another room and then informed Dr. Goldstein that, though they were only humble businessmen, they would try to make the venture succeed without his help. Thus ended Dr. Goldstein's identification with the project.

The remaining New York trustees resigned, and the University became the sole responsibility of George Alpert, as chairman of the Board of Trustees, Morris Shapiro, as president of the Brandeis Foundation, and their six New England colleagues.

Alpert and his fellow trustees had put on a bold front with Dr. Goldstein during their humiliating experience with him, but they felt cornered, indeed, trapped. They had legal title to a campus and a charter, but almost no resources with which to convert technical control into practical reality, and they were facing the hostility of powerful elements in the Greater Boston community. They determined to make one last attempt for support by presenting the case for Brandeis at a special meeting of key Boston families. It was planned for December 26, 1947, in the Somerset Hotel.

About fifty men gathered for the showdown. Only a few were really committed to the venture; the rest were either skeptical or indifferent, present because friends whom they could not refuse had asked them to attend. One of them, Yoland Markson, a respected community leader, probably voiced the sentiment of all the doubters. He noted that the little bastion in Palestine was at that moment battling desperately to stay alive, that the displaced persons' camps were crowded with the survivors of the Holocaust, that inevitably the University would become a Boston responsibility, and that limited resources ought not to be depleted at such a time to the detriment of prior causes.

Thus far Markson probably was expressing the sentiment of the majority. Then he added a gratuitous note, insisting that college education, unrelated to the professions, was a very much overrated need, that those who had practical common sense and stamina — the main ingredients for success — would always come through without ornamental degrees. Joe Ford had been sitting quietly, already determined that his contribution would be influenced by the reaction of the other community leaders. But Markson's comment touched a raw nerve. He rose in anger, scolded Markson for denigrating one of the great privileges of American freedom, and then announced that he would pledge $25,000. His statement transformed the mood of the audience. Within a few minutes more than a quarter-million dollars had been pledged, including a major gift from Markson himself. Alpert and his colleagues had not only their mandate but a new reserve of courage with which to go ahead. Later, as they looked back upon the many dispiriting vicissitudes that the venture had undergone, they counted the Somerset meeting and Ford's response as the turning point in the task of giving reality to the dream of a Jewish-founded university.

III

"We Knew We Were Pilgrims"

Now the search began in earnest for a president so that the University could open in the fall of 1948 with a faculty and student body under assured leadership. The trustees sought the advice of the two men they most respected: Dr. Paul Klapper, president of Queens College, and David K. Niles, who had served as administrative assistant to President Roosevelt and had continued in the post under President Truman.

Dr. Klapper had been chairman of the academic advisory committee and had supervised the survey of campus needs. The presidency of Brandeis had been offered to him after Dr. Goldstein's contretemps, but he quickly begged off. He did not believe that he could undertake such pioneering hazards in his middle sixties, especially since, as he put it, "he was a member of the coronary club." He suggested that the trustees invite me to the campus to explore my availability to be president.

David Niles was based at the White House, but he returned regularly to Boston for weekends. There he directed the nationally famous Ford Hall Forum and held court for the young New England leaders in far-into-the-night discussions on the issues of the day. My friendship with Niles went back many years to when I was on the faculty of the University of Illinois and had been invited several times to speak at the Ford Hall Forum. When consulted by the Brandeis trustees, Niles suggested that I be promptly approached. The next day, Niles called me (we had moved to Sherman Oaks, California, in 1947) to say that he had proposed me for the presidency of Brandeis, and he urged that I come to Boston to be interviewed by George Alpert and his fellow trustees. I had just begun to unwind after retiring from twenty years of administration, travel, and fund-raising as national director of the Hillel Foundations, and I was also quite aware of the troubles that had beset the Brandeis project. I asked for some time to think out the implications of the invitation, for I was not sure that even a trip was warranted. In the meantime I wrote to Dr. Stephen Wise, a devoted friend who, a number of years before, had done me the honor of asking that I consider succeeding him as head of the Jewish Institute of Religion, which he had pioneered and created in New York. His reply was a devastating appraisal of the entire project, citing the curse that hung over it after Einstein had been driven out of its sponsorship. Dr. Wise's letter of March 26, 1948, predicted pain, hurt, and shame if I permitted myself to be associated with the sponsors of the University.

While my wife and I were weighing the significance of another transcontinental uprooting, David Niles called again and I shared with him the alarming admonitions of the Wise letter. Dr. Wise was one of his most intimate and respected friends and he made no attempt to refute his advice. But he insisted that, however great my misgivings, I owed it to the validity of the concept at least to come for the interview. I agreed to make the trip east, planning to stop in Washington for a preliminary discussion with Niles and then to fly on to Boston.

I met with David Niles in his White House office. He reminded me that the issue was not whether there should be a Jewish-founded university, for that issue had been settled; the commitment had been made. The only remaining question was whether the university would be a pedestrian undertaking, shaming the American Jewish community, or a high-quality institution that would meet the hopes of generations who had so long waited for fulfillment. He paid me the compliment of expressing confidence that I would have sufficient prestige and leverage in the American Jewish community and in academic circles to counteract the wrangles of the past. But he urged me to be firm with the trustees, insisting that there must be sufficient independence in the presidency to make sure that the highest academic standards would be met and that internal bickering be contained. I then flew on to Boston.

The trustees had apparently called me in not to look me over, nor to determine whether I was their man. The conference turned into an undisguised appeal for me to take over the Brandeis presidency. As each one spoke, he emphasized different aspects of the projected university, but all of them revealed how deeply committed they were to the venture. America had been good to them, immigrants or the sons of immigrants, and because they remembered the restrictions and the humiliations of their people in Eastern Europe, they could not take for granted what they had been free to achieve in their adopted land. The Lowells, the Cabots, the Eliots, the Coolidges, the Saltonstalls — they were secure in their status; there was no call upon them to demonstrate gratitude. But an Abraham Shapiro, whose accent was pure Slobodka, felt impelled to express appreciation for the freedom and the dignity of American life. How better than by becoming the host in a great academic enterprise, open to all, in the fellowship of the best universities? As I listened to them, they reinforced the conviction that there was enormous power in the constituency that they represented, a power that had been completely misunderstood and overlooked by those who glamorized letterhead names. These remarkable men all had the traditional Jewish awe of education and the educated man. Most of them had no university of their own. Here they found an ideal identification and they were determined to fashion it into the proudest of symbols, regardless of what it required in energy and resources. I made no decision that night, asking for a quiet week of reflection at home. To this day my wife contends that she knew when I alighted from the plane and she saw the look in my eyes that I had made up my mind to enlist in the venture (even though I didn't realize it then).

Within the week I concluded that, however serious the public relations damage of the two acrimonious years of prehistory, the concept of the University had sufficient inner power to overcome the basic obstacles. I was ready to accept the offer of the presidency, but there were several conditions that had to be met, which I outlined in a letter to George Alpert before returning to Boston to complete the negotiations.

First, the trustees would have to pledge to underwrite whatever deficit might develop in the first four years of the University's existence. There had to be protection for the precarious beginning years, and this could be provided only by the founding trustees. A second condition had to do with the pledge of a free hand for the president and the administration in the academic affairs of the University — curriculum, degrees, admissions, honors. The third condition related to the expansion of the board so that it would become nationally representative. "At present," I wrote, "Brandeis is virtually a Boston project and even in Boston much of the 'official' leadership is either skeptical or downright opposed. For a while it may be possible to push the project in the face of such opposition, or in spite of the limitation of support to Boston. But the project must soon burst out of such confining limits. It must be developed into a national enterprise with a flooring of national support, with the sustained interest of national leadership." The final condition had to do with the responsibility for fund-raising. In my conference with the trustees I had been assured that this would be "a very minor part" of my duties, that the trustees would do most of the essential cultivation and legwork. I was realistic enough to know that a president of a modern, privately sponsored university could not avoid the tasks of interpretation and fund-raising. But I dutifully noted the promise of the trustees, knowing that this was an illusion and knowing also that they knew it. I must confess that I set down this understanding with tongue in cheek.

A few days later I flew east again for the definitive interview. The trustees gladly accepted all the conditions I had set forth. I was not surprised by their ready acquiescence to respect the administration's complete freedom of action in academic matters. But I was surprised by the alacrity with which they agreed to underwrite the deficits that might develop over the next four years of inevitable expansion. None of the trustees were men of limitless wealth, yet they were undertaking a guarantee that might call for substantial personal sacrifice. Though they were never called upon to meet that guarantee, it was a magnificent act of faith that, in my judgment, entitled them to be designated as the founding trustees who turned rhetoric and aspiration into responsible commitment.

On May 1, 1948, I moved into the Parker House in Boston and it became my residence for the next few months. My family remained in California so that the younger children, Edward and David, could finish their year's schooling. Howard, our oldest son, was studying and travel-ing in Europe after graduating from Swarthmore. I commuted to Califor-nia every fortnight until the entire family could be reunited in the fall, settling into a Brookline apartment hotel while the search for a presi-dent's house was under way. At last an old New England home in New-ton was located, but it took many months to renovate and redecorate it. The furnishing became a cooperative effort, a special committee under-taking the responsbility to solicit contributions from selected firms. The living room was equipped by one, the dining room by another, the study by a third. Individual articles came in for an enlarged institutional kitchen, the bedrooms, the sunroom, the garden. At the end, the presi-dent's house had become a lovely center not only for personal living but for major university entertainment, and all virtually without cost.

On May 8, 1948, I was introduced to the Boston Jewish community at a general rally in the Statler Hotel, where one thousand people gathered to meet the new president and to hear his conception of the University and the plans for the future. I had two objectives in the scheduled address: first, an affirmative interpretation of the University and the rationale for its support; second, an attempt to dissipate what I con-sidered misunderstandings about its objectives that had been put for-ward by some of its earlier supporters. The affirmative theme, a quality university underwritten for the first time by American Jews, needed little further buttressing; it had already been widely publicized.

I turned instead to the distinction between a Jewish-founded univer-sity and a Jewish university. Some of the early sponsors leaned to the concept of a university that, while offering general studies, concentrated on Jewish values and was intended to train students for Jewish leader-ship. After his resignation, Dr. Goldstein published a volume in which he expressed the hope that the administration would be concerned with the University as "the inculcator of uniquely Jewish values, an intellec-tual and cultural center of Jewish import, and the training ground for American Jewish leaders of tomorrow."

I pledged, of course, that Brandeis would be vitally concerned with Jewish studies, that there would be a close relationship to the educational institutions of Israel, and that there would be proper respect for the Jewish tradition. But there was no expectation that the University would become a parochial school on a university level. The model was to be not the Yeshiva or Catholic University of America or Baylor, but Harvard or Princeton or Columbia. At no point in my address did I directly refute the earlier sponsors of the University, but I made it clear that I would always keep in mind that Brandeis was not intended to be a refuge for students who fled from discrimination elsewhere, and that, while the temper and climate of the University would reflect the traditions of the host group, there would be no attempt at indoctrination of any kind. The enthusiastic response of the audience, and afterward of the press and other media, made me feel that these expressed purposes struck a responsive chord in a proud and sensitive constituency whose support we hoped to enlist.

Meantime, renewal work on the campus that had been going forward all through the spring and summer of 1948, to prepare for the opening of the school year, was accelerated. A small white stone house, once the private residence of Dr. John Hall Smith, was converted into an administration center and inevitably was dubbed the White House. The architects struggled with the other facilities that had been meant for a medical and veterinary school. There was the Castle, a series of interconnected buildings that had been constructed by Dr. Smith without an architect. The dissecting chamber and the vault for the cadavers became a commons room. Some of the laboratories were made over into a cafeteria. Classrooms were combined to create a makeshift gymnasium and rumpus room. All the other spaces, down to the last nooks and crannies, were transformed into dormitories for approximately 150 students. The one general classroom building of old Middlesex was remodeled to include several science laboratories, and its open inner court was roofed over to house a lecture hall with a capacity of about 500; later, as Nathan Siefer Hall, it became the school auditorium. There was an apple orchard and a wishing well that the first students vowed must never disappear. Later, when nostalgia had to be sacrificed to the relentless pressure of the needs of a modern university and sophisticated science laboratories displaced both orchard and well, there were anguished letters of protest to *Justice*, the school newspaper.

As in the case of the president's house in Newton, the call went out for assistance in renovating the campus. Gifts in kind poured in — carpeting, linoleum, draperies, kitchenware, kegs of nails, bundles of plywood, desks, chairs, beds, mattresses, lamps, microscopes, Bunsen burners — equipment that was indispensable and equipment that was useless but that could not usually be refused. Of course, it did become necessary occasionally to decline gifts, though with tact and finesse. One tenderhearted nature lover offered to purchase 150 birdhouses so that Brandeis could become a major sanctuary for the birds of New England. I asked for the counsel of the Audubon Society and was advised to be cautious about gifts that eat. Bird feed would be quite a drain on the narrow resources of a young school and, within an hour after ingestion, there would be problems for the maintenance staff and for the more idyllically inclined students lounging under the trees.

Now applications for admission began to trickle in. We had decided to enroll only freshmen, taking no transfers in the first years, so as to create our own tradition. By this plan it would take four years to complete a full undergraduate cycle, giving us welcome leeway to stagger the development of the curriculum, the appointment of the faculty, and the investment for the physical facilities. We had no way of knowing whether there would be enough applicants to form even a very small freshman class, so each day's mail was an adventure. Ruggles Smith, who had been named director of admissions and registrar and who maintained his office on the campus, kept me informed after the daily morning and afternoon mail deliveries. Sometimes the message would be "Not much this morning, one applicant," or "Good word today, four inquiries and three matriculations." It was an anxious count, for we were fully aware that only a very special type of student would be attracted to a college that was not accredited, and could not be for at least the six qualifying years, and whose degree, if we ever reached the point of granting degrees, might not have any academic value. Those who applied obviously had diverse motives. Some intrepid souls were intrigued by the prospect of becoming part of a pioneering class in a pioneering school. Some expected to find a comforting, compatible climate in a Jewish-founded university. Some may not have been accepted in the schools of their first choice. Ultimately 107 enrolled, and in later years, when they became respected alumni, many of them leaders in their professions, they took pleasure in referring to their youthful selves as "kooks with a passion for adventure."

The inauguration of the University and the installation of the first president was scheduled for October 8, 1948, in Symphony Hall in Boston. The invitation was sent to university presidents and the heads of learned societies around the world. There was a cordial response, and we were gratified to be host to one of the largest university convocations of the twentieth century.

The unusually large representation was, of course, not a tribute to anything that had yet been accomplished. The campus had barely been settled and a small freshman class prayerfully enrolled. There was no certainty about the monthly payroll for even modest expenditures. We had to conclude that participation by representatives of the oldest universities was obviously a tribute to an assured potential. The academic world knew the Jewish community and had deep respect for its generosity in every communal undertaking. The president of Brown, Henry Wriston, perhaps spoke for all his colleagues when he called me aside at the reception that followed the convocation. He wished me well and then added: "How fortunate you are. Just think of being president of a university that will never have any financial problems!" I was startled, for taken by itself, the comment seemed to be repeating the old canard that Jews are affluent enough to undertake anything. Wriston caught himself, for he had not meant this at all. He added that it was his experience, over a long lifetime, that Jews had an unusual sense of communal dedication. When they undertook anything, they could always be counted on to see their objective through. "Yes, Sachar, you are a lucky man."

But though, apparently, our Christian friends had undeviating confidence in the capacity of the Jewish community to meet its responsibilities, the Jewish establishment was not nearly so sure. Even our trustees still held their collective breath and were awed by the responsibility they had assumed. Most of them probably did not realize that Brandeis was located on Boston Rock, the highest point of land due west from the heart of the city on the perimeter of what is metropolitan Boston. It was from Boston Rock that Governor John Winthrop had surveyed the site of the future city more than three hundred years earlier. I could not help paraphrasing a sentence from Governor Winthrop's history of the Massachusetts Bay Colony, relating it to our situation as Brandeis began its academic journey: "We *knew* we were pilgrims."

IV

Formulating Academic Aims

I T was a challenging time to come in as the president of the newly created American university. But it was bewildering too. For the country had been fundamentally transformed by the war and its outcome, not only in its foreign relations and its economic policies, but in its social mores, its moral outlook, its responsibility for citizens whose survival with minimal dignity called for government concern and help. Transformed, too, was the whole field of education, its objectives as well as its techniques.

To begin with, the G.I. Bill, surely one of the noblest instruments of gratitude ever devised by a government, fired untold hundreds of thousands of young veterans with the determination to begin new lives and to fulfill newly stirred ambitions. Most of them came from families who had never even dreamed of the prospect of a college education. Now, earned in the crucibles of war, it was their right, perhaps the most precious of the fringe benefits that society offered. Every institution, Ivy League or what was once quaintly called "freshwater college," would have to do its share to absorb the 1946 armada of students.

Among the returning veterans there were, of course, some good-time Charlies along for the ride, but for the most part the new students were seriously motivated and more critical and demanding than their prewar counterparts. They were not to be fobbed off with lecture material that had not been reworked for twenty years or the threadbare witticisms that no longer entertained or stimulated. Ill-prepared professors were likely to be hissed at. College administrators, inured to students as inveterate shirkers, were astounded at petitions demanding longer library hours.

The college world was also dizzy with proposals for experiment, for scrapping, if need be, much that went by the name of education. What, after all, was so sacrosanct about the time-honored curriculum that emphasized the classical humanist tradition? It came under heavy fire from those who now boldly insisted upon more practical preparation for "the world of reality." "Empty knowledge" — literature, the arts, philosophy, and "dead language" books that seemed unrelated to contemporary problems — all this was derided as anachronistic in the brave new world.

Now and again someone like Henry Steele Commager would point out acerbically that Jefferson and the other founding fathers had never studied civics or political science. Instead, they had read Latin and Greek and the classics. A future American President, James Madison, remained an extra year at Princeton to read Hebrew. But to the utilitarians this was sophistry and totally irrelevant. Even those who maintained a modicum of loyalty to the humanistic heritage conceded that considerable revision was called for. Many felt that the conventional curriculum of the undergraduate schools was too oriented toward students who would enter graduate or professional schools and therefore shortchanged the vast majority who had no intention of giving still more precious years to obtain advanced degrees.

As the cauldron bubbled, we who were trying to plan Brandeis simmered too. We had but one uncompromising objective. Brandeis could not be commonplace or mediocre. John Roche, one of the early deans, who believed this fervently, said: "There are in theory two ways to create a first-rate university: start out at the bottom and inch upward from third rate to second rate to first rate; or at the outset strike for the top. In practice mediocrity reproduces itself, so that, unfortunately, third-rate schools remain third rate." We recognized that the risks were great, but we knew also that it is unwise to try to get over a chasm in two leaps.

The first decision to be made obviously had to do with the size and range of the school, for this would influence all other planning. What was our aim? We could opt for a large student body, ultimately many thousands, on the model of our neighbors, Boston University, Northeastern, the University of Massachusetts. Or we could determine to remain a small university, at first exclusively undergraduate until we had earned accreditation, with a small faculty-student ratio, and then, in time, adding graduate programs, never unduly expanding enrollment so as to lose the character of intimacy.

It was the latter option that we adopted. Indeed, the choice seemed inevitable. The academic world would be watching with more than perfunctory interest what the contribution of Jewish pride and sensitivity was to be. Some years later I explained the Brandeis decision in a baccalaureate address that was published in the *Journal of Higher Education*. The case for expanded enrollment, enlarged classes, and what was virtually mass merchandising in higher education had been eloquently presented by a highly successful business executive, Beardsley Ruml, and my article served not only as a reply to his views but as the rationale for Brandeis's concept of its educational role.

Ruml suggested that much more mileage could be obtained from a university faculty simply by doubling or tripling the size of its classes. He saw no magic in small, intimate groups, and student-faculty ratio in a college of quality could be raised, without jeopardy, from eight to one to twenty to one. Furthermore, too many colleges, in Ruml's opinion, were plagued by superfluous courses that represented ever more recondite areas of knowledge, which, in turn, siphoned off the teaching time of the faculty. There should be drastic pruning in the number of such courses, he said, so that a smaller faculty could cope with a basic curriculum when the pedantry or the proliferation had been shorn away. Ruml noted that his suggested reforms would materially cut expenses, and would make it possible to augment faculty salaries without the always painful chain reaction of increasing tuition fees.

In my response I acknowledged that there was considerable validity in much of what Ruml had to say. There is no special magic in small classes. I believe it was a president of Fisk who said wisely that unless there is really good teaching, the small class merely assures the transmission of mediocrity in an intimate environment. "The happy faculty of easy communication," I noted, "is not exclusively related to numbers; it is related to character and temperament. All of us have probably known people who are incapable of intimacy, even with themselves. But while we cannot manufacture intimacy by some cabalistic faculty-student ratio, we must avoid the opposite educational pitfall of viewing education as a mechanical process." I had no quarrel with Ruml's game of numbers. "It is indeed as easy to speak to two hundred as to fifty, but the essence of the educational experience is not the lecture; it is the faculty-student personal relationship. When the student body is materially increased at the same time that the faculty is decreased to achieve more economic operation, the personal relationship virtually disappears, except for an infrequent office appointment. For what is the most rewarding experience in the university?" I asked. "Is it not the association with a few exceptional spirits who have a decisive influence on thinking? What students remember most in their lives is not facts and data but the rare incandescent teachers who profoundly affected their outlook."

I remembered that my own career was transformed because I came to know Roland Green Usher, who headed the history department at my alma mater, Washington University. It was his teaching of history, combining interpretive brilliance with dramatic presentation, that sent me into the field of history. When he burned Joan of Arc at the stake I smelled the smoke and fire in the room. If occasionally a member of his family could not use a symphony ticket, he would invite me to accompany him. I later became his assistant in his omnibus survey of western civilization and I soon realized, if I were to concentrate on British history, that I must continue my graduate studies at Oxford or Cambridge. As it happened, I fetched up at Emmanuel College, Cambridge, on an

1851 Exhibition Fellowship, set up by Queen Victoria. There another great teacher, John Bury, the classical historian who edited Gibbon, took me under his wing. Two such personalities, deeply interested in their students, patient with their questions, opened fascinating new worlds with their sense of perspective and were a university experience in themselves. Their views and their influence were vividly before me as I read Ruml's memo, and I was more than ever persuaded that his whole philosophy of education was misconceived when he advocated an economy program that would reach more with less. "A university is not a department store," I continued. "It is a fellowship of teachers and students in which the personal relationship must be maintained. For otherwise, the teacher is merely a voice on a platform, and the student is only a name in a roll book — or worse, a product to be merchandised as cheaply as possible. . . ."

When I reached Ruml's recommendation to cut courses drastically for purely economic reasons, I wondered whether he was not eliminating warts and blemishes by amputating limbs, thereby jeopardizing the whole educational organism. Of course, I agreed, not every piddling specialization should become an undergraduate course to satisfy the vanity or the research program of a professor. Courses should be carefully screened to prevent sterility. But to reduce courses to meet an economic problem is rearranging a body of knowledge to gain maximum piece-goods efficiency. This scheme sounded like H. G. Wells at his worst and was little less than a caricature of educational technology. Specialization, even when expensive, is part of the blood and bone of a university. We must think hard before eliminating the course that represents the thorough, disciplined mastery of a small, controlled academic field. It is one of the special glories of the educational process, fully as vital as the broad, synthesizing, general course which provides perspective. We need breadth, but we also need depth. This is what Thoreau probably meant when, hearing a friend boast of the many branches of knowledge taught in his college, he exclaimed, "Yes, indeed, all the branches but none of the roots."

The reasoning on size for a school like Brandeis was simple and virtually noncontroversial in comparison with the long discussions on the nature of the curriculum and the pace of growth that it would inevitably influence. Here we were embattled in the educational arena that rang with the names and the ideas of John Dewey, Irving Babbitt, Albert Jay Nock, Alexander Meiklejohn, Robert Hutchins, and newer names that included Stringfellow Barr, Sidney Hook, James Conant, and scores of others. Everyone, it seemed, even those who had lived faculty lives for two generations in the oldest Ivy League schools, seemed to have notions about what was to be done in the postwar world and the need to do it promptly.

If the temptation to go Ruml's mass merchandising route was quickly dispelled, there was also little inclination to go the way of the experimental schools that caught most of the headlines of the day — Sarah Lawrence, Bennington, Reed, Antioch — though they had much to admire. Every part of the country had its laboratory of exciting educational experimentation, aimed at people who had special interests. They had many failures to discourage them and their eager sponsors but also many exciting successes to give them new hope. These bold ventures validated again the belief that in a huge country like the United States, with more than two thousand colleges, there is a place for almost any kind of career preparation and temperament and ambition.

In the end, of course — or rather, the beginning — we would imitate no single model. We would not relinquish the commitment to becoming, in time, a university with the very best graduate programs we could devise. In undergraduate education, we would strive for a college that would approximate the ratio of faculty to students and the breadth of options offered by such schools as Swarthmore and Oberlin. We would not stake the entire destiny of our venture on the experimental projects that highly specialized schools offered.

Fortunately, there was ready access to a major report that Harvard had financed and sponsored over a two-year period that had reviewed the whole educational scene, and it included recommendations that could be adapted to fit almost any college that preferred the tradition of the liberal arts and sciences. A commission had been appointed in 1944 after many years of dissatisfaction with the elective system that President Charles Eliot, a revolutionary in his day, had introduced more than half a century before. Eliot had reacted sharply against the rigidity of the imported German university system, with its hidebound curriculum. He had established an elective system that gave students wider latitude to organize their courses, choosing what appealed to them, avoiding what seemed irrelevant or what they found too difficult. All that had been required was for them to amass the required number of official credits for classes attended and work turned in. The task force was unanimous that such free choice, often carried to ridiculous "smorgasbord" extremes, was now completely outmoded.

The Harvard General Education Report, published in 1946, was the work of twelve outstanding senior professors who were released from formal teaching duties for two years. It unanimously recommended a core curriculum for the first two college years, about half of which would include basic courses that related to the humanities, the social sciences, and the natural sciences. Students would find sufficient leeway for specific subject choices in each discipline, and even for one or two survey courses in history or literature or general science. When the studies in the core curriculum had been satisfactorily fulfilled, the student would then be free, with faculty advice and collaboration, to choose a concentration and devote the rest of the undergraduate career to it. The report frankly discussed the possible criticism of "superficiality" in an introductory curriculum that gave students so much leeway. But it was agreed that a college career was a travesty where a student could walk off with a diploma at Commencement without at least an introduction to the vocabulary and general concepts of basic western thought. All that was hoped for was "to take a limited amount of subject matter and show how a discipline works." In any case it was worth trying, since the last two years were planned as grueling ones, with a heavy load of demanding work in the chosen field.

The General Education Report was a basic influence in the development of the Brandeis study program, but in a few instances we diverged radically. We added a fourth area, the creative arts, to the core curriculum, on the assumption that at least an overview was essential in music, theater, the fine arts, and even, perhaps, the dance. We were one of the few colleges to include this area in its requirements, for in most established universities, the creative arts were still struggling valiantly to attain respectability as academic disciplines. From the outset, Brandeis was determined to become preeminent for study, research, and performance in the arts, and we refused to limit their scope to extracurricular activities. We could not start too early to cultivate interest, even in the general student who had come to us for science or the social sciences.

We also undertook another major commitment that had been left merely implicit in the General Education Report. In the first two decades after World War II the great student protests against indifferent teaching had not yet begun. Faculty, on the whole, still labored under the compulsion of "publish or perish," and their writing and research meant much more to their careers than devoting time to undergraduates — to answer their questions, to explore their interest, to clarify their thinking. Brandeis refused to distinguish between good teaching and individual creative research. Thus far, and for some years to come, Brandeis was likely to remain an undergraduate school, dedicated to the distribution system of general education. But the day would come, sooner rather than later it was hoped, when graduate departments would be added. Surely there need be no dichotomy between good teaching and sound scholarship. Indeed, the best teacher was most often the creative scholar. It therefore became a fully understood commitment that faculty who were brought in primarily for graduate studies and research would also teach undergraduates. The lowliest freshman would not have to wait until his junior or senior studies or his graduate years to be exposed to the experience of the stars of the school. And it was understood, too, that those who combined teaching and research would not come reluctantly or sullenly to the former. I always cringed when I heard a faculty man talk about "a teaching *load*."

Still another decision came early, the determination to make the University an instrument for special services that it had the resources and the capacity to perform. Its primary obligation as a quality teaching and research institution of course remained. But, it was assumed, there was also an obligation to undertake projects that could be socially useful.

Indeed, this was exactly the course that was followed by many of the scientists, who applied for grants from the great national agencies to link some of their basic research to the problems of health and social welfare, to develop methods to cope with the pathology of the cell, or diseases of the heart, or the riddles of aging in its medical and social consequences. Dr. Sylvan Schweber, one of the prioneers of our Physics Department, put it well when he wrote:

> In recent years, there has [also] been a growing tendency on the part of universities to include in their functions an ever increasing range of *applications* of knowledge. The traditional functions of universities are thus being altered by the interaction of the new knowledge and technology which they have helped to develop, with economic and political processes, changing values and the assumptions of new moral responsibilities. This merely attests to the fact that universities are not static but evolving institutions.

Hence, from the beginning the University gladly accepted such responsibilities if they could be fulfilled without depleting our general funds.

Some of them are later described — the Wien International program that brought gifted students to the campus from every part of the world; the Lemberg Center for the Study of Violence; institutes to sponsor research in the problems of television communications; special projects undertaken by the Florence Heller School for Advanced Study in Social Welfare; semester seminars for people in careers related to civil rights and civil liberties; tutoring programs for blacks and other minorities who had been culturally deprived in inferior high schools.

These and many other projects were not established without dissent that was often quite strident. Many of the faculty were opposed to the expansion of the University's role beyond the purely cognitive. They were wedded to the tradition of the university as a teaching and research center, believing that "utilization projects," however socially useful, were diversionary. To be sure the projects often provided dramatic visibility, and undoubtedly appealed to donors. But such temptations, these critics insisted, had to be resisted, because the ultimate cost in encumbering the basic aims of the University would be too high. Besides, the argument ran, if donors were ready to make gifts to the University, why not persuade them to assign them for faculty salaries and scholarships, not for peripheral programs that government ought to undertake. The irony of such reasoning was that the faculty would be outraged if instructed how to use their personal resources, but they had no objection to telling donors how they should use theirs.

In my inaugural statement of October 1948, I had made a threefold pledge that related to the quality, the spirit, and the open opportunity to be offered by the newly founded school. The statement was really a hope, for when it was made the University had not yet opened its doors; indeed, we did not know whether there would be enough applications for the school year to begin. Apparently the components of the University already in being — the trustees and the faculty — were determined that the pledge must not remain as rhetoric.

All efforts were now turned to its fulfillment. It was a frenetic experience to raise the immense extra funds to maintain a small faculty-student ratio, to meet the highest salary standards, to expand the curriculum so that there were sufficient offerings to maintain an effective balance between electives and required subjects, and to telescope into a few years acquisitions for the library that had taken other universities decades to achieve. But it was accomplished. We set the end of the fifth year of Brandeis as the first academic deadline; the absolute minimum time required for full accreditation by the New England authorities was the graduation of two classes. Our performance must have been adequate because not only was the accreditation voted in this minimum span, but the president of the accreditation body, Nils V. Wessel, then president of Tufts, accepted the invitation to be guest of honor at the celebration dinner. He congratulated Brandeis for an exemplary academic achievement "rare in academic annals" that made it an honor for the oldest schools of New England to welcome it into their fellowship.

V

The First Faculty:
Beginners and Retirees in Tandem

T HE problem of organizing a faculty called for unusual recruitment. If the University had been content to remain a local effort, offering a competent but undistinguished educational experience to run-of-the-mill students, it would not have been too difficult to enlist men and women to fulfill its goals. But we had undertaken a national responsibility that carried with it a very special symbolic significance. We therefore could not settle for mere adequacy. Yet what had we to offer to scholars of stature or young people of promise to induce them to cast their destinies with the beginning years of a precariously financed, unaccredited school? I saw the task as twofold. Brandeis required a permanent nucleus of young and feisty faculty who had the courage to join our experiment early in their careers. And it needed a leaven of sagacious men and women whose scholarship had ripened, whose stature was national and international, and whose wisdom and experience would give us balance.

The primary task was the most difficult, to seek out young people whose scholarly fulfillment, with time and perceptive encouragement, was likely. This became a major challenge, and the counsel of friends and well-wishers in the academic world was crucial. In the main, we were fortunate. We had our share of meteorites and falling stars, but a very high proportion of our risks turned out well. A goodly number went on to distinguished academic posts elsewhere, but I may be forgiven for believing that Brandeis bred them. When Phi Beta Kappa accreditation was conferred in 1961, only thirteen years after the University's founding — the shortest period of self-proving since the eighteenth century — the achievement in faculty recruiting was cited as outstanding. The report noted: "The pattern is clear: aggressive recruitment of younger men whose scholarship has been indicated but not fully demonstrated, and rapid advancement when they have produced as expected."

One of the most impressive examples was Saul Cohen, a scholar who had been trapped in the tontine effect of the longer-established universities, which decrees that in the scramble to the top more will fall off than reach the summit. His sparkling originality in research, particularly in chemistry, remained unencouraged in his first university positions. When he did not rise beyond the rank of instructor or lecturer at Harvard, where he had received his degree summa cum laude, or later as a National Research Council fellow and lecturer at the University of California in Los Angeles, he turned away from an academic career to move into applied research with industrial corporations. These positions were apparently very lucrative, but the academic life was in his blood; when, ten years after his impressive doctorate at Harvard, he was offered an associate professorship at Brandeis, he welcomed with visible delight the opportunity to return to campus life. He was promptly named head of the School of Science and within two years, in 1952, when the first Brandeis class was graduating, he was appointed full professor. When the faculty had grown sufficiently to warrant its formal organization and the appointment of a dean, Cohen was the inevitable choice.

He was a hard driver, often seemingly abrasive, stern in his demands, but he asked for nothing from others that he did not ask of himself. He was single-minded in his devotion to the highest academic standards for the University, and he was generally perceived by his faculty colleagues as scrupulously fair and considerate. He supported me when there was criticism of the fast pace of construction, tens of millions poured into plant and facilities. He responded caustically that modern teaching and research, especially in the sciences, was no longer a blackboard experience and could not function without adequate tools. Ours was never a quiet or docile faculty. Yet the policy of surrounding ourselves with strong and independent-minded men and women amply justified itself, and never more so than when Cohen gave farsighted leadership in structuring the expanded curriculum as the Brandeis graduate programs began to evolve.

Meantime, he had been elected to the American Academy of Arts and Sciences, and when his work as dean was completed he returned to teaching and research and service on the Faculty Senate. He was among the first members to become a faculty representative on the Board of Trustees. His preeminence garnered major grants for his research from the National Science Foundation, the National Institutes of Health, and the Atomic Energy Commission, now the Energy Research and Development Agency. It was a proud and thoroughly deserved climax when he became the first faculty member named as University Professor.

Another example was that of Leonard Levy, then a young instructor at Harvard, a protégé of Henry Steele Commager, with whom he had taken his graduate work at Columbia. Commager recommended Levy, who joined the Brandeis faculty in 1951, with enthusiasm. Levy quickly demonstrated that our expectation of preeminent scholarship and painstaking teaching would not be disappointed. His promotion was rapid and, when he was thirty-four, the chair in constitutional studies that had been established as a tribute to Chief Justice Earl Warren was assigned to Levy. When his book *The Legacy of Suppression* appeared in 1960, Justice Frankfurter wrote to him that he would rather have been the author of the volume than to have been appointed to the Supreme Court. Levy startled the uncritical American public with his study of Thomas Jefferson when he balanced the wisdom and vision of the Monticello sage with his cavalier treatment of civil rights. The flow of learned articles and scholarly volumes never stopped. In 1969, Levy won a Pulitzer Prize for his book *The Origins of the Fifth Amendment*. In the interim he had served as dean of the Graduate School and then as dean of faculty. His administrative judgments, tough but always fair, matched his academic preeminence.

Levy could have had the presidency of Brandeis after my retirement, but his wife, Elyse, was troubled with respiratory problems and required the drier climate of the West. The family therefore moved to California in 1970 and Levy joined the faculty of Claremont as head of its Department of History.

In contrast to Cohen's and Levy's tough academic and administrative stance, John Roche could be termed a Merry Andrew. Like them he was uncompromising in the austerity of scholarly standards, but he was almost raffish in his unconventionality. He liked to work person to person, across the board, defying or ignoring the jurisdictional traffic signals. He came to Brandeis in 1956 from Haverford, where, though his classes must have often unsedated quiet Quakers, he was one of the most popular teachers. He had grown up in Brooklyn during the Great Depression and he never forgot his roots.

In those early days, with Brandeis but eight years old, the president's recommendations for faculty positions were still received with more than a modicum of respect. I had, however, some considerable difficulty with the Political Science Department, where the redoubtable Herbert Marcuse exercised a certain *éminence grise*. Marcuse himself, of course, had been recruited on the strength of his undeniable scholarship at a time when many universities were cautious about employing committed and articulate Marxists. Roche, on the other hand, was an equally unabashed New Deal liberal. Indeed, within a few years, he had become the national president of Americans for Democratic Action. He also had directed the Fund for the Republic study of Communist infiltration into opinion-forming groups. Marcuse resisted the appointment. "I will not have this renegade," he stormed, "rammed down our throats." But

Roche came, and in time he was elected by the faculty to head its senate, and served as dean of the faculty. Inevitably he was dubbed "Abie's Irish Roche." He claimed never to have understood how a strong-willed president ran the risk of bringing in as dean one whose views would invite almost daily challenge. "Sachar," he wrote later, "must sometimes have wondered why God had punished him with an Irish anarchist for a dean." After a particularly revolutionary and expensive innovation that he badgered me with unrelentingly for weeks, "the president," he said, "simply pulled the sheet over his head and began the Prayer for the Dead." But the tenacious Roche had his way. He was equally out of harness when he dealt with the more conservative faculty who were apprehensive about innovation in governance; "To say don't rock the boat," he warned, "is so often actually saying don't rock the hearse."

Roche wrote prolifically on American politics, the American presidency, and the Supreme Court, several volumes in collaboration with Leonard Levy. His volume on civil rights, where he discussed the Abrams case, the Gitlow case and other Supreme Court landmark decisions, was widely acclaimed as a model of perceptive interpretation. Both Lyndon Johnson and Hubert Humphrey had a high regard for Roche. He was often called in as a consultant on the problems of Southeast Asia, and he made frequent investigatory trips for the administration. In 1966 he asked for and received a two-year leave of absence to become what was jocularly termed "intellectual in residence" at the White House. He served mainly as a speechwriter for the President and the Vice-President, and as liaison to the academic community. The final years of the Johnson administration were bitter ones, and when the President announced he would not seek renomination the loyal men around him began to send out feelers for new positions. Their association with the Johnson administration, however, had become a major liability. Many liberals who had insisted during the McCarthy years on drawing sharp distinctions between a scholar's academic competence and his political views suddenly began merging the two. Dean Rusk, longtime secretary of state, found that there were no faculty offers from any of the leading universities, and he had to settle for a post in a small Georgia college. Walt Rostow found he could not return to MIT, where his former faculty colleagues discovered, after his long tenure there, that he was not meeting the highest standards as a scholar. A weary John Roche called from the White House one day saying that he too wanted "to come home." Because he was on official leave of absence there was no need to clear his request with the faculty. I simply told him, "The key is under the mat, John, and you do not have to knock."

Nor did he. But the climate had changed. Most of the faculty respected his stature as a writer and teacher and his experience in the top advisory echelons of the government. He was deeply disappointed, however, by the way others, who had been ADA colleagues, reappraised his scholarly credentials because of his views on international affairs and American foreign policy. Nor was it easy to teach a student body that had once loved him but among whom there were now activists with a completely different doctrinaire complexion. Roche struck back, especially in the syndicated articles that he was now writing regularly for the national press. He noted that the only difference between doctrinaire liberals and cannibals was that cannibals ate only their enemies. In 1973 he accepted a call from the Fletcher School of Law and Diplomacy at Tufts to head its Department of International Politics.

No faculty member in our beginning years elicited more respect and affection from colleagues and students than Irving Fine. He had been a young instructor of music at Harvard, but though he had dazzled the faculty there, his promotion was blocked by the unavailability of tenured positions in a star-studded department. He was quite remarkable, as a composer and a musicologist, and as a teacher. The memory of his own gropings, of the encouragement given him by his mentors, Walter Piston, Serge Koussevitzky, and other titans in the world of music, made him especially sympathetic and effective with students. He was so deeply indebted to the patience of his mentors that he spared no effort whenever he found latent talent.

A problem in writing of Irving Fine is to find a way to say, without causing pain to those who loved him most, that he was a driven young man — in the sense that Mozart and Schubert were driven young men of music. When he was in the heart of composition, he taxed himself relentlessly, for he was incredibly demanding in his standards. The cruelty of perfectionism that he expected from others was imposed even more rigidly upon himself. One would have liked to put up one's hand and say, "Irving, there is plenty of time." But for Irving there was never enough time — for teaching, composition, performance. In everything he was like a high tide in the Bay of Fundy. Unusually, perhaps, for so creative a genius, he was a superb administrator and an ideal interpreter for the needs of his growing department and the school council for the creative arts. He was ever worrying over curriculum and faculty, over festival and concert. He was one of the most distinguished American composers, but his calls came through for more pianos, more classrooms, more secretarial assistance, and above all, for more funds to encourage graduate students, for more help to perform the compositions of gifted young people. He was most resourceful in his administrative battles, and when one door closed because of practical difficulties, he came in through another. He usually got what he wanted — rarely for himself, always for his people.

Irving Fine died in 1962, in his forty-seventh year, after presenting the latest of his works at Tanglewood. Mine was the heartbreaking task of delivering the eulogy at our Berlin Chapel, an assignment unmitigated by the presence of his parents, widow, and uncomprehending little daughters, with Leonard Bernstein and Aaron Copland among the pall-bearers. As more than a footnote, it should be added that Fine himself would have exulted at the establishment of an endowed chair in his name by his parents, the first incumbent of which has been his colleague and fellow composer Arthur Berger, whose own distinction continues to grow.

Meantime we turned to the pool of exceedingly talented and capable people who, for one reason or another, were virtually unemployable by then current university procedures. In some cases it was simply a matter of chronology; either the individuals had passed the mandatory age of retirement or were so close to it that the usual college pension plans then in effect could not afford to take them on. Others, of whom Herbert Marcuse was an example, were victims of the political climate of the times, when even universities with long traditions of academic freedom thought it foolhardy to venture into the eye of a hurricane. Whatever the reason, it seemed that precious talent was going to waste. And Brandeis, young and yearning, had need of it.

For with all our good fortune in the high proportion of young faculty who lived up to highest promise, we believed that it was still necessary to seed our newly established departments with scholars who had already become authorities in their field. Many of them in their late sixties and even in their seventies were in excellent health and at the peak of their reputation and effectiveness. They were becoming emeriti not because of decline or incapacity, but to make room for younger scholars whose opportunities for promotion and tenure could not be obstructed. But in a school where the entire faculty could be entertained in the living and dining rooms of the president's house, there was no problem of fore-closing opportunities for its younger members. Hence it seemed wise to offer key posts to a few distinguished scholars who had made their reputations elsewhere and who could offer not only their competence in special areas, but also their mature judgment for the planning of the University's formative years. Such appointments would also create visible prestige for the University. Above all, the earliest students would be brought into personal relationships with personalities of great stature, a rare experience in even the elite institutions of the country.

In the initial faculty of thirteen, one man of international stature stood out, Ludwig Lewisohn. When we invited him to Brandeis, he was already past the conventional retirement age, but his steady productivity continued in articles and books that more than sustained his reputation as one of the most brilliant contemporary men of letters. He had endured many years of discrimination in Germany and in midwestern American universities, and he welcomed the post of professor of comparative literature at Brandeis for the sheltered base that it offered in his twilight years. He and his wife, Louise, and their cat, Cupcake, took up residence in the Castle as unofficial campus hosts. They lived with the students, often ate with them in the dining hall, and entertained them in their remodeled apartment, usually in memorable bull sessions that lasted far into the night. Lewisohn was scintillating in discussing the works of Shakespeare and Goethe and other immortals of literature, and he was incomparable when he ranged over his personal experiences with the giants in the old and new worlds. When Lewisohn spoke of Alexander Pope's "feast of reason and flow of soul," he could have been describing those evenings in the Castle with his fascinated student audience. When the University library attained sufficient eminence to attract collections and documentation, Lewisohn was named librarian and exercised his magisterial acumen in determining what would be enduringly valuable. When he died in 1952, his widow contributed his priceless personal library of belles lettres to Brandeis.

Cupcake Lewisohn also deserves at least parenthetical recognition in any history of early Brandeis as the first in a long line of campus animal characters. One of the University guests was the publisher and commentator Bennett Cerf. In a hilarious article in the *Saturday Review*, he recalled his first stay at Brandeis, the high point of which was the co-rescue of Cupcake from one of the extremely tall campus trees.

"Ludwig Lewisohn," wrote Cerf,

> was in the middle of telling me how he had finished his scholarly two-volume *Goethe: The Story of a Man* on Goethe's 199th birthday, when his wife, Louise, uttered a shrill cry of alarm. Cupcake, the Lewisohns' outrageously spoiled cat, just had knocked over a priceless Ming vase and escaped through the casement window. Ludwig was in hot pursuit before you could say Mister Crump. Around the campus at an ever madder pace sped Cupcake and her pursuer. Suddenly the playful feline shinnied up a Massachusetts variety of giant Redwood tree. Ludwig went up after her — and captured her, too — on the highest branch, while students, faculty, and Cerf cheered a brilliant maneuver, faultlessly executed. Of course, there remained the minor formality of getting Ludwig and Cupcake down from the tree. The student body was equal to the emergency, producing the tallest ladder I ever saw to facilitate the descent. "You handled that well," I told the boys. "We ought to by this time," answered one. "After all, this is the third time we've done it since Saturday." "With your propensity for exaggeration," said Dr. Lewisohn as he bathed deep gashes in his arm and threw his ruined new Abercrombie & Fitch sport jacket into the incinerator, "I suppose this innocent little chase

will turn into a wild elephant hunt in the jungle." When he reads this, he will see how unjust were his suspicions.

There was old wine, too, the rarest French vintage, represented by Albert Guérard. An expatriate from France, he had spent his teaching career in this country at Williams, Rice, the University of California, and mainly at Stanford. Upon statutory retirement, he gladly accepted the Brandeis bid. His son was professor of comparative literature at Harvard and he welcomed the opportunity to be closer to his family. His classes in French literature and civilization, where his teaching was marked by old world charm, went beyond the facts of French culture. He was primarily concerned with interpreting the traditions of the humanities, the sensible use of freedom. "It is evident that in certain countries, knowledge had far outstripped wisdom; and the peril is with us too." He stressed the need to avoid glib judgments as true simply because they were wrapped in glittering prose. He encouraged dissent: "The curse of the moderates," he said, "has ever been their incurable timidity." "I believe with Heraclitus that change is the only reality. I even admit the possibility, if not the desirability, of sudden change: love at first sight, conversion, crisis, revolution, catastrophe, adventure, miracle." He cautioned his students not to be overwhelmed by authority, not to admire ideas or policies simply because the pundits of the moment pronounced them wise or valid. "This," he said, "argues a servility which is demeaning. A man must have the courage of his own taste; or, in Blake's words, he must not allow himself to be connoisseured out of his senses." His counsel was most useful for a highly cerebral student body that was often unduly fascinated by rhetoric, especially critical rhetoric. While at Brandeis, Guérard brought together in a valedictory volume, *Fossils and Presences,* many of the essays he had written earlier, and there he summarized his view of history as made by "creative, accelerated gradualism." Many of his students went on into university careers in French history and culture with the indelible mark upon them of Guérard's training and outlook.

There were others of an older generation who came to us in this way — Alfred Kroeber and Paul Radin, who gave depth and imagination to our offerings in anthropology; Everett Hughes in sociology; Rudolf Kayser in philosophy. Of course the risk of inviting the retired to come to Brandeis sometimes boomeranged. Kurt Goldstein was one of the giants in the area of psychology. He had won international honors for his research in disorientation and his *The Organism* was one of the classics in psychology. He had served as director of various neurological and psychiatric divisions in European hospitals and had taught at Columbia Medical School and other American universities until his retirement. The Department of Psychology included a number of his most loyal disciples and they wanted to have him at their side. He was already in his middle eighties, and this was really tempting fate too severely. His chief influence was with his faculty colleagues rather than with the undergraduates. At the midway point in the school year his vitality gave out, and his classes had to be suspended. But there were very few such disappointments.

In a few instances we agreed to make concessions in order to bring in highly desirable faculty members. A new school is not bound by rigid institutional procedures, and we could more easily cope with such special arrangements. In our second year we reached out for Max Lerner, who was successfully combining academic identification with adventurous journalism. When he was only twenty-five he had been named assistant editor of the *Encyclopedia of Social Sciences* and then had become its managing editor. He had taught at Harvard, Williams, Sarah Lawrence and at the New School for Social Research. As an editor of the *Nation* and as a regular columnist for the *New York Post*, he had covered the world's trouble spots. When he was approached in 1949 to take a professorship in American civilization at Brandeis, he welcomed the offer but retained his New York base. His class schedule was therefore telescoped into a day and a half, so that he could fly from New York on the morning of one day and return by the evening of the next. He asked to be free every other semester for world travel, and this wish was also granted. Thus we had only a part of his talents; the students could take advantage of only a fraction of his after-class time. But even a small piece of Lerner was a boon for the University, especially in its first years. He was a spectacularly successful teacher, lively and provocative, prodding the latent capacities of the very best students. This temporary arrangement turned into one of the most permanent, and he remained a faculty member for nearly twenty-five years, retiring at seventy when he jauntily entered early middle age, determined to give more of his time to the twenty volumes that he said he still had in his belly.

Our relationship with Mrs. Franklin Roosevelt as a faculty member was a genuine love affair. When she joined the Board of Trustees, and then served for three years as hostess of a national television program on contemporary affairs with the University as its base, there was a general impression that she was merely lending her name for whatever prestige it would bring. But as it turned out, Mrs. Roosevelt took all of her duties quite seriously, and her identification with the University, structured to meet her amazing schedule, was gratifyingly productive in every way.

But it was when she joined the Brandeis faculty as a visiting lecturer that her capacity to communicate her passion for world peace and to explore practical ways to achieve it was most clearly manifest. She agreed to offer a credit course that dealt with the many nonpolitical agencies of the United Nations — the Human Rights Commission, the

Educational and Scientific Commission (UNESCO), the World Health Organization (WHO), and many others. The enrollment was limited to six American and seven foreign students who had come to Brandeis on Wien International Scholarships. Mrs. Roosevelt held a seminar once a month, and the other sessions were directed by Lawrence Fuchs of the politics faculty. It was a rare experience to study the operations of the United Nations agencies and to have one of its most knowledgeable figures discuss its inner workings. Each year one of the seminars was conducted in Mrs. Roosevelt's Hyde Park home, where the students moved among the memoirs of the great days of the Roosevelt incumbency. When one of the Swedish students was asked about the class, he responded, with a measure of awe, "It was thrilling to have Mrs. Roosevelt talk casually about 'Franklin' and 'Winston' and their contemporaries, in the most intimate terms, and we felt that we were in a living room with the greats of our times, listening to a family discussion." Mrs. Roosevelt took personal interest in all of the students, explored with them their career goals, and helped several of them with influential recommendations and contacts.

When it came to identifying Eleanor Roosevelt in the University catalogue, she refused to be listed with professorial rank. "I have no college degree," she said, "and I am not an academic specialist." We compromised on "Lecturer" and her name appeared in the alphabetical order among the Rs.

Certainly no discussion of our unceasing effort to strengthen our academic structure should omit a unique piece of good fortune that came to us quite early in our quest. We could not hope to persuade many of the gifted men and women to leave permanent posts of established prestige and security. But some of them could be tempted to come to us for visiting periods of a semester or a year while they were on sabbatical or on leave. At the outset such appointments were only occasional, for their support had to be wrung out of extremely limited general funds.

It was during the search for a way to establish this program on a less precarious level that, in 1954, I approached the trustees of the Jacob Ziskind Foundation in the hope that its guidelines might permit a gift to accomplish our purpose. The trustees were most favorably disposed. They allocated the sum of half a million dollars, whose income and portions of whose principal could be used for visiting professors, especially from foreign lands. The Jacob Ziskind Visiting Professorship became one of the most productive developments in the academic life of the University. It not only fulfilled a vital curricular need but it brought fresh views and insights to the University. The roster of men and women who came to our young school includes E. H. Carr of Cambridge, a former editor of the London *Times* and an authority on Soviet

Russia; Pierre Emmanuel, the brilliant French poet and Resistance fighter; Erich Heller of the University of Wales, in German and comparative literature; Arnold Hauser of the University of Leeds, in the fine arts; Lewis Mumford, who was pioneering new concepts to protect our cities and our environment; Israel Efros of the Hebrew University, professor of Hebrew literature and philosophy; Stanley Kunitz, the poet who was awarded a Pulitzer Prize during his incumbency at Brandeis; John Passmore, professor of philosophy in the University of Sydney in Australia; Philipp Frank, professor of physics from the University of Vienna. Some of those invited as visiting professors were sufficiently intrigued to wish to stay on, and several became permanent members of the Brandeis faculty, notably Alexander Altmann, professor of Judaic studies at the University of Manchester, and Cyrus Gordon of Dropsie College, professor of archaeology and Mediterranean studies.

At first it was possible to invite only two or three visitors each year. Fortunately, the Ziskind Fund was most resourcefully invested and its capital doubled within seven or eight years; hence it was possible to bring in more and more visiting faculty. In the fifteen years until my incumbency as president ended, it was perhaps the most influential factor in the enrichment of faculty offerings; beyond 1968, as the capital continued to grow, its influence further deepened and broadened. I often referred to it as our academic Gulf Stream.

Perhaps one other supportive teaching innovation should be noted here since it proved, in the beginning years, to be most productive. Called Education S, since it was originally intended as a special course for seniors, it was an adaptation of the program that had long existed at All Souls College at Oxford, where statesmen, scholars, and professional people were invited as Fellows for various periods during a school year to discuss their views with those in residence. About twelve or fifteen notable visitors were scheduled for the year, and they were chosen by senior representatives in collaboration with me. They were to talk about the turning points in their lives, their great decisions, why they made them, how they evaluated success or failure.

We were gratified that no matter how high we reached we usually had a welcome, affirmative response. The sessions were unstructured, with no class recitations. The one requirement was an evaluation paper, based on the discussions in the course and on reading from suggested lists that were distributed when the lecturers were announced. In the week following the visit, a faculty panel gave their reactions to the message and their participation deepened the significance of the visitor's message. During the first few years I presided over the sessions, acting as a moderator, keeping the discussions from trailing off, and offering a summary at the end. Afterward Max Lerner, and then Milton Hindus, took over as moderator. The Commons Room in the Castle was invariably filled for the sessions that began at seven in the evening and often ran on beyond midnight. A student editor, reviewing one of the evenings, wrote that of the one hundred fifty seniors for whom the course was meant, all four hundred turned up. The desire for attendance and participation was understandable, for the course featured a *Who's Who* of men and women of extraordinary attainments.

A memorable evening was spent with Leo Szilard, the Hungarian scientist who had settled in the United States and joined Albert Einstein in warning the American government that Hitler was well on the way to the completion of an atomic bomb. Szilard persuaded Einstein to appeal to President Roosevelt to accelerate the research on nuclear power, for if Hitler won the race, the Nazis would control the world. So Roosevelt authorized the Manhattan Project. This research involved America's leading scientists and such men as Einstein, Szilard, Fermi, Bohr, and others who had fled from Nazi Europe. The bomb was perfected and the secret test at Alamogordo in July 1945 meant that America had control of the most destructive weapon in history. By then the Nazis had surrendered and Hitler had committed suicide, but the war against Japan was not yet over.

Szilard described for his tensely listening audience his futile attempts to persuade the top American policymakers not to drop the bomb upon Japanese cities. Roosevelt had died a few months earlier, and the awesome responsibility for the decision rested with President Truman. Szilard could not reach him but he did get to James Byrnes, then the assistant to the President. Byrnes told Szilard that it would be "political suicide" to have spent more than two billion dollars on the bomb, without authorization, and then not to use it. Szilard commented bitterly that President Truman's action was at least based on his Christian concern over the heavy human cost of the invasion of Japan, the possible loss of half a million lives if the Japanese did not surrender. But Byrnes was apparently more concerned with the political consequences of an immense expenditure for a weapon that was not used.

The discussion that followed centered on the rationale that justified Hiroshima, on the morality of saturation bombing, and on the judgment of Jean Rostand, who had written: "Science has made us gods before we are even worthy of being men." The evening with Szilard and the conversations with him became, for many of the students, their most vivid experience at Brandeis. Szilard, too, was immensely impressed with the student body, not as research experts, but as the vital, passionately concerned, intelligent representatives of the new generation upon whom the destiny of the world would depend. He returned later for a full semester as a visiting professor.

When we asked Norbert Wiener, the father of cybernetics and the author of *Ex-Prodigy*, to come to us, there was the liveliest curiosity and the expectation that we were to meet a *Wunderkind*. Wiener's childhood and boyhood had been a horror story. His father, a brilliant Russian immigrant who had become the first professor of Slavic languages and literature at Harvard, was an irascible perfectionist who had driven the precocious Norbert with a relentlessness that almost destroyed him. Wiener had an unusual childhood and early manhood. At seven he was performing advanced experiments in chemistry and physics in a home-built laboratory. He entered high school at nine and Tufts College at eleven. He received his undergraduate degree at fourteen and his Ph.D. from Harvard at eighteen. There were five prodigies at Harvard at the same time and all of them lived in a blaze of cruel publicity. It took Wiener years to adjust to the realities of normal social life, and it was not until he was nearly thirty that he shed his otherworldly bewilderment to begin truly productive work as a professor of mathematics at MIT.

The audience of Education S was introduced to a shy, unpretentious scholar, the prototype of the classic absentminded professor, ill at ease during the introduction, so hopelessly nearsighted that, in addressing the jam-packed Commons, he often faced in the wrong direction. When questions were asked, he would hurry up to the seat of the questioner to talk directly to him. But once he began speaking, completely uninhibited, all thought of his eccentricity disappeared. He was witty, self-deprecatory, and amazingly tolerant of the egomaniacal father who had pushed him so hard. As he outlined the problems of a prodigy who was advanced too fast intellectually in a rigidly conventional society, he was speaking to an audience whose I.Q. was also amazingly high. There were many transfixed youngsters sitting before him who identified closely with him. Wiener had no quarrel with the early involvement of children in serious matters; there was no harm in introducing them to foreign languages, the discipline of mathematics, and the miracles of science. But he was envious of the gifted youngsters of the present generation who could enjoy the enlightened programs of an enriched curriculum with boys and girls of their own age, instead of being propelled, usually by exhibitionist parents, into an environment where they were completely maladjusted, neither man nor boy.

Wiener devoted most of his discussion, however, to the growing power of automation in our society and its likely impact upon the future. He described how far the world of applied science had already gone in the development of the mechanical brain. He had coined the name for the process, "cybernetics," from the Greek root for "steersman." Some of the results — the thermostat, the governor on engines, the computer — had already been integrated into daily living and were taken for granted. They had revolutionized not only procedures and techniques but the essence of research. They solved equations with lightning rapidity. They gathered information from more sensitive sources than man's own brainpower could, by the use of strain gauges, voltmeters, photosensitive tubes; these never slept nor became sick nor tired and, if properly designed, never made mistakes. Wiener forecast infinitely expanded uses of the mechanical brain, not only for speed and accuracy, but for the solution of problems of space and health and the production of food.

Of course not all the guests who came for Education S were received with enthusiasm, although all were given a courteous hearing. The purpose of the course was to present men and women who had unique outlooks on life and who had influenced their generation. Obviously some of them represented values that were highly controversial. Their presentations and the questions and answers that they elicited made for dramatic confrontation, as when the head of the Central Intelligence Agency, Allen Dulles, came for a tough give-and-take evening. He had to move through the gauntlet of a picket line manned by students who were outraged by CIA operations.

Dulles noted that the CIA had originally been created as an information-gathering agency to guide top officials who conducted American foreign policy. But the realities of the Cold War had compelled the agency to go far beyond its original mandate. During the ten years under his direction, the United States had been locked in a struggle with the Soviet Union to prevent the engulfment of large parts of Europe and the rest of the world. The Soviet secret service carried out continuous infiltration and engineered government coups and kidnappings and assassinations. The CIA was therefore called upon to carry out missions that attempted to thwart and confound the secretive activities of America's enemies, and it moved quite deliberately into espionage and counterespionage.

Dulles did not look the cloak-and-dagger part. He was a quiet, restrained man who spoke temperately, unemotionally, as if he were reciting a trade report. In the dinner hour preceding the Education S session, he had told Thelma that his son had been desperately wounded in the Korean War and was living out his years as a vegetable in a veterans' hospital. Dulles presented the case for the CIA as an indispensable operation in a no-holds-barred world, where the very openness of a democracy compelled safeguards to protect its vulnerability against the machinations of totalitarian enemies. As he related little-known incidents, the listeners were taken through an Ian Fleming thriller. There was a barrage of questions, most of them pointedly critical, for this was an audience that could not easily square the methods of spying and subversion with the ideals of a democracy, even a democracy threatened and beleaguered. The questioners wondered how an agency that was virtually uncontrolled could protect itself against falling into the hands of unscrupulous or arrogant politicians who would use its power for personal political purposes; how it could be insulated so that its techniques would not corrupt the legal routines of domestic life. These were troubled observations offered long before Watergate, when all such apprehensions came to tragic fulfillment. At the end of the evening Dulles had won few converts, but the youthful audience must have been sobered by their introduction to the complexities that confront modern leadership as it wrestles with the problems of means and ends.

The inclusion of Education S in the curriculum inevitably provoked intensive discussions among the faculty and its validity was often challenged. There were many who held that the presentation and the questioning of a succession of personalities, however interesting or influential, did not add up to a university course, and that it diluted rigid academic standards which called for structured learning and accompanying tests to maintain the discipline of study in depth. There were others who welcomed the course as a valuable supplement to the prescribed work of the curriculum. I shared their view that if 117 of 120 credits were assigned to conventional lectures and classes, term papers, and laboratory experiments, three could be spared to bring the students in close association with great personalities drawn from every stratum of national and international life.

After five years Education S was dropped as an accredited course, but not because of the criticism that it did not meet curricular standards. A number of special-interest groups had been organized mainly for politics and social issues, and they also brought men and women of stature to the campus. A loyal Quaker supporter, Harry Helmsley, established a fund that underwrote the appearance of half a dozen national personalities each year who conducted a dialogue with the students on problems of racial and religious understanding. The head of radio station WMCA in New York, Nathan Straus, created two trusts, one in memory of Stephen Wise and the other to honor the Israeli diplomat Abba Eban, and each year the students chose world figures for a stay on the campus. Visiting lecturers came in such numbers — scientists, artists, statesmen, poets, social welfare technicians — that they made up a supplementary university experience in themselves. Above all, the growing sophistication of television and its documentaries and panel discussions with world figures fulfilled some of the original purposes of Education S, with more ample resources. But in the beginning, Education S helped immeasureably to enhance the University's innovative programs.

After the University obtained full accreditation in 1954 and launched its graduate program, we no longer needed to build exclusively on the hope that emerging talent would fulfill its promise, or on the reputation of retirees and visitors. Brandeis's reputation as a major institution of learning was sufficiently established to attract scholars of national and international stature. It was an exciting intellectual center: its facilities, especially for the sciences and the creative arts, were exceptional; its salary scale gave it highest rank even by AAUP standards. There was an additional inducement in its geographical location — where seventeen colleges and universities were established within an area of seven or eight square miles. Here one's social life could be enjoyed with peers in one's field. As the funding for chairs proceeded at a gratifying pace, as graduate programs were added at the rate of one or two a year, faculty leaders were encouraged to recruit vigorously with no inhibiting expectation that a particular scholar "could not be moved." Within ten years, many of the departments of the University — biochemistry, chemistry, physics, mathematics, Judaic studies, music, psychology, and others — were given top rank by the American Council on Education.

VI

Completing a Campus in One Generation

I N the past century less than a dozen privately founded universities, including Brandeis, achieved almost immediate national stature. Among them were Johns Hopkins, the University of Chicago, Rice, Duke, Vanderbilt, and such women's colleges as Vassar, Smith, and Wellesley. All but Brandeis were launched with substantial endowments. Johns Hopkins, founded in 1876, was built on the $3.5 million of Baltimore and Ohio Railroad stock bequeathed by Hopkins. Chicago began in 1892 with a $35 million endowment in oil stock from John D. Rockefeller, who had dreamed of a Baptist-founded university. Within a few years his gifts reached more than $80 million. The nest egg of Rice Institute was $10 million from the cotton fortune of William March Rice, although the school was not launched until 1912. The eccentric Rice had been murdered in 1900 by his valet and litigation tied up the estate for years. When the sensational trials ended and the bequest was validated, Rice Institute was so substantially protected that until very recently it was not necessary to charge tuition at all. Stanford, in the beautiful Santa Clara Valley near Palo Alto, was born of a $30 million endowment from the Central Pacific Railroad tycoon Leland Stanford. Organized almost as a personal fief, Stanford became the cautionary example of paternalistic control. Ambrose Bierce took an impish delight in printing the name as £eland $tanford. Conceived as a memorial to Stanford's only son, his widow was vigilantly obsessive in her concentration on buildings — to the exclusion of teaching and research. A faculty member remarked, as salary standards declined, "It's too bad men can't feed their families on buff standstone; it seems to be the one plentiful thing."

The tobacco millions of James Buchanan Duke and his family persuaded North Carolina to change the name of precariously financed Trinity College and move it to Durham, where, as Duke University and solidly reinforced, it began a new lease on life in 1924. Vanderbilt was incorporated in 1875 as a model university for the Southern Methodists.

Its financial founder was the buccaneering Cornelius Vanderbilt, who relied upon his friend Andrew Carnegie's help and upon the General Education Board for the Church for an additional $18 million. Vanderbilt's own share was so overwhelming that, at the inaugural services, the president turned without a qualm to the portrait of the old pirate, and the text of his invocation came from the tenth chapter of Acts in the New Testament: "Cornelius, thy prayer is heard, and thine alms are in remembrance, in the sight of God."

Three women's colleges, Vassar, Smith, and Wellesley, received substantial seed money from farsighted individuals who defied the prevailing resistance to higher education for women. Matthew Vassar, a brewery magnate of Poughkeepsie, wished "to build and endow a college for young women which shall be to them what Yale and Harvard are to young men." Henry F. Durant, whose only child died as a small boy, founded Wellesley in 1875 because he was confident that women were as capable of serious study as men in the Ivy League schools. Time would reward him with some of the first women astronomers, a pioneering aviatrix, and, among other influential alumnae, Madame Chiang Kai-shek. Smith also came into being in 1875, almost by accident. Its female Maecenas, the spinster Sophia Smith, had written five wills, and on numerous occasions she nearly followed the advice of her pastor to make over her inherited wealth either to Amherst or to an established female seminary.

Brandeis, as ambitious and aspiring as these older schools, began poor as a church mouse, or, rather, as a synagogue mouse. Justice Brandeis's name was a powerful moral asset, but no endowment came with it or was expected. Support had to be won from a vastly dispersed constituency that in 1948 was almost unendurably overtaxed for philanthropic purposes. Yet Brandeis could not afford to grow slowly. We needed everything at once — faculty support, student scholarships, buildings, equipment, administrative and maintenance assurance. Tuition and room and board income provided only a fraction of our resources. The deficits compelled appeals for supplementary support. Our competition for philanthropic attention came not only from established schools but from the endless and urgent causes supported by American Jewry in the postwar period.

We could not follow conventional fund-raising patterns. Our first graduates, barely more than a hundred, would celebrate their tenth reunion in 1962, when they would be still on the lower rungs of their professional and business careers and in the midst of mortgage payments and pediatricians' bills. Professional fund-raisers could only offer counsel on strategy. Volunteers and dedicated lay people were needed to exert their influence for the University.

I was extremely fortunate that all through my long incumbency I had at my side an able, resourceful lieutenant, Clarence Q. Berger, who served as a confidential assistant. His assignments ranged well beyond the specific duties that he carried or the titles that he bore. A Bostonian whose family circumstances were precarious in his youth, he had to stretch and drudge for everything he achieved. After his father's untimely death, he had transferred from the University of Maine to Harvard in the nadir of the Depression. He remained at Harvard after graduating in 1933 to take a master's degree under the redoubtable Pitirim Sorokin. Later he became one of the young protégés of David Niles. I met Berger when he was director of the New England division of the Anti-Defamation League. He had invited me, in April 1945, to give a memorial address in a citywide tribute to Franklin Roosevelt, and I was impressed with his organizing ability. When we began to recruit staff in the summer of 1948, Berger was offered the post of public relations director; in the next twenty-five years, he boxed the compass in administration assignments and titles. Growing up during the Depression had left an indelible mark on Berger's personality. His view of human nature was, to me, abnormally dark, and was wary of excessive enthusiasm from whatever quarter. He rarely went all-out in confidence or trust. This sometimes made our association painful, but it had its positive values for the University. He was usually realistic in spotting, early on, those individuals — fortunately few and far between and not always from rough-and-tumble backgrounds — who sought to use Brandeis and its growing prestige for their own ends under the guise of philanthropic intentions. While he was broadly tolerant of human frailties, his psychological seismograph registered high when he encountered phonies.

Berger was a valuable colleague, therefore, and not only in the knotty problems of fund-raising and public relations. His counsel was extremely useful in the crucial task of identifying men and women as potential trustees, with whom he often maintained long-standing relationships of respect and affection; in organizing major proposals to submit to foundations; in recommending top executives for major administrative departments; and, above all, in projecting the image of Brandeis as an institution of quality.

Physical facilities at first offered the strongest appeal for major gifts, for they were immediately identifiable. This was nothing new in the history of generosity to universities. As far back as the thirteenth century, when the first colleges of Oxford were founded, it was buildings such as Balliol College, given by a Scot to afford the students a place of dignity and to rescue them from the hostels or inns where they had been compelled to find abode, that held out the largest appeal. Some of our more unctuous faculty professed themselves superior to this form of philanthropy and made supercilious noises about "bricks and mortar." One graceless individual even painted over the plaque in his room. (It has since been restored.) Yet these detractors were usually the first in line for assignments to more adequate buildings, laboratories, and offices.

A master plan for the physical growth of the University in its first ten years took early priority. We at first chose as the architect Eero Saarinen, the brilliant Finn who had designed some of higher education's loveliest and most imaginative buildings. Saarinen died lamentably soon after taking the assignment. Only the dormitory quadrangle surrounding the old Middlesex ice pond is his. The commission then went to the firm of Harrison and Abramovitz, a personal gratification for me, since Max Abramovitz had been a student at the University of Illinois during my Hillel days there.

Abramovitz revised the Saarinen plan not only to incorporate his own views but also because the original plan quickly became obsolete as the tempo of construction accelerated to keep pace with academic needs. The bulldozer was rarely off the campus during our first twenty years. Since most donors could not redeem a large pledge all at once, we readily granted extended time schedules and construction bills were covered by loans. Audacious as this policy may sound in the light of later economic developments, it proved prudent during the 1950s and 1960s, when costs mounted much more sharply year by year than did interest rates on institutional loans. Had we deferred construction, academic progress would have been slowed, and the ultimate costs would have become prohibitive. By 1968 Brandeis had a $70 million investment in physical plant, connecting utilities, and landscaping – all entirely paid for or covered by valid pledges. Estimated replacement value, in the same year, was $200 million.

It would have been comforting had we been able also to build into our gift schedule for construction a sum to ensure maintenance. But a young university desperately in need of facilities could not prescribe total support conditions. Indeed, virtually no university could. Even Harvard was quite content to accept the pledge for its Widener Library, a memorial to the young heir who went down with the *Titanic* in 1912, and its support became a formidable charge on its annual general funds. When, after World War II, Thomas S. Lamont offered to underwrite a new undergraduate library facility, the need for a simultaneously established maintenance fund was better understood and Lamont volunteered it.

In the pioneering period, our multitudinous needs dictated resilience in negotiating for gifts. The first lecture auditorium constructed at Brandeis was assigned as a memorial to a family on the basis of a pledge that could not have been accepted for a minor seminar room ten years later. The first chairs at Brandeis were gladly named for families who could offer partial, often very partial, endowment.

The exigencies of pioneering were responsible also for the apparently capricious schedule of construction. Logically, the library would be given first priority along with classrooms and laboratories. Accommodations for student living, office space, recreational facilities, student lounges — all necessary but not indispensable — would then wait their turn. Every effort was therefore made to link a donor's gift with the facilities or the academic offerings most urgently needed. But often the donor, a modest contributor toward general funds, had a special interest for a long-range permanent identification that he wanted on the campus for his family.

Thus an impressive athletic center was constructed years before an adequate library and major science facilities could be made available. Abraham Shapiro was the most generous of the first trustees. His zeal and tenacity were crucial during the heated controversies and dissensions that plagued the prefounding years. But his dream of Brandeis included a well-rounded student body, made possible by a diversified program where the American tradition of sports and competitive athletics could also be pursued. He was convinced that the image of the university would be irreparably blemished if Brandeis attracted a student body that was overwhelmingly bookish. He feared classrooms filled with "grinds," all too often identified with Jewish intellectualism. It was suggested that it would not be fatal if all students were not well rounded; they did not have to roll. Shapiro would then draw himself up to his full height of five feet five and insist that purely academic facilities had much more glamour for a Jewish constituency and there would be little difficulty in obtaining them. He wanted the athletic center, and he wanted it not only for its functional service but because it would carry the message to the general public that Brandeis was a normal, wholesome American institution. And he was ready to make a substantial grant to bring this about. So a spacious athletic center facing the main highway, bearing the name of Abraham Shapiro, was among the first new buildings to be dedicated, in the presence of the governor of the Commonwealth, the secretary of labor, and the outstanding sports figures of New England.

Fortunately in most instances it was possible to persuade the donors to identify their gifts with the facilities that more immediately fulfilled our primary mission. Nevertheless, since major benefactions often came by bequest, it was not always possible to anticipate them. Many of the most essential facilities therefore came to fruition in most unconventional ways.

Each year the University sponsored a gala dinner at one of the Boston hotels as a reunion for its New England donors. The great majority were part of what was called the Brandeis Associates, a loosely organized club whose membership consisted of those who made annual contributions of one hundred dollars or more. In regular attendance was a quiet, unassuming, shy little man, who would come up to the dais after the affair in order to shake hands with me and the special guests. I often wondered how he could afford even his modest contribution to the Brandeis Associates. I always greeted him and inquired about his welfare, and I always got the same answer, that he had no complaints. No one seemed to know him. Apparently the Brandeis gathering was the only public function he ever attended. In 1956 he died and we learned that he had no family, no heirs, no friends, and that he had made the University his sole beneficiary. When his estate was appraised, it was revealed that he owned considerable real estate in Boston, and his ultimate bequest reached about $1.8 million. The first graduate programs were soon to be launched and the most essential need was a science research center. The decision was quickly made to build it with the proceeds of the bequest and to name the building, in his memory, the Julius Kalman Science Center. Often as I passed it I could not help thinking of this lonely man's tragedy. He never got the slightest satisfaction from any of his holdings. So long as he lived, despite his hidden paper wealth, he was Shakespeare's "O, without a figure." He came to life only after his death, through the invaluable facility that his resources made possible. I kept thinking also of what even the few words of greeting at an annual meeting must have meant to him, if his response was to name the University his beneficiary.

At the 1953 Associates dinner, the dramatic announcement was made that Brandeis had earned accreditation by the New England Association of Colleges. The occasion was further highlighted by the announcement of a grant of half a million dollars from the Charles Hayden Foundation, the University's first major gift from a non-Jewish source. The gift had been carefully cultivated by one of the Brandeis Fellows, Sidney L. Kaye of Boston, a wholesale food distributor. He had won the personal friendship of J. Willard Hayden, the head of the foundation whose educational grants had, until then, been limited to the largest and most influential universities. Hayden was not an easy man to deal with. He was blunt and could be abrasive, and he knew very little about Jews. But he knew Sidney Kaye and he admired his integrity and his thoughtfulness. When I accompanied him for several conferences with Hayden, to place before him the needs of the University, it was clear that Hayden thought of support for a new venture like Brandeis primarily because it had elicited the loyalty and the commitment of Sidney Kaye. When the grant was announced, Hayden paid a glowing tribute to his old friend and then added a matching proviso for the contribution that was to provide exceptional stimulus in the campaigns for support. His challenge launched a special appeal for life memberships in the Associates, pledges of two thousand dollars to be paid out over a two-year period. The campaign not only quickly achieved its goal, but it substantially broadened the supporting constituency of the University. The Hayden grant and the matching life membership proceeds provided the nucleus for an expanded science complex that was constructed over the next few years.

Thomas Gray and other poets invariably found inspiration in "the glimmering landscape," but to University officials its care and maintenance were a perennial financial problem. Where could the donor be found who was sufficiently perceptive to recognize that keeping the grounds trim and fresh, building and repairing the roads, providing utilities were all an integral part of imaginative landscaping that sustained the beauty of the campus? Until such a donor could be discovered, the oppressive expense would have to be borne from hard-to-obtain general funds.

Hence I was much impressed when I learned how resourcefully Swarthmore College had coped with the problem. I was invited to Swarthmore to spend a few days with the students for a series of discussion groups and a wind-up convocation lecture, what the Quakers termed the collection. The campus was magnificent in its charm and grace, its natural advantages of location and terrain enhanced by meticulous care. I asked how priority had been given to landscaping and was informed that some years earlier one of the trustees, Arthur Hoyt of the Scott Tissue Company, had set up a landscape fund, whose income was to provide for the beautification of the campus.

My search for a similar fund began as soon as I returned to Brandeis. Fortunately, through the intercession of one of our trustees, Lawrence Wien, we were able to interest a successful New York merchant, David Schwartz, the head of Jonathan Logan. He was a tough, blunt-spoken man, self-educated, and an unlikely prospect for such a project. But in his business career he had demonstrated a sure instinct for style, and he was the soul of generosity. His wife, Irene, was intrigued by the thought that the family could duplicate at Brandeis the role of the Hoyts at Swarthmore. It was especially important, she knew, for a new school like Brandeis, since without adequate landscaping, modern architecture can be stark and austere. The Schwartzes gave the University one of its most unusual gifts, a ten-year budget to cover the expenditures for initial indispensable landscaping. Apart from such utilitarian developments as the construction and repair of roads and walks and the installation and maintenance of utilities, each year some portion of the campus was chosen for beautification. Within a decade, the campus had been transformed.

Inasmuch as I had prevailed on so many devoted supporters to lend themselves to functions to advance the interest of the University, I could not very well object when my own name was requested for whatever leverage it could command when I reached my sixtieth birthday in 1959, especially when it was presented as an ideal occasion for raising a very substantial tribute fund. On February fifteenth the birthday party was held in the crowded ballroom of the Waldorf in New York. Representatives of every segment of our diversified constituency participated — trustees, Fellows, president's councillors, faculty and students, alumni — still minuscule in size, but making up for numbers with touching loyalty — members of our National Women's Committee — which had undertaken the maintenance of the library — and of course a large body of supporters. Abraham Feinberg, chairman of the board, presided. Judge Joseph Proskauer, another trustee and a distinguished figure in American Jewish life, now well past eighty, sparkled as always; he could not understand what was so unique about a sixtieth birthday. "This is mere callow youth," he insisted. Indeed, he still regarded me as a child prodigy. Robert Hutchins, another program participant, was in the same age bracket as I, and our friendship went back to the days when he was called to the University of Chicago as America's youngest college president.

Leonard Bernstein was in the full tide of his brilliant career as the director of the New York Philharmonic Orchestra. He reminisced with affection about the earliest years at Brandeis when he had served as a visiting faculty member in our Department of Music. He marveled at the *chutzpah* of a university president who, before even the first class had been graduated, did not hesitate to mount a music festival that featured the American premiere of Kurt Weill's *Threepenny Opera*, arranged by Marc Blitzstein, and starring the author's widow, Lotte Lenya. What he did not add was that the undoubted attraction for the huge audience at the festival was the announcement that he himself was to do the conducting.

Before my response the chairman presented a bracelet to Thelma, each of whose gold charms represented significant parts of our lives. There were charms for our wedding anniversary, my faculty years at Illinois, my long tenure in Hillel, and my inauguration as president of Brandeis. There was a charm for my writings and for those of our sons. There was a charm for Thelma's schooling at Washington University and charms for my years there and at Emmanuel College in Cambridge. Thelma's response was in keeping with the spirit of the occasion. She referred to each of the charms and what each symbolized in our lives together.

There was one other surprise in the program. My mother, who had just passed her eightieth birthday and had flown in from St. Louis for the occasion, was asked to rise in her place to be greeted. She was surrounded by all of her children and most of her grandchildren. To me, the sustained standing ovation she received from the audience was no conventional amenity. There had been many dark moments since the days at the end of the last century when she arrived as an immigrant from Turkish-held Jerusalem, but, fully as much as my father, who died in the University's first year, she had held the family together and had never relinquished her ambitions for them.

I knew better than to go beyond the climactic moments of the evening. I contented myself with a look ahead to tasks that could be undertaken with renewed confidence, now that the foundation was set. The practical postscript to the evening was not inconsequential: more than $350,000 had been subscribed in advance. I asked that it be set up as a scholarship fund until my presidency had ended. It then became part of a five-million-dollar tribute fund that made possible not only a fellowship program for study abroad for Brandeis students and faculty but also the acquisition of valuable acreage for future expansion and the erection of the beautiful International Center.

Still another way of winning productive friendships was inaugurated in the mid-fifties through the initiative of Lawrence Wien. He began a series of "air safaris" to the campus. Every few weeks he would personally lead a group, which ranged from about ten to more than two dozen, in a one-day visit. He also recruited other "hosts" to round up their friends and business associates for such safaris. The party would gather at New York's La Guardia Airport early on a weekend morning; be met in Boston by a car caravan of well-briefed, attractive students; drive to the campus for a tour, lunch at the Faculty Center, where the University's high officials would speak informally about Brandeis's long-range objectives and answer questions; attend miniseminars with distinguished faculty representing the areas that interested particular guests; and be driven back to the airport for the return flight. All the speeches, however eloquent, at affairs held in New York, all the promotional literature, however imaginative, could not compare with such visits to Brandeis, where the beauty of the campus could be seen and the departments' functioning could be interpreted by outstanding faculty. The New York safaris provided the model for those from other cities, some of them beginning on Saturday noon and ending Sunday evening. These preparations required more time and brought more last-minute cancellations, which were disappointing. But on the whole, they too were gratifyingly effective. Some of the most important friendships came through such safaris, and they brought not only gifts and bequests but also the willingness to supply interpretive leadership in the home communities when the need arose.

Since unrestricted funds were always a prime need, Brandeis very early adopted the fund-raising format of the plate dinner testimonial, a peculiarly American invention. This technique made it possible to turn a public tribute to a devoted benefactor into a contribution to a cause close to the benefactor's interest. Invitations were sent to business associates and friends of the guest of honor. The dinner charge varied considerably, depending on the clientele. Once the dinner and drinks and entertainment had been paid for, the rest was the net contribution to the cause. What could better represent American pragmatic ingenuity and the interests of sweet charity?

Brandeis did not hesitate to use this approach, concentrating upon guests of honor who were not merely successful in their industries but who had also played a constructive role in community life. It was rarely difficult to find such guests, for from the very outset Brandeis had attracted men and women who had achieved public recognition. The earliest guests set an impressive pattern: men and women from the University family — Jacob Goldfarb and Lawrence Wien of New York, Louis Salvage of Boston, Ben Swig of San Francisco — and great public figures who were devoted to Brandeis — Eleanor Roosevelt, Chief Justice Earl Warren, Senators Lehman and Ribicoff. Once the pattern had been set it was not difficult to sustain it. The dinners usually brought out large and well-disposed audiences. The charge ranged from about $100 to $500, and when the special gifts of preliminary luncheons and parlor meetings were added, the affair rarely netted less than $100,000 in unencumbered funds.

We were fortunate in having strong friendships in many of the basic industries and it was therefore possible to arrange for about forty dinners a year — in some communities as annual affairs, in others with intervals of two or three years — ultimately building up a solid beachhead of support that could make up for the lack of endowment income on which the much older universities counted. After a few years there were regular gatherings in such areas as beverages, shoes, food products, infant wear, jewelry, petrochemicals, cosmetics, electrical supplies, real estate, banking and finance, entertainment, publishing, and men's and ladies' clothing.

Through the intercession of Jack Poses, one of our trustees and the head of Parfums D'Orsay, we began invaluable relationships with the cosmetics industry. Some of the most successful houses were under Jewish ownership — Helena Rubenstein, Fabergé, Charles of the Ritz, Revlon, and of course D'Orsay. For our first industry dinner, Poses obtained the cooperation of representatives from each of the major houses and many other firms. Leonard Bernstein, then a member of our faculty, was persuaded to serve as the guest of honor, and he was at his mischievous best. He felt very much at home with the purveyors of cosmetics. He revealed that he had almost been part of the industry, for his father had been an impecunious wigmaker in Boston, long before the wig had become a fashionable item. There was a small struggling cosmetics house in New York that was eager to sell out, and Bernstein's father could have purchased the business for six hundred dollars. But he could see no future in a polish that turned women's nails a bloody red. It seemed so barbaric. Old Bernstein, in those pre-Freudian days, had no conception of the subconscious carnality of the primitive female of the species, and the offer was declined. The name of the firm was Revlon.

In the course of many trips to the West Coast, I had established a good working relationship with popular figures in the entertainment world. The theater, the cinema, their actors, producers, writers, investors, included many of the most generous contributors to the causes of American Jewish life. I became almost a conversion favorite, for, when Jews married non-Jews, some of the rabbis would assign my volume *The History of the Jews* as a textbook for the introduction to the fate that the convert was, for good or ill, to share. I was told by Danny Kaye that, on a plane one day, he was startled to find Carroll Baker deeply absorbed in the chapter on Judaism and Christianity. Elizabeth Taylor, in her flirtations with Judaism, made several attempts to master the intricacies of the section on prophetic Judaism. Sammy Davis, Jr., referred in his autobiography to "Dr. Abe," who reminded him of the common sorrow of the disinherited that was shared by Jews and blacks. Hence, when the guests at our plate dinners included these and such other highly visible and popular personalities as Joan Crawford, Lucille Ball, Jack Benny, Leo Jaffe, Eddie Cantor, Bess Meyerson, Sam Spiegel, Joe Levine, and Alan King, standing room attendance was always assured. Virtually all of these performers, whose services were often cheerfully donated to many good causes, were ideal interpreters for the University in their large circle of influence.

Danny Kaye appeared at several functions as guest of honor. He demonstrated his remarkable versatility when, at the tail end of the evening, he took the addresses of the participants who had preceded him and used them as texts for an extraordinary spontaneous potpourri of wit, ridicule, schmaltz, and zany humor. One year, during the Passover holidays, Danny was filling an engagement in Boston as a benefit for the symphony orchestra, and we invited him, his wife, Sylvia, and their daughter to our family Seder. He had not attended one since his boyhood in his parents' home and the nostalgic memories that were evoked apparently gave him so much joy that we were happily embarrassed to learn that he had invited his accompanist and all the Jewish members of his retinue to come to our home for the second night. He showed his appreciation by coming to the campus the next season to address a large, informal bull session where one serious youngster refuted his inveterate optimism by quoting from Aristotle. Danny kept referring back to his questioner as Morris Aristotle, a name the young philosopher found difficult thereafter to shake off. Later, Danny Kaye received the University's honorary degree for his contributions to UNICEF, having brought laughter and good cheer to hundreds of millions of children when he traveled in their interest to the remotest parts of the world.

Perhaps the most dramatic example of princely generosity came out of the Palm Beach Country Club in Florida, one of the most luxurious resorts in the world, whose standards for membership include adequate community philanthropy. The rationale was simple. Any family that could afford the stiff fees of the club and the scale of living in Palm Beach was expected to meet its responsibilities to the community. The fulfillment of duty here was as much an indication of character as business or professional intregrity or social graces. Such a constituency was a natural magnet for every important cause in Jewish life, and here the emergency appeals for Israel received spectacular response. Hospitals, seminaries, rehabilitation centers, schools — all found exemplary support. Millions of dollars must have been contributed each year in intervals of teasing conversations in a locker room or at a luncheon table or between strokes on a golf course. These were much more effective sites for persuasion and fulfillment than formal, structured meetings or rallies. Indeed, the club frowned on fund-raising affairs. The members insisted that they had been endlessly involved in such functions at home, and when they escaped routine for a well-earned holiday, they ought not to be diverted with the same round of pressures and appeals.

It was Morris Brown who first opened the club's cornucopia to Brandeis. Brown was a successful New York plastics manufacturer who, as president of the club, gave at least half a year in full time to its welfare. In supervising each detail of the club's administration, he came to know every member intimately. Genial, buoyant, and hospitable, he made it a personal concern to have the members enjoy every advantage that the club offered. His solicitude was returned with affectionate goodwill and no request of his could be easily denied. Old Joe Kennedy, who spent his winters in Palm Beach and held an honorary membership at the club, sensed this and asked Brown to lead the annual campaigns for St. Mary's, the community's Catholic hospital. The hospital's final affair was always held at one of the country clubs that excluded Jewish membership. An exception was regularly made for Brown and it was always pointedly declined, but the results of his quiet, personal campaign were always astonishingly successful.

Brown became a devoted supporter of the University in 1955 and was soon one of its most enthusiastic advocates. Later, having become a trustee, he was the cochairman of the three-year campaign that raised sixty-five million dollars for the University. He readily agreed to invite the top leadership of the Palm Beach Country Club to a luncheon for me in his lovely home, and this informal function was the beginning of many years of productive parlor meetings in Palm Beach, where some of the most important gifts to the University were completed. It was at such a luncheon that the friendship with Nate and Frances Spingold developed. It led to a visit to the campus by the couple and their decision to contribute more than $4 million to construct the magnificent

Theater Arts Center. It was also here that other necessary facilities and academic programs were underwritten. And it was this extraordinarily generous response to the University's needs that impelled the Board of Trustees to hold its February meetings in Palm Beach and to link them with a preliminary week of privately planned conferences and a Saturday night affair that became the social climax of the Palm Beach season.

Brown died suddenly in 1964 and was succeeded as president of the country club by a Boston shoe manufacturer, Louis Salvage, another University trustee. Salvage was held in the same high regard and affection by the country club membership, and his devotion to the University was equally unfaltering. He took pride in the cancer research laboratories that he underwrote for the University and, since he set an example of generosity when he approached others, the response to his appeals did not waver. Toward the end of his life his health failed rapidly, but he looked upon his chairmanship of the Brandeis weekend almost as a sacred responsibility and, though it often meant getting out of a sickbed, he presided at the luncheon and the evening banquet. His staff would give him a prepared speech. Invariably he would glance at it with cataract-ridden eyes, throw it away with a brusque "To hell with it," and talk in the plain homespun vernacular that his friends knew and loved.

Because so much depended on the results of the Palm Beach effort, the strategy for the week had to be planned far in advance. Trustees and Fellows who had winter homes in Palm Beach held private sessions with selected prospects, and if help were needed in their interpretive tasks University officials would join them. The Saturday luncheon would be the occasion for the announcement of such gifts as had been secured. There were usually about one hundred guests present, and the program for the afternoon would be planned for their benefit. I usually joined with Lawrence Wien in this appeal and apparently we were an effective team. I would provide the prologue, half banter, half serious, interpreting the concept of the University and its most recent developments; Wien would then announce a special project that would become the Palm Beach designation. One season the objective was the purchase of highly valuable acreage contiguous to the campus, whose cost was divided into syndication units. In another season plans were revealed to construct a social science center on the campus, and it was suggested that this would become a most appropriate tribute to Morris and Pearl Brown. In still another season the appeal was linked to the vastly increased need for fellowships, since the University had launched several new graduate programs. Wien and a few trustees and Fellows set the level of pledges with their own generous commitments, and the bidding from the audience was fast and spirited. The average amount realized at such luncheons came to over one million dollars, and, when added to the commitments that were quietly secured in the preceding weeks, the Palm Beach week could almost be listed with tuition and sponsored research as "assured income" for about 25 percent of the University's general operating expenses.

VII

The Three Chapels

FROM the outset, Brandeis had been set squarely in the framework of the nonsectarian schools and had meticulously striven for complete objectivity in the choice of faculty and staff, in the enrollment of students, and in the development of curriculum. Yet it did not follow that the religious experience, so basic in our lives, should be ostentatiously ignored. It was believed that many young people on a college campus were eager for some opportunity to express their faith, to link themselves with the enduring values of their traditions. The solution that was chosen at Brandeis to express the religious experience turned out to be dramatic and innovative.

There were many historic models for religious expression on privately sponsored campuses. The most common was to build the chapel in the image of the host group. At my own school, Washington University in St. Louis, the Graham Memorial Chapel reflected the Episcopal tradition of the founding and supporting groups. Hospitality was gladly offered to students and faculty of any denomination who wished to use the chapel for their own religious purposes, but there was never any doubt that Graham was an Episcopalian chapel. Since worship is largely a matter of mood and sentiment, it was difficult for other than Episcopalians to evoke the ethos, the nuances of their own tradition, however gracious the hosts. A Jew, away from home, could not enter fully into the mystique of the sacred Yom Kippur liturgy when he worshiped at Graham amid the Christological symbols that came out of the Episcopal experience. Swarthmore's Quaker chapel was at the disposal of all groups, but though its austere symbolism literally breathed humility and reverence, an alien quality clung to the worship of the students reared in other traditions. Such a model, therefore, of creating a Jewish chapel and offering its use to all other groups, was not followed at Brandeis.

Some attention was given to the example of the chapel at Cornell, a gift to the university from Myron Taylor, a distinguished Quaker diplomat who had spent many years as the special ambassador of the United

States to the Vatican. Behind the altar wall, each denominational group arranged its own symbols for worship. The chapel was equipped with special electronic controls that spun these symbols into place as they were needed. When the Jews gathered for worship, a button was pressed and an Oren Kodesh and its Torahs hove into view. Catholics rarely use facilities that are shared by other religious groups; hence at Cornell, as elsewhere, they preferred the Catholic churches in Ithaca itself. The Cornell pattern held little appeal for us. Apart from its diverting gimmickry, there was no feeling that this was one's own house of worship, that it belonged emotionally as well as physically to the group using it.

Hence, this concept, and others that had been devised for other campuses, did not meet the needs at Brandeis. It seemed more appropriate for the first Jewish-sponsored nonsectarian university to be understanding and sensitive hosts, avoiding the connotation that every worshiper was somehow beholden for access to religious facilities. The architects, Harrison and Abramovitz, were therefore commissioned to develop a concept that would include three separate chapels, one for each of the great western faiths, to stand side by side, none to cast shadows upon the others, all linked within an interdenominational area that could be used when common purposes were to be served. Thus each group would have its own chapel, designed to fulfill its own tradition, with no need for electronic devices, space allocations, or time schedules. And what went into the chapel would be there permanently to sustain the religious climate each group counted as precious and unique.

It was quickly determined that the costs for construction were not to come from the general funds of the University. Each denomination would seek support from its own coreligionists for its chapel, and its officials and student leaders would remain in complete charge of their own affairs. But since campaigns to finance all three chapels might stretch out inordinately, it was at first suggested that at least the Jewish chapel be built, with the others to follow as soon as their funding was assured. Here the student leadership intervened. There were strong protests in the Student Council and in the columns of *Justice*. The students insisted that the Jewish chapel might stand by itself for a long period and the first intuitive impressions would be difficult to overcome later. It was better to wait, however long, until all the funding had been assured and then the three chapels could rise in their places together. Fortunately, the students' arguments prevailed, and the architects were instructed to draw the plans for the total concept; the appeal for construction and supporting funds proceeded simultaneously.

As expected, the campaign for the Jewish chapel was completed first. It took the form of a tribute to one of New England's most beloved surgeons, Dr. David Berlin, a world-famous thyroid specialist. Scores of his grateful patients undertook to finance the construction of the Jewish chapel to celebrate Dr. Berlin's fiftieth birthday by honoring the memory of his parents, Leah and Mendel Berlin.

When it came to the design of the chapel and its equipment, the architects studied the plans of some first-century synagogues that had recently been discovered by the Israeli archaeologist Sukenik and his gifted son, Yigal Yadin. The eternal light and the menorah were modeled on those that had been unearthed in the dig in Israel. The window curtains took the form of a *tallith*, a prayer shawl; the ark was a replica of the tabernacle that was carried by the Israelites in the desert; the design for a specially woven cover was created for it by Mitchell Siporin of the Brandeis Art Department, who studied the directions for the *perochoth* (the ornamental cover for the ark) described in the Second Book of Chronicles. Several Torahs were contributed for the ark. One of them had been retrieved from a burning synagogue in Germany during the Black Thursday of November 1938, when Hitler launched one of his early pogroms. Another was purchased in Israel as the gift of Nate and Frances Spingold, who later underwrote our Spingold Theater. Other families competed for the privilege of contributing the facilities to be used in the chapel — furnishings for the chaplain's study, an organ for the services, prayer books, an outdoor altar. A symbolic piece of sculpture by Elbert Weinberg, representing Jacob wrestling with the angel, was commissioned by a devoted patron of the University, Mrs. Harry Cline, as a memorial to her husband. It was placed at the entrance to the chapel.

Simultaneously campaign plans were launched to obtain the funds for the Catholic chapel. The former governor of Massachusetts, Paul Dever, gladly accepted the honorary chairmanship. Louis Perini, one of the country's great building contractors, took the active chairmanship, and many of the Catholic lay leaders of New England were brought into the campaign committee. The architecture and the symbolism in the sanctuary were meticulously planned with the cooperation of the highest Catholic authorities. Indeed, the vestments were the personal gift of Archbishop, later Cardinal, Cushing. The organ was a memorial tribute from the family of William Callahan, a courageous young man who gave his life during World War II. Archbishop Cushing compared the architectural restraint and unpretentiousness of the chapel to the one in Assisi where the Franciscan Order was born. With fine sensitivity he named the Catholic chapel Bethlehem, to link the traditions of the Old and New Testament.

Some early problems developed, even before the dedication, because of the opposition of some bigoted Catholic dissidents. A fundamentalist group in Boston, the Feeney sect, disavowed by the Catholic church, was greatly disturbed that there should be a Catholic chapel on our campus. How could good Catholics permit the Savior to be captive to the Jews whose ancestors had crucified Him! There were ominous warnings that there might be an "invasion" of the campus and a king-sized protest to disrupt the dedication. That the threat did not material-ize was due almost entirely to the courage and gallantry of Archbishop Cushing. The projected Feeney invasion was, he told me, *his* problem. He was prepared to meet it. Rightly perceiving that even Feeney would not raise his hand physically against his bishop, Cushing announced that he would himself bless the chapel and conduct its first mass. So he did, and the united service was held in peace and dignity, with no further problems from the Feeneyites.

The Protestant chapel, like each of the others, was built in the form of a Bible, an open Bible, as eloquent a sermon in stone as the imagina-tion of the architects could devise. Its symbolism reached back to the noblest models of the Protestant tradition. It was made possible by the goodwill of Protestant families in every part of the country, whose generosity was spearheaded by the leadership of C. Allen Harlan, a Detroit communal leader. He was a kinsman of Justice John Marshall Harlan, whose grandfather had also sat on the Supreme Court of the United States in the late nineteenth century. The elder Harlan, in the case of *Plessy* v. *Ferguson* in 1896, was the lone dissenter from the decision to establish separate facilities in public educational institutions for blacks and whites; "separate but equal," the writ decreed. His grand-son had the satisfaction, sixty years later, of sitting on the Warren court, which, in *Baker* v. *Board of Education of Topeka*, unanimously over-turned *Plessy* v. *Ferguson*. Allen Harlan agreed to take the chairmanship of the campaign for the erection of the Protestant chapel, which was to be named for his distinguished forebear, whose views were appropriate for a University bearing the name of Justice Brandeis.

As the construction of the chapels was nearing completion, offerings poured in from families everywhere, not only altar cloths, candlesticks, prayer books, skullcaps, chalices, and flowers, but major gifts such as organs, a communion table, and furnishings for the lounges and chap-lains' offices.

Uniting the three chapels, an interfaith area was developed, its many acres of immaculately tended lawn stetching across the inner campus up to the science cluster. It had an outside altar that was to be used for occasions when all groups came together, usually for baccalaureate ser-vices or similar all-University functions. Its construction and mainte-nance became the project of the alumni of a New York high school fraternity, Mu Sigma, through the persuasion of General Bernard Bar-ron, who served with distinction in World War I and World War II. He was joined in leadership by fellow officers he had met in wartime and the Kriendler family, who were the proprietors of the renowned "21" Club of New York.

In 1958 General Barron, "Pete" to his classmates, proposed that the interfaith area become the memorial to Jack Kriendler, one of the brothers who had recently died, and that the next reunion of Mu Sigma be held at "21." Those who accepted the invitation to attend would be asked to contribute to the memorial fund. The Kriendlers and their partners were delighted with the idea and insisted upon being the personal hosts for the dinner. There were three such reunions at "21," by which time the pledge for the interfaith area had been fulfilled.

The relationship with Mu Sigma was a fortunate one beyond the interfaith project. The friendships that emerged from the reunions resulted in major future gifts when the lawyers, the accountants, and the tax specialists in the group served as friendly interpreters to their clients in the interest of the University. Many of the members continued their visits to the campus on its great days, especially those whose children came as students. Invariably they made their pilgrimage to the interfaith area of the three chapels, to be reminded again of the unusual way in which a high school fraternity's reunion was made to serve the long-range interests of the University where they had all become foster alumni.

Meantime, several years before the interfaith area had been funded, the formal combined dedication of all the chapels was held. It took place on a beautiful fall day in 1955, and it was much more than a Brandeis event. It stirred national interest, for the three chapels had become a dramatic symbol of practical interfaith amity. The *Boston Herald*'s lead editorial summarized the significance of the occasion:

> The magnificent thing we seem to have partly achieved here is a comfortable coexistence of diverse faiths, cultures and individualities. There have been a lot of failures and there will be more. But the ideal we mostly practice, the ideal that is embodied in the protections of the Constitution, is the ideal of a communion of diversities. . . . We have not the strength of conformity on which the totalitarian nations rely. We ought not to put our trust in any attempt to match it. Our strength is the far greater strength of accepted diversity.

Justice Harlan was invited for the dedication ceremonies to receive an honorary degree. He was joined by three internationally distinguished religious leaders, representing the Jewish, Catholic, and Protestant faiths. There was Rabbi Leo Baeck, who had been the chief rabbi of Germany all through the Hitler period and had refused to leave the country, sharing concentration camp horror with his people until the collapse of the Nazi regime. He was invited to bless the Jewish chapel. Unfortunately he became seriously ill on the eve of the convocation and died soon afterward, so his honorary degree had to be accepted by his granddaughter. Jacques Maritain was invited in honor of the consecration of the Catholic chapel. He was the profoundest interpreter of the scholastic system of Saint Thomas Aquinas and had been former ambassador of France to the Vatican, teaching at Princeton since his arrival in the United States. Paul Tillich, the erudite theologian, represented the Protestant tradition. He had taught in the great universities of Europe and was now in a joint appointment at Union Theological Seminary and at Harvard.

In the dedicatory address I summarized the rationale for our chapels:

> Our concept was developed after patient introspection and exploration. It came out of the consciousness that a campus experience must be a preparation for the tasks of life. Our world is tragically fragmented, disrupted by bitter ideological disputes, nationalist rivalries, racial antipathies, religious bigotry. When we say that the world is crazy we are using the word in its very literal sense, for crazy stems from the French root, *ecrasé* — broken, shattered. And the illness of our world comes from the fact that it has been so broken and shattered. The great task of the religious experience is to help restore cohesiveness by rechanneling the forces which break and shatter. . . . Here at Brandeis we shall each respect our own faith, draw strength and meaning from its survival values, and carry this respect with pride in the presence of each other.

Through the years the chapels served the Brandeis family in their worship, their glad days and their sad ones, their weddings and confirmations and funerals, their study groups and their conferences. We were especially pleased with the large number of student romances, and the weddings were very often planned for the college chapels. There was scarcely a week without such a joyous occasion, and on some weeks all three chapels were exuberantly busy. Our chapels became a model for other universities that were ready to abandon the tradition of a single denominational chapel for hosts and guests, and hardly a year passed without a visiting committee coming to explore the Brandeis example. There was little need for explanation or briefing. The existence of the chapels, side by side, fulfilled the message that had been sounded at the dedication. Here, without the degrading nuances of forbearance or tolerance or obsequiousness, a tradition of understanding and mutual regard had been built, which drew from the experience of religious faith its most precious quality.

Undoubtedly the students and faculty and their chaplains can relate scores of incidents when the chapels became the central point of an unforgettable experience. Much depended, of course, on the caliber and character of the individual chaplain. In the main, I believe, we were remarkably fortunate in the quality of our representatives. Most were young men, often not long ordained and almost as often involved in doctoral or advanced-degree study at Brandeis or some other nearby college or university. Whether their predominant youth was a deciding factor or not, in general our chaplains identified themselves with prevailing student interests in different eras. I think particularly of the combined involvement of students and chaplains in the civil rights movement of the 1960s, and of the reaction to the Vietnam War.

A later Hillel chaplain, Rabbi Al Axelrad, serving mainly in the sixties and early seventies, was most resourceful in committing scores of students to community projects as a means of applying religious zeal to practical purposes. He organized teams of students to visit the Hebrew Rehabilitation Center for the Aged once a week in a kind of "adopt a grandparent" program. Another project involved visits at hospitals, mental institutions, and prisons. Still another involved students as assistants to the part-time Jewish chaplain at Massachusetts General Hospital. Some of the students began corresponding with crippled youngsters at the residential Alyn Orthopedic Center for Crippled Children in Jerusalem. Others conducted Jewish holiday parties and services at the pediatric and adolescent wards of mental institutions and hospitals, as well as at the Perkins School for the Blind. Clusters of students and the Hillel Singing Group paid Jewish holiday visits to nursing homes in the area. Students and faculty came together for weekly letter-writing sessions to Soviet Jewish activists ("Refusniks") and their families. They reached out to befriend and assist Soviet Jews who had been resettled in the Greater Boston area.

Perhaps the most moving observance, which became a Hillel chapel tradition, was the Remembrance of the Holocaust. It was developed by one of our Canadian students, David Roskies, and it was based on his script, "Night Words — A Midrash on the Holocaust." Subsequently it was published by the National Hillel Commission and adopted by Hillel foundations and Jewish organizations throughout the United States and elsewhere. Rabbi Axelrad recalls the enthusiasm of his student congregation when a new form of service was developed, a *havurah*, emphasizing fellowship, with continuous participation by the congregants mainly through group singing. Axelrad wrote:

> A regular member of the *havurah* service was an outstanding and courageous female student who suffered polio in her childhood, just before science managed to eliminate that dread disease. As she had braces on her legs and had to walk with crutches, it became especially difficult and hazardous for her to negotiate Brandeis's terrain by herself during the winter months. I therefore gladly accepted the obligation to call for her when we planned services on special occasions. Several years later, after she had graduated from Brandeis, I had the in-

comparable thrill of officiating at her marriage in her home-town synagogue.

There were many other experiences, sometimes brought to me by others, that I have cherished over the years: the Sunday morning when the Protestant chaplain, a tall, commanding young man, came rushing around the pond shouting, as the wings of his gown flapped wildly, "Father, Father, can we borrow your organist? Ours didn't show." Or the day a distraught student burst into my outer office with the alarming report that the menorah was gone from Berlin Chapel. My assistant, Larry Kane, himself a Catholic alumnus of one of our early classes, strolled in and said, "It's all right, Dr. Sachar, Rabbi loaned it to Father until Friday for the Advent Wreath in Bethlehem." There was the Jewish graduate student in our Department of Music who composed a Catholic liturgy as a part of her doctoral studies, which was given its premiere performance in Bethlehem.

Two memories remain most vivid. One was the joyous tenth anniversary rededication in the autumn of 1965. The program included panels and symposia, involving our own faculty and distinguished visitors drawn from various fields. There was even a reunion of former chaplains. The day-long affair culminated in a major banquet that was so well attended it had to be held in the Athletic Center. The speakers were men of international repute. I cannot remember any of their remarks now. Neither, I am sure, can they. But none will forget what was to be one of the last appearances of Cardinal Cushing at Brandeis, when he agreed to help us climax our celebration. He arrived quite late, and we could all see how the ravages of the fell disease that would erode all but the beauty of his courage and faith had made themselves manifest. His face was ashen. He was both unusually subdued and apparently extremely tired. He merely played with his food, for he had already begun to experience difficulty in swallowing. Nevertheless he listened patiently and pleasantly to the three internationally acclaimed speakers. At last he rose to deliver the briefest speech any of us could remember. He professed an admiration for the previous speakers and their theological insights. His own theology, he insisted, had barely gone beyond that taught to children via the catechism. "And what," he asked, "have I been doing all day?" Dramatic pause. "I've been giving away *fish*." There had been a strike that had left tons of fish in danger of rotting on the wharves. Someone had called the cardinal's residence and said he might have the fish for his poor if he could find ways of giving it away. The audience roared, for didn't "Cush" always make us laugh! But the point was not lost in the laughter. He admired, respected, and encouraged education, but his portion of God's work was, though he would not have used the phrase, *g'milleth chesed*, the charity of grace and favor that asks no thanks.

The other remembrance is of the tragic afternoon when young President Kennedy was assassinated. That crisp November day had begun pleasantly, outwardly at least. I still remember, incongruously, how green the playing fields were across the road from the president's office, how unusually mild it was. However, I had a particularly difficult faculty meeting scheduled for three o'clock, which I was not anticipating with any delight. I was at lunch when news was brought me of the shots in Dallas, and I immediately hurried back to my office. There I found my staff in various stages of bewilderment. One even later confessed she thought *I* had been shot. People congregated around radios. When we heard through the static that the priests had left the hospital, one of my assistants said, "Then he's gone, sir," and got up and walked away weeping, bumping into the furniture as she went.

Somewhere in the ensuing confusion I directed that someone get in touch with all three chaplains. I need not have done so. All were at their posts. As the word spread, students, faculty, and staff began stumbling and streaming up the hill toward the chapels. Hastily we prepared an order of service. The chapels were not only filled to overflowing with sorrowing members of the Brandeis community — groundsmen, students, kitchen helpers, and senior faculty — but the neighborhood folk came over, clotting in grief-stricken groups on the lawns and pathways leading up to the chapels. As all, in their hundreds, went reluctantly on their way, I reflected how, in such moments of unspoken grief — now for a fallen President, but equally for a stricken faculty member or a youngster scarcely past his teens — it seemed so natural to make one's way to the chapels, where only the hearts need speak.

VIII

Academic Endowments:
The University Itself Wins Tenure

Before the sixteenth century, chairs, as we know them, were unusual articles of furniture. Common folk and even members of
the rising merchant class rarely nurtured household expectations that
went beyond the unmitigated oaken hardness of bench or stool. Gentle-
women enjoyed the luxury of silken cushions on the floor, and the
principal room of a nobleman's castle contained but one recognizable
chair, on which the lord of the manor sat to govern. Chairs also took
the form of thrones, sometimes provided with a canopy or side curtains
to shield the monarch or bishop from icy drafts. Thus, invariably, the
chair betokened authority. The connotation has persisted into our own
day, and the leader of a meeting "takes the chair" and is known as the
chairman. Women's lib advocates have repudiated the exclusive male
suffix, but they have not quarreled with the symbolism of the chair.
By the time of the Renaissance, chairs, evolving into more utilitarian
uses, had become more common. But in the academic world the term
retained its magisterial connotation and, equally significant, it represented the dignity and the prestige of a named professorship.

It was in 1502 that the Lady Margaret Beaufort, the mother of King
Henry VII, provided endowments at both Oxford and Cambridge to
support eminent scholars. By her generosity Lady Margaret changed the
fiscal organization of the English universities, and thus had a far-reach-
ing effect on the colleges and universities of the New World, which
owe their origins to English rather than to Continental models. In the
medieval university a senior scholar was obliged to collect his fees individually from his students. Even the great Abelard, in the twelfth century, had to shoo away nonpayers and try to collect arrears from others.
But scholars, then as now, were rarely blessed with business acumen.
Moreover, then as now, the popular lecturer or teacher drew the larger
crowds, while the equally gifted scholar whose subject was more de-

manding, or whose delivery was often somnolent, attracted fewer students and a smaller income. Endowed chairs allowed a man to be evaluated by his peers rather than by the often fickle regard of those he taught. Thus, Erasmus, the first occupant of the Lady Margaret Chair in Divinity and Greek at Cambridge University, may well have been the first academician in the history of western higher education who did not have to dun his students.

Lady Margaret's action left a more enduring legacy than her son's victory over the Plantagenets. Wealthy nobles and prelates followed her example, and the tradition was heartily endorsed in the New World, even when other trappings of royalty and nobility were eliminated. John Hancock founded a professorship at Harvard in Hebrew and theology. The will of Dr. Ezekiel Hersey provided for two chairs in medicine that have become coveted appointments. A wealthy merchant of Boston created Harvard's Nicholas Boylston Professorship of Rhetoric and Oratory, whose stipend was set at $1,500, a considerable sum in the eighteenth century. It carried the added privilege for the incumbent to graze his cow in the Harvard Yard. The Boylston Chair was first held by John Quincy Adams, twenty years before he became President of the United States, and the chair sustained its tradition of prestige long after the literal meaning of rhetoric and oratory had been transformed. Yet such endowed chairs were rare; there were only six in all the colleges of the country before the American Revolution, and four of them were at Harvard.

In the four and a half centuries since a king's mother sought to release scholarship from mendicancy, the cathedra aspect of the endowed professorship has become purely symbolic, but the aura of distinction has never been lost. Every privately supported university reserves its named chairs for its outstanding tenured faculty, and scholars treat their appointment to endowed chairs as a high honor. And from a purely practical point of view, the endowment that supports a chair guarantees that the salary of an incumbent will not be subject to the vagaries of university fund-raising income.

From the earliest days of Brandeis, the quest for the endowment of faculty chairs was given high priority. But such gifts were very difficult to come by. It was much easier to interest even the most philanthropically motivated families in the underwriting of buildings, science laboratories, or centers for the humanities, the social sciences, and the creative arts. Fortunately, each year there were imaginative and sensitive supporters who were sufficiently concerned about a particular academic field to channel their philanthropy, by outright grants or bequests, to express this interest. Endowments for chairs were also created through carefully planned testimonial affairs that saluted a national figure, or a highly regarded communal leader. Tribute gifts were encouraged for the endowment that was to bear the name of the honored guest. The

establishment of chairs could follow no master plan; fulfillment depended on the unpredictable timing when wills or bequests matured, or
on the caprice of a particular testimonial opportunity. Nor could the
amounts for the endowment be rigidly set. The venerable universities
could command a figure; Harvard now insists upon a capital fund of a
million dollars. Brandeis was too young, at the threshold of national
prestige, to be so requisitory. The acquisition of each chair, therefore,
usually represented an adventure, often burdened with frustration,
whose happy ending was by no means assured. How much depended
upon factors extraneous to academic planning can best be demonstrated
by describing how some of the earliest endowed chairs came about.

In the late spring of 1948, before I took up my duties as president, I
was on the scheduled program of the Town Hall of New York. I was
introduced as president-elect of the newly conceived University and,
though my lecture topic related to European political developments, the
open forum that followed elicited a number of questions about the
concept of Brandeis and its projected orientation. When the program
was over, a little old lady came up to me, introduced herself as Mrs. Max
Richter, and expressed great interest in what I had outlined. She hoped
that I could spare the time on my next visit to New York to confer with
her attorney.

Within the week I was in touch with Charles Segal, Mrs. Richter's attorney, who was to become one of the University's first Fellows and a
devoted friend through the next quarter century. He explained that Mrs.
Richter had recently been widowed. Her husband had been a wealthy
silk merchant and had left a substantial foundation whose income Segal
was prepared to assign to colleges and universities that met high standards. Segal's main interest was Swarthmore College, but he shared Mrs.
Richter's enthusiasm for the concept of Brandeis, and he was prepared
to explore with me how the Richter Foundation could be helpful. Our
conference resulted in the establishment of the University's first assured professorial salary, an annual pledge to support a distinguished appointment, the actual endowment to become available after the passing
of Mrs. Richter. The capital fund was received by the University some
years later, one of the three or four largest in our portfolio. The immediate annual commitment enabled us to recruit an outstanding incumbent. The chair was offered to Max Lerner, who became a member of
the faculty in our second year as the Max Richter Professor of American
Studies.

Twenty-five years after the establishment of the Max Richter Chair,
Charles Segal attended the Commencement where his granddaughter
graduated with high honors. In the intervening period he had counseled
many of his clients to include Brandeis in their listing when they
planned testamentary gifts. Our twenty-five-year association was a

happy and productive one. But the disquieting thought often occurred to me: what if I hadn't been booked for Town Hall, or had not been booked on that particular day, or what if Mrs. Richter had had a cold and decided not to attend? When I related to Max Lerner the capricious circumstances of the funding of the chair, he concluded that he became a professor at Brandeis because a little old lady did not have a cold on that fortunate Town Hall day.

The circumstances that resulted in the establishment of an endowed chair named for Harry Austryn Wolfson, the Harvard savant and one of the world's most respected philosophers, were light-years away from the concerns of scholarship. The initial negotiations began with a real estate deal between one of our trustees, Lawrence Wien, and a highly successful New York realtor, Erwin Wolfson, who conceived, among other major enterprises, the Pan American Building project above Grand Central Station. The commission for the complicated transaction that Wien had worked out would normally have amounted to approximately a quarter of a million dollars. Wien refused to accept the commission; Wolfson insisted that he had more than earned it. Wien then suggested that Wolfson could make the sum available to Brandeis University, setting up an endowed chair in Wolfson's name. Wolfson demurred. "I am just a real estate operator," he said. "A chair bearing my name would carry little meaning except that money was contributed toward it, and not even my money, for the grant would really be your earned commission. But, if you want to go through with this, I would much prefer to have the chair named for my cousin, Harry Wolfson, who is a famous professor of philosophy at Harvard."

In great glee, Wien called me. I shared his exultation, but cautioned him that a number of preliminary steps were required before the chair could be established and named. Certainly it was necessary to obtain Harry Wolfson's permission, and this might not be easy. Wolfson was the shyest and most self-effacing of scholars; there was no assurance that he could be persuaded to accept the designation. Besides, all of his half-century academic career had been spent at Harvard. How would he react if a chair in his honor went to another university, and how would the Harvard authorities react?

I called on Wolfson in the basement of Widener Library, where he had labored for a lifetime on his research and writings. He was a fragile-looking, gnomish man whose erudition was awesome. His magnum opus was the twelve-volume *Structure and Growth of Philosophic Systems from Plato to Spinoza*. His *Philosophy of the Church Fathers*, a two-volume study of religious philosophers from Saint Paul to Saint Augustine, published when he was sixty-seven, had become an instant scholarly classic. A Harvard colleague, Donald C. Williams, recalled in Wolfson's obituary in 1974 how, many years before, a British scholar had been completely flummoxed when asked to review an article of Wolfson's. The essay was thirteen pages long, written in six languages, and had seventy-two footnotes. Its terrifying title was "An Unknown Pseudo-Democritean Fragment and the Muslim Unextended Atoms." The learned Briton eventually "surmised that Harry Austryn Wolfson might be the name of a committee or an institute."

When I found Wolfson's office, it was difficult to spot him quickly, for, as usual, he was almost buried under the helter-skelter of books and manuscripts. Once trapped by a tenacious visitor he was always the soul of courtesy, although one sensed that he was anxious to get back to his research. I dispensed with amenities and apprised him of my purpose. I told him that his cousin Erwin was eager to establish a chair in philosophy at Brandeis and we would be honored if it carried the name of Harry Wolfson. Wolfson blinked for a few moments and then remarked, "The chair should really be named for the person who most deserved it, our Uncle Mendel. It was Uncle Mendel who had the vision and the courage to pull up stakes in Lithuania at the turn of the century and to pioneer his way to the New World. It was Uncle Mendel who brought over Erwin's father and it was Uncle Mendel who brought me over. Yes, the chair should be named for him." I agreed that Uncle Mendel deserved the love and gratitude of the family, but Erwin had been responsible for the gift that made the chair possible. Wolfson refused to be interrupted. I doubt that he had even heard me. He continued, "Uncle Mendel had the genius that was responsible for the business success of the other members of the family. Where would Erwin's father be without Uncle Mendel and where would he be?" I still persisted. "The chair should have an illustrious incumbent," I pleaded. "Then surely," he argued, "his erudition would be unaffected by the name of the chair." How could I compete with the master in logic? In despair I aimed a low blow. "Harry," I said, "Brandeis is a very young school. It would add immeasurably to its prestige if the chair honored the philosopher rather than the actual donor." Apparently I touched a vulnerable spot. "Well," he said, "if it would be more helpful for Brandeis, a school that I very much admire, then I withdraw my objection." But as I left, I could still hear him muttering that full justice was not being done to Uncle Mendel.

I then arranged to see federal Judge Charles E. Wyzanski, Jr., an old friend, who was serving as the chairman of the Overseers of Harvard. I wanted to sound him out on the possible reaction at Harvard if, after an incumbency of more than fifty years, Wolfson permitted his name to be linked with a chair at another university. Wyzanski quickly put me at ease. "Brandeis is not just another university," he reminded me. "It is Jewish-sponsored; it bears the name of one of Harvard's most illustrious sons. The gift has not been diverted from Harvard. If it did not go to Brandeis, it would not be made at all. The Harvard community would assuredly respond only with admiration and would rejoice with the authorities at Brandeis that the chair strengthens the academic quality of the young University that bears such an honored Harvard name."

In 1968 I read an unusual story in the daily press that one of the great publishing lords of West Germany, Axel Springer, had offered a million marks to Prime Minister David Ben-Gurion to help create an art museum in Israel. Springer was a devout Christian who had escaped the fate of dissidents in Nazi Germany during the Hitler regime because of what had been diagnosed as a terminal illness. He had not been involved in the Nazi apparatus; and when the regime collapsed in 1945, he was one of the men on whom Chancellor Adenauer counted for service in reorganizing Germany on a firm democratic base. He had inherited a modest newspaper and magazine chain and had built it into one of the major publishing empires of Europe. He shared Adenauer's deep sorrow and shame over the Holocaust, and used the columns of his influential newspapers and magazines to advocate strong ties with Israel and just compensation for the victims of Hitlerism. There was considerable dispute in Israel over the acceptance of his proffered gift, just as there had been many emotional protests over the restitution funds that West Germany had offered to Israel to help strengthen its economy. The latter funds had been accepted and had helped decisively to stabilize the Israeli economy. They were accepted, not as compensation but as a gesture of national contrition; and the Springer gift was interpreted as having been offered in the same spirit and was also accepted.

When I read this story, I wrote to Axel Springer to explain the concept of Brandeis and the symbol that it represented in the American Jewish community. I expressed the hope that he would wish to extend his program of reconciliation to the Jews of America. Such letters rarely survive beyond a secretary's perfunctory processing. But in this instance, within a week there was a transatlantic call from Ernst Cramer, special assistant to Springer, who indicated that his chief had been deeply impressed with the suggestion and that he, Cramer, was prepared to fly to the United States for a detailed exploration of what might be a practical action. Within a month he was on the Brandeis campus and I was negotiating with the affable, highly intelligent aide, one of a few Jews who had returned to Germany after the Nazis had been eliminated. I suggested that both Springer's wish and the long-range interests of the University would be best served if a chair in contemporary history were endowed by him. Occupied by a distinguished historian of contemporary affairs, it would encourage study and research in the period that most interested Springer; it would also reinforce one of the areas that Brandeis, a growing center of international studies, was most anxious to strengthen.

Cramer readily agreed that such a project would most likely intrigue

Springer and he flew back with the assurance that he would warmly recommend it. Springer quickly accepted the recommendation and made available a million gold marks to endow the chair that was to be named for his mother, Ottilie Springer. He understood fully that the gift carried with it no authority to influence either choice of incumbent or the individual's freedom in teaching or research. Indeed, Springer would not have had it any other way.

When the gift and its purpose were announced, two small groups on campus vigorously dissented. One was similar to the protestors in Israel, who insisted that this was "blood money" and should not be accepted no matter what rhetoric of reconciliation was used. The other group, mainly militant leftists on campus led by Herbert Marcuse, professor of politics, and Heinz Lubasz, assistant professor of history, also a German refugee, excoriated the administration for accepting such funds from the leading "reactionary" publisher in West Germany. Springer's politics, they declared, were a menace to the liberal socialist movements of the New World. These dissidents carried their opposition to extremes in the violence and scurrility of their protest. I was saddened that there was no restraining counsel from either Marcuse or Lubasz, who had always been quick to attack censorship when it affected their views, but who apparently believed that, because a donor represented a differing point of view, it was immoral to accept gifts from him even though the project was fully protected in its freedom and objectivity.

The first incumbent of the Ottilie Springer Chair was Geoffrey Barraclough, who came to Brandeis from Oxford. He was one of the best respected historians of the contemporary world. He gladly accepted the assignment, noting that Springer had published the German translations of many of his writings. When the chair was officially installed, Axel Springer and members of his staff came to the campus for the occasion. Springer was delighted with Brandeis itself and was particularly moved by the creative way in which the memorial to his mother was to be established.

During the summer of 1964 Thelma and I were vacationing in a New Jersey spa, and we noted that Miss Fannie Hurst, a novelist who had enjoyed considerable popularity in the pre–World War II period, was also a guest. She seemed very much alone, abstracted and uncommunicative. I remembered her well not only for her best-sellers, especially *Back Street*, but because she was a graduate of Washington University, Thelma's alma mater and mine, and had been quite a celebrity in her heyday. I approached her before dinner one evening and asked whether she would like to join us. Her face lit up and she accepted with alacrity. During the few remaining days of our holiday we looked forward to our evening meals together, when our conversation touched upon matters of mutual interest — creative writing, education, travel, literary friendships — that brought her back to her great days. We parted the best of friends, though she, it seemed, rather sadly. Her marriage had been guided by the principle of "freedom from binding ties." She and her husband were in accord that they would lead completely independent lives, with meetings and associations for themselves only by appointment. The permissive marriage had not lasted; she had no family, she had built no intimate, concerned friendships, and she knew her writing days were over. Apparently she knew also that she had not long to live. Now as a lonely, elderly lady, her reputation in eclipse, she spoke glumly of the time ahead, quoting at our parting from her favorite Tennyson: that the future meant only "to live forgotten and love forlorn."

A few months later I received a call from her New York attorney, Harry Buchman, who informed me that Fannie Hurst had died that morning. He transmitted her request that I deliver the memorial address at the funeral services. He also informed me that her rather substantial estate was to be divided between Washington University and Brandeis, which she had written into a revised will after our summer meeting. The very modest service was attended by a small group of old friends, mainly from the world of letters and the theater, one of the Washington University representatives, Thelma, and me.

When her estate had been probated, the Brandeis share came to more than $800,000. Her attorney accepted my suggestion that two endowed chairs be set up in Fannie Hurst's name, and that each year two visiting professors be invited to join the faculty in creative writing. In the years that followed the humanities and creative arts curricula were immeasurably enriched as these provisions were fulfilled. These visitors included the kinds of spirit with whom Fannie Hurst would have been most comfortable. Adrienne Rich had received the Shelley Memorial Award by the Poetry Society of America and had published eight highly praised volumes. John Williams had been a faculty member of the Bread Loaf Writers' Conference in Vermont for many years, was the author of several novels, and had won the National Book Award in fiction. William Gibson, author of the plays *The Miracle Worker* and *Two for the Seesaw*, was a valuable asset in our Theater Arts Department. Israel Horovitz, one of the rising young playwrights in the United States, had won the OBIE award twice and worked diligently with our own budding playwrights, helping several of them to earn tryouts in New York theaters. Maxine Kumin, who published many novels and books of poetry, was a Pulitzer Prize winner. And there were many others of similar caliber. This form of enduring tribute seemed most appropriate for the strange, lonely, gifted woman who could write so fervently of love but who somehow missed this kind of happiness for herself.

Sometimes inexplicable family tragedies followed the biblical tradition of converting the Valley of Weeping into a Place of Springs. Sidney Wien, Lawrence's younger brother, and his lovely wife, Ellen, of Atlanta, Georgia, had been prime benefactors of the University. They were deeply interested in its art program and late in 1961 had set up a special fund to permit the museum to acquire unusual paintings and sculpture. In December 1962, many of the art lovers and leading citizens of Atlanta organized a tour of the outstanding museum centers of Europe. The group's chartered plane caught fire on its return takeoff, and all perished in the flames and explosions. Sidney and Ellen Wien and one of their two daughters, Toni, were on the ill-fated plane. Their surviving daughter and sister, Claire (Mrs. Richard Morse), joined with her Uncle Lawrence in establishing an endowed chair in the history of art as an enduring memorial.

In the spring of 1964 I received word of another plane crash, which involved Richard Koret, a New York manufacturer who was one of the University's most devoted patrons. The call came to me from one of our trustees, Joseph Mailman, who was Koret's closest friend and one of the executors of his estate. Koret had no family. His whole life had been devoted to his business in which he had been remarkably successful, building a famous fashion name for the beauty and originality of the Koret handbags. Mailman was arranging the funeral services, which were to be symbolic since no physical remains had survived the crash. Koret left a sizable estate that was bequeathed to Brandeis, and after negotiations with the executors, it was determined that two fully endowed chairs would be established, one in Judaic studies, the other in the history of ideas, an experimental program in which the University was pioneering. When the decision had been reached, I could not help thinking how completely without meaning Koret's life would have been except for the survival value that was assured through the teaching and research that would give his name significance in the generations ahead.

Though the University had established an important center for Jewish studies, many of us felt that it was important to broaden our offerings to include Christian religious and philosophical thought. Our objective was not only to give fuller meaning to the nonsectarian image of the University; it was clear that there were so many Christian-Jewish interrelationships in religious philosophy that it was mutually advantageous to bring to the faculty some outstanding scholars in the field. After one of our staff strategy meetings, I was approached by a young assistant, Emmanuel Goldberg, who had come to Brandeis from the Public Relations Department of neighboring Boston University. There he had worked closely with a deeply religious Protestant board member, Albert V. Danielsen, a Wellesley realtor who had made large contributions to strengthen the Protestant service at Boson University and had helped to establish its Methodist chapel as a tribute to a former president, Daniel Marsh. The Danielsens had also been generous benefactors at several of the Catholic-sponsored colleges and had provided financial assistance for some of the colleges for blacks in the South. Goldberg invited them to the campus to meet with me, and we spoke of the usefulness of adding a missing component to the Brandeis curriculum, a chair that would become the teaching center for a better understanding of Christian thought. They responded with enthusiasm; and they not only established the chair but gave an extra half-million dollars to make possible the substantial strengthening of the offerings in philosophy and ethics. Danielsen was very proud to become a Fellow of the University, and thereafter hardly a public function took place on the Brandeis campus without his presence and the eloquent benediction that he was often called upon to offer.

When I was succeeded in the presidency by Morris Abram, he learned that Danielsen, then in his late seventies, was still playing tennis regularly. Abram, a tennis enthusiast, made an appointment for a match with him. Before the game Abram asked my advice as to the kind of score he should permit this generous donor to run up. In the match that followed, the president, twenty-five years Danielsen's junior, had to play the game of his life to keep up with his septuagenarian opponent, who entered and completed each set with prayer. Danielsen was the only one who was startled and surprised by the ovation that he received from the Commencement audience of 1973, when he accepted the University's honorary degree for the catholicity of his religious and philanthropic interests.

One of our most effective interpreters was Eleanor Roosevelt, especially when she joined our Board of Trustees and our part-time faculty. She willingly undertook special assignments either by addressing our functions or by conferring with families whose support we sought. One day I learned from the nephew of Helena Rubinstein, the queen of a vast cosmetics empire, that she was ready to endow a chair in chemistry at the University. She asked for one privilege, to make the pledge personally to Eleanor Roosevelt, one of the few persons in the world who truly fascinated her. I called Mrs. Roosevelt, explained that I would not ordinarily intrude on her crowded schedule, but that a visit to Helena Rubinstein's apartment to take tea with her would confirm a very generous endowment for the University. Mrs. Roosevelt's response was almost a reflex action: "I would go to China if it meant such a service to the University." At the appointed hour, Lawrence Wien and I called for her in his limousine. We drove to the sumptuous apartment of Helena Rubinstein, which was virtually an art gallery. En route Mrs. Roosevelt asked innocently, "By the way, who is Helena Rubinstein?" The two ladies met and spent a delightful hour discussing their world travels. At the end, the commitment was made for the Helena Rubinstein Chair in Chemistry.

It seemed to us that many good purposes could be simultaneously served if we established the tradition of creating endowed chairs not only through family benefactions or legacies but as enduring tributes to significant public figures. Chairs bearing revered names would honor the University; the designation of the chairs would call attention to the academic commitments of the University; participation in the tribute, broadly distributed, with gifts ranging from the most modest to the most generous, would extend the supporting constituency and enlist new sources of enduring friendship and devotion. Every few years, therefore, a campaign would be mounted to honor an illustrious public figure, such as Earl Warren, Christian Herter, Harry Truman, Adlai Stevenson.

It was after Chief Justice Warren had come to dedicate the statue of Justice Brandeis that we began planning the strategy for setting up a chair in his name. Warren had consistently refused honors of any kind. He believed that, as Chief Justice of the United States, his position made it mandatory for him to avoid any identification that could be even remotely interpreted as becoming beholden. In addition, in a long political career he was very little concerned with personal honors. I realized that there would be no hope of success if we used any conventional persuasion to obtain his consent for an appeal to obtain an Earl Warren Chair endowment. But I remembered his warm lifelong friendship with a West Coast trustee, Ben Swig, the owner of the beautiful Hotel Fairmont, atop Nob Hill in San Francisco. Swig had always avoided calls upon the Justice for any personal advantage or political purpose. But he agreed with us that the appeal to help a young University that bore the name of Louis Brandeis — who had been the inspiration for Warren's own outlook on the law — might break through Warren's resolve. Swig made the approach. How he couched it I never knew; but from the lilt in Swig's voice when the long distance call came through, I knew that he had succeeded.

Inevitably Swig became the chairman of the campaign, and at his side was Dan Koshland, head of the great Levi, Straus empire and one of San Francisco's most respected and beloved citizens. Swig later confided that, though he had raised millions for every variety of cause — other universities, hospitals and welfare funds, Israel — he had never had the experience where funds were so readily subscribed. They came from the oldest friends of Warren's days as governor of California, when he had been nominated by both the Democratic and Republican parties; from those who had supported him in his race for the vice-presidency on the Republican ticket with Thomas Dewey (the famous kangaroo ticket where the back part was stronger than the fore); from loyal supporters of the University; from admirers of the crucial *Brown* v. *Board of Education* decision of 1954.

The chair was designated for constitutional studies and it was assigned to Leonard Levy, one of the youngest men on our faculty. As noted earlier, we were following the practice that became a major factor in the reputation that the University achieved, trying to spot men of promise early and giving them major responsibility. The name on the chair and the caliber of its first incumbent let Chief Justice Warren know that the reluctant deviation from his fixed principle had been fully vindicated.

A chair in the name of President Harry Truman was a natural. His most trusted presidential aide had been David Niles, who was the main architect of Truman's policy that placed the United States squarely behind the establishment of a sovereign Israel. Niles had been one of the founders of Brandeis and, in the earliest years, perhaps its most influential advocate. He died in 1953, but his chief never forgot his loyalty and conscientiousness. When we invited Truman in 1957 to accept an honorary degree and reminded him of Niles's kith-and-kin relationship to the University, the former President promptly consented. It was at the Commencement that I broached our wish to raise the endowment for a chair in history in his name. Truman had been an avid student of American history and had often surprised his advisers by his understanding of the forces that had shaped the national destiny and of the men who had carried decisive roles.

Truman was clearly moved by our desire to establish a chair in his name, for no other university had ever offered him such an honor. I asked several of the national Democratic leaders to assume leadership: Jacob Arvey of Chicago, Sam Rayburn, Lyndon Johnson, Governor Harriman, and members of our own board, Senator Herbert Lehman and Mrs. Eleanor Roosevelt. All of them recognized, even before the longer-range verdict of history, Truman's unique qualities, which made him one of our strongest Presidents. The gifts, however, were not limited to Democratic supporters. Contributions came from all groups — from common folk whose loyal response had effected the stunning political upset of 1948, from trade unions who remembered Truman's social welfare legislation, and from Jewish leaders who could never forget his aid in the creation of an independent Israel. Within a few months the mission had been accomplished and the endowment was in hand. The chair was assigned first to Merrill Peterson, the Jefferson historian who won a Bancroft Prize, and then to Marvin Meyers, one of the best-respected authorities on the foundations of the Republic, an editor of *The Sources of the American Republic*, and the winner of the coveted Dunning Prize of the American Historical Association.

The ready willingness of the entire American diplomatic corps to help us establish the Christian Herter Chair was a good example of the friendships that the University could now command. Herter was a Republican Brahmin from one of the oldest Massachusetts families. He had served a long apprenticeship in diplomacy and government and had a brilliant incumbency as governor of Massachusetts. After the death of John Foster Dulles, President Eisenhower tapped Herter to become secretary of state, and few men in public affairs were more esteemed or beloved. The idea to honor him on his seventieth birthday through an endowed chair came from my assistant Emmanuel Goldberg, who had initiated the campaign for the Danielsen Chair. Goldberg had been on Herter's staff in the governor's office and had won his chief's confidence. He approached Herter with the hope that, though an alumnus of Johns Hopkins, he would permit a campaign for a chair in international studies at Brandeis. Here, too, the factor that obtained Herter's consent was the reputation of the young school in living up to the symbol that Justice Brandeis represented.

Goldberg then demonstrated his resourcefulness for capitalizing on his advantages. He went directly to President Eisenhower and obtained his permission to use his name as the honorary chairman for the campaign. Goldberg added to the sponsoring committee many of the major officials in the state and federal governments. Then a strictly limited appeal, a model of sensitive understatement, was addressed to the men and women in the diplomatic services around the world. The response was extraordinary. Contributions came from virtually every embassy and consulate, and they were usually accompanied by letters of affection that went far beyond the routine of acquiescence. Unhappily, Christian Herter died in December 1966, at the very beginning of the solicitation. We were all deeply touched when the family's obituary notice indicated that memorial tributes in lieu of flowers could be made either to Johns Hopkins or to Brandeis University. The endowment fund was quickly completed. When the chair was dedicated, Governor Herter's oldest son spoke for the family, expressing appreciation that the memory of Christian Herter was to be perpetuated in this creative way.

There was special appropriateness in the decision to establish an endowed chair in legal institutions in the name of Judge Joseph Proskauer, to honor his ninetieth birthday. Proskauer's brilliant legal career stretched back to the earliest days of the century. He had been chief justice of the Superior Court of New York, an adviser to Governor Alfred Smith, many of whose most significant speeches he had written when Smith was the Democratic candidate for the presidency; and he had given resourceful leadership to many major Jewish organizations, especially the American Jewish Committee. He was one of the first national leaders whom I tried to reach for moral support when Brandeis was founded, but his excessively busy schedule prevented an appointment until the University's tenth year. One day I broke through the battery of protective secretaries and got him on the telephone. I asked for just half an hour in his office, uninterrupted, and to this he finally yielded. It proved to be a significant thirty minutes for, at the end of it, he offered not only his blessing but the pledge to call his friends and colleagues together to listen to me at the Lotos Club in New York. Out of that meeting came many powerful new supporters for the University from a social group that had been extremely difficult to penetrate. Judge Proskauer joined our Board of Trustees soon afterward and was one of the most influential interpreters of the University. He remained remarkably active all through his eighties. As he approached his ninetieth year, there was little diminution of vitality. When called upon at any public gathering, his wit was keen and his observations pertinent. It was one of the board's most popular decisions to have a public celebration of his ninetieth birthday and to have the tribute take the form of an endowed chair in legal institutions.

We had a very knowledgeable committee to supervise the campaign, but it ran into an unusual obstacle. Proskauer, a nonagenarian, really belonged to a generation that was very much a part of the past. To members of his own firm — and even to the senior partners who now managed exceptionally important litigation — the judge was a legend, remote and impersonal. The plate dinner attendance was much smaller than a man of Judge Proskauer's attainments deserved. In the long run we accomplished our purpose. We turned to one of the judge's oldest friends and admirers, Dr. Maurice Hexter of our own board. Hexter had been the head of the Jewish Federation in New York for nearly half a century, and quite apart from his profound understanding of changing social welfare currents, he had an encyclopedic knowledge of the thousands of important families who were the pillars of support for the agencies that served the largest community in the world. Hexter had the deepest sentimental reasons for cooperating in our mission. He had known Proskauer for more than forty years and his admiration for the judge bordered on reverence. He knew that the trustees of the Harry Kaufman Foundation were ready to follow any counsel that Proskauer offered; and there was no more effective way to express appreciation for all that the judge had meant to Kaufman in his philanthropies. Hexter suggested that I appeal to the foundation to complete the endowment for the Proskauer Chair. Indeed, he sent me a draft letter to write to the foundation; and, as I remember it, I changed only a "which" to a "that." The full amount needed was voted by the trustees.

Meantime, we enjoyed a gala testimonial evening, where the birthday program included a constellation of legal and governmental luminaries, including Justice Harlan, who, between hearings at the Supreme Court, had made a special trip from Washington. I do not know how Judge Proskauer was impressed by all that was said about him; he was very busy making notes as each speaker detailed an illuminating episode. But, as usual, he stole the show. He revealed the secret of how, despite his habit of vigorous dissent and no-nonsense responses when he found himself in disagreement, no resentments or recriminations were uttered anywhere. "The reason is easy," the judge chuckled. "I outlived all the bastards."

In 1962 the audacious decision was made to attempt an overall, three-year effort that would minimize the University's reliance on the caprice of annual public fund-raising. The goal, set at sixty-five million dollars, was perhaps the most daring ever undertaken until then by a university. Twelve million would be assigned for the completion of construction still to be done under the master plan. Ten million would be used over the three-year period to cover the excess of expenditures over the assured income of tuition and room and board. But it was planned to allocate nearly three-quarters, about forty-three million, as endowment for faculty salaries, scholarships, and fellowships.

Our campaign was announced just as the Massachusetts Institute of Technology was launching one of its own, with a goal set at approximately the same amount. Brandeis was then fourteen years old, and its venture seemed more like quixotry than responsible resolve. But we pinned our faith on the leadership that gladly assumed responsibility: Joseph Linsey as general chairman, Morris Brown of Palm Beach, Ben Swig of San Francisco, and Sam Lemberg of New York as cochairmen; Dr. Sidney Farber, the head of the Children's Cancer Fund, Eleanor Roosevelt, Senators Benton and Ribicoff, and other outstanding public figures who did not limit their service to letterhead identification. The planning, under the expert supervision of Clarence Berger, took more than half a year and included the recruitment of committees in nearly a hundred cities. I flew thirty thousand miles in sixty flights to meet with those who were asked to accept responsibility for participation, and afterward for the actual fund-raising drives. Most of our trustees, Fellows and president's councillors gave whatever time they could steal from their own concerns. Apparently, through the years we had built solid friendships in every section of the country, for within six months it was possible to announce that more than twenty million dollars had been committed. The pledges ranged from the modest amounts of young alumni to several million-dollar grants for specified designations. Then, about a third of the way into the campaign, came a providential development through two magnificent challenge grants from the Ford Foundation, totaling twelve million dollars. If the required matching were met, it would successfully wind up the campaign, virtually complete the physical master plan, and add enough endowed chairs and scholarship support to end the vulnerability of the University's academic objectives.

The Ford Foundation had selected a limited number of universities that were quite clearly on their way to national eminence. It had undertaken to provide major grants that would permit these institutions to make commitments for academic programs, research, and construction that might otherwise have to wait for decades. The objective was further emphasized when the condition was attached that the universities were to generate matching gifts in cash, twice or three times the grant amounts, from private, nongovernmental sources. As the news of the Ford plan percolated through the educational world, there was a great stir among institutions eager to qualify for consideration. Brandeis, too, determined to make its bid, although it seemed like a very remote hope. We had been in existence barely a dozen years. We had only just established a few graduate programs. Our alumni body was small, the oldest among them hardly out of their twenties and few having yet made any mark. But the University had demonstrated spectacular progress; only thirteen years after its founding it had achieved Phi Beta Kappa accreditation, and our master plan — physical and academic — betokened an ambition that had every possibility for early fulfillment if such a grant could be achieved. I therefore welcomed the appointment that was set with James Armsey, the Ford Foundation grants director.

It was a brisk autumn day in 1962 when I met with Armsey in New York. Though I came armed with a general proposal for expansion in many academic and physical areas, I expected that this would be a preliminary visit, to be followed by the formal presentation of our plans. When I was ushered into the office, Armsey came forward to greet me most cordially. "Do you remember me?" he asked. Assuming I had never met him, I responded, "Should I have?" He then noted that he had been at the University of Illinois during the late 1920s when I was teaching in the History Department. His roommate had been James Reston, who later went on to a distinguished career with the *New York Times*. Reston had taken my course in modern history and had often discussed my lectures when he returned to his room. Armsey had not taken any of my courses, but Reston's complimentary evaluation had given him an introduction to my work that he had not forgotten. The exchange of Illini reminiscences gave us an informal rapport that made it much easier for me to discuss my mission. Obviously the Brandeis proposal would have to make its own way, but it did not hurt that Armsey was so friendly and well disposed from the outset. Indeed, the meeting opened up a personal friendship that included our wives and has been affectionately sustained to the present.

The documentation required by the foundation gave us a superb opportunity to think through our plans for the next generation. For the requested funds were not meant to meet current expenditures nor to cover ongoing obligations. They were meant as seed money or, as the Ford prospectus put it, "to build on excellence and realistic aspirations for the future." Hence the proposal outlined plans for a much-expanded undergraduate curriculum, a somewhat larger student body, resources for scholarship and fellowship aid that would attract even better-qualified applicants, launching several new graduate departments, boosting salary levels for faculty to retain our best people and to recruit new faculty clearly on their way to distinguished careers, expanding the program of the Florence Heller School for Advanced Studies in Social Welfare, doubling the acquisitions for the university library, making available more generous subsidies for faculty research. All these objectives were in the master plan, but the pace of achievement had to be linked with funding. We hoped the Ford grant and its matching inducements would bring these objectives to much earlier fulfillment.

The proposal was developed by a task force of sixty faculty and administrative staff members under the executive direction of Clarence Berger, who spent many months gathering supporting data. What emerged was a volume of more than four hundred pages that included immediate projections and long-range objectives. When it reached Armsey, he noted that it was the best proposal of any that had been submitted. In November 1962 he called me personally to indicate that six million dollars had been assigned, with the proviso that eighteen million dollars was to be raised by us within a three-year period. There was dramatic timing in the call, for it came just as the trustees were at their regular meeting on campus. I tried to be casual in making the announcement to them but I failed completely. Meanwhile, the announcement had reached the Faculty Dining Center, and the cheering was joined even by our foreign Ziskind visiting professors. Seven other universities were awarded grants in varying amounts and with different matching requirements: Notre Dame, Stanford, Johns Hopkins, Vanderbilt, the University of Southern California, Brown, and Denver. Brown was 198 years old, Stanford was 77. Brandeis was the youngest and the smallest. The criteria for the choice as detailed in the letter of transmission indicated where Brandeis had concentrated its strength. It had built "a solid structure of support in its unusual Jewish constituency"; it had developed "independent administrative and legal control, free of legislative and political influence"; it had recruited "eminent and generous trustee participation"; it was favored by "resourceful and aggressive presidential leadership"; "its academic planning was in the best tradition of sound scholarship"; "the quality of its faculty and student body augured well for a future dedicated to the highest objectives of liberal education."

The Ford announcement was hailed as a major breakthrough for the young University. The *New York Herald Tribune* editorialized that it was the recognition of Brandeis's proven ability to create new outposts of excellence. "Brandeis University is marching toward a pinnacle of prestige in the academic world. Herein lies one of the educational stories of the century." The campaign that was mounted to raise the matching funds had a galvanic unifying effect on the entire Brandeis family — trustees, Fellows, president's councillors, National Women's Committee, faculty, students, alumni, administrative staff, and thousands of friends and well-wishers. There were meetings in scores of cities — house parties, luncheons, telephone appeals. In the first year three-fourths of the goal had been achieved; and then a major new incentive emerged. Apparently, Notre Dame and Stanford had achieved their goals very quickly and received a second grant. Of course, they had thousands of well-established alumni. But the university world took it for granted that, for Brandeis, miracles were commonplace. In any case, the very hope that a successful first campaign might lead to a second grant worked like a shot of adrenaline. Within eighteen months the message went to the Ford Foundation that all conditions for its initial grant had been fulfilled.

In our second proposal, the commitment was undertaken to encourage matching contributions for academic purposes. Government agencies had frequently participated in underwriting physical facilities, usually health-oriented: science buildings, laboratory equipment. And Brandeis had received more than its proportionate share for such expanding needs. Why not extend this matching principle to academic designations to help endow chairs, fellowships, and scholarships? The University in its first sixteen years, up to 1964, had received contributions — primarily by bequest — for the endowment of fifteen chairs mainly in scientific areas. This rate, averaging one a year, was a tolerable pace so long as we were not yet in the elite company of universities that were centuries old and had built impressive endowments. Was it too ambitious to aspire to twenty-five new endowed chairs in a three-year period and to right the balance so that the humanities, the creative arts, and the social sciences could also be materially strengthened? The proposal aimed to encourage the donor to contribute $250,000 for a chair designation, his gift to be supplemented by a Ford "bonus" of $150,000. If a total of $3.75 million were used for this purpose from the Ford funds, twenty-five endowed chairs could be established.

It was a Herculean undertaking, compounded by boldness and confidence, for the campaign to match the first foundation grant had scarcely been completed. It was a proud moment when Brandeis again found itself in the select company of the few universities that, having successfully matched a first grant, were to receive a second. Armsey was the guest of honor at the function in December 1964, when the completion of the first grant and the challenge of the second were simultaneously celebrated.

The new campaign went into high gear at once and was even more intensively conducted than the first one. Substantial fillip was provided when the influential *Comparative Guide to American Colleges*, noting the impact of the first grant, listed Brandeis among the twenty most selective colleges and universities in the United States. With the help of thousands of volunteers across the country, the second campaign was successfully completed in less than two years. Twenty-two chairs had been underwritten, and by the end of the full three-year period, negotiations for several more were well under way. During the time span that had been set by the Ford Foundation, the original eighteen chairs had been expanded to more than forty, relative to every discipline. Four were in the field of science; the others righted the endowments' balance by seeding the humanities, the social sciences, and the creative arts. They included chairs in the arts of design, Judaic studies, economics, politics, social planning, history, legal institutions, behavioral science, theater arts, sociology, philosophy, and the fine arts. It became possible to conduct seminars jointly with MIT in urban policy and social planning, and to collaborate in mathematics colloquia and theoretical physics with Harvard and MIT.

The wisdom of the Ford grants was vindicated when the American Council on Education, in its 1968 report based on data gathered through 1966, ranked seven of the Brandeis departments among the top twenty graduate programs in the universities of the country. Equally gratifying, the campaign had secured many millions of dollars for scholarships and fellowship endowments. These took many forms, some sufficiently ample to see students through their entire university career, as in the case of the Chernis grant, which was assigned to a young refugee who became the valedictorian of our first Commencement and went on to a distinguished academic career at Yale. Others were designated for special fields of concentration, such as the one set up by Harry and Mildred Remis of Boston that offered encouragement to young people of great promise in the creative arts, or by Mary and Abbey Hirschfield for graduate students in the humanities. Such grants were indispensable in a University where more than 30 percent of the student body required financial assistance.

Of course, such fulfillments carried sobering responsibilities. Armsey had warned that this would happen. "The grant," he said, when he announced the second Ford challenge, "may solve a few immediate problems, but it will create others. It won't make your life happier. The wholly new level of excellence the grants are designed to help you reach, while it is comforting to contemplate, is disturbing and disruptive to achieve."

I had no illusions about the burdens that the unending quest for excellence would impose. Brandeis, at least in its founding years when precedents were set, could not plan and function timidly with a bookkeeper's mentality. I was convinced, however, that the occasional risks were not irrresponsible so long as we could rely upon an astonishingly sensitive and generous constituency. This conviction was implicit in my reply to one of my friends, a midwestern college president. He asked me how our trustees and I could sleep nights when our obligations kept growing and there was no undergirding endowment to protect them. "Oh," I replied, "but we do have an endowment and it is better than blue chip capital funds. Our endowment is people."

IX

Building the Sciences

THE historian and university president walks softly when he approaches the vast and constantly evolving organism that is contemporary science. Howard Mumford Jones, saddened by the gulf that seemed to be widening between the scientist and the humanist, wrote: "Men of good will, desirous of opening channels of communication, look back with nostalgia upon the nineteenth century when Arnold and Huxley could debate liberal education, Tyndall explain why he was a materialist, Sir Charles Lyell write so that even clergymen could understand him, and Charles Darwin create masterpieces of literature that were also masterpieces of science." Loren Eiseley has said that the two loneliest creatures on earth are man and the porpoise: man because he has memory and history, the porpoise because he wants to talk to man and cannot make himself understood. There are times when one or another sector of the academic community swims in the porpoise's element, and all of us must be sometimes lonely because we too cannot make ourselves understood. C. P. Snow, after lamenting the apparently unbridgeable chasm that has developed between the "two cultures," concluded that it is "the scientists who have the future in their bones."

I think the existence of such a sharp dichotomy is overstated, often the product of polemic semantics. Certainly at Brandeis we did not feel compelled to choose sides. We found no incompatibility between structuring the curriculum to make available the best in the scientific tradition and the legacy of the arts. Obviously, the University could not seek preeminence in every discipline. It was mandatory to be *competent* in all offerings, but special achievement would have to be limited to selectively chosen areas. It opted early, therefore, to share its resources among fields in the sciences and in the arts where a unique contribution was likely, and it recruited gifted faculty who were eager to take fullest advantage of a school where the two cultures could flourish side by side.

In our first two years, we had too few faculty to think of a departmental structure. Indeed, there was strong sentiment to avoid the "fragmentation" of departments altogether as a principle of organization. Even later, when graduate studies were inaugurated and demanded departmental specialization, the schools turned into councils, on which sat the heads of the various departments to deal with interdepartmental matters and the problems of general education. In our beginning years, we combined our disciplines into four schools — the sciences, the humanities, the creative arts, and the social sciences — each school usually headed by the senior faculty member who commanded the widest prestige. We expected that such organization would provide leadership in the recruitment of the key appointments that we sought.

Saul Cohen, whom we brought in from his California research in chemistry, was the first chairman of the School of Science, and though he concentrated on the needs of his own field, he cooperated fully to give the other sciences equal stature and visibility. He shared our determination that quality must never be compromised, hence avoiding expansion into every subdivision in the bewildering diversity of modern science. But he accepted no limits in areas that he defined for major Brandeis contributions. Within a few years he had gathered a nucleus of scholars and researchers with original casts of mind, some already renowned, but mostly younger people whose potential for distinction he confidently predicted. The dozen or so colleagues whom he recruited for chemistry became a well-integrated team, intensely loyal to their chief and proud of the University that had brought them together. Sidney Golden, the scholarly theoretical chemist, was concerned with the quantum statistical theory of chemical kinetics and with atomic and molecular structure; Paul Dorain explored in depth electron paramagnetic resonance; Henry Linschitz did most of his research in the physical mechanisms of photobiological processes and the reactions of excited molecules; Robert Stevenson investigated the solution and structure of natural products; Myron Rosenblum was mainly involved with organometallic compounds; Kenneth Kustin, later department chairman, took responsibility for the courses in chemical kinetics and mechanisms of inorganic reactions; James Hendrickson concentrated on the synthesis of natural products and the development of new synthetic reactions. Ernst Grunwald came from the Bell Telephone Laboratories; his research in solution chemistry and the kinetics of proton transfer reactions added distinction that was recognized when he was elected to membership in the National Academy of Sciences. Indeed, an unusual number of Cohen's choices in chemistry were early honored by the American Academy of Arts and Sciences, when Golden, Linschitz, Grunwald, and of course Cohen were all elected.

The time was opportune for significant progress in the areas in which such a faculty was preeminent. The enormous needs of World War II had stimulated vast research programs to develop synthetic materials, such as rubber and nylons, medical products and insecticides, and the field was wide open for the application of fundamental knowledge to practical chemistry.

Because of its successful science program, the University was consistently able to attract the ablest high school students. Subsequently, when they found themselves in frenetic competition to gain admission to the good medical and dental schools, they did very well. Indeed, in relation to its size, Brandeis generally ranked very near the top in placement. The caliber of the faculty also drew graduate students and post-doctorals from some of the most important universities. By the early 1960s, we had between sixty and seventy postdoctoral students in the sciences. The most sophisticated electronic and spectroscopic equipment was made available, not only to them, but even to the freshmen and sophomores. Early in the semester, students taking introductory chemistry were taught to evaluate laboratory data and to present them effectively in well-structured reports.

By 1967, the chemistry faculty was confident enough to apply for a Center of Excellence grant from the National Science Foundation to add essential new equipment to the laboratories, to strengthen even further its staffing, and to open its facilities to a much larger group of students who hoped to go on in medicine, the health sciences, and public health. And though only a handful of grants was later awarded, Brandeis was included among them, receiving nearly $900,000.

Meantime, the explosion of knowledge in the immediate postwar period gave biological research a dynamic quality that exhilarated all who were part of the adventure. In some, it even bred a kind of arrogance that seemed unseemly in a scientist. "Molecular biology," said Max Perutz of Cambridge in all seriousness, "is the basic science of life; it is now the only way one knows what one is talking about." Dr. James Henrickson would not agree; he reminded his colleagues that it was the study of chemistry that made modern biology possible. The friendly competitive chaffing over which discipline was more important enlivened the luncheon breaks and added to the awe of the younger men and women, who were further prodded by the rivalry of academic pride.

In such a heady climate, the biology faculty and their most advanced students worked with mounting excitement. For the dramatic developments of the previous few years were only a prelude to even more fantastic discoveries in enzyme research, in the role of bacteria and viruses, in the nature of complex structures and their relationship to the control of all living systems, in the fast merging of animal and plant ecology into a sort of social ecology. Herman Epstein concentrated on radiation biology and virus genetics. Maurice Sussman and his wife, Raquel Rotford-Sussman, worked together in microbiology, exploring cellular differentiation and microbial genetics. Edgar Zwilling conducted experiments in vertebrate development and tissue interactions that were watched with fascination. Tragically, he died, a comparatively young man, before he could take satisfaction in the results of his pioneering research. Albert Kelner concentrated, along with Sussman, on microbial genetics and also on radiation biology. Attila Klein became a respected authority on the complications of plant development and metabolism. Jerome Schiff opened out unrealized research opportunities in sulfur metabolism and in photobiology. Later the department, aided by substantial new grants, was augmented when we coaxed Martin Gibbs away from Cornell to bring added strength to the field of photosynthesis and plant physiology, and when Andrew Szent-Györgyi was persuaded to transfer his research in the chemistry of muscle contraction from Woods Hole to Brandeis. The scientific world once again recognized the faculty's caliber when it elected Gibbs to the National Academy of Sciences and Szent-Györgyi to the American Academy of Arts and Sciences.

The biologists, like all their colleagues in science, did not regard their research and teaching as mutually exclusive. In their research they fully involved not only their graduate students but their more highly qualified undergraduates so that they too could enter the new world that biology was opening and charting. Students were taught the functions of the newest, most sophisticated tools: analytical ultracentrifuges, radioisotope counters, electron microscopes, chromatographic and fractionating devices of all sorts. With these skills they moved into the eerie world of viruses, single-cell plants and animals, slime molds, chick embryos, fruit flies. Studies were in fact structured so that the students would be exposed to the rich cargo of scientific discovery and descriptive data inherited from the past while they worked beside their faculty mentors to become part of the research in progress. "In effect," wrote Zwilling, "many of our courses are actually two in one; with the students aided in their efforts to master descriptive material by means of independent study, while the lectures are largely devoted to modern experimental biology."

The quick national recognition of the departments of chemistry and biology was paralleled by the development of advanced programs in mathematics and physics. Research in mathematics had proliferated during and since World War II and top-level faculty were much in demand. It was early determined, therefore, to concentrate, insofar as graduate work was concerned, on algebra and topology, and so to make Brandeis a major center in these areas. Vigorous recruitment enlisted a brilliant team of about ten men who, though quite young, had already distinguished themselves. The nucleus included Oscar Goldman, Maurice Auslander, Arnold Shapiro (who died not much past thirty), Heisuke Hironaka, Felix Browder, Joseph Kohn, and Edgar Brown, who were mainly concerned with homological algebra and differential topology. Hironaka won the Fields Medal, a recognition that some scientists regard as equivalent to a Nobel Prize. This original group was joined by Richard Palais, David Buchsbaum, and Harold Levine, working with Brown in differential topology; Robert Seeley, in singular integrals; Hugo Rossi, in functional analysis and complex geometry; Paul Monsky and Teruhisa Matsusaka in algebraic geometry; and Jerome Levine in differential topology and Krest theory.

Research for such a faculty was the breath of life, but they did not downgrade their work with undergraduates, who found themselves in a rarefied atmosphere where it was academically fatal to think carelessly. Nor was there any disdain manifest for applied mathematics. While abstract research was the faculty's pride and the main reason for their eminence, they recognized the obligation of mathematics as an indispensable instrument for all the other sciences. This was the age of major advances in solar and space research, and in the exploration of the mysteries of elementary particles and their interaction. To these men, therefore, it was not demeaning for the queen of the sciences also to serve as handmaiden to them.

Ironically, the very eminence of this gifted team created a problem for the University. The faculty knew that they were in great demand and regarded themselves as a very special group, as indeed they were. There was quick promotion for them and for their newer, younger colleagues, and salary advancement somewhat beyond the University's general guidelines. But as they gained visibility and as offers poured in to them, it was natural that they would become restless. As stars, the mathematicians were not seeking benefits that they did not deserve, but it was not possible for us to go too far beyond the limits that had been set for other outstanding faculty. The budgetary decision periods each year were often quite difficult, and the administration won no popularity for its mandate to hold the line. I often wished that I could pledge the commitment of a special donor angel for them, since I fully shared T. H. Huxley's irrefutable theorem: "What men of science want is only a fair day's wages for more than a fair day's work." Fortunately, only a few of the men who came to Brandeis in those early days were attracted elsewhere, and mathematics at Brandeis retained its preeminence in the academic world.

Initially, there was little expectation that Brandeis could quickly build an important department of physics, since eminent faculty and sophisticated facilities would call for a prodigious investment when the financing of the total university was still so precarious. Nevertheless, in a period revolutionized by the explosion of the fission and fusion bombs and the spectacular penetration of space, it was understood that emphasis on the sciences would be seriously handicapped unless at least a minimum program were launched, and unless at least a few men of prominence in physics were recruited. It was after all the Nobel Prize winner Isidor Rabi, who, when asked why he chose to be a physicist, replied: "Physics is the only basic science there is. Everything else is to the right of it and depends on it. Nothing is to the left of it." The chemists and biologists were not the only imperialists!

Apparently, however, there could be no "minimum programs" at Brandeis. For, to the astonishment of the academic world, when an invitation was extended in 1954 to the world-renowned physicist Leo Szilard to join the minuscule group at Brandeis, he accepted without cavil and gave us one of our most exciting and productive courses, a seminar in the frontiers of science. Apart from the gratifying visibility that his presence on the faculty gave us, Szilard was most generous in offering counsel on the development of the science departments.

I held my breath when the colleague of Einstein and Fermi and Bohr and the pioneers of the Manhattan Project visited the campus for the first time, in 1953, and I had to show him the meager laboratory facilities that we then had, hardly sufficient for a good high school. But Szilard was not nonplussed. He rather admired the pluck of the little David among the Goliaths of higher education. His own thinking had always been audacious, and he was eager to be helpful in what he confidently expected would place the school, in less rather than more time, in the forefront of scientific institutions.

With such encouragement it was not difficult to be adventurous. Every effort was now bent to procure the funding that would enlist a corps of brilliant theoretical physicists and to reinforce them speedily with equally resourceful experimentalists. I am afraid that there was more than a touch of audacity in the recruitment. Somewhere I had read the comment of a laureate in physics: "There are only two categories of men who become theoreticians: the geniuses and the men who are merely brilliant. Those less than brilliant needn't bother to come around." And how could we be blamed for reaching for the best when the University, virtually in its infancy, had been able to capture a prize like Szilard.

The original team consisted of a trio of young men who matched discernment with penetration. There was David Falkoff, soon to be taken by early death, who came to us from MIT's Lincoln Laboratory. He had produced startling results in his research on fluctuations and irreversible processes and had just been elected to serve a second three-year term as associate editor of the *American Journal of Physics*. There was Robert Thornton, who came to us in 1950 after fifteen years at Talladega College and a short stint at the University of Chicago. We could not hold him long, since high-level positions were opening for blacks, and after only three years Thornton went to Dilliard to become its dean. Sylvan Schweber, who in his early years had thought seriously of the Orthodox rabbinate, had turned his sharp, Talmudic mind to the mysteries of science and had won a national reputation for his work in theoretical mechanics. His volume *An Introduction to Relativistic Quantum Field Theory*, published in 1961, educated a whole generation of young theorists. The original faculty and their students, graduate and undergraduate, overflowed classrooms and offices and lecture halls. Then others, keen and fervid in their versatility, came to broaden the initial beachhead, each need bringing the insistence from the faculty committees (budgets, they insisted, are problems only for the administrators!) that the highest competence must be the irreducible minimum. Eugene Gross began dazzling his colleagues with his research in plasma physics and electrodynamics. Kenneth Ford, a nuclear physicist, won a national reputation for his imaginative undergraduate text, *The World of Elementary Particles*. Stanley Deser was hard at work seeking the elusive bridge that might cross the chasm between the quantum theory of fields and general relativity. Fifteen years later he was still patiently pursuing the link that had eluded generations of his most distinguished predecessors. The young Swiss Max Chrétien filled our slot for particle physics; Jack Goldstein, later to become dean of faculty, opened out the vistas of astrophysics; Howard Schnitzer, nuclear theory and elementary particles; Marcus Grisaru, mathematical physics; and Hugh Pendleton, the quantum theory of atoms, molecules, and solids. Edgar Lipworth, brought in from the radiation laboratories of the University of California, was a major recruit. Since coming to Brandeis he made some of the most sophisticated and accurate measurements in atoms, using an atomic beam apparatus which he had conceived and built himself. He won world fame for testing the fundamental principles of physics time reversal.

Above all, there was young Stephan Berko. He had escaped the Holocaust and had been one of the students spotted by the Hillel Foundation, who had sought out the most gifted survivors for opportunities in American universities. Berko had ranked all of the candidates who had competed, and after his doctoral training he had risen to front rank among the younger scientists, concentrating on nuclear and solid-state physics. At Brandeis he not only became a dedicated teacher and a brilliant researcher in experimental solid-state physics, but, with Edgar Lipworth, he made a major contribution in planning the facilities that had become indispensable if the teaching and research were to go forward.

The department now not only included the traditional patterns of physics, which sought to understand man's experience in nature, but also the relationship to medical problems and research. It was this thrust that encouraged the establishment of a biophysics subdivision that enlisted the cooperation of Kenneth Kusten, Henry Linschitz of chemistry, Andrew Szent-Györgyi, and other leading members of the biology department. Perhaps nowhere was the value of investing in talented young people more completely vindicated than when Brandeis took calculated risks in accepting the assurances of distinguished scientists that their protégés should be given the encouragement of early visibility and quick promotion. There was a ready answer to those who worried that too much was being risked when so much responsibility was shouldered by scholars in their twenties. As the scientists themselves often reminded us, Kepler was only twenty-four when he created modern cosmology, and Isaac Newton was twenty-four when he arrived by induction at the law of universal gravitation; he said wryly: "I was at the prime of my life." Above all, Einstein was twenty-six in 1905, when he propounded the general theory of relativity and the proof of mass-energy equivalence. We did not hope to develop such authentic geniuses, but we were persuaded that to discover and encourage unusual talent was our responsibility in laying the foundations of the science departments.

Inevitably, men with such research records received impressive grants from the major federal agencies. Indeed, Brandeis was cited as a Center of Excellence in physics as well as chemistry, and was assigned more than a million dollars for its program. When graduate studies were evaluated every few years by the American Council on Education, Brandeis was invariably on the honor list.

The physics faculty made another basic contribution. They were intensely interested in improving teaching methods and materials, and with their colleagues in other scientific areas, they were leaders in improving demonstration and laboratory experiments and in creating more adequate textbooks and films, which were widely adopted in science classes throughout the country. The impact was felt, not only in American schools at all levels but in schools throughout the world. Jack Goldstein was called regularly to Africa for seminars with science teachers; Stanley Deser journeyed to Latin America, Europe, and Russia. Our scientists served on government and foundation commissions that were sent to every continent. And there was a constant interchange with institutions of higher learning in Israel in all areas.

In the mid-1950s, I called a conference of senior professors and asked if Brandeis could sponsor summer institutes where some of the world's leading scholars could gather to update their colleagues on the status of their research and to flint each other's ideas. One of our physicists, Dr. Schweber, suggested that we emulate the famous Summer Institute of the University of Paris that convened world-famous physicists for summer colloquia, where their most recent work could be discussed and critically evaluated. Our first Summer School in Physics was organized in 1958 by Dr. Schweber, with over eighty participants. It was supported in part from a grant by the Raytheon Corporation. The importance of the venture was promptly recognized and was largely responsible for winning continuity for the program through subsidies from the National Science Foundation and NATO. Each year it brought to Brandeis about seventy outstanding theoretical physicists from all over the world for seven weeks of seminars and colloquia. The lecturers and resource consultants included Nobel laureates and others in the forefront of physics research. In addition, scores of carefully chosen graduate and postdoctoral students were invited.

The sessions in the seminars and classrooms, the discussions that centered on the most recent physics breakthroughs, the interchange during the long walks amid the lovely surroundings of the University, the table conversation during lunch and dinner hours, the bull sessions — all these made the fleeting weeks as productive an experience as these gifted men and women could hope for. Since books and articles were often obsolete as soon as they appeared, the annual publication of the lectures and discussions became valuable reference works on current research developments. The institute became an annual summer pilgrimage to the Brandeis campus, lasting for nearly fifteen years until with dubious concern for economy, federal budgetary cutbacks eliminated support for such enterprises.

At the other end of the spectrum, another imaginative and useful program was an arrangement with the Newton High School that brought selected youngsters to the campus for six weeks, full time, during the summer, each associated in the ongoing research of a Brandeis faculty member. It was geared to give the students early exposure to current research in heart disease, cancer, radiation sickness, and other basic health problems. The first year provided the pilot project; it was most successful and was gradually broadened to include several other advanced high schools in New England.

Our most ambitious scientific development came in the field of biochemistry. It was planned as a graduate discipline, even though the considerable investment in faculty and facilities required special daring. But the area was a natural one for Brandeis, whose supporting constituency was always intrigued by the hope that the University would sponsor medical research and training. Besides, biochemistry was one of the youngest of the sciences and Brandeis would not be at such a disadvantage in seeking a respected place in so new a field. Only after World War II was biochemistry included in the departmental structure of universities (until then it was mainly limited to medical schools). The American Biochemical Society was not organized until 1908, with just thirty members, and when Brandeis was founded in 1948, the society had only seven hundred members. It has now grown beyond three thousand.

If the program were to meet its promise it would have to be assured imaginative direction. We sought the counsel of the ever helpful Dr.

Fritz Lipmann, a Nobel laureate and one of our Fellows. Lipmann went over our own faculty's suggestions, added some of his own, and then narrowed the list to five. He was doubtful that the top two recommendations would be willing to cast their lot with so young an institution, but he was sure that any of the others, if they agreed to come, would be almost equally valuable. We had never been reluctant to reach out for the so-called unattainable, so the first names on the list were approached, Dr. Nathan Kaplan, then at Johns Hopkins, and Dr. Martin Kamen, a key member of the chemistry faculty at Washington University, with a long record of research and discovery in bio-energetics, and a pioneer in the attempts to apply to medical problems the physical properties of radioisotopes. Intrigued by the dynamism of the University and by the promise of a vigorous campaign to acquire the necessary facilities, they both accepted our invitation and formed the nucleus of what they vowed would become a superb department. They recruited a group of gifted younger men and women, who, in turn, attracted the most promising graduate and postdoctoral students.

The early faculty included William Jencks, later elected to the National Academy of Sciences. Trained as a physician, he had been one of the pioneers in the kinetics of enzyme catalysis. His in-depth study of mechanism enzyme reactions led to the training of a large number of scientists both at Brandeis and in other universities and research centers. One of these, Dr. Julius Marmur, who later joined the faculty of the Albert Einstein Medical School, began his important studies of nucleic acids at Brandeis. Dr. Serge Timasheff, who headed one of the few pioneering U.S. Department of Agriculture laboratories in an academic setting, brought the skills of physical chemistry and thermodynamics to bear on biochemical problems. The addition of Lawrence Levine, who was soon awarded a career grant by the American Cancer Society, introduced us to the excitement of immunochemistry and immunology, with its many applications to medical research. His wife, Helen Van Vunakis, was his research colleague, and the two became national figures in their field. Lawrence Grossman was among the early researchers to investigate the enzymatic reactions involving DNA synthesis and repair. The implications of his work on repair stimulated major attention in the possibilities of its application with mammalian cells. Since one of Dr. Kaplan's early interests was in enzyme cofactors, he sought an outstanding associate to share it with him. Dr. Robert Abeles, then at the University of Michigan, and formerly at Harvard and Ohio State, was primarily concerned with Vitamin B_{12} and, together with Kaplan, he continued his general interest in cofactors and applied studies on reaction mechanisms to a wide spectrum of enzymes. There were many others: Gerald Fasman was concerned with the conformation of biological micromolecules and the biological properties of polymino acids; Farnsworth Loomis, whose research took him into the biochemistry of differentiation and growth in primitive animal systems; Gordon Sato, who concentrated on the specialized function of cultured mammalian cells; Mary Ellen Jones, whom we recruited from the Biochemical Research Laboratories of the Massachusetts General Hospital and whose research took her into the role of carbamyl phosphate in microbiology and mammalian systems; Morris Soodak, affectionately referred to as "our Christian Arab," and Farahe Maloof, who were concerned with the biochemical pharmacology and the biochemistry of the thyroid; John Lowenstein, whose research centered on metabolic regulation of carbohydrate utilization and fat synthesis; and William Murakami, who worked in the biochemistry of virus-infected cells.

The leader of this impressive team, Nathan Kaplan, refused to rest on his laurels, nor did he permit his colleagues to ease off. The American Cancer Society had the fullest confidence in him, and when he began to develop a device — called an automatic serum enzyme analyzer — in the hope that it could detect the presence of cancer before the usual symptoms appeared, every request for grants was honored to facilitate his search. Other grants, ultimately totaling millions, came pouring in from the Public Health Service and the National Science Foundation.

Such men and women were not just gifted specialists. They were animated and prodded and goaded by a mission. They agreed with the critic who said: "Philosophers have only *interpreted* the world differently — the point is to change it." As they worked together, the laboratory lights burning far into the night, they made biochemistry at Brandeis, as fellow biochemists did in a very few other select universities, a crusade that could shape the destinies of mankind.

Before concluding the story of twenty-odd years in the sciences, it may be appropriate to add a word about the special arrangements that were completed with the Carnegie Institute of Technology (now Carnegie-Mellon) and the California Institute of Technology for five-year joint degree programs, in which the students earned both their bachelor of arts and bachelor of science degrees. The arrangement, known as the 3-2 Plan, enabled the student to obtain a solid grounding in the liberal arts, with science as the area of concentration, and then to go on, after the third year, for two years of specialization in the various branches of engineering. The program was maintained for several years, and it was terminated only when the technical institutes determined to bring in faculties of their own for the undergraduate work in the liberal arts. Since this type of partnership was limited to a select group of high-level liberal arts universities, it was reassuring to know that Brandeis had earned early the reputation to be among them.

In our recruitment of the peers in all the sciences, we had promised to give every priority to obtaining the physical facilities required. A campaign involving many millions was undertaken in 1960. Only an institution as brash as Brandeis would have dared to plan one concentrated effort for eleven buildings with all of their astronomically expensive, sophisticated equipment. We went along with *Venus and Adonis:* "Things out of hope are compassed oft with venturing." Happily, our boldness was rewarded and the goal was oversubscribed.

The required funds pledged, construction went forward briskly for several years, and by 1965 the entire science complex was completed. It included a special library of science, with a capacity of a quarter of a million volumes, which was named for the donor, Leo Gerstenzang, who had pioneered a fortune from the sale of Q-Tips. Many other families from various parts of the country had cooperated in the venture, each helping to underwrite one of the units. They included three physics buildings, skillfully interconnected, that came from Harry Bass of Boston, Charles Yalem of St. Louis, and the Abelson and Getz families of Chicago. A biology center, which included the most advanced equipment for teaching and research, came from a New York merchant, Charles Bassine, and his brilliant son-in-law, Arthur Cohen, who was named by *Fortune* magazine as among the most promising business entrepreneurs of the younger generation. A lovely, well-equipped home was at last provided for the mathematicians through the gift of a New York stockbroker, Horace Goldsmith. Chemistry, which had been impatiently waiting since graduate studies were inaugurated, came at last into its own through a complex of buildings provided by Herman and Rose Lecks of Miami Beach and Harry and Mae Edison of St. Louis. Biochemistry fascinated many families, and their interest resulted in a profusion of gifts — from Robert Wolfson of St. Louis, Stanley Rosenzweig of Washington, and Joseph Kosow of Boston. The philanthropic cornucopia overflowed when Lewis Rosenstiel, the head of Schenley's, provided the most generous gift in the history of the University, leaving an impact that warrants fuller detail in a later chapter.

The dedication, set for early November 1965, was more than a University celebration; it became a major salute from the world of science. The reputation that the University had now earned was indicated by the acceptance of invitations from among the most honored scientists in the land. Hoping that our traditional good luck in convocation weather would not desert us, we planned to hold the dedication outside. The site chosen was the roof of the Gerstenzang Science Library, with the science complex rising all around us. From this vantage point there would be a spectacular view of the campus in all directions. Would have been! The Sunday morning dawned wet and drizzly. A year earlier this caprice of weather would have spelled disaster, since we would not have been able to seat all our guests in any amphitheater or lecture hall.

As luck had it, however, the final touches had been put on the interior of the Spingold Theater just the previous Friday, so the center's first "onstage cast" included five Nobel laureates as well as other world-renowned scientists. The twelve honorary-degree recipients were Carl Cori of Washington University, Nobel laureate, with his late wife, for research in the regulation of carbohydrate metabolism; Ernest Nagel of Columbia, whose teaching and research bridged the gulf between the natural and social sciences; Oscar Zariski of Harvard, editor of major journals in mathematics; Jerome Wiesner, science adviser to President Kennedy and at that time provost of MIT, later its president; Chaim Pekeris, Israeli geophysicist, professor of applied mathematics at the Weizmann Institute; Torbjorn Caspersson, director of medicine and cell research at the Nobel Institute for Medicine in Stockholm; Severo Ochoa, chairman of the Department of Biochemistry at New York University's College of Medicine and Nobel laureate in medicine; Gerard Piel, editor and publisher of *Scientific American* and winner of the UNESCO award for service to science education; Isidor Rabi of Columbia, Nobel laureate in physics and former chairman of the Atomic Energy Commission; Albert Szent-Györgyi, Hungarian-born director of the Woods Hole Marine Biological Laboratory, who had presented his gold Nobel medal to Finland in her hour of need; and Robert B. Woodward of Harvard, who had only days before been informed he would receive the Nobel Prize in chemistry for his work in synthesizing complex substances such as reserpine and chlorophyll. The address was to be given by James E. Webb, director of the National Aeronautics and Space Administration.

Despite the weather (Dr. Wiesner was discovered walking around outside with his pipe upside down, puffing merrily), no convocation proved more colorful. Several of our guests had earlier been honored by Oxford, and they wore their flaming red gowns and wide soft velvet hats. Dr. Caspersson was arrayed in a frock coat of unusual cut, striped trousers, a very high-colored shirt over which a handsome decoration was suspended on a wide blue ribbon, and a tall silk hat that was also of unusual shape, more sugarloaf than stovepipe. Since the Swedish scientist was well over six feet tall, the hat permitted him to tower over even such tall men as Robert Woodward and Severo Ochoa, let alone the diminutive Isidor Rabi!

A word about the honorary-degree citations for this occasion. They were among the most difficult with which we ever worked. Just to catalogue the achievements of those men was to use a vocabulary that, to say the least, was not caviar to the general. Our science faculty, especially Larry Grossman in biochemistry, were generous with time and suggestions as to which achievements each recipient treasured most. I have always believed that honorary-degree citations should be something more than catalogues, and that each should contain some quotation or reference that, while intelligible to the public, holds a special meaning for the recipient. With the Nobelist Severo Ochoa, this was particularly difficult. Spain had produced this remarkable man, but Spanish contributions to science had been poignantly infrequent in the last five hundred years. I had assistants scouring Spanish literature in translation for days to find something felicitous. Finally we settled on a few words from a poem by Miguel de Unamuno, the philosopher-poet-novelist whom even Franco had not dared to oust from the faculty at the University of Salamanca, Unamuno's "golden Salamanca." Ochoa, a regal man with the bearing of a true hidalgo, was strikingly handsome with snow-white hair and a long, dark, Spanish countenance, severe in appearance compared, for instance, with Szent-Györgyi, whose face crinkled with laugh lines. As I reached the Unamuno quotation, I glanced up at Ochoa, whose Spanish austerity had lighted for a moment with a smile like all the sunshine of Iberia. Such minimoments were the treasured extra remembrances of our exercises that raised them far above the level of perfunctory back-patting.

In summary, the University's record in science in its first two decades had carried us quickly into front rank. The undergraduate student body was one of the most highly selected; College Board scores in the very high 700s were not uncommon, and graduate students sought admission after undergraduate preparation in the best colleges. Between ninety and one hundred full-time faculty members were actively engaged in teaching and research. All of the departments were housed in a newly completed science complex, providing over 200,000 square feet of space, furnished with modern, sophisticated equipment. There was now a special science library containing nearly fifty thousand volumes, and the Women's Committee was working at its usual frenetic pace to bring the number to a quarter of a million; scientific journals in their hundreds were regularly received from throughout the world. Our philosophy of teaching validated the pledge that the entering undergraduate would have access to the most highly reputed faculty if capacity to warrant the privilege was demonstrated. The students were actively involved with the faculty in some of their experiments and were taught, almost from their freshman days, the austere, uncompromising disciplines of research. By the early 1960s, grants for research from the major national agencies were averaging $8 million annually, and the character of the research in each field was winning the highest acclaim from the peers in each of the sciences. The climax in the progress of science at Brandeis came in the final year of my incumbency, when a major biochemistry grant of $19 million was given to us by Lewis Rosenstiel that made possible, within the next few years, a new major biomedical facility and a much extended program in the medical sciences.

X

"Get the Best Brains and Don't Interfere"

THE program in biochemistry, and later in all of the biomedical sciences, received its major thrust from the encouragement and support of Lewis Rosenstiel, a rather remarkable industrialist who had built the Schenley liquor empire. He was a hard-nosed business tycoon, a tough competitor, and a shrewd judge of men and their motivation. He was authoritarian in his managerial approach, but he elicited undeviating loyalty from his staff, drawing their best efforts by handsomely rewarding enterprising initiative. His interest in medical research was awakened by the desperate struggle of his first wife, Dorothy, who fought a losing battle against cancer.

I came to know Rosenstiel primarily through one of our trustees, Joseph Linsey, who had the franchise for Schenley products for Greater Boston and who was one of Rosenstiel's most devoted friends. In the early years of the University we had received a few contributions from Rosenstiel, token gifts for scholarships usually set up in deference to Linsey's requests. In the fall of 1956, with our plans well advanced for the development of a graduate and postdoctoral research program in biochemistry, Linsey and I agreed that the time was right to approach Rosenstiel for a major grant.

The appointment was arranged and Linsey and I flew down to Miami, where Rosenstiel usually spent the winter months. On the plane, Linsey and I discussed our goals and a strategy of approach. When we arrived at the Fontainebleu Hotel and were ushered into Rosenstiel's suite, we learned that he had not been too well and, after several restless nights, had finally fallen asleep late in the afternoon. Our appointment was for nine o'clock, but we considered it unwise to have him awakened. Linsey and I therefore drank coffee, watched television, and chatted until late into the night, when Rosenstiel was ready to receive us. He gave me no opportunity to make the presentation we had planned. All I could do was to indicate that the University was vitally concerned with bio-chemistry and needed the seed money to organize a creditable department. Rosenstiel asked for no details. He simply announced that he would give the University a million dollars and he hoped that, if it were spread over a ten-year period, principal and income, it could help launch the program we had in mind. He also suggested that we follow his own business practice: "Get the best possible brains and don't interfere."

Active recruitment began at once, and when we succeeded in luring Dr. Nathan Kaplan from Johns Hopkins and Dr. Martin Kamen from Washington University, we were on the way. Soon a whole series of appointments was announced that catapulted the department into the front rank of biochemical research. During the next few years we kept Rosenstiel fully informed of the progress of the research in the life sciences, and he was elated that the continuous flow of government grants that our faculty was able to generate multiplied his seed money tenfold. Whenever there were important milestones in his life — birthdays, anniversaries, conferences — and I could get away, I would join Linsey in driving to Rosenstiel's summer home in Greenwich, Connecticut. Rosenstiel made several visits to the campus, and his discussions with the science faculty indicated clearly that his knowledge of their work was not superficial.

The years, however, were also crowded with sadness and tragedy for him. In February 1960 his son David, only thirty-nine, succumbed as his mother did to cancer. A daughter, Louise (Skippy), the only survivor of his marriage to Dorothy and upon whom he had pinned his hopes for love and understanding in his lonely later years, brought him little consolation. She was a brilliant woman, greatly resembling her father in business acumen and in organizing capacity. He had demonstrated his confidence in her judgment by naming her a trustee of the Schenley Foundation, along with his attorney, Judge Marx of Cincinnati. But she had married one of the officials of Schenley, Sidney Frank, and there was continuous friction between Rosenstiel and his son-in-law. Skippy inevitably sided with her husband, and the alienation between her and her father grew continuously more serious. In the fall of 1960 Judge Marx died. A violent battle erupted when Skippy and her father were at odds over the appointment of a successor trustee. Since each had one vote, a stalemate developed, and the quarrel went into litigation. The lawsuit was not only costly but it embittered Rosenstiel, as he was confronted by the embarrassing press stories that he imagined were initiated by his daughter. Rosenstiel's ongoing interest in the University was not affected by his domestic problems. He continued to visit the campus and took pride in the rapid tempo of its science development.

In June 1967, when he turned seventy-six, the University sponsored a birthday party for him to which the inner family of Brandeis, his business associates, and representatives of his many philanthropies came to pay tribute. The affair gave me the opportunity to discuss Rosenstiel's mature perspective, which had influenced him to turn the many sorrows of his personal life into service to others instead of indulging in the sterility of self-pity and fruitless grief. In response he sent a very touching letter that offered a view of the man which those who had no intimate association with him never realized. He wrote:

> To my deep respect and esteem for you I want to add sincerest gratitude for the wonderful Brandeis evening you caused to be in my honor. . . . I want to say this to you. You are a very perceiving man. Your remarks touched me deeply. . . . While you were talking . . . I was churning inside. . . .
>
> My own interest in serving others started with my dearly beloved wife, Dorothy, and goes back to the first days of our marriage. This lovely girl of great stature, statesmanship, ability and character, suspected then, I believe, what the future might hold for her. So our lives were spent, Dorothy's particularly, in trying to learn what life really meant.
>
> We lost two children within a short period of time early in our marriage; Lewis Jr. was fifteen months old when he died. I had to face the unbearable tragedy of losing my beloved after a long illness, at forty-four years of age, and then years later, David was struck down with Hodgkins disease. Although we did everything possible to prolong his life — he finally succumbed at thirty-nine.
>
> I can honestly say I do not know how much all of this affected my daughter, Louise, who came to the Dinner the other night. Nor do I believe I will ever find out. But I was deeply impressed with your perception in visualizing what it can mean if one permits reverses of life to be destructive, to alienate one's sense of responsibility and one's need to love. If life's sorrows have any meaning at all it is to be found in the renewing of the desire to give of oneself to one's fellow human beings.
>
> I learned that lesson and as long as the good Lord gives me the strength and the means I hope to continue to help the dedicated people of the world, the researchers and their teachers, so that others may not have to suffer so much. . . . In this connection it is my fond hope that I am going to be able to dissolve the Foundation while I live and give all the monies away during my lifetime, and this for the very selfish reason that I would like the joy of witnessing much of the good that is accomplished. . . .
>
> P.S. I would like to add one thought. It was the want and the will to help his fellow human beings . . . coupled with his

simplicity and his serenity . . . that I have always found so attractively overpowering in Joe Linsey.

Late in 1967, a serious illness incapacitated Rosenstiel for months at a time. He therefore determined that he would retire as head of Schenley, sell out his interests in its far-flung industries, and give all of his attention to the disposal of the assets of the foundation, which by then had reached a total of about $54 million. He found a legal way to bypass his daughter's objections and planned to make the distribution quickly, so that if death should intervene, his wishes would not be thwarted.

On January 23, 1968, he invited me to his Florida home to discuss the foundation and his plans for the disposal of its assets. "I am now ready," he wrote, "to sit down with you to finish formulation of the plans for the liquidation of the Rosenstiel Foundation." I flew down to Miami and he outlined an imaginative plan to make major gifts to the institutions and causes that had meant the most to him personally.

Near the end of the evening he turned to the future of the life science research program at Brandeis, and I detailed the developments that had been largely influenced by his earlier gifts and by the federal grants they had stimulated. Then I spoke of our hopes for expanded biomedical research. He listened intently and then indicated that he would not let much time pass before he reached final decisions. A few weeks later he called me from Greenwich, Connecticut, asking if I would come down to discuss further his plans for the foundation and specifically for Brandeis.

We met on February 19. He expressed his satisfaction over what had been done thus far with his original gift. I did not have to name any figures for our biomedical plans: he had apparently decided what he wished to do. He announced quietly, almost casually, that he would contribute ten million dollars, and he hoped that this could "give us a favorable start" in the expanded research program that we had discussed in January. When I attempted to evaluate the impact of such generosity, not only on research in the field but on the future of Brandeis, he turned the conversation. He was always uncomfortable when praise was attempted, and apparently now more than ever.

The timing of Rosenstiel's extraordinary gift provided a dramatic climax to my tenure as president. A few months before, approaching the completion of twenty years at Brandeis, I had asked the trustees to accept my resignation and to begin the search for a successor. They had settled on Morris Abram, a distinguished New York attorney, a partner in the firm headed by Judge Simon Rifkind. The announcement of this news had already been prepared and was to be released the morning after my conference with Rosenstiel in Greenwich.

I was to be driven back after dinner to New York so that I could take an early plane to Boston the next morning. Rosenstiel was in a jovial, relaxed mood and he decided that he would drive to New York with me. During the hour's trip, Rosenstiel mused: "You know, I don't believe that the quarrel with Skippy is really her fault. I think she must be stirred up by that _____ lawyer of hers, _____ _____ _____ Morris Abram." My heart skipped several beats. There were thousands of lawyers in New York, and out of all of them, the one serving Skippy in the case against Rosenstiel had to be Morris Abram! It required no prescience to guess Rosenstiel's reaction when he read of Abram's appointment the next morning. Late as it was when I got to the hotel, I called Thelma to tell her that I had probably just seen ten million dollars fly out of the car window.

I returned to Boston early the next morning, knowing full well that the date, February 20, 1968, was fated to be a decisive one in the life of the University. The phone in my office rang at eleven. It was Rosenstiel. His voice was cold and grim. "I note by this morning's *Times*," he said, "that the Brandeis trustees have made a choice of a new president. You know what my opinion of him is, don't you?" "Lew," I replied, "I know how you must feel. But you should remember that there is nothing personal in Abram's assignment to the case where he represents Skippy. There must be a hundred lawyers in the Rifkind firm. Any one of them could have been assigned." "True," Rosenstiel said, "but the one assigned is Abram. Can you really believe that I would entrust the largest gift of my life to a college headed by this _____? How much do you people really know about him? Have you checked his record in Atlanta where he spent most of his professional life? Since he has been the opposing attorney, I had him checked out carefully. I have had plenty of experience with lawyers in constant battles in a long business career. I have often taken on men like Abram. I have expected no quarter from them. But the qualities that make him effective when he seeks advantage in a trial are not the qualities that I would look for in a college president. In any case, I don't want my gift to be administered by the man who has turned my daughter against me and has vilified me publicly. I must withdraw the pledge." He spoke with such finality that there was no point in interrupting him or offering any rebuttal.

A few hours later a follow-up telegram was delivered. It read: "Dear Abe: Kindly accept my resignation as Fellow of Brandeis University and permit me to refer you to Carl Sandburg's preface to his volume of poetry, as follows: 'All around us is the inexplicable, also the incomprehensible and the unintelligible.' My personal warmth for you continues. Most sincerely. LSR." After studying it carefully, I took heart from the very fact that Rosenstiel had offered a rationale for his resignation and had dressed it up with a literary quotation. His assurances of continued personal friendship made me hope that the situation was not irretrievable. But I knew that I must not argue with a man who had been so deeply wounded by the break with his daughter, whom he really loved.

I wired back: "I do not have it in my heart to blame you for your reaction. My ardent hope is that your esteem for the University will some day overcome your misgivings about the man who was doing his professional duty to a client. You quoted Sandburg; let me quote Philo: 'Scrutinize the facts rather than the litigants so that neither affection nor hatred becloud your decision.' Meantime I am deeply touched by your assurance of continued personal affection which I heartily reciprocate. Fondest regards. ALS."

The next hours were anxious ones. That night the only half-expected call from Rosenstiel came through. He said: "I still believe that the trustees have made a serious mistake in their choice of Abram as president. In character and objective he is not cast for University leadership. Yet I cannot penalize the University for an administrative judgment. Brandeis is a great institution and you have built too solidly for any successor to jeopardize its progress. How about you and Abram flying down to Miami, where I now am, so that we can spend a day together to reappraise the situation." The heartwarming call was followed by a letter that elaborated on his decision not to permit personal misgivings to influence a gift for a major science research venture. "On more sober reflection," he wrote,

> it is my opinion that it would be wrong of me to deprive Brandeis of any assistance I would be able to continue. . . . Subject to meeting with Mr. Abram, and with you, at an early time to crystalize some decisions, I just want to say that I deal in facts, too.
>
> If this new Abram undertaking be his life's work, and he is dedicated to that end (I have made some exploration of his talents which are represented as many), it would then be my hope he could in measure follow in your footsteps . . . a most difficult task.
>
> I send my warmest regards. I cannot help remembering how hard my friend, Joe Linsey, worked for Brandeis and encouraged my interest, and it would be most unfair of me to forget.

I called Morris Abram to explain that Rosenstiel was contemplating a major gift, but was inevitably upset, knowing it was to go to a University that would soon be headed by the man who he believed was harassing him in an intrafamily lawsuit. Abram recognized the bizarre complexities of the situation and readily agreed to join me for the conference with Rosenstiel. My counsel was that he should not try a public relations approach with charm or flattery and that he ought to let Rosenstiel do most of the talking. The few hours with Rosenstiel were externally pleasant ones, with no discussion of the lawsuit or of family matters. Rosenstiel talked broadly of his interest in science research. He drew Abram out about his views on higher education and on his faith in the younger generation to cope with its problems. Quite clearly he was taking the measure of the man who would lead the university through the complexities of the years ahead. Abram rose to the occasion with all the skill that had served him well in the causes he had headed with distinction. After I had returned to campus, Rosenstiel called to say that he was quite willing to give Abram the benefit of the doubt and that he hoped he would make a good president of Brandeis. "My gift stands, and good luck to all of you."

All through the summer and early fall, both Rosenstiel and I were busy winding up long incumbencies, I as president of Brandeis, he as chairman of Schenley. In August, Thelma and I invited him and his wife, Blanka, to a dinner that would be a kind of affectionate valedictory as we retired from active administration. Thelma made sure that every Schenley product was at hand for the cocktail hour. When Lew and Blanka Rosenstiel arrived and he was offered his choice, he chuckled, "I never drink."

The evening went very well. His visit to the campus and his conversations with some of our most brillant faculty strengthened his faith that his substantial gift was to be used well. After dinner he called me aside and asked when my incumbency was officially over. I told him that at the beginning of the new school year, on the first of September, Morris Abram would assume the presidency and that I was to be named chancellor; "I am going from the House of Commons to the House of Lords." He said almost casually, "I plan to give you a going-away gift. Let us raise the ten-million-dollar allocation to the University to fifteen million. I believe you can do much better then, without having to scrimp and scrape." By now I should have adjusted to his nonchalant way of making exciting announcements. But this new gift was too large to be taken in stride. I excused myself to search the Bible for an adequate reaction and I found a verse in the Book of Psalms. I quoted it in the telegram that went to the chairman of the board:

> August 15: Our negotiations with Lewis Rosenstiel for medical research program successfully completed with gift of fifteen million dollars to be publicly announced later in month. Hallelujah. Psalms 126, verses 5 and 6. ("They that sow in tears shall reap in joy. Though he goeth on his way weeping That beareth the measure of seed, He shall come home with joy, Bearing his sheaves.")

A fortnight later, as we made ready for the public announcement, I called Rosenstiel to clear the details. I noted that we could now think in terms of both a well-protected research program and adequate facilities in which to house them. "Perhaps therefore," I said, "we ought to assign the income of eleven million dollars for research and use the other four million dollars for the building that will provide the laboratory and office facilities in which the teaching and research will go forward." "What building?" he almost shouted. "What building? The allocation from the foundation was not intended to include funds for any building. I want the entire fifteen million dollars to be assigned for the academic program. Brick and mortar have never interested me." "But Lew," I protested, "you are a practical enough man to know that a science program cannot operate in a vacuum. We can bring in some of the world's best-endowed research people, the brains that you refer to, but they must have laboratories in which to function, and sophisticated equipment for their experiments, and office space to evaluate the results. Our existing space is completely inadequate for the expanded efforts that you are making possible." Rosenstiel did not hesitate for a moment. "I told you that I would contribute fifteen million dollars for research and this must stand. If you have to have additional physical facilities then go ahead, but you must not encroach upon the research funds for this purpose. I'll up the ante with a special grant of four million dollars to take care of your goddamn brick and mortar."

The unspoken language behind this apparent ingenuous exchange was fully understood by each of us. Rosenstiel was not naïve enough to believe that research could be mounted with chalk and a blackboard; he had apparently intended all along to augment his gift. But he had his own eccentric way of indulging his very carefully thought out philanthropic objectives. In any case, the "going-away gift" had now climbed to $19 million dollars, and I was running out of biblical quotations. I followed with my letter of acknowledgment, and invited Rosenstiel to become the chief sidewalk superintendent.

The expanded program in biomedical research did not get under way for several years, because faculty dissension developed over the administrative control of the program. Senior faculty members in the existing life science departments saw in the Rosenstiel research grant, yielding $900,000 annually, an unprecedented opportunity to obtain funding for their own research, which had been seriously jeopardized by the curtailment of government grants. A director could not be named until the problem of his authority and jurisdiction had been settled, and the arguments were long and drawn out.

Unfortunately, after only a little more than a year in office, in February 1970 the new president suddenly resigned to become a candidate, unsuccessfully, for the Democratic nomination as senator from New York. He explained that there was a very close deadline for filing and he was therefore unable to give longer notice. In the light of his assurances when he accepted the presidency, his action was widely criticized as opportunistic. I could not believe that it was political ambition that was responsible for the precipitate resignation. I interpreted it as the means for a quick withdrawal from his post at Brandeis when he realized that it required duties and commitments quite different from what he had expected. He had accepted the presidency in good faith, but now he wanted out. I expressed this belief to the chairman of the board, who conveyed my inference to Abram. He sent me a handwritten note of appreciation for not joining in the chorus of condemnation. "Larry told me," he wrote, "of his conversation with you of yesterday. I deeply appreciate the spirit of understanding and acceptance of good faith in intentions I expressed when I became president."

In the ensuing months of administrative confusion very little could be done to firm up long-range decisions. Rosenstiel demonstrated great patience, but, as he was approaching his eightieth birthday and his illnesses multiplied, he became increasingly restive. Though I had relinquished all administrative responsibility, he appealed to me for action. I brought home to the acting president, Charles Shottland, that we must not betray our word to a donor who had expressed unlimited confidence in the University by making available the securities for the total amount of his obligation. Once before our grant had nearly been lost by circumstances beyond our control. It would be the height of folly to risk alienation because of actions that were very much within our control. The infighting would have to stop and a director be named promptly.

At last, in the spring of 1971, the full potential of the program was achieved. A blue-ribbon committee of outside scientists recommended the appointment of Dr. Harlyn Halvorson, a distinguished biochemist, as director of the center, and he assumed his responsibilities in the fall. The biomedical research program was set up as an autonomous unit, with all policy matters firmly in the jurisdiction of the director. Halvorson welcomed the cooperation of a committee of faculty members in the life sciences. He solved the nagging problem of providing supplementary research support for the life sciences faculty by assigning up to one-third of the Rosenstiel income to the regular university graduate departments, with the understanding that only those research applications would be considered which fell directly into the categories of the programs of the biomedical center. Halvorson and his advisers concluded that perhaps the center's most important role would be in the continuing exploration of the secrets of normal and abnormal cells. Biochemistry concerned itself with the study of small molecules in cells; biology with the physiological behavior of cells in development. Halvorson hoped to create a bridge between the clinical responsibilities of the center and the academic training provided by the graduate science departments.

The first appointments were widely hailed. A team was encouraged to come from the Children's Hospital in Boston, Dr. Carolyn Cohen, Dr. Donald Caspar, and Dr. Susan Lowery, brilliant young scientists who had been doing extensive research in cellular structure and function.

They were quickly reinforced by Dr. David DeRosier, whose interest lay in image analysis. It was a real coup also to induce Dr. Alfred Redfield to join the group. His earlier career had been given to physics, where his research broadened the understanding of nuclear magnetic resonance. He then switched to the study of the structure of biological molecules, hoping to strengthen the interaction between physics and biology.

Dr. Halvorson simultaneously recruited another interdisciplinary team in molecular and cell biology for the genetic study of higher cells and their chromosome organization. He was himself an internationally respected authority in the field and he brought in as colleagues Dr. James Haber, Dr. Michael Rosbash, and Dr. Pieter Wensink. Dr. Halvorson looked forward to launching still another program in cellular immunobiology, and with this and related areas of intensive research commitment, the bridge that he had planned took solid form in the first years of his direction.

Meantime, construction of the biomedical center was accelerated and was completed during the 1972 school year. "The goddam brick and mortar" of Rosenstiel's teasing reproof was the envy of all the science research centers of New England. The dedication ceremonies were held in a period when government research grants were being drastically curtailed. Dr. Sol Spiegelman, head of the Columbia biochemistry division, spoke for all his colleagues in winding up the exercises: "Now more than ever," he said, "we need free institutes peopled by men and women of talent who choose their problems and solve them. The lights are going out across the land in the laboratories of America; they are being turned out by the bureaucratic policies which have been established in guiding and controlling our medical research. We can be grateful that by Mr. Rosenstiel's generosity a new light is being lit here and it will burn brightly for all of us."

XI

The Humanities

IMMEDIATELY after World War II, no area of curriculum in university life was as much under fire as the humanities. More than ever the pressure mounted for education that would lead to "practical" career results. The term "relevant" kept creeping into public discussion, and those who defended a major place for the humanist values of language and literature, of philosophy and the classics, found themselves on the defensive when they advocated the indispensability of such training for a truly civilized life.

As noted earlier, at Brandeis we were not drawn into the struggle. We decided from the outset that, while we were very much concerned with the social and natural sciences, equal status would always be assured for the humanities and that we would seek the very best faculty to interpret them. I later summarized our view, when we dedicated a major science complex, in the presence of half a dozen distinguished Nobel laureates. I said then: "Great as the Brandeis commitment is to accent the sciences, we will not allow the arts and humanities to wait below the stairs, like the housemaid. . . . We must teach the future biochemist to taste the salt beneath the laughter of Volpone, the physicist to delight in Mozart, the chemist to place his knowledge in the perspective of history, the mathematician to see the beauty in paint and marble as in the binomial theorem. Only thus will we avoid a race of fragmented men."

We built the faculty in the humanities, as diversified in special interests as such a group could be — Ludwig Lewisohn hard at work on a volume for the two hundredth anniversary of Goethe's birth; Milton Hindus caught between his running battles with Céline and editing a volume on Proust (which he almost titled *Remembrance of Things Proust*); James Cunningham laboring to compress his cool, astringent poetry into such tightness that a London *Times* critic concluded "that his language is deliberately remote from speech" (in truth, no one could devastate with such effectiveness the wordy and the windy); Robert Preyer mining away on the treasures hidden in the works of the Victorians; Osborne Earle gallantly maintaining the glories of Chaucer; Victor Harris resurrecting the enduring significance of Spenser and Milton and other praised but often neglected English classics, then swinging to the present to analyze the very much read but often unpraised works of contemporary novelists; Joseph Cheskis transmitting the mellow charm of French and Italian literature. In the 1952 yearbook the story was spread that when the devout Cheskis said his morning prayers, he usually managed to sneak in a canto or two in Italian from the *Inferno* of his beloved Dante. As these gifted men, and others who joined or followed them, gave new dimensions to their specializations, they found a common bond in their determination to fulfill the main purpose of a humanities curriculum: to expose their students to the very best that had been thought or written. They were tough individualists, quarreling, arguing, exposing, challenging, almost as if they loved the intellectual battle for its own sake, but uniting at once against the invasions of mediocrity. I was inevitably reminded of John Stuart Mill's famous prayer addressed to his intellectual adversaries: "Lord, enlighten Thou our enemies, sharpen their wits, give acuteness to their perceptions and consecutiveness and clearness to their reasoning powers: we are in danger from their folly, not their wisdom: their weakness is what fills us with apprehension, not their strength."

It was Robert Preyer who wrote me later when he outlined his objectives as English and American Literature Department chairman:

> We might not agree on morals, politics, the meaning of texts; but we did agree that our ideal aim was to put students in complete possession of all their powers. As practical classroom teachers we wanted them to have access to the productions of first-rate minds, to enable them to experience what that meant. . . . Our negative purpose was to insure that they recognized and developed a proper disesteem for the meretricious and the third rate. . . . Above all, we feared the inculcation of what Whitehead called "inert ideas," that is to say, ideas that are merely received into the mind without being utilized, or tested, or thrown into fresh combinations."

Preyer was really describing why many of our faculty accepted a bid to a precariously supported, still unshielded Brandeis. They were in flight from institutions, many older and safer, that were filling up with people who were captive to such "inert ideas"; they wanted to escape from this sort of mental torpor. I remembered interviewing a lively young applicant for a post in Romance languages. Dr. Cheskis was present at the interview and after it was over, I asked him what he thought. "Ah," he chuckled, "there's the kind of man it will be a pleasure to keep fighting with."

The department kept bringing in other authentic stars, each addition making the recruitment of the next a little easier. A major coup was achieved in 1953 with the arrival of Irving Howe, the literary critic and editor of *Dissent*, who, though scarcely in his forties, already had three or four teaching posts behind him. When he disagreed — and he disagreed more often than not — his sharpness rarely cut superficially. It left deep gashes. He took special delight in exposing what he termed "the flabbiness of such post-God-era entrepreneurs as Norman Mailer and Arthur Miller." He reserved tolerance and patience only for his students, and then only for the ones who demonstrated genuine promise. He wrote always with social purpose, and his literary evaluations of Faulkner and Anderson and other modern luminaries were interspersed with volumes on current politics and international affairs. He was deeply interested in proletarian Jewish life, and he edited anthologies that brought together the classics of Yiddish literature. A department could take pride in its considerable stretch and ballast when it included such men as Howe, a literary guerrilla marksman, and the stately, austere Osborne Earle, with his scholarly devotion to Chaucer.

The department also harbored, until his untimely death, Philip Rahv, founder of *Partisan Review*. One of the many writer-editor-critics who started out in the thirties when writers like Edmund Wilson, and Mary McCarthy, to whom he was briefly married, and so many others were coming into their own, Rahv had known and worked with most of the major figures of American letters. What he had to give students, therefore, was not knowledge distilled from long hours in the library, but flesh-and-blood experience. He had been, so to speak, present at the creation of many of the works he assigned to his students. In his teaching he revered the tempestuous days when as editor he took over Kierkegaard's conception of the real critic: "to keep the wound of the negative open."

Aileen Ward was a later arrival who had achieved national distinction when she was awarded the John Keats prize for her biography of the poet. Influenced by the psychological insights of Erik Erikson, Miss Ward took Keats through his tragic adolescence, buffeted by problems too overwhelming for the strongest spirit, and indicated how, in his finest hours, he emerged into an extraordinary poet. The compassion that she demonstrated in her interpretation of Keats shone through her patient teaching experiences with an unusually restless and highly strung student body.

The seventeenth and eighteenth centuries were creditably interpreted by John Smith and Benjamin Hoover. They had a particularly difficult task to make their material meaningful to our unique student body. In one of the student evaluations, where the youngsters sit in candid judgment on their teachers, there was an illuminating comment on their subject matter and the difficulties encountered by the average Brandeis student when confronted with the classics of Milton and Spenser. "Some familiarity with Christian theology would be helpful, since metaphysical poetry may not mean too much to the Jew who must consult footnotes for every reference to the New Testament."

It was the presence of such people on our faculty that, I believe, allowed us to draw an august roster of visiting professors and lecturers. Milton Hindus recalls how often Robert Frost returned and how thoroughly he enjoyed the beauty of the campus. "I remember showing him around the grounds and coming upon a lovely grove of trees with their familiar-looking silver bark. 'There are some of my bushes,' Frost exclaimed." He evidently felt that if only God could make a tree, it still took a poet to put it into memorable verse. To oblige old friends, Mary McCarthy would protect time for Brandeis during a brief visit to the United States, even though she had to make the visit do double duty by bringing along her brother Kevin, the actor, so that they could at least have a breakfast together. Hortense Calisher, the novelist and short story writer, was visiting lecturer for a year, as elegant in her person as in her prose. There was one banner year for poetry when Pulitzer Prize winner Stanley Kunitz came as a visiting professor. Alfred Kazin offered a stimulating, highly popular minicourse one summer in the adult education program.

We were fortunate that only very occasionally were we taken in by the flashy dilettante, the glib pseudoliterate. They are to be found on every campus, cultivating eccentricity to attract visibility. On the whole, however, our English literature offerings were magnificently represented, and many of the better students became faculty members in important colleges and universities, helping to sustain the quality image of their alma mater.

To our surprise, there was growing interest in Yiddish. The surprise came because the language had been associated by the children of the first Jewish immigration with ghettos and alienation and insecurity. The children of émigrés from Yiddish-speaking lands were usually eager to shed Old World associations, and their determination to demonstrate their complete assimilation into American life often impelled them to look upon Yiddish as shameful, scrubby baggage. But the third generation was apparently much more secure in its American acculturation. To many of them Yiddish meant a reaffirmation of identity, and this feeling was strengthened when they learned that the literature was rich and robust. When Maurice Samuel, the gifted interpreter of the matrix from which most Jews in America had emerged, wrote *The World of Sholom Aleichem* immediately after World War II, it became a bestseller as the literary world discovered the rich ore in a culture too long neglected. H. L. Mencken revealed that he had sat up through a whole night reading the volume, which opened a totally new world to him.

Samuel, Irving Howe, and other gifted, enthusiastic interpreters began to translate the masterpieces of the nineteenth- and early twentieth-century giants, and the sociological phenomenon of most immigrant groups was revalidated: what the second generation wishes to forget the third generation strives to remember. When the sons of Jacob Berg of New York, who were part of the generation that had been caught up in the richness of the old Yiddish culture, set up a fund, in memory of their father, to make possible the teaching of the Yiddish classics, we responded with enthusiasm. The first instructors had to struggle to sustain enrollment, for they were old-fashioned pedagogues, the only ones then available. It was when Robert Szulkin, an easygoing, unruffled, witty, Old World émigré, who later became a popular dean of students, brought his own warm personality into the teaching of the language he loved that his students responded with excitement. Soon there was no longer fear that at least these young people would forget the world of their grandfathers.

One of the bonuses of our literature faculty was the remarkable proliferation of publications among the students. The school paper, *Justice*, was inevitably the conventional college gadfly, although the term "conventional" in relation to *Justice* would have infuriated the editorial guardians of the fortress of dissidence. Conventional, indeed! They seized upon every issue where administration could be clobbered. They developed a genius for detraction. They reminded me of the Irish immigrant who landed on our shores whose first words were: "Where's the government? I'm agin' it!" The editorials would drip with sarcasm and with charges that their ideal of Brandeis was being compromised by opportunism. Dr. Aiken of the Philosophy Department was sure that nothing would satisfy such students "short of the whole university community living together in one great academic kibbutz!" But their barbs were phrased meticulously, with concern for style that their faculty had minted into their discussions. "The network of highways on campus," one wrote, "was the work of a Tibetan monk who had built mountain passes in his native land for Yaks so that two of them could never pass each other." Another wrote: "The dining hall is ideal; it is dark, damp and crowded. This creates a situation where one is unable to see the food on one's plate, thus permitting a person to eat through four years of college meals and call everything rice pudding." In fairness, the editors were as sharp with each other and with contributors as they were with the establishment.

It was frustrating to read a scathing editorial after I returned, often on a night plane, from a fifteen-hundred-mile trip whose mission was to secure scholarship support, a large share of which went to our critics. But the irritation never goaded the administration into any kind of censorship. *Justice* remained an unchallenged, scolding conscience, and all the journals and yearbooks followed its tradition.

While we did not count our foreign language offerings as an area for major development, they were not neglected, and the young faculty labored conscientiously to make up with devotion to their best students for the budgetary limitations that constrained expansion and the establishment of a graduate department. German and Slavic languages were linked to form one department. Harry Zohn, who headed the German area for many years, knew he was bucking the tide in trying to keep up tolerable enrollments in German. But he persevered, even introducing the singing of German folk songs in his classes. As the years passed, and even the students who were born after Hitler's horror could still not forget the Holocaust, Zohn consoled himself by giving more play to his unusual talent for translation and editing, and his literary output in this direction was impressive. Russian, from the early sixties, became the additional responsibility of Robert Szulkin. He was thoroughly at home in the classics of the nineteenth- and early twentieth-century Russian literary golden age. But though there was increasing interest in Russian history and political philosophy, the students were handicapped by little knowledge of the language, which was rarely taught in the high schools. The giants of Russian literature — Tolstoy, Dostoevsky, Turgenev, Chekhov, Gogol — had therefore to be taught in English and the reading assignments were in translation.

The Romance language literature offerings did not suffer from this disadvantage. French and Spanish, and often Italian, were staples in most good high schools, and admission to Brandeis required a reading knowledge of at least one such foreign language. James Duffy, who doubled in African history and was often consulted by the State Department because of his knowledge of Portuguese Africa, and Dinah Lida, who headed the Spanish program, were enthusiastic teachers and scholars. They never wearied in their campaign to include graduate offerings. Who could counter their argument that, since the University had achieved worldwide recognition as a center for the study of international affairs, the Romance languages had to be given the legitimacy of fullest expansion? Their campaign received major reinforcement when Edward Engelberg was lured from the University of Wisconsin. He had migrated from Germany as a boy of ten at the outbreak of World War II. Most of his education had been in this country, and he had earned a brilliant doctorate at Wisconsin and taught for eight years at the University of Michigan. He came to Brandeis in 1965 to take over the chairmanship of the program in Romance languages and comparative literature. He soon added his voice to those of his colleagues to make comparative literature one of the University's academic priorities. I had little doubt that time was on their side if it was only the lack of funds that blocked the way. It would assuredly be opened when a generous donor was discovered who was sensitive to the vacuum in the curriculum that gave insufficient emphasis to foreign cultures.

We knew from the outset that the University could not excel in every field. We were content that an unusual number of departments had earned a superlative reputation and were resigned to be judged competent in the others. But there was disappointment that we could not include general philosophy among the areas of distinction. The historic Jewish community had produced towering personalities — Philo, Maimonides, and Spinoza in earlier centuries, Henri Bergson, Martin Buber, and Harry Wolfson in our own day. So there were inevitable expectations that Jewish-founded Brandeis would make every effort to sustain this proud tradition. Judaic studies responded to the challenge when the world-renowned Simon Rawidowicz was appointed and sent forth disciples who bore the marks of his meticulous scholarship. But we had no such good fortune in the general field. Most of the senior faculty carried out their duties conscientiously, but few in the academic world looked to Brandeis, as they did for literature or biochemistry or mathematics or history, as an exciting center for new philosophical insights.

Henry Aiken was perhaps the only exception, but he too seemed so preoccupied with problems of personal identity that the clarity of his thinking was undoubtedly affected. Where he shone was in a gentle skepticism that was transmitted to his students more by manner than by thought. Get involved with the great causes that challenge our complacency, he seemed to be saying, but don't expect too much. He concluded one of his later volumes, *Predicament of the University*, on a note that was dangerously close to utter futility: "As it is, I am bound to say it, it is entirely problematic whether American universities, deeply interpenetrated as they are by the spirit of rationalism, and the American social system, overwhelmed as it is by the cant and by all the status symbols of a rationalist ideology, are very much better fitted than their 'totalitarian' counterparts to be the objects of a philosopher's piety and love." This gloomy view was of little help except theoretically to give body to his courses in ethics. Two of the younger men on whom we based some of our hopes turned early to deanships. Aiken suggested that it was their preoccupation with administration and faculty politics that submerged whatever talent they may have had for serious scholarship.

It was a great pity that the Philosophy Department could muster no real strength, especially since we had been fortunate enough to obtain full support for the endowed chair named for Harry Wolfson, perhaps the world's most learned scholar in comparative religion and philosophy. A chair bearing such a revered name called for an appointment of rare distinction. The dean was apparently overawed by the reputation of the candidate, an art entrepreneur–turned–philosopher. In the interview, the candidate skillfully wangled an oral pledge that, he later insisted, gave him the right not to teach when he was involved with his own business concerns and to take leaves of absence whenever he pleased. He not only shortchanged his classes, but the knowledge of the privileged arrangements that he had contrived created difficulties with other more productive and cooperative faculty members. Fortunately, the general climate at Brandeis was not enjoyable for such goldbricks, and after blustering about legal recourse when he was given regular teaching assignments, he went on his way.

One unexpected bonus came from an earlier appointment. In 1951 we invited Rudolf Keyser, who had achieved a reputation in his native Germany for scholarship on Spinoza. He was a son-in-law of Albert Einstein, and knowing of the early feud that had embittered his father-in-law, he sought his advice about coming to Brandeis. The old man offered no objection, which represented the first thaw in Einstein's relationship to the University. Keyser, however, died after only a few years in the Philosophy Department and as the University librarian.

In the middle fifties a unique interdisciplinary program was launched by the University, designed to give graduate students a broad understanding of the historical development of ideas in several fields of thought. We termed the program the History of Ideas, structuring it to lead to the doctorate for candidates who planned careers in teaching intellectual history. We were fortunately well prepared, for we drew senior faculty from the areas of the sciences, history, sociology, anthropology, Judaic and Christian studies, and philosophy to undertake teaching and the guidance of research. Students were expected to acquire a good general understanding of the theoretical and methodological problems involved in the comparative historical study of ideas and the intellectual climate of a given period. But within this framework the student was also required to concentrate on a special area. In essence, the program was intended to introduce the student to the conceptual side of the great disciplines, the basic ideas that had influenced the progress of western civilization.

Those who taught and guided the studies of the doctoral candidates were among the most distinguished senior faculty. In the earlier years they included Frank Manuel and Paul Alexander of History, Herbert Marcuse and John Roche of Politics, Lewis Coser and Philip Rieff of Sociology, Abraham Maslow of Psychology, and Nahum Glatzer and Alexander Altmann of Judaic Studies. In later years the participants included Stephen Toulmin and Peter Diamondopoulos of Philosophy, Richard Held of Psychology, and Marie Boas of the History of Science.

A listing of typical courses would perhaps be the best way to illustrate how the program operated. There was a course that dealt with the major figures in the Christian tradition, including Saint Paul, Saint Augustine, Saint Thomas Aquinas, Luther, Schleiermacher. There was another in modern religious thought that examined the classic works of

Kierkegaard, Buber, Tillich, Barth, Teilhard de Chardin. Still another concentrated on the Book of Job and the eternal problem of evil. There were courses in political thought from Machiavelli to Marx and from Marx to Mao Tse-tung. Another covered the intellectual history of Europe from 1890 to 1930 and from then to the present. There were still others in the history of science in various centuries, with study in depth of seminal thinkers who set the theoretical premises and the interaction and flow of ideas between the various disciplines.

One grave obstacle in assuring the continuity of the program developed early and called for tactful diplomacy to overcome it. Like many interdisciplinary, unendowed programs, it had to draw its faculty from established departments. Even the chairman of the program had to be borrowed for his teaching and administration from the department that represented his permanent responsibility and the guarantor of his tenure. This meant that the History of Ideas was a kind of orphan in the storm, and every year there was a hassle over which faculty would be assigned out of specific departments to contribute their teaching and their supervision of the students' research. Yet it hung on, perhaps because during my incumbency I was deeply committed to its continuance. It was hoped that after a few years of productive operation its unique quality would give it less challengeable viability, and that an imaginative donor would appear to ensure its permanent budget. It would then be freed from the mendicancy that was so often the price of cooperation.

It was perhaps primarily because we had an extraordinarily versatile archaeologist-classicist on the faculty, Cyrus Gordon, that we were influenced to establish an area that we called Mediterranean Studies, really a combination of the Classics and archaeology. Gordon was a brilliant scholar who had been trained at the University of Pennsylvania and filled teaching posts in Bible, archaeology and Oriental studies at Smith, Princeton, and his alma mater, Johns Hopkins, until he became professor of Assyriology and Egyptology at Dropsie College in Philadelphia. He came to Brandeis in 1956 to fill a chair that had been endowed by a Leominster plastics manufacturer, Joseph Foster. He made his courses in archaeology an ongoing drama and led teams of students, almost every year, on digs to Crete and other Mediterranean islands. In 1957 he startled the academic world with the announcement that in his study of ancient tablets of 1600 B.C. that he had unearthed in Crete, mainly receipts for food and grain and military supplies, he deduced a positive link between the Hellenic and Hebraic cultures.

Gordon's thesis precipitated an enormous archaeological controversy. Most scholars repudiated his conclusions, claiming that he was spinning out a theory from much too flimsy evidence. But he had loyal supporters, too, and the vigorous dispute made him a world figure. Soon he was embroiled in an even more rancorous controversy when he announced that he had proofs that the first landings on American soil had not been achieved by the men of Columbus, nor even by the tenth-century Vikings, but a thousand years earlier by the ancient Hebrews. One can imagine the popular imbroglio that this precipitated. At the height of the controversy I was sharing a platform with Senator Edward Kennedy in Kansas City. He had just been reelected for another term in Massachusetts. With delightful banter that brought down the house, he thanked us for not breaking the Gordon story until after the election. As a sophisticated politician, it would have been difficult for him to express his views without alienating either the Italians or the Jews, two powerful voting blocs in Massachusetts. He added a speculative note that if the newcomers were indeed wandering Hebrews, the reaction of the Indians must have been: "Good God, there goes the neighborhood!"

XII

The Social Sciences

PERHAPS the liveliest faculty were in the various areas of the social sciences. This was to be expected. Not only were the sociologists, the historians, the political scientists, and the economists involved in the gut issues of this turbulent period, but the psychologists and the anthropologists turned into a very different breed from earlier generations and joined the activists for whom the campus was a staging area.

After World War II the sociologists were not only lively; they were explosive. Their discipline was a comparatively new one, scarcely yet respectable, fighting for recognition in the academic hierarchy. It came into being to reexamine the sanctions of society with no sentimentality, no inhibitions, and no obligation to tradition. It inevitably drew to itself the temperaments and the dispositions that fulfilled themselves best when they were critical of the status quo. Hence we knew very well that we were opening the doors, and windows too, to all kinds of persistent gadflies when we determined, almost before we had an establishment, to include a Sociology Department in our table of organization. From the point of view of the originality and competence of the teams that we brought together, there could be no question that our choices were of a high order. David Riesman, the renowned author of *The Lonely Crowd* and the doyen of sociologists, rated the department in the 1950s, in relation to its size, as one of the most productive in the country.

We invited our first sociologist, Lewis Coser, in 1950, when we had only just admitted our third class. Coser fulfilled completely the role that he assigned to the profession, that of dutiful martyrdom. Born in Germany and brought up just as Hitler was coming to power, he was educated primarily in France and never returned to his homeland. He immigrated to the United States in 1941, completing his studies for the doctorate at Columbia. After a short stint at the University of Chicago as an instructor in sociology, he was invited to Brandeis. Coser was a prolific writer and was known as one of the leading interpreters of social conflict. He was a maverick in his views of American life and its social system and became one of the editors of *Dissent*. University governance was an ideal target, and he gave me and my administrative colleagues many opportunities to savor the full meaning of Shelley's ode: "I fall upon the thorns of life: I bleed." The continuing battle was not personal. Coser had no quarrel with me other than that I was an administrator. In his later volumes he summarized his views of the rebellious intellectual's role in contemporary society: in the industrialized twentieth century an intellectual was an alien and alienated. If he compromised, he was lost. If he fought back, he could take comfort in knowing that he was at least bloodying the enemy. He despaired of ever winning. If, to make a living, he joined government, or the civil service, or a university faculty, he resignedly accepted the role of a voice crying in the wilderness. As an intellectual, therefore, Coser had to be in opposition. He was the leading member of the small committee that considered young Clifford Geertz for a post in anthropology and, despite the pleas of our senior anthropologist, turned him down. Geertz went on to Princeton and a brilliant career that was climaxed when he won a Pulitzer Prize for his highly original writings.

In less combative moments Coser may have admitted that abstract criticism could not solve practical problems when there was a world of building and creating to do by mere mortals. But this was never conceded. It was safer for a censorious temperament to be critical within the framework of the security created by the very forces that it was his duty to excoriate. Hence he stayed on; indeed, he remorsefully enjoyed one of the longest incumbencies, eighteen years. He was determined, he often said, not to give in, for conscience had a duty to defend principle. But when the tax-supported university at Stony Brook was created in the New York system, and a position was offered to both him and his wife, he yielded to the fleshpots of the suburbs.

Soon we were ready for another appointment in the department, and Coser highly recommended a young instructor, Maurice Stein, who had apparently performed satisfactorily in a junior capacity at Dartmouth and Oberlin. He was a faithful protégé of Coser, and the volumes that he wrote while at Brandeis reflected his mentor's social orientation. In 1960 he published *Eclipse of Community* and *Identity and Anxiety*. A few years later he followed with *Blue Print for Counter Education*. The difficulties he had in obtaining tenure from his colleagues, who judged his scholarship pretty thin, and the blasting that his volumes received in the journals of sociology made him wonder whether he perhaps belonged in some other area. He accepted a two-year assignment as dean of critical studies in the newly organized California Institute of the Arts in Burbank. I was amused when, after a year as dean, with the problems that he encountered between the Scylla of trustees and the Charybdis of faculty, he asked to see me while I was on tour on the West Coast. There he was quite sheepish about his earlier unappreciative evaluation of Brandeis and relieved that he had not burned his bridges, for he had taken a leave of absence rather than having offered his resignation. He returned to Brandeis somewhat subdued, perhaps now with a glimmer of realization that great institutions cannot be built without combining the strength of the mortar and the hatchet.

Other faculty members were added as the University expanded and as the appeal of sociology grew among the students. In their technical tasks as teachers they ranked high and were often called upon for papers at their learned societies. But almost invariably they joined Coser and Stein as institutional scolds. It was now almost impossible for an applicant to be considered who would not fit into the pattern that had been set. By 1960, though some of us had wakened to the infiltration that was taking place, it was too late to stop the process. This became even clearer when the department recommended Everett Hughes, former editor of the *American Sociological Review*. Hughes had been at Chicago for more than a quarter of a century, and since it was one of the freest institutions in the country, the sociologists under Hughes had taken fullest advantage of this freedom. At Brandeis, surrounded by compatible colleagues who accepted all his fractious premises, he looked forward to serene political and social years in a critic's paradise. After he reached the age of retirement, despite all the shortcomings he had attacked at a very young Brandeis, he gladly accepted the invitation of his former colleagues to come back every few years as a visiting professor.

Anthropology was a blood brother to sociology: indeed, in many universities the two were joined in one department. But when Robert Manners was invited from the University of Rochester to launch the discipline at Brandeis in 1952, he interpreted his role very differently from that of his colleagues in sociology.

Manners's earlier fieldwork had been among the American Indians of northern Arizona, Utah, and eastern California and had resulted in important ethnohistorical monographs. His main research, however, concentrated on primitive African communities. He was also very much interested in the Caribbean. His colleagues thought highly enough of his competence to name him editor of the *North American Anthropologist*, the official anthropological journal. Manners, too, was a political activist and must have found himself very much at home amid left-wingers on the faculty who were disenchanted. But he was a meticulously fair teacher and never permitted his political views to influence his choice of faculty. As the school grew and more faculty was required, he nominated men and women of every point of view: Elizabeth Colson, as a senior colleague, and younger scholars of promise — Helen Codere, David Kaplan, George Cowgill, Benson Saler, Robert Hunt — all performing solidly and working their way to national prominence.

Anthropology was one of the departments that we hoped to buttress, until it came of age, with some distinguished retirees who still had good years in them in which to transmit the fruits of their mellowed scholarship. Alfred Kroeber, the dean of American anthropologists, could come for only one year, but we were more enduringly fortunate when we persuaded Paul Radin, at seventy-five, to join the faculty as a permanent member after a long and fruitful career in teaching and research. I had first met him in the early twenties, when I was a student at Emmanuel College in Cambridge, and he was completing a five-year lectureship at one of the other colleges there. Soon to appear were his landmark volumes *Primitive Man as Philosopher* and *The Method and Theory of Ethnology*, and they marked him as one of the genuinely original minds of his generation. For such a man and for such a technique of teaching, Brandeis, with its small enrollment of highly motivated youngsters, had an irresistible appeal. In the foreword to the *Festschrift* that was affectionately sponsored by his former students to salute his seventy-fifth year, I wrote:

> It is further evidence of his still resilient and pioneering temper that this internationally eminent anthropologist should now bring his wisdom and his skills to the youngest of American universities. What Brandeis in its youth will give this veteran would be a little presumptuous to state. On the other hand, what he can offer us is clear. "One who learns from the old," said a Talmudic master, "is like one who eats ripe grapes and drinks old wine." In joining the salute and congratulations accorded Dr. Radin by the academic world, I congratulate, too, the new generation of Brandeis scholars who are privileged to take the cup of learning from his hand and in turn pass it on to their successors; for in it is the wine of life.

The most influential and the most widely known of the social scientists was Herbert Marcuse. It was virtually impossible to catalogue him, for he was a remarkably versatile scholar, equally at home in politics, sociology, and philosophy. Like so many of his colleagues he was an émigré, fleeing Hitler's Germany in 1934. He taught at Columbia and Harvard and joined the Brandeis faculty in 1954 when the first graduate schools were established. The secret of his appeal to young people could not have been in his teaching manner or in his writing style. He spoke ponderously, pretentiously, the convoluted German syntax carried over into English. His writing was equally turgid and prolix. One critic said that the relationship of his thought and his written English was like that of a horse to a hurdle. Yet he stimulated students everywhere, undoubtedly because his bitter denunciation of the social structure fitted so perfectly the frustration of young people in the sixties. Marcuse dressed up all the disenchantment in Freudian and Marxian terms. He was contemptuous of free speech, treating it as a hypocritical ploy by the power group who used it as a form of repression. He became a guru for the offbeat youth movements that had already set up Mao Tse-tung and Ché Guevara as idols, and his volumes were a staple for radical writers and thinkers of the sixties. He stayed at Brandeis for twelve years, leaving only because of mandatory retirement.

We were fortunate that we could launch our Economics Department with a nationally distinguished incumbent, Svend Laursen. This tall, handsome, urbane, pipe-smoking Dane came with an impressive record both in writing and in consultant service. He had been on the staff of the United Nations International Monetary Fund in Washington and was a senior economist and economic attaché at the Office of Strategic Services in the Department of State. He was valued as an expert on fiscal controls and was given leave for a year to set up the monetary system of the newly established government of Pakistan. He had been widely published on monetary problems, especially in the scholarly journals of his native Denmark, and had degrees from the University of Copenhagen and the London School of Economics; his doctorate was taken at Harvard on a Rockefeller fellowship. He began his teaching career at Williams and then came to us. He was our sole economist until we had completed the first undergraduate academic cycle. But as the University grew, he began intensive recruitment, and he was able to persuade some of the ablest economists in the country to throw in their lot with us. To our sorrow he died suddenly, in early middle age, and the department and the University lost one of their most vaulable assets.

Through the years there were a number of other fine scholars, representing widely different fields, who came into the economics faculty. One of the most popular among them was the Sovietologist Joseph Berliner. He came in the later years, in 1963, by which time the department had pretty well jelled. He added considerable distinction to the small but tightly knit group that included Louis Lefeber, Romney Robinson, Richard Weckstein, Trenery Dolbear, Barney Schwalberg, Robert Evans, Jr., and others. They were of a caliber that could easily have offered and directed graduate studies, but we had to wait for donors to make possible adequate fellowship support and library offerings. When the International Center was constructed, I was pleased that a special wing was added through the generosity of the Bostonians Edward and Sayde Goldstein, and that the Economics Department could move into it to become close neighbors.

We began building our Politics Department around the presence of Max Lerner. As earlier noted, he was more of a presence than an incumbent. Lerner could give us only a day or two in each week, and usually for only one semester in each year. For he doubled as a columnist for the *New York Post* and each year traveled on foreign assignments for his writings. He could, therefore, take on no responsibilities that required sustained attendance. We always regretted that during his entire quarter century at the University he never undertook the guidance of a graduate student in doctoral research. But whatever concessions were made to fit his schedule seemed worthwhile, for he was a brilliant lecturer and his courses were invariably sought out, as much by nonconcentrators as by those who chose politics as their major. His wide contacts also helped immensely in recruiting faculty and in persuading world figures to visit the campus either for Education S, in whose direction he collaborated with me, or as permanent members of the faculty.

Meantime, the Politics Department filled up rapidly, mainly with younger people who brought vigorous teaching to their classes and a healthy climate of social awareness to the whole University community. John Roche, whose influence has been noted earlier, was a prolific writer, but he gave considerable time to teaching and to administration as an early dean of faculty and chairman of the Faculty Senate.

I. Milton Sacks was another welcome member of the department. A rough-and-tumble character, Sacks was brought up in the Bronx in the poverty and social distress of the Depression. He took his undergraduate work at the City College of New York in its great days and his doctorate at Yale. Sacks came to Brandeis in 1955, just as we were completing requirements for accreditation. He had begun specializing in the problems of Southeast Asia and was to be called upon more and more often as a government consultant. He made frequent visits to the area and, on a special grant, would teach at the universities of both Hue and Saigon when each was under fire. Sacks was utterly devoted to Brandeis, and in the early 1960s I had enough confidence in him to ask him to take the onerous assignment of dean of students. Although he served with meticulous integrity, I have sometimes wondered if I did him any favor. Milton's deanship coincided with a time when student protest arose from personal issues rather than from larger humane and social concerns. Passionately honest himself, and the product of an environment where the necessities of life, let alone the luxuries, were painfully won, Sacks had a short fuse for adolescent silliness. When some students, few if any of whom had earned the purchase price of their secondhand automobiles, rebelled against his parking regulations, Milton simply blew. This did not diminish his popularity as a teacher, however. Even the most easily swayed detractors among the students admitted, as one of the yearbooks acknowledged, that to "drop your pen or pencil in Sack's class meant that you've lost a month's information before you pick it up." His short fuse, too, did not affect his standing with his colleagues. He was elected by them to serve as the faculty representative on the Board of Trustees, and he had the longest tenure of anyone as head of the Faculty Senate.

There were other carefully selected appointments in these turbulent but exultant years of growth, and an exceptionally strong department emerged. It included Roy Macridis, a young scholar of Greek origin with an expert knowledge of contemporary Europe and especially of French politics. His volumes on Charles de Gaulle grew out of his intimate friendship with many of the men around the general. Donald Hindley was thoroughly versed in the problems of the South Pacific, and he wrote the definitive history of the Communist party of Indonesia. Lawrence Fuchs began with general history, but branched off to head a special division that we organized for American civilization, combining politics and history. Ruth Schachter Morgenthau came to us from Boston University with a superb reputation in African politics. As an aside, I should note that when she married Henry Morgenthau, then part of our administrative staff and managing our communications program, the wedding was performed in the Berlin Chapel with Henry's father, the former secretary of the treasury, on the platform, sitting near the Ark trying to cope with a skullcap, and with Mrs. Roosevelt smiling benignly at him and the couple from her seat in a front pew.

There were a good number of other young faculty to round out the department, tough individualists holding tenaciously to their ideological positions, but with deep respect for the views of their colleagues. All of them were eager to be called on by the government for counsel in their specialization, and most of them were. They used their sabbaticals or were given leaves of absence to fulfill such responsibilities in Washington or in foreign lands.

There were sentimental as well as practical reasons for giving high priority to the building of a strong Department of History. My association with superb teachers at Washington University, Harvard, and Cambridge had launched me into the field professionally, and all my writing had been related to history. I knew personally many of the creative people in the field and I was sure they would be willing to help us in recruiting able young scholars. In the first years we concentrated on American history. The assignment for the European field had already been given to a young medievalist before I became president. It was quickly obvious that he had little promise as a creative scholar and his duties were reorganized so that his main efforts would be concentrated on our early construction program. The first major appointment went, therefore, to a young Kansan, Merrill Peterson, who had done his undergraduate work at the University of Kansas and then went on to Harvard for his graduate work. Even before he received his Ph.D. he was offered a berth at Brandeis, with the promise that promotion would come quickly when his doctorate had been achieved.

Peterson was a low-keyed, deliberate, circumspect, laconic personality, and he may have been a little bewildered by the intense, uninhibited type of student and faculty colleague with which he had to deal. Hence, when in 1955 an invitation came from Princeton for him to join the faculty there, he responded. But after three years he was eager to return. "It's good to be home again," he said. He was named to the recently established Harry S Truman Chair in American History. Further, he had sufficiently adjusted to the climate of Brandeis to warrant his collateral appointment as dean of students. In conformity with our policy of encouraging administrative officials who emerged from the faculty to retain some teaching assignments, Peterson continued to conduct a seminar. These were highly productive years for him and his students. His volume *The Jefferson Image in American History* won the Bancroft Prize in History and the Gold Medal of the Thomas Jefferson Memorial Foundation. He remained at Brandeis until 1962, when a call came from the University of Virginia to head the Department of American History, a call he could not resist, since Virginia was the nation's acknowledged center for Jefferson studies.

It should be added that an invitation was extended in 1950 to Henry Steele Commager. His year as visiting professor meant much more than a teaching assignment, for he was an invaluable counselor for a school just setting its foundations. He gladly joined the luncheon kitchen cabinet where, at fairly regular intervals, a group of us, including Lewisohn, Cohen, Cheskis, and later Fine, Roche, and Rawidowicz, would take lunch informally, not only to discuss problems but to spin dreams.

As the years passed and enrollment rapidly increased, other promising young scholars were added to round out the offerings in American history: Marvin Meyers, Morton Keller, David Fisher and Donald Bigelow. Soon the courses had multiplied so substantially, and the relationships with literature, economics, urban studies, and related fields had been so intertwined, that it was determined to reorganize this area and make it interdisciplinary, offering graduate as well as undergraduate studies. It was given a special autonomy of its own under the general rubric of American civilization. Apart from the high caliber of its faculty, there was a later development to support graduate students concentrating on American studies. Through the generosity of Irving and Rose Crown of Chicago, a major twenty-year trust fund was established that provided ten graduate fellowships annually, at $7,500 each, with assurance of renewal where needed. I jubilantly wired the chairman of the board that "I had just made off with the Crown jewels," and noted that such a gift, establishing one of the best-funded graduate programs in the country, would guarantee a steady flow of superb graduate talent that would probably be destined for university teaching or government service or diplomacy.

During our first two years the offerings in European history remained minimal since we had only one European medievalist. But in the summer of 1950 I received a call from one of the University's most loyal supporters, Paul Smith, a noted criminal lawyer and an old, cherished friend whom I had met through David Niles. He inquired, with a measure of embarrassment, if there were a vacancy in history that might be filled by his brother-in-law, Frank Manuel, who had completed brilliant graduate years at Harvard but for whom only a part-time position had opened. For more than ten years thereafter he had filled government positions, but never for long, and he was eager to return to academia. Smith admitted that Manuel had a somewhat abrasive personality that had won him few friends, and he could get no useful recommendations for more permanent placement. But he assured me that an interview would soon demonstrate his extraordinary capacity. We were not yet really ready for a second European historian; the student body was much too small. I had expected to wait for a more adequate budget for the 1952 year, with a much larger enrollment.

The interview with Manuel was most satisfying. He was obviously a very gifted man, learned, articulate, profound, and refreshingly witty. His sharp tongue and quick temper must have been the product of a severe physical disability: he had lost a leg in a war-related misfortune. Since we would need another European historian a year later anyway, we brought Manuel in earlier than originally planned; the University never made a more fortunate and mutually advantageous bargain. Manuel turned out to be one of the two or three most stimulating members of the faculty and a most productive and respected scholar. His studies and biographies on the eighteenth-century mind were extraordinarily well reviewed by his peers. He was, to be sure, a difficult colleague, dogmatic in discussion, who taught with cutting sarcasm. But his scholarly standards were austere, and students who entered his classes in dread ended up with the deepest respect for demands upon them that elicited their best. However, I had considerable difficulty with members of his own department, whom he would blast unmercifully whenever crossed. At last I had to call him in, after a particularly painful and ruthless tongue-lashing that he gave one of his colleagues, a modest, not-so-sparkling historian whom we had brought in from Nebraska. I reminded Manuel that one could disagree intellectually without destroying the personal dignity of a scholar, even if one did not think much of his scholarship. Surely he could suffer ordinary competence more gracefully. Apparently Manuel did not forgive me for the private dressing-down, and it was after this that he accepted an offer from New York University. We regretted his loss after sixteen years, both because he added immeasurably to the distinction of the department and because of his yeastiness as a teacher.

During the next few years more offerings were continually added with parallel faculty increases. Marie Boas, a niece of the world-famous Franz Boas and herself an authority on Robert Boyle and seventeenth-century chemistry, was added to introduce the students to the history of science and the scientists who both enriched and shook up their generations. In 1954 we welcomed Paul Alexander, a German émigré, who had taught briefly at Harvard and then for ten years at Hobart. He was a Byzantine scholar and he strengthened our offerings considerably in medieval history. For a few years he served as chairman of the department. Almost simultaneously we invited George Fischer to come to us, a specialist in Soviet history, who followed in the footsteps of his father, the journalist Louis Fischer. Fischer's volume *Soviet Russia Today* was adopted as an authoritative text in universities across the country, and Harvard's Houghton Library assigned him to arrange, catalogue, and analyze the private papers of Leon Trotsky.

Alexander remained with us four years and then accepted an offer from Michigan, landing finally in California. Fischer moved on after a few years to Cornell. But by the middle fifties our enrollment in the many history courses had grown so substantially that, when all the replacements were made and new fields were opened with outstanding authorities to cover them, the department met the austere standards of the ranking evaluation agencies.

I cannot close this section on the Department of History without noting my own happy experience in it. One of my greatest pleasures in the presidency was the teaching assignment that I undertook for a course in the twentieth century open to advanced undergraduates. It was scheduled as a two-hour weekly session, with a young assistant to take the third hour for the supplementary assignments and the quizzes. I knew that the responsibility would entail endless inconvenience since my travel schedule was always exceptionally heavy. I determined, however, never to cut away completely from teaching, not only because I wanted to retain a direct relationship with students, but also as a welcome relief from the tiring routines of administration. I succeeded in structuring my schedule to ensure my presence at the class hours, and when a commitment in the Middle West or on the West Coast had to be fulfilled the night before, I often took the night plane home so as to be on hand for the class. I began my teaching in the early fifties, and I don't believe that I missed more than one or two classes in History 36.

Since I was dealing with personalities and events that followed World War I, I added an optional hour to the class schedule to show documentary films that dealt with the classroom assignments. A whole series of such documentaries had been developed by the major television networks. We had many devoted friends in the industry and, since the programs had been transferred to kines, which could be shown on any good home projector, the films were readily made available to us. I realized that history as recorded by television technicians could not be taught with the discipline and integrity that credit courses demanded. But I felt that it was important for the students to watch the great historic personalities in action, to know them better than could be possible out of the best written texts or the most carefully prepared lectures. The films were not meant to substitute for historic analysis; they were supplements, to give more reality to the personalities we were dealing with. What could take the place of actually hearing Churchill in the House of Commons, defying Hitler after Dunkirk, or seeing Nehru and Jinnah as they watched the lowering of the Union Jack and the raising of the flags of India and Pakistan when their nations won their independence. The experiment was successful beyond all my expectations. Very few students left when the lecture was completed, and many visitors joined their classmates for the films.

Few of us who began planning for the area of psychology, even before Brandeis had earned its accreditation, imagined that the day would come, within less than a decade, when the curricular offerings would include the whole field of clinical, experimental, comparative, and social psychology. There were no misconceptions that such breadth of coverage, from the elementary principles of psychology aimed to initiate undergraduates to the most diverse theoretical and experimental areas of associationism, structuralism, functionalism, behaviorism, and scores of their modern derivatives, would not require massive budgets both for teaching and for the necessary facilities. The misconceptions rarely arose because, as in other of the Brandeis ventures, there was faith that the program would produce the support. What did create apprehension was that a faculty of strong-minded individualists, often in tough ideological wars with their colleagues, might not exercise sufficient discipline and cooperative resilience to work together as a team.

Much of the credit for creating a climate of amicable dissidence belongs to the two men who had the most to do with developing the program and who, between them, chaired it for twenty years, Abraham Maslow and Ricardo Morant. Maslow came in 1951 with an impressive reputation, leaving a secure post at Brooklyn College. Underlying all his interpretations of psychology, especially in dealing with motivation, was his concentration on values that came from the best and noblest spirits, men and women who, in his words, had "wonderful possibilities and inscrutable depths." In later years he referred to his motivation approach as the psychology of "self-esteem." His principle of encouraging diversity of outlook in a department as the best means of exposing students to every point of view was the exact opposite of the procedures of the sociologists.

He brought in Morant a year later to develop the experimental aspects of the psychology curriculum and to plan what was to become an innovative graduate program based on the premise that graduate students should be treated as colleagues and research collaborators. Morant was a young scholar of Spanish origin who had just earned his doctorate at Clark University and who was deep in his studies on space perception and body orientation. His experimental approach complemented Maslow's humanistic ideas and, since each was personally devoted to the other, they formed an ideal pioneering team.

Psychology, one of the first departments to add graduate studies, soon expanded into the largest in the University. It included many of the divisions of social psychology, child psychology and development, and offerings in educational psychology that were needed to strengthen the background of those who planned teaching careers. The faculty kept growing to keep pace with the expanded catalogue listings. An entire division in psychological counseling had been set up under Dr. Eugenia Hanfmann, who came in 1952 after many years as a lecturer at Harvard and a member of its Russian Research Center, where she was in charge of the clinical studies of the Soviet Displaced Persons project. She had also been a practicing psychologist with children at the famed Judge Baker Guidance Center. How far the department had progressed in the esteem of peers in the field could be measured when, in less than ten years, at the annual meeting of the Eastern Psychological Association, the Brandeis department — one of the smallest units in terms of outside research grants — presented six papers, more than any other college or university in the nation. And in the following year its members presented seven papers.

For a few years we were able to hold onto Richard Held, who was concentrating on problems of spatial orientation and sensory motor coordination, an area especially valuable to the air force and the technicians working on air flight problems. But an offer from MIT was too attractive for him to resist. But by then David Ricks, Richard Jones, and Ulric Neisser had come to join us from teaching positions at Harvard, and in the next few years the department was augmented by other young, research-oriented faculty. In 1965 we had the good fortune also of adding George Kelly, who came to us from a brilliant incumbency at Ohio State. Kelly was sixty at the time and past president of both the clinical and consulting divisions of the American Psychological Association. His two-volume work, *The Psychology of Personal Constructs*, had given him a worldwide reputation and laid the foundation for a new discipline, the personal-construct theory. He eschewed the prevalent model of mental illness as disease and saw it rather as a problem in education that had to be approached through educational techniques. The impact of his ideas has yet to be felt.

The department was at its zenith in achievement and reputation when death cut down both Kelly in 1967 and Maslow in 1970. With both gone, strains began to pull the department in conflicting directions and many of our ablest faculty accepted other posts. The plan that had been so patiently nurtured — of a department with equal representation of humanistically oriented psychologists on the one hand and experimentalists on the other — was becoming difficult to sustain. The conflicts that had been contained at Brandeis during the first twenty years were increasingly manifesting themselves as young Ph.D.'s, themselves products of disrupted departments, joined the faculty in the late sixties and early seventies. The statesmanship of Maslow and Kelly was sorely missed. The primary task for the period ahead became one of restoring and maintaining the equilibrium that the earlier leadership had established.

XIII

The Creative Arts:
Music, Theater, Fine Arts

Few major universities, I suspect, have made music their first graduate program. But ours was an unusual situation. Once we had determined that the creative arts were to be required of all students, music
inevitably was given a special place in the curriculum. We were encouraged further by the expectation that there would be no lack of
substantial support. In disproportionate numbers American Jews were
patrons of the creative arts, particularly music. Since the days of
August Belmont, Jewish names were always on the patrons' lists for
symphony orchestras, museums, opera companies, theaters, and the
whole range of the creative arts. When Brandeis announced its objectives we were not disappointed in the response.

Initially the "Department" of Music was comprised of one unforget-
table character, Erwin Bodky. He had been born in Germany, and as a
youth was one of the very few students accepted by Richard Strauss.
Bodky became a world authority on the keyboard works of Johann
Sebastian Bach shortly before Hitler sent him, his wife, and his daughter
on the trail of uprootings, from Holland to England, eventually to the
United States. Bodky first obtained a minor position with the Longy
School of Music in Cambridge. There he organized a Friends of Early
Music committee, and for a number of years he presented concerts in
the Busch-Reisinger Museum of Harvard for select but distinguished
groups of patrons headed by Elizabeth Sprague Coolidge. Within three
years, the membership of the committee had grown to over a thousand,
and it not only sponsored concerts and recitals, but gave scholarships to
talented students and the use of musical instruments to those who could
not afford them. Moreover, the committee acquired the entire recorded
works of Bach, Beethoven, Mozart, and Brahms to assist in teaching.
Later, the committee helped in the adaption of classrooms and lecture
halls for the special requirements of music.

Two families deeply interested in Brandeis, the Adolph Ullmans and the Samuel Slosbergs, had become friends of Bodky. It was on their recommendation that he came to Brandeis in 1949, and he brought with him the loyalty and commitment of the Friends of Early Music. Just beginning our second year, we had only a small enrollment, but this discouraged Bodky not at all. Of the 250 freshmen in the Class of 1950, 40 had been active in their high schools as members of orchestras, chamber music groups, and school bands. These and many others flocked to Bodky, and the concerts he inaugurated drew audiences from far beyond the University family. Meanwhile, he was writing the definitive work on Bach's keyboard works. Tragically, he did not live to see it published with the Harvard University Press imprint. He died suddenly on holiday in Switzerland in 1958.

Meantime, in 1950, when Bodky had been with us for a year and we lacked only a senior class to make up a legitimate college, it was time to bring in another figure in music to help expand the curriculum. Bodky welcomed the young Irving Fine, whom we winkled away from Harvard. Through this team — the not very old master and the still very young composer — Brandeis earned its early reputation for major concern with music and creative arts. Indeed, Aaron Copland gladly joined Fine in offering a joint course, "The Anatomy of Twentieth-Century Music." By 1951, when we were at last a four-year school, I was sufficiently sanguine to suggest to Fine, now the head of the School of Creative Arts, that we ought to dare a quantum jump. We had won the goodwill of well-wishers in many parts of the country, and among them was Leonard Bernstein. Would it be presumptuous, I asked in all innocence, for us to approach Bernstein for at least part-time service at the University? Bernstein was by then living in New York, where he was working with the New York Philharmonic, and traveling all over the world as a guest conductor. Fine was at first nonplussed, and thoroughly dubious that Bernstein could be induced to leave New York. I suggested that we could make concessions for a man of his caliber. Surely a commuting arrangement, similar to that worked out with Eleanor Roosevelt, might be persuasive. Fine reluctantly conceded that there was no harm in trying.

Subsequently, Adolph Ullman and I drove up to Tanglewood for the interview with Bernstein. We made an unabashedly sentimental appeal. I emphasized to Bernstein what Brandeis meant as a symbol, how important it was for us to fulfill highest expectations in the areas we had charted as unique for our concentration, and that he would be making an enduring contribution if he joined the music faculty in our beginning years. At that time I did not know what has since become common currency. It seems that Koussevitzky, himself a Russian-born Jew who had encountered difficulties in his own early career, had often urged Bernstein to Anglicize his name, if only to reduce resistance to his talent. Bernstein steadfastly refused. He would make it as Bernstein or not at all. Perhaps it was this quality of unintimidated pride, as well as some of the glittering unrealities I put to him, that helped to bring about his decision. We had, for example, high hopes for an annual creative arts festival, where Bernstein's direction would be given unlimited scope. When Ullman and I made it clear that he would be expected on campus only about once a month for a succession of days, that assistants would carry the supplementary assignments, his enthusiasm grew. But he wondered about our facilities. Did we have a music center? We did not. Did we have an amphitheater for festivals? We did not. Did we have instruments for orchestra and ballet programming? We did not. "But, Leonard," I urged, "just let us announce that you are coming as part of our faculty and as director of our festivals. I'm sure that we shall very quickly obtain the necessary facilities and the donors will consider it a privilege to make the gifts." Bernstein was never one to ponder important decisions. His consent was given there at Tanglewood, only moments before he went on stage to conduct.

On the long drive back to Boston, Ullman, who had been a fascinated party to the whole proceedings, asked ingenuously, "What kind of facilities did you have in mind?" I had been waiting for the question. "By a strange coincidence," I replied, "I have the plans for an amphitheater in my pocket." And I passed over to him some rough sketches that had been drawn up for me before the trip. Ullman hesitated only fractionally longer than had Bernstein. Before we reached Boston, he had determined to underwrite the construction of the Adolph Ullman Amphitheater.

Bernstein's course in modern music, offered in 1951, was a tour de force. It was anything but a conventional introduction to music appreciation. Many readers will remember his *Omnibus* programs on music that came later, and that drew at least in part from his Brandeis experience. His approach to students was essentially the same one that he used on these immensely popular television programs: "You think you hate modern music? I cannot promise you will like it at the end of this program, but at least you will know why you hate it." Then, too, Bernstein was wonderfully eloquent. I remember his referring to "the whole Milky Way of possibilities inherent in the twelve tones of the chromatic scale; and the color and shimmer and thunder of the Romantics who nourish our sense of wonder and give us back our moon which has been taken away by science and made into just another airport."

Bernstein and Fine joined now in stepping up recruitment for the department where they hoped, in Fine's words, "to maintain a precarious balance between scholarship and performance." They persuaded old friends to join them, and when they did, they established an area unusually strong in composition. Harold Shapero was on the Harvard faculty, but held there to a junior position. The head of the Koussevitzky

Foundation spotted his rare talent and commissioned his well-received *Symphony for Classical Orchestra,* which early augured a distinguished career. Arthur Berger taught at Juilliard before coming to us and was also music critic for both the *New York Herald Tribune* and the *Saturday Review.* He was already the chief interpreter of Aaron Copland's work and later published the definitive study on his old friend.

Bernstein's presence made it possible to start planning creative arts festivals on a most ambitious scale. Our debut in this field was scheduled for our first Commencement, in 1952. Work on the Ullman Amphitheater began at once, the commission going to Harrison and Abramovitz, who became the University's master planners. The amphitheater was designed principally for open-air affairs — convocations, Commencements, and, of course, the summer Creative Arts Festival. Constructed on three acres with seating for two thousand, but with space on the grassy slopes for seven or eight thousand more, it was equipped with a huge stage and an orchestra pit for forty musicians. Beneath the staging area were facilities for dressing, storage, and utility, as well as a number of classrooms. Though it seemed impossible to meet the Commencement deadline, carpenters and electricians eventually walked off the stage with minutes to spare before Bernstein raised his baton for the opening.

By any standards, it was a *ne plus ultra* week for a first Commencement. Every day was packed with seminars and workshops, and the evenings were filled with music. Opening night saw the American premiere of Kurt Weill's *Threepenny Opera.* Brilliantly performed, *Threepenny* went from its Brandeis premiere for a run of eight years in the Theater de Lys off Broadway. The next night provided a second premiere, a specially commissioned Bernstein operetta, *Trouble in Tahiti,* which the following November was presented by NBC on a coast-to-coast television broadcast. The new production of Stravinsky's choral ballet *Les Noces,* choreographed and danced by Merce Cunningham, was the third evening's offering. On still another night there was a special performance of Pierre Schaeffer's *Symphonie pour un Homme Seul.* There were poetry readings by Karl Shapiro and William Carlos Williams and Peter Viereck, a jazz festival, an afternoon of art films and an exhibition of artworks that the University had already acquired. Throughout, the University was host to leading critics from around the nation, and it was their consensus that Brandeis had given enduring significance to its first Commencement. One critic wrote: "Not in our time, in this part of the country, had there been any such comprehensive and knowing attempt to appraise and stimulate the arts of America." And all of this as the University was graduating its first 107 students.

The following year the Creative Arts Festival was devoted to the

Comic Spirit, and this happy theme was explored in many of its art forms. Leonard Bernstein led the planning and was easily able to persuade an extraordinary cast of celebrities to participate. For the opening night, produced by the Lemonade Opera Company of New York and again conducted by Bernstein, we presented the American premiere of the comic opera *Les Mamelles de Tirésias,* by Francis Poulenc, which had created a furor at its Paris debut. Later in the week Morton Gould's exciting new *Concerto for Tap Dancer and Orchestra* was given its American premiere, featuring Danny Daniels.

By 1957, the Creative Arts Festival had become an eagerly awaited part of the Commencement festivities. Indeed, the 1957 festival, dedicated to an appraisal of six art forms — chamber music, dance, jazz, poetry, orchestral and operatic music, and the fine arts — represented a kind of climax. Pearl Long and her fourteen-member dance company interpreted two new works. This was the first time that a University had commissioned composers to write original jazz music for a campus program. Three artists from the world of jazz, and three including Harold Shapero of our own faculty, gave their jazz premieres. Works by Irving Fine, *Fantasy for String Trio,* and by Arthur Berger, *Duo for Clarinet and Piano,* performed by the Juilliard String Quartet, were also given their New England debuts.

One of the largest art exhibits ever mounted on an American campus, more than two hundred carefully screened works, were displayed throughout the festival period and for a week thereafter. There were seven exhibitions by leading artists, including one-man shows by Stuart Davis and Jimmy Ernst, who had been Brandeis Creative Arts award winners. Works by Max Weber were also on display, and during the Commencement exercises he was given an honorary degree along with former President Truman. Two Pulitzer Prize winners, Richard Wilbur and Robert Lowell, led a group of New England poets in a high-level symposium. Aaron Copland, who also received an honorary degree at Commencement, conducted a concert of his own works as a tribute to Adolph Ullman, who had died recently. The program included a concert version of Copland's only opera, *The Tender Land.*

The momentum of the early exciting years never slackened. To be sure, we lost Erwin Bodky and Irving Fine by death, and the duties of the concert season in New York became too onerous for Leonard Bernstein to make regular trips to the campus. But Shapero and Berger continued with their impressive teaching schedules; they reached out for an ever-expanding faculty, keeping meticulously to the standards that had now become the irreducible minimum. There was Paul Brainard, who came in 1961 and became department chairman a few years later. He had been trained in Heidelberg and Göttingen, and was an internationally acknowledged Baroque scholar, who contributed to ongoing editions of the works of Bach and Tarfini; Seymour Shifrin, one of America's most widely respected composers, whom we brought from the University of California at Berkeley in 1966; Robert Koff, violinist and conductor, whom we took from Juilliard to direct our performance activities; and Caldwell Titcomb, who introduced his students to the instruments of the orchestra and their use by major composers and led those who were more advanced to a better understanding of Beethoven. We were especially fortunate in recruiting Kenneth Levy, historian of liturgical chant and Renaissance music, who inaugurated the Ph.D. program in musicology.

Meantime, in the early spring of 1954 we had launched the first of a series of annual Beaux Arts balls, and the large group who were drawn into the sponsorship developed a camaraderie that served the University well. The first ball, held at the old Somerset Hotel, was typical, in its imaginative planning, of those that followed. Under the general chairmanship of Mrs. Paul Smith, the hotel ballroom was transformed into a Spring Extravaganza by Alfred Duca, one of New England's famous decorators. Two Bostonians who were officers of the Friends of the Creative Arts undertook the production of a special souvenir art book. On each of the one hundred pages was the reproduction of an advertisement done by a gifted artist, commissioned by firms who paid $1,000 a page. Most of the skillfully devised advertisements were works of art and the book itself became a collector's item. A special Costume Service Center was set up to offer counsel on the design of costumes or on how to obtain them. At a gaily planned midnight supper, the cartoonist Al Capp judged the costumes and awarded special prizes for the best. When all expenses were deducted, the University, in addition to giving its patrons one of their most enjoyable evenings, substantially augmented its art scholarship program.

Brandeis was only eight years old when it undertook to present Creative Arts awards for distinction in the fields of music, theater, painting, and sculpture, later adding fiction and poetry. The Brandeis awards were specifically meant to pay tribute to excellence in the creative arts, and the announcement was heartily welcomed. There was no semblance of arrogance in establishing the project for, although the University was among the nation's youngest, its reputation had few peers in the creative arts in the academic world. Besides, no national university-sponsored awards were then in existence.

Two types of annual awards were presented: medals for the artists whose career achievements were judged to have left an enduring mark upon their times, and citations and generous grants-in-aid for younger people whose present work offered promise of future eminence. Adapting Columbia's Pulitzer Prize pattern, the Awards Commission, consisting mainly of our faculty leadership in the creative arts, received the

The old Castle, inherited from the Middlesex Medical School.

Above. *Ludwig Lewisohn and Cupcake in his Castle apartment. 1949.* **Below.** *Justice William O. Douglas meeting with student leaders in advance of the Education S. forum.* **Opposite.** *Statue of Justice Brandeis, executed by Robert Berks.*

Leonard Bernstein rehearsing for American premiere of **Three Penny Opera.** *1950.*

First enlargement of Board of Trustees. 1951. New members include Adele Rosenwald Levy, Eleanor Roosevelt, and standing, extreme right, David Niles, Administrative Assistant to President Truman.

Below. *1960. Informal session before Eleanor Roosevelt's program, "Prospects of Mankind," is televised. Senator Kennedy announced his intention to seek the Democratic nomination for President during this campus visit.*

Cardinal Cushing at service dedicating the Catholic Chapel.

The Three Chapels.

Inaugurating the Wien International Student Program at special convocation in 1958. Lawrence Wien, who endowed the program, the President, Senator John F. Kennedy, one of the first Wien students, Senator Leverett Saltonstall, George Kennan, and Abraham Feinberg, chairman of the Brandeis Board of Trustees.

The first intercollegiate football season included game with Harvard freshmen at Harvard stadium.

David and Paula Ben-Gurion on visit to Campus. With Israeli Ambassador to
the U.S. Avrahm Harmon and Dr. Sachar.

1961. Convocation to celebrate Phi Beta Kappa accreditation. Ralph Lowell,
Nils Wessell, Leo Szilard, Lady Jackson (Barbara Ward), and Adlai Stevenson.

Valedictory Commencement 1968. President Sachar receives his Brandeis hood from the Secretary of the Board, Dr. Sidney Farber.

Previous pages. *By 1968 the campus had grown to 260 acres. More than eighty buildings for the fully developed Brandeis program had now been erected.*

nominations of a jury whom they selected. It was contemplated that the impeccable reputation of such juries would be perhaps the most important factor in lending prestige to the awards. In the first years, the funding for the project came from a few families who were persuaded to provide seed money. Later, a donor who preferred to remain anonymous underwrote the project until his death in 1973. Then the program was placed on a permanent basis by a trustee family, Jack and Lillian Poses, who had already established the Poses Institute for the Fine Arts.

The first awards went to William Schuman, in music; Stuart Davis, in painting; Hallie Flanagan Davis, in theater; and William Carlos Williams, in poetry. The caliber of such recipients set a pattern of virtuosity that gave the awards instant recognition as a very high honor. After the tenth year another category was added to pay tribute to those whose talents ranged over all of the creative arts, and medals went to such figures as Martha Graham, Buckminster Fuller, Meyer Schapiro, and Dr. Alfred H. Barr.

It required unusual perceptiveness for the juries to spot budding talent for the grants-in-aid that were intended to encourage younger people. The judgments were rarely disappointing; within a decade after the awards many of the recipients' had moved into the select circle of assured preeminence. In the very first group the grant-in-aid for musical composition had gone to Robert Kurka. He composed a new American opera, *Good Soldier Schweik*, which was performed by the New York Opera Company, and the reviews generally agreed with the prophetic Brandeis citation that "here was a superb talent at the threshold of greatness." Unfortunately Kurka died of leukemia within a year, at the age of thirty-five. The 1960 grant had gone to Gunther Schuller, then thirty-five, but already impressing his peers in music by the versatility of his compositions. Within seven years he had reached top rank and was named president of the New England Conservatory of Music.

The award presentations were always notable occasions, the audience, comprising the most loyal patrons of the arts, crowding the ballroom of one of the major New York hotels. The first such affair was held at the old Ambassador Hotel, and the awards and citations were made by Nelson Rockefeller, then chairman of the board of the Museum of Modern Art. The arrangements were under the expert supervision of Mrs. Edith Steinberg, who, for more than fifteen years until her death in 1972, directed special events for the University in the New York area.

By 1968, the Creative Arts Awards had won a permanent place in the honors listings of American cultural life. Allen Tate, named as a medal winner for his stature as a poet, was undoubtedly speaking for many others who had been chosen when he acknowledged that though he had an impressive array of citations, he cherished two above all, the Pulitzer Prize and the Brandeis Creative Arts Award.

All this time, the Music Department functioned in the cramped underground space provided by Ullman, which also served an expanding theater program. The need for an adequate center became so pressing that even the most persistent critics of the bulldozer conceded that occasionally it justified its existence. Fortunately, by 1956, the generosity of the Slosberg family of Brookline, Massachusetts, helped solve the problem. Samuel Slosberg, a New England shoe manufacturer, had been a trustee for several years. He was involved in many philanthropic activities and was soon to be the dynamic president of the Beth Israel Hospital. He and his wife, Helen, were the earliest music and art patrons of the University and, with Adolph Ullman, had created the Friends of the Creative Arts to give the initial impetus to these activities at the University. A music center was authorized by the family as a memorial to the Slosberg parents, Jacob and Bessie, and construction on it began at once so that it could be completed and dedicated by April 1957.

It was designed by Harrison and Abramovitz as a beautiful, two-level glass and red brick structure, matching the color and melding into the unity of the campus architectural master plan. Glass-walled offices and classrooms were constructed on the main floor; directly below were the many sound-conditioned rooms for instruction and practice. Provision was made for a projection booth for films and slides. But the heart of the building was the 250-seat recital hall, with perfect acoustics even for the most delicate chamber music. The main lobby of the recital hall became an art gallery bathed in natural light from the plastic skylight.

But even as the excavations began in the summer of 1956, we knew in our hearts that the building would be outgrown all too quickly. And, indeed, within two years it was bursting at the seams. The Slosbergs then provided the necessary support to double its size. The Music Center never really outgrew its outgrowingness. One evening, at a special concert, I discovered to my chagrin that, almost lost in the crowded audience, Sam Slosberg and his wife were standing quietly in the overflow at the rear of the recital hall listening intently to the performance. I went up to apologize for the poor work of younger assistants, who had apparently made no provision for the patrons of the center. I was stopped short in my apology when Slosberg chuckled, "Apparently the center is getting plenty of use. Let it always be that way, and we won't mind standing." And it always was.

Concerts and festivals, spectacular as they were, nevertheless did not eclipse the unique teaching contribution that Brandeis offered. The department was extraordinarily successful in integrating its academic, scholarly, and performing activities. Every effort was made to provide opportunities for music concentrators to receive advanced instrumental or vocal instruction, even though they were not enrolled in a conservatory. To accommodate them, arrangements were made for private study with highly qualified teachers, usually drawn from the Boston Symphony Orchestra. Music M, as the course was named, kept up the quality of vocal or instrumental achievement within the framework of a liberal arts college. Limited grants-in-aid were allocated on a competitive basis to those who, in an audition before a faculty panel, exhibited unusual talent in performance. No credit was offered for this special instruction. Within a very few years the department had produced a considerable number of successful professional musicians along with many teacher-scholars who went on to coveted college and university positions.

A gratifying seal of approval for the quality of the music program came when William Schuman was given an honorary degree for his own highly rated compositions. Schuman was usually as austere in his evaluations as he was in his creations. Yet he offered the judgment that Brandeis, with its superb faculty, had become, in less than ten years, the best musicological center in the country.

Art departments, museums, and exhibitions have usually been regarded as the luxury aspect of a university's table of organization, even in the supposedly affluent Ivy League. But in our third year we were ready to bring in a teaching artist-in-residence, and we encouraged him to think of his program and its needs as a basic University commitment.

Our artist pioneer was Mitchell Siporin, who had grown up in the poorer sections of Chicago during the Great Depression. Siporin had early demonstrated talent of a high order, but there were few outlets for it when hunger and despair were the order of the day. It was Franklin Roosevelt's imaginative WPA project that first offered employment with dignity and salvaged talents such as Siporin's. His frescoes for the WPA achieved critical acclaim, and later, as a result of a national competition under the aegis of the Treasury Department, he was commissioned (together with the painter Edward Millman) to execute the frescoes for the Central Post Office in St. Louis, Missouri, the largest government mural commission to that date. After three years of military service in North Africa and Italy, he won a Prix de Rome in 1949 for painting. Soon his forceful Expressionist art found its way into the permanent collections of the most reputable museums in the country. He accepted the Brandeis invitation in 1951, and remembering his earlier experiences as a soldier-artist in North Africa and Italy, he took in his stride the makeshift facilities in which he was forced to teach and paint. The army expression "improvisation in the field" was the order of the day, and studios and lecture halls were established first in the Castle, then in the first-floor offices of the gymnasium. Siporin served as a one-man department, teaching courses in painting and drawing as well as a survey course in the history of art, for which the slides were borrowed from the Educational Department of the Boston Museum of Fine Arts. Borrowed, but not for long! The Brandeis collection now consists of well over 100,000 slides and has its own curator.

Unlike the practice of most eastern universities in the early fifties, Brandeis placed as much emphasis on the making of a work of art as on criticism and historical research. Both studio and history courses were given in the same department and students were exposed to and participated in the seeing, feeling, and making processes. The faculty was similarly integrated and artists and scholars worked and planned side by side.

In 1952 a noted art historian, Professor Leo Bronstein, was added to the faculty. He came to Brandeis from the Asia Institute, where he served as an expert in Islamic art. A student of Henry Focillon's at the Sorbonne, he seemed an unworldly character, often lost in reverie but remarkably perceptive in his interpretation of the arts of many countries and periods. Whether lecturing on Islamic miniature painting, Greek sculpture, or John Singleton Copley — an enthusiasm acquired in Boston — he was an inspired lecturer, performing for and swaying his student audience into an acceptance of the poetic vision. It said something for our determination to expose our students, and our faculty too, to every variety of art orientation that at Bronstein's side, for two years as visiting professor, was Arnold Hauser, a professor at the University of Leeds in England, author of *The Sociology of Art*, and the outstanding Marxist interpreter in English of the history of art. This diversity was further emphasized by the later addition of the Indian scholar Walter Spink, the Sinologist Richard Edwards, the Renaissance scholars Creighton Gilbert and Ludovico Borgo, and the medievalist Joachim Gaehde.

Meantime, in 1953 Peter Grippe joined the Fine Arts Department, and we were able to add sculpture and graphics to our teaching activities. A native of Buffalo, Grippe's experiences had been similar to Siporin's with the WPA. He was close to the Abstract Expressionist movement in New York and was an artist of great versatility. He had, in fact, headed Stanley Hayter's Atelier 17 at one time and was an able printmaker as well as ceramist.

Our permanent faculty was further broadened when one of the most generous couples of Cleveland, Maurice and Shirley Saltzman, sophisticated art collectors themselves, set up an endowment to enable the University to invite visiting artists for a year of teaching and art guidance. The Saltzman endowment made possible the presence of Philip Guston, Jacob Lawrence, Frank Stella, Elaine de Kooning, and Anthony Toney, and the sculptors Philip Pavia, Ibram Lassow, and Richard Lippold.

All through these earlier years, gifts of art were being routed to the University, including quite valuable works of Stuart Davis, Fernand

Léger, Milton Avery, George Grosz, Willem de Kooning, and others then very much in vogue. Before we graduated our first class, more than three hundred paintings had arrived, and we hastily organized a Brandeis Art Collection Committee to evaluate the works, both for teaching and for exhibition. These were stored in the basement of one of the residence halls, and when a raging hurricane (artlessly named Edna) flooded some of our buildings, a portion of our collection suffered water damage. Fortunately most of the better paintings survived and were satisfactorily restored. But "the act of God" strengthened our conviction that until we could build at least a modest museum, further gifts would have to be declined and teaching seriously handicapped as a result. A museum, therefore, went onto our expanding list of priorities. I am sure there were murmurs on and off campus at the imprudence of a university for hankering after an art museum when it needed so much else in terms of "basic" commitments. As often before and since, the dilemma was resolved because we followed, loosely to be sure, Thackeray's sanguine guideline: "Keep an eye on heaven, and one on the main chance."

The heaven-sent main chance in this case turned out to be Edward and Bert Rose. Rose was a successful New England manufacturer of mattresses for children's cribs. His wife, Bert, had studied music as a very young woman and was devoted to all the arts. I first became acquainted with Rose when a complicated lawsuit exacerbated the relations between his firm and the giant Simmons Company. After considerable legal fencing, Rose came up with a Solomonic solution. Ed wrote to the president of Simmons, a Roman Catholic, "Why should we keep quarreling and piling up legal fees? Let us take the amount in dispute and divide it between a Catholic philanthropy that you will name, and a Jewish philanthropy that I will name. In this way the dispute will be amicably resolved to the advantage of causes close to our hearts." The proposal was eagerly accepted by the Simmons president, who designated a Catholic-sponsored hospital in Connecticut while Rose named Brandeis.

This gift brought the extra dividend of a warm personal friendship. I soon came to appreciate the art interest of the Roses and felt I could open out to them Brandeis's need for an adequate museum. Their response was immediate and enthusiastic. They agreed to make provision in their wills not only for an art museum and its complete maintenance, but also for an endowment whose income would support exhibitions and scholarships. When the wills were drawn in 1958, Ed Rose was nearing seventy, Bert, sixty-four. Each readily took on the role of interpreting the University to a large circle of business associates and friends. Ed soon became a trustee of Brandeis, while Bert accepted responsibility as national chairman for life memberships in the Women's Committee.

As our personal friendship deepened, and the ties of the Roses to the

University strengthened, it seemed appropriate to urge them not to wait for their wills to mature. The University had immediate need for the museum. Besides, I argued, the Roses were both vigorously healthy people and childless. Why should the pleasure of helping to plan the museum be left exclusively to strangers who would get all the gratification that really belonged to those who had spent a long lifetime in making the resources available? Wasn't a little bit of taffy now better than a great deal of epitaphy later? Once this redoubtable pair had agreed, *they* became the impatient prodders. They served as sidewalk superintendents with what can only be described as fastidious passion.

With a museum on the horizon, or at least on the periphery of our vision, it became important to recruit a teacher-cum-administrator with the special knowledge and skills of a curator and critic. Our first choice was Sam Hunter, who, while quite a young man, had built a formidable reputation in these areas. In his early twenties he had been an art critic for the *New York Times* and an editor for Harry Abrams, the art publisher. He had taught at Barnard and UCLA and had held curatorial posts at the Museum of Modern Art in New York and at the museum in Minneapolis. Hunter came to us in 1960, just as our program was moving out of its modest beginnings into a major activity. In developing our art collections, he concentrated on both the French Impressionists and avant-garde, contemporary works, and evaluated the hundreds of art gifts that were offered to the museum. Yet he found time and energy for a whose succession of critically acclaimed interpretive volumes in his own special fields: modern French painting, modern American painting and sculpture, Picasso and cubism, David Smith, Piet Mondrian, the graphic art of Joan Miró, Larry Rivers, a volume called *New Art Around the World*, and another on that most luminous of abstract painters, Hans Hofmann. Hunter was chosen to select the works of contemporary American artists to be shown at the Seattle World's Fair, which later came to Brandeis as a special exhibition. He brought to Brandeis other important exhibits, including one-man shows by Hans Hofmann, Franz Kline, and a retrospective of the Belgian surrealist René Magritte. Each of these and many other special exhibits were previewed in champagne receptions for invited guests.

Hunter had been brought in as curator with the understanding that teaching was an integral part of his duties. Unfortunately, he gave the impression that the time and energy given to students were a waste of precious talent for a creative artist. In his biography of Hofmann he lamented that so gifted an artist should have been curbed by the routinized discipline that teaching required. Such a reaction to teaching may have been influenced by the fact that Hunter made little effort to get along well with ordinary people. A perfectionist in his own field, he could run roughshod over the feelings of donors or would-be donors who did not share his artistic enthusiasms. He left Brandeis in 1965 and, after a series of briefly held posts, found a satisfying niche as professor of art and archaeology at Princeton.

When Hunter had left the Museum of Modern Art to come to Brandeis, he was succeeded there by William Seitz, who followed him once again, to Brandeis. Seitz, too, came with an impressive record as a teacher, critic, and art administrator. He had taught at Buffalo and Princeton, where he had been curator of the university museum. Bill Seitz was a prodigious worker. He was himself a practicing artist, whose works reached some of the most important galleries, as well as a perceptive critic of his personal favorites — Monet, Toulouse-Lautrec, Turner, Mark Tobey, and Arshile Gorky. Others of his volumes received wide acceptance in the best tradition of teaching: *The Art of Assemblage*, *The Art of Israel, Kinetic Art, Sculpture: Its Image in the Arts.* He was constantly on call to direct the mounting of exhibits for universities, museums, and governments. Indeed, it was because this activity gave him his greatest satisfaction that problems were created during his incumbency at Brandeis. His frequent and prolonged absences, often without administrative clearance, meant that his basic responsibilities at Brandeis were not always fulfilled. His inevitable rejoinder, in argument, was that his critics were Philistines. He should have remembered that when Lord Salisbury was annoyed by a dinner partner who kept stigmatizing as Philistines those who crossed him, he offered the critic the literal biblical reference: The Philistines had been assailed by the jawbone of an ass. After five years of a tempestuous love-hate relationship, Seitz accepted a post at the University of Virginia, but died there before his sixtieth birthday.

In retrospect, where all things come together more harmoniously, each of these men, whatever their personal and administrative idiosyncrasies complicated by their artistic temperaments, helped to enhance the reputation of Brandeis as one of the nation's art centers.

A note should be added about the Rose Art Museum itself, which was dedicated in 1966 as part of a major community art festival. It is often, and appropriately, referred to as a jewel box. It is most pleasantly situated on a rise, with its glass front making an illuminated picture after dark. The design is severe, but adaptable. A cantilevered stairway leads from the main, ground-level gallery to the lower level, where there is a decorative pool with a fountain. In the fortnight before examinations, the pool harvests hundreds of pennies thrown by students as a good-luck gesture. For permanent display on the main floor is a collection of early ceramic ware patiently gathered through the years by Mrs. Rose. The collection includes important specimens in several categories. Chief among them are several pieces of very fine and rare French faience (decorative earthenware) from the Napoleonic era, as well as outstanding examples of English creamware. Of particular historical significance are English pieces of the period featuring caricatures of Napoleon.

Some years later, to celebrate their sixtieth wedding anniversary, the Roses added an annex to the museum that doubled its capacity for exhibition, storage, and administration. Before it was completed, Rose had not only covered all the pledges on the original building, but had fully financed the additional construction. At the dedication Rose, eighty-six, bantered with charm and wit and gaity; none knew that he was to have a serious operation the next morning. It was an ordeal that would have terrified a much younger man. When I went to see him at the hospital afterward, he apologized that I would have to do all the talking since he now had only one lung. But he did manage to comment that the nurses at the hospital were not as pretty as they used to be. When I returned to the office I ordered a five-year diary for him, only because none of the shops had any ten-year ones. But while his stamina never gave out, it could not overcome the ravages of cancer, and it was one of the saddest tasks of my life to deliver the funeral eulogy when he died soon afterward.

The judgment that emphasis on the fine arts at Brandeis would multiply its friends and patrons was amply vindicated as soon as the Rose Art Museum had been dedicated and was in full operation. No year passed without gifts of important artworks. They came from the families of Senator Benton and Larry Aldrich, from friends very close to the University, and from total strangers who were impressed by what the art program at Brandeis had become. Equally important, art patrons now wished to underwrite other facilities, and we were placed in the extraordinary dilemma of an embarrassment of competing offers. The Fine Arts Department rejoiced, however, for all their physical needs were soon fulfilled. A teaching center that included imaginatively illuminated studios and a lovely outdoor sculpture court was commissioned by the Goldman and Schwartz families of New York. Our first Canadian gift for a physical facility was contributed by the Pollock family of Quebec, for another teaching center that included an archive for art slides and an auditorium fully equipped for art lectures. One of New York's glass manufacturers and an art collector himself, Albert Dreitzer, in honor of his wife, Mildred, underwrote the conversion of one of the main halls of the Theater Arts Center into a beautiful art gallery.

In deciding to give a high priority to theater in the curriculum, Brandeis was instituting no revolutionary change; it was really returning to an almost forgotten tradition that linked the theater arts to student life. To be sure, in recent times the university has relinquished playwriting and performance to the rialto. But never completely, and several fine universities have won high honors as heirs of the old tradition. Yale established a nationally famous drama center in 1926, when it spirited away the redoubtable George Pierce Baker from Harvard. Even Homer nods, and Harvard had apparently reached the conclusion that playwriting did not belong in its curriculum. Before his departure for Yale, Baker's 47 Workshop had nurtured the talents and, indeed, the genius of Eugene O'Neill, Thomas Wolfe, Philip Barry, Sidney Howard, and many others. Now Yale supplanted its archrival as the most exciting drama center in the academic world. By mid-twentieth century, university theater had become an important profession in itself, and those who hoped for careers in the theater could add the campus to the entertainment industry as a possible option. Play production in colleges and universities involved far more people and many more productions annually than took place in all of the commercial theaters of the nation.

Brandeis therefore was in very good company when it planned to give major emphasis to the theater arts, and it was ready for such responsibility since its sponsoring constituency included some of the most generous theater patrons. They needed little prodding to join in the adventure; indeed, they took the initiative in urging Brandeis to strive for leadership and not to be fearful about support. The most successful New York producer, David Merrick, gladly assigned to Brandeis a share of royalties for its theater program from his Broadway productions. The main entrepreneurs of the cinema world were also quickly drawn in. The stage and screen actor Paul Muni demonstrated his high regard for theater at Brandeis by bequeathing his considerable estate for the program and the scholarships of the department. Leo Jaffe of Columbia and Samuel Goldwyn and Louis Mayer of Metro-Goldwyn-Mayer set up scholarship and fellowship opportunities and gave their names for fund-raising affairs that brought gifts from hundreds of their colleagues. A New Jersey industrialist, Irving Laurie, lost a talented daughter, Barbara, who had begun writing for the theater; in her memory he and his wife underwrote an experimental theater, where the plays of students and faculty could be given their first critical tryouts.

The recruitment of faculty went forward vigorously with the understanding that the program was not to be structured as a vocational school in theater. To be sure, there would be training — expert training, it was hoped — in designing, directing, and producing. But these technical aspects of theater were to be developed within the context of a liberal arts curriculum. The first faculty included Edwin Pettet, who had achieved an impressive record as the director at Amherst's Kinsley Memorial Theater. Howard Bay was recruited from Broadway, where he was counted as one of the theater's best designers. He later won a coveted national award for his design of the set of *The Man of La Mancha*. John Matthews was really a commuting member of the department. He had to keep his base in New York, for he had earned a solid reputation as a "play doctor." After his skillful surgery on *Anastasia*, it had an extraordinarily long run on Broadway. One of his own early plays, *The Scapegoat*, based on *The Trial* by Kafka, won the Arts of the Theater Award just before we invited him to our faculty. He was invaluable for students, as he applied patience and experience to guide their talents in play composition.

Charles Werner Moore, cited by the League of Professional Theater Schools "as one of the two best acting teachers in the country," was brought in as the anchorman for the acting courses. James Clay, the first American ever to be invited to teach a full term at the Royal Academy of Dramatic Art in London, took charge of productions. The commitment to give our undergraduate theater majors good preprofessional training in a liberal arts context was emphasized when Louis Kronenberger joined the faculty. For many years he had been a critic for *Time* magazine, a playwright, and the author of many volumes that ranged from art history to a classic study of stage comedy. It was equally indicative of intent that among the first directors who were invited to join the faculty was Eliot Silverstein, who won national importance later when he directed the film *Cat Ballou*.

As it turned out, the Laurie Theater played an ever more important role in maturing the talent of our most gifted students. It is pleasant to realize that an alumnus, Joshua Mostel, who titillated us all during his undergraduate years by his almost aggressively youthful and endearing resemblance to his father, Zero, went from Brandeis to the innovative Proposition Theater in Cambridge. More recently, he created a charming cameo role in *Harry and Tonto*. And, speaking of cats (since Tonto is a cat), another Brandeis alumnus in the field was Michael Weller '65, whose play *Moonchildren* did well off Broadway and in Boston. The *Boston Globe* not only praised the play, but made much of the series of "auditions" for a cat to play an important role. Meanwhile, Jeremy Larner '58, who began his professional career as a novelist, won an Oscar in 1973 for his screenplay of the film *The Manchurian Candidate*. Still another alumnus, Allan Fox '68, was given a contract in Joseph Papp's Public Theater as a director. Perhaps the most popular and successful cinema personality is Barry Newman of our first class, who, as Petrocelli, became a national celebrity.

Not all problems were solved, even with such impressive talent. There were members of the English Department who wished to play down the technical aspects of the theater programs; indeed, some of them could not understand why "drama" needed a theater department at all. Since Brandeis was not to be a professional theater training center, surely the general drama courses belonged in the English Department. There were heated disputes and much faculty infighting that added to the provocative climate of the University. The students joined in the battles and joyously fought out their views in the columns of their papers and in their bull sessions. But the main problem related to facilities. The Ullman Amphitheater, which served very well for open-air festivals, convocations, and Commencements, opened opportunities also for ventures in summer theater and enabled us to present well-known American plays. But we were always at the mercy of the capricious New England weather. During our first summer program, we came off well. There were virtually no rain-outs, although I well remember otherwise exciting evenings when the temperature, ninety degrees at five or six o'clock, fell to Siberian depths before the play had ended. In the second year, the Yankee weather gods turned petulant, not only depriving enthusiastic audiences of opportunities to see plays like Christopher Fry's *The Lady's Not for Burning*, but creating havoc on box office receipts and, therefore, on the budget. Even more disheartening was the inadequacy of Ullman as a teaching center. It was half jocularly referred to as the Brandeis Manhattan Project. In the early years, all theater teaching was scheduled in the basement of Ullman. To the public, who saw only the exterior, it was a handsome open-air auditorium. It was rarely realized that during the school year, especially in the fall and winter, when the huge rolling doors were closed, the teaching proceeded in the windowless rectangular band shell underneath. Nevertheless, theater studies and productions somehow thrived.

H. D. F. Kitto, an authority on Greek tragedy, was there from time to time, leavening his lectures with a repertoire of hilarious limericks. The actor-director Douglas Campbell, now mainly identified with the Tyrone Guthrie Theater in Minneapolis, could have been found there teaching and staging fight scenes for a production of *Romeo and Juliet*. Jasper Deeter, founder and head of Hedgerow Theater, one of America's finest repertory companies and theater schools, spent a season in Ullman, oblivious to the snow drifting in under the doors, while he directed a most memorable *Hedda Gabler*. And — better known to the profession than to the public — men like the mime Carlo Mazzone-Clementi, director Jack Manning, and playwright-teacher Howard Stein, presently associate dean of the Yale School of Drama, contributed to the small but vigorous theater program.

The "secret" aspect of all this derived, of course, from the fact that Ullman was too small to open to the public. The theater set up within saw five major productions a year, and a number of these would have attracted attention if they had been advertised, but that was hardly feasible. For example, the American premiere of Pirandello's *Man, Beast, and Virtue* was staged at Brandeis, attracted some producers who had been informed about it, and led to a production of the play in New York, but since Ullman's seating capacity was not even enough to accommodate concerned students and faculty, the public never knew.

Obviously, the full potential of the theater arts could not be attained, and certainly no graduate studies, until adequate facilities became available. Each year the hunt for the "angel" became more intensive. At last, at the tenth anniversary of the founding of Brandeis, we could announce that Nate and Frances Spingold, a New York couple who were devoted to the theater and the arts, had become the patrons whom we had sought for so long. Spingold, a Chicagoan, had trained for the law but was early drawn into public relations, and he became a leading member of the William Morris Agency, whose clients included the stars of the cinema and the theater. An early first marriage for Frances ended in divorce; she and Mr. Spingold were married in 1911, and they conducted the Madame Frances designers' salon together until it was sold in 1932. Spingold was later identified with Columbia Pictures and became its executive vice-president, and he helped to develop the motion picture as an art form. The couple established homes in New York and in Palm Beach that were also virtual private art galleries; the collections gathered there rated among the best in the country, including French Impressionists and works·by artists who were experimenting with the newer art forms. In 1957 they made their first visit to Brandeis and were enchanted by its beauty and academic quality. When Spingold died the following year, his will assigned the major portion of his estate to the University, subject to a life interest for Frances, and it was designated for a theater arts center. The benefaction totaled many millions, and it therefore became practical to think of a center that would offer the facilities not only for theater but also for the performing arts, including dance and film.

The commission for the theater was given to Max Abramovitz, who treated it as an unparalleled opportunity to fashion a major facility for the University and also to offer a model for the performing arts in the New England colleges. Many conferences were necessary before a program of requirements developed to provide for the varied spectator, stage, and support spaces. Numerous plans for the shape of the theater were reviewed — the square, the rectangular, the hexagonal, and the circular — until the last form was decided upon. Its versatility permitted the various spaces to open off the central stage, as spokes do from the hub of a wheel. The sturdy and simple materials of brick and concrete were used, because they seemed to relate well to the campus atmosphere. When completed, a magnificent building emerged, dominating the west part of the campus adjacent to the music and art centers.

The dedication was planned to climax the 1965 commencement. It became a major festival and dramatized the commitment of the University to the creative arts. Eliot Norton, the New England theater critic, wrote: "Some of the older universities are cool to the theater, or even indifferent. . . . Brandeis, aware and alert, and friendly to the arts from the beginning, has made plans to embrace the American Theater with new ardor in what well may be a significant union."

A whole series of exhibitions was planned, under the auspices of the Poses Institute of Fine Arts, to supplement the dedication exercises. For weeks before, visitors thronged to the campus to take advantage of the exhibits and to inspect the new building. Not surprisingly, the opening was covered by the national press and attended by several of the most eminent and concerned people in American theater and films, among them David Merrick, Harold Clurman, and John Gassner.

The caliber of the men and women who accepted the invitation to receive honorary degrees as part of the dedication was an index of the importance attached to the occasion and its national significance. They included Alfred Lunt and Lynn Fontanne, Sir John Gielgud, Brooks Atkinson, George Balanchine, John Ford, William Schuman, Lillian Hellman, Allardyce Nicoll, Richard Rodgers, and Roger Sessions. It was appropriate for such an occasion and in such distinguished company to include Samuel Slosberg, a Brandeis trustee, who had been its outstanding patron of music and the creative arts since the University was launched.

The dedication over, all energies were now directed to the inauguration of a graduate program when the new school year opened in the fall. The program leading to Master of Fine Arts degrees in acting, design, or playwriting had been approved, the faculty had been increased, and all seemed serene — but as so often happens at birth, there were some difficulties. Most awkward was that only the exterior of the building was really finished. Classes were scheduled, actors had been hired, a season of fine productions had been promised, yet the building was unavailable. Veterans of summer stock, two-week repertory, and Broadway openings are fanatical about meeting deadlines, and they remain unfazed by obstacles, even those that border on calamity. So the department members sneaked into the building under showers of sparks from the welders and set to work. The construction foreman, horrified at the risks these people were taking, stuck to the spirit of the law and allowed occupation of each section of the building only when sudden death seemed at least a few yards away from the occupants. The distinguished actor Morris Carnovsky, who had joined the Brandeis faculty to round out a brilliant performing career, was to direct the premiere production, and as part of the plan to develop first-rate training, he had hand-picked a full company of seasoned, professional actors. There they stood on the main stage, calmly rehearsing *Volpone* as if for the silent screen, their voices utterly lost in the Niagara of construction noise. There was not yet a place to build costumes, no area free in which to paint scenery, and now, because of the general chaos, no possibility of carrying through the original plan for the whole season of plays. To make matters worse, the theater manager failed to materialize.

As it turned out, James Clay, one of the theater faculty's directors, took over the manager's job while teaching a full load of classes and "winged" it through the first season, managing somehow to get the campus, public, and press in, as the department was forced to decide one play at a time what would happen next. Amazingly, and beyond even the expectations of the most demented hopefuls, the season opened on schedule and the curtain rose on a first-night audience of more than a thousand who came to salute the new resource for the theater arts in New England, and it included John Volpe, governor of the Commonwealth, John Gassner of the Yale School of Drama, and Joseph Papp, who had pioneered the popular Shakespeare Theater for the general public of New York. Donald Cragin of the *Herald* praised Carnovsky's performance as "the marvelous trouper leading the troupe." The hard-to-please critic of the *Boston Globe*, Kevin Kelly, wrote: "The production is worth its weight in Volpone's gold."

Other openings could now be announced with more confidence. Carnovsky's favorite role was *King Lear,* which he performed to perfection annually to climax the Shakespeare festival in Stratford, Connecticut. The play was billed as part of our first season's offerings at Spingold. Carnovsky preferred an audience for his dress rehearsals, more especially what he called a "schools audience," that is, young people of high school age and even younger. This information reached my office belatedly, but members of my staff, Marylou Buckley and Larry Kane, in spite of a blizzard, conjured up a full house of high school and junior high school children and even of Jesuit seminarians from nearby Weston. For many of the youngsters this was not only a free night out at the theater, but their first taste of Shakespeare. Needless to say, they did not approach *Lear* with any of the reverence accorded Shakespeare by more adult members of the audience. In fine, they demonstrated their approval — and disapproval — quite without inhibition, as if they were at the movies.

Meantime there were serious internal problems to be solved. Having fifteen or twenty professional actors in a company entirely separate from the classroom training of students was not working out. Other universities had tried it and failed, but the advantage of a standard-setting permanent company was so attractive, that, with fingers crossed, the effort was made. However, it became clear quickly that students, both graduate and undergraduate, were being neglected as the needs of the resident company were given priority, and the decision was made to shift to an artist-in-residence system, which would select a few artist-teachers to perform and work with the students in the studios as well as in plays. The idea was to make a sharp change and organically integrate every aspect of the teaching. Only older actors would be engaged, so that graduate actors could be sure of opportunities to play roles in their own age range. The Equity actors would have to agree to play as cast, to play in anything, even classroom exercises, and to teach. Casts would be deliberately mixed in a flexible master-apprentice system that would include undergraduate concentrators. All productions were to be chosen and handled so that performance would be equal to classroom work in instructional value. It all sounded thrilling and not too difficult to achieve, but making it work turned out to be harder than opening a season in an unfinished building.

It took more than three years to move completely from the separate company idea to full integration, and there was much hauling and shoving, not only with the problem itself, but between members of the department who often enough could not see eye-to-eye on how to get where the majority wanted to go. But, by the third season, 1967–68, the work in Spingold had begun to take its characteristic shape and was of sufficient stature to be noticed by the new National Endowment for the Arts in Washington. The foundation made a grant to mount a play by Don Peterson, *Does the Tiger Wear a Necktie?*, whose theme was the terrifying problem of drug addicts.

Peterson had taught in a rehabilitation center for addicts in New York and he was writing from life. His prizewinning script had been chosen from more than two hundred that had been submitted for the Bishop Award of the American National Theater and Academy. Its premiere at Spingold was an augury of what the future held. Eliot Norton saw the play as an example of "what can be done by a combination of government, university and the professional theater, all acting in concert." Alta Maloney in the *Herald* wrote: "Brandeis University is circling in on the true function of the University Theater, to provide a public place where unproved playwrights may have a hearing. And the words of Don Peterson, with his *Does the Tiger Wear a Necktie?* ring surely in the Spingold Theater." And the drama critic for *Newsweek* wrote: "While the American university's contribution to theater has been as superficial as a flick of greasepaint . . . the tradition is now changing. Some change is already visible, from UCLA to Ohio State University, from Boston's Brandeis to the University of Michigan, where new drama buildings are already open or on the rise."

It was equally gratifying to the University that its first crop of masters of fine arts were sought after; they were well trained and they were getting jobs. And those undergraduates highly recommended by the faculty could be sure of acceptance in the best advanced programs elsewhere.

In the summer of 1968 the department produced an audacious international festival of avant-garde theater companies and fairly turned eastern Massachusetts upside down. There were misgivings among the theater faculty, who were concerned that the cynicism of the period was driving out the disciplined integrity that good drama should have. Herbert Shore deplored the trend that set up the way-out writers as the models to be followed. "I watch the plays of Albee and Gelber and Richardson, I read the fiction of Updike and Malamud, Bellow and Nabokov, and I wonder what has happened to the vision. Where have we lost the human heart?" Many patrons and no small number of reviewers thought the pieces presented were outrageous in their use of nudity, and I had many explanations to make to the more staid of our loyal supporters. But *Time* and the *Saturday Review* praised Brandeis for courage in bringing together so much that represented experimental activity in world theater.

The theater program was expensive, of course. The escalating maintenance costs, the budget for high-level faculty and for quality performance, the curtailment of scholarship and fellowship allocations that attracted some of the very best students — all contributed to the perennial financial problems. But the gratifying reputation for pioneering in the theater arts and for the superlative teaching contribution of the University seemed to make the investment worthwhile.

XIV

The Library: *Cherchez la Femme*

I F there was any one moment of doubt about the good sense of my decision to accept the presidency of Brandeis, it was when I had my first view of what passed for the library that we had inherited from Middlesex. It consisted of approximately a thousand volumes, mainly medical and veterinary texts, most of them obsolete. They were housed in what had been the veterinary school stable. There were seats for about seventy-five readers. Even though our first class of little more than a hundred were only freshmen, and it was planned to take four years to achieve the full undergraduate cycle, I wondered how the school could function, especially with our high-quality objectives. I remember the sinking feeling that came over me as I stood in front of the pathetic little structure, too incredulous to make any comment to the three trustees who had driven me to the campus to evaluate our assets and our needs. One of my first actions when the shock of the visit wore off was to explore with some of our neighboring universities the possibility of using their facilities until we could create some of our own. The response was heartening. All who were approached welcomed the newcomer in their midst; they invited our faculty and students to use their stacks; they promised to supply occasional volumes on loan. But, of course, these could be no more than temporary courtesies, and it was painfully clear that a well-stocked library had to take priority over all our other considerations.

It was a stroke of genius for the first chairman of the Board of Trustees, George Alpert, to conceive the plan of marshaling women's groups throughout the country and to persuade them to adopt as their responsibility the Brandeis library and to pledge its maintenance. A few months before the first class was to be received on campus, in the summer of 1948, Alpert appealed to Mrs. Harry Michaels of Boston to take the leadership in developing such auxiliary groups. Mrs. Michaels, a former president of the Boston chapter of Hadassah, with demonstrated organizational skills, had the time and energy to devote to the heavy tasks that would be required. In collaboration with another dynamic community leader, Mrs. Irving Abrams, a founding committee was selected whose members were drawn from special-interest groups. It was hoped that each of the women would be able to muster recruits from their own constituencies for what would become the Brandeis University National Women's Committee.

The early months were critical, for there was almost instant resistance. While the power structure in most of the larger communities did not oppose the concept of Brandeis, it was argued that the proliferation of causes would inevitably siphon off support for budgets that were already strained to the limit. To counteract such opposition it was necessary, before launching a chapter, to identify and make full use of personal friendships. Their advocacy would be indispensable to assure conciliatory persuasion in community councils. The initial strategic breakthrough would have to depend on *Who's Who* and, even more, on Who Knows Whom.

The women in Greater Boston who had been active in national organizations called upon their associates to take assignments for Brandeis. Even before the first students had been enrolled, Mrs. Abrams, prominent in the Women's Scholarship Association of Greater Boston, secured an allocation that made possible the purchase of the librarian's priority list of approximately a thousand volumes for the incoming freshman class. Memberships poured in, and the Boston chapter, headed by Mrs. Abrams, in its first few months became one of the Big Four in the Boston community. Its organization was soon followed by thriving chapters in Providence, New Bedford, Fall River, Springfield, and other New England communities, which, as expected, provided the momentum for expansion elsewhere.

During the many years of campaigning for the United Jewish Appeal, George Alpert had established relationships in many southern communities — Houston, Memphis, Louisville, and others. He appealed effectively to his many friends there to provide founding leadership for the women's chapters. I had been located for many years at the University of Illinois, as a member of the history faculty and then as national Hillel director, and there were now hundreds of former students in positions of responsibility in communities throughout the country, especially in the Middle West. Many of them had been welcomed into our home; there were even baby-sitters for our children among them. When Brandeis came into being, this body of former students was among our most enthusiastic and loyal allies. Initially the Chicago chapter of the Women's Committee was virtually a Hillel alumna group, and the organizational affair was a sentimental reunion for Thelma and me and for our first members. In Cleveland the dean of the Jewish community, Alfred Benesch, a Hillel commissioner and president of the Cleveland Board of Education, and his wife, Helen, offered help. They teamed up with

Adeline Kane, whose husband, Irving, was a leader in national philanthropies, and with Mrs. Leah Mellman, and these three most influential women in the community soon built up one of the largest chapters in the country. In St. Louis, Rae Sachar, my sister-in-law, brought in a circle of socially prominent women, and around this nucleus several thousand women joined to make the chapter a powerful community force. Indianapolis, Kansas City, Milwaukee, Cincinnati, Columbus, Pittsburgh, Detroit, Minneapolis, and St. Paul were all early bastions in the Middle West. Chapters in Los Angeles, San Francisco, San Diego, and Denver soon opened the West for the program. And New York, Philadelphia, Baltimore, Washington, and Miami were beachheads for us up and down the Atlantic seaboard. By 1949 it was possible to convene a national conference in Boston with representatives from many cities across the country. As the years passed, the report of each national president, whose term was normally two years, glowed with the enthusiasm of geographical expansion and mounting membership. The membership escalated rapidly from 25,000 in fifty-two chapters in 1951 to 72,000 in one hundred and twenty-five chapters in 1969.

Recognition that the Brandeis library was moving into the front ranks came in several ways: the speed of acquisition, mounting circulation figures, and the use of research materials by increasing numbers of scholars. One of the most impressive acknowledgments of excellence was the invitation from the Association of Research Libraries for Brandeis to play a key role in the newly launched Farmington Plan, a cooperative effort among selected libraries to coordinate the acquisition of research materials from every part of the world, with each institution assigned a specific area. Brandeis gladly joined and began to acquire the materials from Egypt, Jordan, Iraq, Lebanon, Syria, the Arabian peninsula, and, of course, Israel. Later, the political tensions and the wars in the Near and Middle East made it difficult to sustain the flow of scholarly materials from the Arab states, but what did get through, directly or through intermediaries, was centered at Brandeis and was extensively used.

The pace of acquisition made it clear that an adequate library building could not be long postponed. While there was still no complete undergraduate student body, the old veterinary stable, hastily renovated, could serve as a makeshift library. By 1954 Brandeis had been accredited and had launched its first graduate programs, and the National Women's Committee sponsored a special campaign to add a wing to the converted stable. But thereafter, if the University was to rank as a first-class institution, no further temporary measures could suffice.

A library that fitted the image that Brandeis now projected would require an ultimate capacity of at least half a million volumes (soon the goal was expanded to a million), with reading and research space to accommodate the augmented student body and faculty of the future.

There was no expectation that a donor would be found to parallel the munificence of a Widener, a Lamont, a Firestone, a Harkness, or a Rockefeller. But an adequate library for a mid–twentieth-century university would still call for many millions for construction and support. The attainment of full accreditation brought pride, but with it a note of near desperation crept into the search for the indispensable library benefactor.

During the spring recess of 1956 I arranged for an appointment with a New York merchant, Jacob Goldfarb, whose reputation for enlightened philanthropy was legendary. He was already a generous patron of the University, but he had not identified any special area for long-range support. I had established a warm relationship with him many years before through our mutual interest in the Hillel Foundations. I was received most courteously and affectionately, and was asked to outline the University's needs and the commitment they would require. I had no notion of what would appeal to him or how substantially he would wish to be represented. I therefore spoke of the priorities that had to be quickly met by what a national magazine reporter had hailed as "a young university in a hurry." They ranged from academic chairs and fellowships to major physical facilities, including the University library. He listened without interruption, a smile lighting up a cherubic face, but there was no reaction to any specific proposal. Apparently, however, a chord had been struck "like the sound of a great Amen." Several days later Goldfarb called me. He told me that at the Seder the night before he had discussed his contemplated gift to the University with his wife, Bertha. Their first impulse had been to assign a million dollars in their wills. But, after sober second thought, they decided to make the money available at once to help underwrite the library. "So go ahead and don't delay further." I tried to cover my stunned delight by chiding Goldfarb for not at least reversing the telephone charges. When the exciting decision was transmitted to the officers of the Women's Committee, they agreed that the best way they could make love to Goldfarb without creating connubial problems in the family was to pledge a matching sum. They already had raised half a million dollars above their assigned budget in their first eight years, and it had been held for just such a possibility. They now were determined to double this zealously guarded amount quickly so that they could be worthy partners with the Goldfarbs. At the National Conference in June the delegates enthusiastically accepted the commitment, beyond the regular budget, and it was made good in a series of whirlwind life membership campaigns. Goldfarb insisted that he was infinitely better off than the biblical Solomon, who had only a thousand women in his entourage.

We called in Harrison and Abramovitz, and commissioned them to design a library whose scope was to remain undefined until we knew more clearly what other donors would contribute to this most ambitious construction venture. While the concept of the library was taking form, we continued to explore the interest of other families who might be induced to underwrite special areas; donors were persuaded to sponsor reference halls, seminar rooms, carrels, and reading rooms. Samuel and Rieka Rapaporte, of Providence, Rhode Island, underwrote a special wing as the Treasure Hall, fully equipped with temperature- and humidity-controlled vaults to house precious manuscipts, incunabula, rare volumes, and other archival materials.

When three million dollars had been pledged, the architects were authorized to turn their imaginative design into definite specifications. But before the building was halfway up, Goldfarb, while attending a trustees' meeting, called me aside and, almost shyly, noted that we must not modify any of the plans for the library simply to fit budgetary limits. He therefore asked that we put him down for another half-million dollars. During the next year of construction, he quite spontaneously kept adding similar allocations until his own contribution approached three million dollars. As the building neared completion, he said to me one day, "Bert and I are honored that the trustees plan to name the library for us. I want you to know, however, that if a major donor is obtained who is primarily concerned with the library, please give it to him. We have had our satisfaction in making our gift. The designation really is not personally important." This was not spoken with mock humility, but was characteristic of an extraordinary couple. Obviously, it was the University that would be honored if the Goldfarb name were linked in perpetuity to its library. How completely it had entered the University vocabulary was made clear after the library had been completed. There was a reception for foreign students and the Goldfarbs were in the receiving line. A youngster from Nigeria was introduced to them. "Goldfarb," he exclaimed excitedly. "Oh, you are the library!" The Goldfarbs beamed.

The library was completed in time for the opening of the school year in 1959, and the special convocation on November 8 brought thousands of friends and supporters to the campus, including representatives from the women's chapters. The special guests who received honorary degrees included the librarian emeritus of Harvard University, Keyes DeWitt Metcalf, who had been an invaluable consultant during the planning stages, the sculptor Jacques Lipschitz, the historian Henry Steele Commager, and Julius Stratton, president of the Massachusetts Institute of Technology and later chairman of the executive committee of the Ford Foundation. The dedicatory address was given by Archibald MacLeish of Harvard, the Pulitzer Prize poet and former head of the Library of Congress. He was especially eloquent as he defined and dramatized the place of libraries in a dangerously expanding technological world. But the simple, modest response that was made by Jacob Goldfarb was the most moving part of the occasion. He recalled that he had come to the United States as a penniless boy from Austria. His first jobs included messenger service for Western Union, receiving three cents for each telegram delivered. He had worked his way up through the business world until he headed a great mercantile empire. It was a wondrous climax, he felt, to have been able to use the opportunities that his adopted land opened out to him, so that he and his Bert could now make a library available to the University that had been fashioned by his people. These unadorned remarks, spoken with the inner passion of gratitude, were so moving that MacLeish, one of the great masters of the English language, asked the unpretentious merchant-donor for a copy of what he had said.

A word must be said here about Louis Schreiber, who served for nearly twenty years as the director of the library. He died in early middle age in a tragic automobile accident that also injured his wife. I write of him in the context of the library's creation to pay him the respect that he earned by his loyalty and conscientiousness, but that was never really offered to him during his lifetime. Our original librarian had been a conscientious young man, William Leibovitz, whom Fate denied the opportunity to fulfill his ambitions. He died suddenly in our first year, and his duties fell on Schreiber, an assistant. Schreiber was virtually self-trained, with none of the academic credentials that the profession insisted upon for rank and status. Hence, though he carried heavy responsibilities for the physical needs of the library, working unconscionable hours, it was necessary to give the titles to academicians who ostensibly made judgments on acquisitions and library relationships. The women admired Schreiber for his ready accessibility, and for his practical advice on their problems of administration. The memorial collections that poured in from them after his death were sent with unabashed love for a man who found no task beneath his dignity if it served the University.

With the library completed, dedicated, and in full use, the Women's Committees had an impressive symbol to stimulate their efforts. Major drives continued, but they were now supplemented by intensive fund-raising campaigns that had become essential to provide for substantially increased maintenance and acquisition costs for the library.

One especially valuable and imaginative development was a project, mounted annually, to provide for subscriptions to learned journals; these had become a necessity since the launching of graduate departments. Major research developments, especially in the life sciences, were so quickly overtaking earlier studies that books were often obsolete by the time they were published. Even more highly specialized journals had multiplied at such a pace that there was already a digest devoted solely to abstracts and summaries of leading journal articles. Thousands of subscriptions would be needed to ensure full coverage, but at least hundreds were required to keep the faculty and graduate students current.

Many of the journals were almost prohibitively expensive; the annual subscription for *Chemical Abstracts*, an indispensable tool for researchers in the life sciences, was $500. Journals that were published abroad also called for substantial sums.

In 1962, soon after the Goldfarb Library was in full operation, we decided to solicit annual twenty-five-dollar gifts to provide for the average cost of such subscriptions. The project was enthusiastically described at the women's National Conference and one hundred subscriptions were immediately announced. When the campaign was opened to the general membership the response was equally gratifying. The subscription goal was set at 1,500 learned journals, and it was achieved within a few years. Many of the women went quite beyond individual subscriptions; they agreed to subsidize entire back files of the most important journals. By the end of the first year there were already sixty-four complete files.

Capitalizing on this impetus, and with encouragement from the Ford Foundation, the women made a major effort, in 1963, to complete whole centuries of documentation. In a remarkable spurt of acquisition, the library purchased microfilms of all periodicals published in England between 1681 and 1900, all American periodicals from 1800 (42,000 titles), and those published in Britain between 1475 and 1700 (125,000 titles). It was a heartwarming climax to a banner year, in which the class of 1963 offered, as their class gift, all copies of American newspapers published in the eighteenth century.

Meantime, several years earlier, a New Books for Old campaign had been launched, which was especially effective in the larger cities. The idea came almost simultaneously from the leadership of the chapters in Boston and on the Chicago North Shore. Families were encouraged to give up volumes in their private libraries to be placed on sale at virtually giveaway prices. It was hoped that the volume turnover would net substantial sums for the acquisition budget of the library.

By the spring of 1964 the project had achieved the logistical efficiency of carefully planned military operations. The campaign of that year by the Chicago North Shore chapter was a prime example. Two hundred volunteers were marshaled for a Sunday afternoon canvass of listed homes. They were given 8,000 shopping bags and asked to fill them. In the first few hours they had gathered 12,000 volumes. The family of James L. Price contributed an entire library of 4,000 volumes, which included many first editions, hand-tooled bindings, and the autographs of important authors. The volumes were taken to the parking lot of the Wilmette branch of Carson, Pirie, Scott, the Chicago department store. There, in a huge tent, the 60,000 volumes were laid out for mass disposal. Passersby goggled as they watched the fashionable suburbs' most elegant and best-groomed ladies in smocks, ruining their manicures, as they dragged piles of dusty books to their assigned places, sifting, categorizing, pricing. Before the sale began officially, access was given to specially invited booksellers, librarians, and connoisseurs. In the four-day sale period that followed, most of the volumes were sold. Those that remained were sent as gifts to libraries whose budgets did not permit adequate acquisition as well as to institutions for the disadvantaged that had no library budgets at all. In 1965 there was a three-day sale in Dallas, attended by 1,500, and the 2,000 volumes that were not disposed of were sent to Vietnam for the American military. In other years thousands of volumes were sent by various chapters to Books for Equal Education, a nonprofit organization that distributed volumes to disadvantaged rural areas and college libraries. The processing expenses were usually met by donors. Within a few years New Books for Old campaigns became annual events in about sixty-five cities. When the twentieth anniversary of the Women's Committee was celebrated, it was announced that more than three million volumes had been thus "recycled." We learned again, as so often, that the strongest foundation for any community cause is the committed amateur, without whom the trained professional is help-less. After all, the etymology of amateur is "lover." The amateur's job may need guidance and be less skilled, but it is fulfilled with love.

The chapters kept vying with each other for ever more resourceful ways of reaching their communities. There were beautifully planned and arranged luncheons that featured faculty speakers; there were tours of members' private art collections, international art exhibits, and auc-tions. In May 1966 the Washington chapter took fullest advantage of its location and planned a three-day international art exhibit and auction cosponsored with UNESCO. The preparations took a full year and involved the active participation of more than two hundred members. The wife of the Venezuelan ambassador and Mrs. Arthur Goldberg, whose husband was chief of the United States delegation to the United Nations, headed the patrons' group. One or more paintings and other art-works were sent on loan by fifty countries of the United Nations. Hundreds of other valuable paintings were donated for auction, includ-ing works by Renoir, Chagall, Dufy, and Henry Moore. The pre-auc-tion buffet was held in the spacious halls of the World Bank; among the hundreds of visitors were ambassadors, directors of museums and gal-leries, public officials, and artists. President and Mrs. Lyndon B. Johnson graced the occasion, and an internationally famous art auctioneer, Peter Wilson of Sotheby's, was introduced by Roger Stevens, chairman of the National Council on the Arts. More than one hundred and fifty art objects were sold, and the results of the occasion — one of the most distinguished ever sponsored by the University — appreciably aug-mented the Library budget.

The initiative of the women seemed to be inexhaustible. Hardly had one source of income been proposed when another was already on the agenda. Ever new categories were devised for those who were ready to expend more than the nominal dues, and special collections were underwritten when the gifts were made in the sums of $100, $200, $500, $1,000, or $5,000.

Early in the development of the library, one of the national presidents, Mrs. Joseph Schneider, submitted a plan for the creation of an endowment fund that, however slowly built, would increasingly help to stabilize the supporting income. There were initial fears that emphasis on endowment, in a period when there were so many urgent needs, would become diversionary. Mrs. Schneider persisted. She noted that many of the women were in a financial position to render more than modest service to the University and that the completion of one specialized gift often stimulated the desire to move on to another. Many also would be encouraged by the availability of an endowment fund to remember the library in their wills. In the spring of 1957 the endowment program was officially accepted, with the understanding that gifts would be sought primarily from those who had already fulfilled responsibility for more basic priorities. Within a few years, the endowment had grown to more than a quarter-million dollars and each year brought impressive augmentation. By the end of my incumbency in 1968, the fund had passed the half-million-dollar mark.

The first years concentrated almost exclusively on the tasks of fundraising. But since the chapter members were recruited primarily from families who were sensitive to educational objectives, they inevitably began reaching out for ways to serve the members themselves and their own communities. In 1956 study groups were launched that were open to members who were interested in specialized subjects. Begun modestly, these ultimately included the novel, poetry, drama, current educational issues, America in world affairs, contemporary history, Judaic studies, and the whole gamut of the humanities, the arts, and the social sciences. Syllabi were prepared by Brandeis faculty, with bibliographic references that were carefully selected to avoid either the superficiality of the dilettante or narrow specialization. Since participation was restricted to those who had a serious interest in the subject, the study groups were intimate enough to meet in private homes, and a gratifying esprit de corps was often developed. After ten years, it was reported that about 125 study groups were functioning well throughout the country. Virtually every group retained a constant core membership year after year, exploring diverse fields in a pattern of continuing education.

Many of the women found satisfaction in the study tours, which were based on extended trips to foreign countries. There was no originality in the project: many organizations had been sponsoring such group tours, with chartered flights and all accommodations and sightseeing meticulously planned and supervised. But those under the auspices of the Brandeis women included distinguished faculty members who served as knowledgeable tutors and gave the trips special insights that took them beyond pleasure and relaxation. A three-week tour of the Mediterranean basin with Cyrus Gordon, the archaeologist, following the route of the Phoenicians, was pleasant enough in itself, but it became a memorable experience as he described and evaluated the ancient civilizations of the Mediterranean and the Near East.

The existence of a major library facility inevitably stimulated interest in gifts and bequests of valuable book and documentary collections. In 1962 a dozen outstanding publishers and collectors met on campus and were urged to offer their experience and their influence for this side of the University's aspiration. The publishers validated their goodwill quite tangibly; Alfred A. Knopf, Ben Zevin, and Max L. Schuster not only offered counsel but arranged for gifts of hundreds of their firms' volumes. They also agreed to organize a bibliophile affiliate for the University to stimulate the acquisition of rare documents and books and special collections. Leadership was provided by several who, though businessmen, had a lifelong interest in the world of letters.

There was Ralph Samuel, a New York banker who had been intrigued by nineteenth-century British history and had been collecting Disraeli letters, which he now began conveying to the University. Because Samuel knew of my abiding interest in Disraeli (my doctoral thesis at Cambridge was centered in nineteenth-century British history), he sent the letters to the library by way of my office. There was Philip Sang, an ice cream manufacturer of Chicago, whose family had already underwritten the impressive American Civilization Center. He was an avid and extremely knowledgeable collector of American history documentation, with special interest in the colonial and revolutionary periods. Many of his most valuable items were given to the library. His catalogue "The Genesis of American Freedom" was the first volume published by the Brandeis Bibliophiles. It was listed by the American Institute of Graphic Arts as among the fifty best books of 1961 for its design and production.

Above all, there was Bern Dibner of Norwalk, Connecticut, who had developed a very successful engineering firm and had created the unique Burndy Library, which concentrated on the history of technology. He had not waited for a library building to offer his gifts. As early as 1957 he had sent us choice first editions of the writings of Galileo and Kepler, Darwin and Freud. He contributed a rare edition of the works of a little-known, medieval Jewish physicist-mathematician, Rafael Mirami, who had pioneered research on the optical properties of mirrors. This work was thought to have helped Pope Gregory regulate the Gregorian calendar of the sixteenth century. Dibner had new treasures for us almost every year, including choice items dealing with Leonardo da Vinci and his inventions, and a special hall was set apart in the library, underwritten by Dibner, to receive his gifts. He obtained from one of his friends, McKew Parr, the documentation that he had collected in writing a definitive volume on Magellan and the age of discovery, *So Noble a Captain*. It brought to the library invaluable source material that dealt with exploration and discovery in the western hemisphere from the fifteenth to the eighteenth century. The widow of Ludwig Lewisohn, proud of his association with the first faculty of Brandeis, contributed his superb collection of belles lettres, especially rich in German and French literature. His correspondence, including letters from Thomas and Erica Mann, Stefan Zweig, and Edmond Fleg, also came to the library. One of the earliest treasures was the priceless collection of volumes in economics that came from the library of Morris Hillquit, who had played a decisive role in the New York labor movement early in the century. In 1959 the library received from Dr. Oskar Samek, the literary executor of the Viennese publicist and poet Karl Kraus, a valuable collection of 3,000 volumes on history and political science in German and English. The University also acquired the complete library of the Hebrew scholar-educator Leon Slommsky. Actor Joseph Schildkraut, the two-time Academy Award winner and the star of *The Diary of Anne Frank*, died at sixty-seven in 1963, in the midst of rehearsing a new Broadway musical. His will revealed that he had bequeathed to Brandeis his extensive library, mainly in German, and much of the valuable art collection that had been begun by his father, who was a close friend of Justice Brandeis. Approximately 2,400 volumes from the estate of Perry Miller, the distinguished professor of American literature at Harvard, were acquired in 1964. They substantially strengthened our holdings in seventeenth- and eighteenth-century history and literature, with main focus on developments in New England.

A major treasure trove came to the University by the will of Arthur M. Schlesinger, Sr., a member of Harvard's History Department for more than forty years, a Pulitzer Prize winner, and one-time president of the American Historical Society. He had revealed his intention to me at a dinner party in Boston that Alfred Knopf had arranged for some of "his authors," noting that the Harvard library undoubtedly already had virtually all of the volumes he had collected. At the time of his death in 1962, he was completing the editing of a new multivolume interpretation of American history. When the bequest of the main part of his private library came to us, it included hundreds of out-of-print volumes and others virtually unobtainable through regular channels.

Irving Wallace, a popular novelist, began turning over volumes and documents dealing with twentieth-century American literature and provided a generous grant for custodial care. David Borowitz, a lamp manufacturer of Chicago, made available his rare collection of first editions of American and English literature. Leonard Simons, a Detroit public relations executive, had given many years to the gathering of valuable volumes in Judaica, which he had beautifully bound. In 1961 he offered the collection to the University, and visitors to the library invariably stopped on the floor where they were shelved to admire the beauty of the bindings.

Of course, at the outset the library was still too young to identify any priorities for its collections. Hence the earliest gifts followed no identifiable pattern. A Shakespeare first folio was acquired, as were the first printed edition of the Zohar published in Mantua in the sixteenth century, twenty-two letters of Marcel Proust, and many original musical scores.

In 1959, the library had begun to receive from Benjamin and Julia Trustman of Brookline the original prints of the nineteenth-century caricaturist Honoré Daumier. After 1962, the Daumier gifts to the library became ever more extensive until 4,000 items, perhaps the world's choicest collection, had been transferred. The main collection was housed in the library vaults, but selected items were rotated regularly for exhibition in the main lobby. Each year prize items were organized for traveling exhibits that were sponsored by the Women's Committees in most cities.

Meantime, the library continued to acquire collections of historically significant letters. The family of Stephen Wise turned over many cartons of his correspondence. Since he played a dominant role in both American and Jewish life through the first half of the twentieth century, including the long Zionist struggle and relationships with Woodrow Wilson, Franklin Roosevelt, Albert Einstein, Felix Frankfurter, Louis Brandeis, and hundreds of other movers and shakers of the time, the gift provided invaluable source material. The papers were indexed and opened to scholars and researchers of twentieth-century Jewish life.

Another valuable resource came to the library when David Niles died in 1953 and the family placed his papers in my custody. They were organized and indexed but have remained restricted until I can find the time and the leisure to edit them.

Ruth and Lester Glick of Cleveland, through the special interest of their son, Thomas, underwrote the acquisition of a valuable collection of Spanish Civil War material, which has made the University an important center for the study of one of the watersheds of modern history.

The acquired collections were not limited to books, documents, or letters. A Long Island merchant, Eli B. Cohen, had spent a lifetime accumulating a unique collection of watches, some of them hundreds of years old, in the oddest and most extraordinary styles, and they were given to the library. A Boston attorney, Joseph Abrams, contributed his collection of Confederate stamps with the understanding that after his death they could be sold, the proceeds to be turned into a scholarship fund. Leo L. Sheinfeld, a Boston architect, turned over a valuable collection of first-day-issue Israeli stamps, most artistically mounted by him on specially designed panels. The lobbies and corridors of the library were made more interesting by the displays of these articles, and by the frequent exhibition of famous letters and rare coins and stamps and books.

The negotiations for the acquisition from the Vatican of a world-famous collection of Hebrew codices turned out to be a fascinating adventure in both complicated funding and interfaith collaboration. In the fall of 1961, I was called by Father Paul Reinert, president of St. Louis University, an old, hometown friend, who outlined to me an enterprise that had excited his scholarly interest. He had received permission from His Holiness, Pope John XXIII, to obtain a microfilm of the codices in the Vatican Library that represented nearly four hundred years of Hebrew writings in literature, history, philosophy, and religious thought, especially valuable for the Spanish and Portuguese Jewish experience. A microfilm, Father Reinert noted, deposited in the library of St. Louis University, would make it the most valuable reservoir of Jewish medieval learning and thought in the western hemisphere.

I congratulated Father Reinert on his resourcefulness and asked why he was calling me. He explained that while he had the authorization to commission the microfilm, it would require a substantial budget, and he needed help to obtain it. "You have superb contacts," he said, "and surely in an enterprise of such scholarly promise you would be able to enlist their cooperation." He added, as a special inducement, that the Vatican authorities would undoubtedly release a second set of microfilm for our library if the funding were provided through us. Naturally the project intrigued me and I promised to do all I could.

Within a fortnight I called him back and told him that I had obtained the necessary funds. Apparently he had not expected such quick results and he could not restrain a very un-Jesuit exclamation: "The hell you say!" When he recovered he asked, "Where did you get the funding?" "Oh, from Cardinal Cushing," I replied. Then I gave him the details. After Father Reinert's call I consulted one of our trustees, Joseph Linsey, who had been very helpful to Cardinal Cushing in his fund-raising problems, and we both visited the cardinal in his mansion. I outlined the project that Father Reinert had in mind and suggested that, quite apart from making available the resource that the Hebrew codices represented, there was an opportunity here, in the period of Pope John's appeal for an ecumenical climate, to provide a dramatic example of scholarly collaboration by two universities, one Catholic-founded, and the other Jewish-founded. I suggested that the cardinal provide us with the names of half a dozen of his main supporters, with an introductory letter that would indicate his approval of the project. Cardinal Cushing had acute public relations antennae; he needed no persuasion to recognize the extraordinary symbolism of the effort. "No," he chuckled, "I shall not give you any names, nor introduce you to any of my contributors. However, I'll make the needed sum available from my own Cardinal's Fund."

Father Reinert rejoiced with me that the project had been so happily consummated. I did not learn for several weeks that, after our visit, Cardinal Cushing had approached several Jewish businessmen in Boston and had received from them very substantial contributions that went beyond the replenishment of the Cardinal's Fund. Providence, with a little help from His vigilant servants, may do His work circuitously, but often with remarkable effectiveness.

The microfilms were completed within a year and transferred to both universities. Father Lowrie J. Daly, S.J., who headed the Pope Pius XII Library of St. Louis University, on his return from the Ecumenical Council in Rome joined Professor Alexander Altmann of the Brandeis faculty, who was to be in charge of the codices, for the dedication of what had become our most important resource in medieval Hebrew civilization. The guest of honor was, of course, Cardinal Cushing.

One of the most gratifying by-products of the activity of the women's groups was their ambassadorial role. When the wife or the mother or the sister was bending every effort for the library she was an ideal interpreter of the University concept for other members of the family. Some of the most important gifts that came to the University, therefore, emerged from the membership in a women's chapter. Mrs. Irving Crown of Chicago was a leader in the Chicago group. A succession of library gifts flowed from her; she rarely attended a conference without some exemplary announcement. The climax came when she and her husband, Irving, established a heavily endowed graduate fellowship program in American civilization with a capital fund that yielded $75,000 annually. Hardly a year passed without such major gifts to the University whose incubation occurred in a Women's Committee membership.

The reports that were delivered at the annual conferences noted the rapid growth of the chapters and their membership. They noted the services of the library and the expanding activities that were sponsored in communities from Boston to San Francisco, from Minneapolis to New Orleans. Inevitably the question was asked, especially by the professional and lay leadership of other colleges, what were the forces that created this extraordinary kind of loyalty? What motivated tens of thousands of women to give endless time and energy to planning and promoting immediate and long-range activities, all in the interest of a University that scarcely any of their families had attended? Undoubtedly it had been an ingenious decision to assign the responsibility of the library to the women. A highly motivated group could thus concentrate on a special project that carried immense dignity and high quality, theirs to plan and achieve. The most distinguished men and women in the world of letters who came to address the conferences invariably emphasized the place of the library as the heart of the University, and the women who were its patrons and guardians cherished their historic role.

Each year, therefore, in good times or bad, during surges of national prosperity or periods of anguish and disruption and disenchantment, the reports of the women pointed to the consistency of growth and achievement. And when Father Hesburgh of Notre Dame asked me, in awe, how all of this could have been done, my reply was entirely accurate: "*Cherchez la femme.*"

XV

The International Emphasis

I T was natural for Brandeis, in identifying its academic goals, to include an emphasis upon international studies. This commitment was
reflected in the curricular offerings in history, politics, economics,
anthropology, sociology, comparative literature, the history of ideas,
and related areas. It was further manifested in the recruitment of
visiting scholars from abroad and in the support program that encouraged our faculty to apply for Guggenheims, Fulbrights, Fords,
and other fellowships that underwrite teaching and research in foreign
lands. But above all it was clear that our objective would be substantially advanced if we could ensure a steady flow of foreign students
to our campus to study, to be introduced to the patterns of American
life, to exchange views with their American classmates and each other,
and to return to their homelands as more knowledgeable interpreters
and ambassadors. To mount such an ambitious program would, however, require a substantial fund to provide the scholarships and fellowships for assignment to the ablest and most promising foreign students.
The man who I hoped could help us obtain such support was Lawrence
Wien, who had joined the Brandeis board in 1957 and became one
of its most influential members.

Wien was an extraordinarily able and attractive man. He was the son
of a middle-class New Jersey family and had taken his undergraduate
and his law degrees with high honors at Columbia. While practicing law
in New York most successfully, he pioneered a technique in real estate
investment known as syndication. His holdings became ever more substantial and ultimately included major hotels, apartments, and office
buildings in many parts of the country, including the Empire State
Building in New York. The Wiens lived well, with lovely apartments in
New York and Palm Beach and an eighty-acre country estate in Weston, Connecticut. They traveled widely, using as their base an elegant
apartment in London. They were most gracious hosts and sophisticated
connoisseurs of art, owning some important works. Having achieved an

enviable standard of living and fulfilled all family responsibility, Wien concluded early in his career that there was little else that money could give him in personal satisfaction. This led him to adopt what he called a philosophy of "reasoned philanthropy." He became a generous contributor to Columbia and a patron of Lincoln Center and of the Institute for International Education. He gave dynamic leadership, along with major contributions, to the Federation of Jewish Philanthropies in New York and headed several of its campaigns. It was in this period of expanding community service that he was first introduced to Brandeis University.

I had been scheduled to address a group of potential supporters in Westport, Connecticut. My hosts, Jack and Lillian Poses, invited their neighbor in Weston, Larry Wien, to come to the interpretive affair. Wien was having second thoughts about too many communal involvements, which might have an adverse effect on the causes to which he had given priority, and he tried to be excused. He offered a pledge of ten thousand dollars to the University "if I do not have to come out to hear Dr. Sachar." Poses told me later that he had adroitly turned down the "bribe," and it became the largest sum that had ever been offered for me not to be listened to! Wien finally attended the function where, in discussing the obligation of Jews to make a corporate contribution to American higher education, I must have touched a responsive nerve. He came up to the lectern afterward and asked if we could have lunch together in New York within the next few days. The luncheon clinched his identification with the University and, as he often said with affectionate ruefulness, it turned out to be the most expensive of his life. I was reminded of the mock contrition of Meyer Weisgal, who garnered tens of millions for the Weizmann Institute in Israel. "To have lunch with me is a very enriching experience," he said, "but it can also be very impoverishing."

In the years that followed, Wien became chairman of the Board of Trustees, and hardly a season passed without some major underwriting from his family for facilities and programs. But his most significant gift was of himself, his initiative, his eloquence on a platform, his generosity, and the leverage that he had with so many influential families.

In 1958, when we became serious about launching a foreign student scholarship program, Wien believed that he could interest his good friend Henry Crown of Chicago as a possible patron. He was a most generous philanthropist and he had been sufficiently impressed with the concept of Brandeis to have established, several years earlier, a science laboratory complex in memory of his parents.

The appointment with Henry Crown was readily arranged and Wien and I flew out to Chicago. It was agreed that the presentation would be made by Wien. It was a fascinating experience for me; I had rarely listened to such a persuasive appeal. It was neither a sales talk nor a contrived performance. Wien was earnestly pleading a cause and he did it as a committed evangelist. Apparently our timing was not propitious. Crown explained that he was deeply impressed by the project but he was in the midst of discharging major commitments that he had assumed for a number of universities in this country and in Israel. He promised that Brandeis was on his list for another family gift, which did indeed materialize a few years later when an endowment was established, named for Irving and Rose Crown, his brother and sister-in-law, to subsidize fellowships in American studies.

In the early part of our return flight Wien was unusually reticent. I attributed the mood to disappointment, and I tried to make the point that, in presentations for major objectives, it was inevitable that only a fraction of the attempts came to fruition. I too was disappointed, but not discouraged. Surely there were many other families who could be approached. I soon realized that Wien was hardly listening. It was not comforting that he needed. He was turning over in his mind his capacity to make room for the program in his own long roster of philanthropic commitments. He had presented the case of international scholarships with such eloquence and effectiveness that he had persuaded himself that this was a project that he should undertake! I don't remember whether we were over Kokomo, Indiana, or Akron, Ohio, when he turned to me and said quietly, "We won't wait for Crown or for anyone else. Mae and I will do the job ourselves." It was a commitment that involved an immediate annual expenditure of $300,000, which was to rise to $420,000 annually for 112 students, fully supported, and which ultimately required an endowment of between six and seven million dollars.

Wien did not feel that he had fulfilled his responsibility, however, if he did not simultaneously make a substantial contribution to Columbia. Within the week, therefore, he called up the dean of the law school, William Warren, and introduced himself as an alumnus. He said that he planned to establish a scholarship program for foreign students at Brandeis. "But I have a compelling obligation to the Columbia Law School and I would like to contribute a million dollars for scholarship purposes there." The dean afterward admitted that he nearly suffered a heart attack. What university official ever had a telephone call that announced an unsolicited gift of a million dollars from an alumnus with whom he was personally not acquainted!

In preparation for the launching of the program, I set up an appointment with Dr. Earl Dennis, director of the International Educational Exchange Service Office under the State Department. I was eager to explore how to use the experience of our American cultural attachés so as to be assured that we were giving the scholarships to students who would later be of service to their own countries, for the program was meant to be much more than a resource by which foreign youngsters could advance their own careers. Dr. Dennis was most enthusiastic. He noted that the usual foreign scholarship was limited to one year: a Wien scholarship offered, if need be, several years to fulfill an educational objective. It provided full support for tuition, room, board, and personal expenses related to academic needs. And the number of annual scholarships meant that the program could become truly international in scope. Dr. Dennis instructed the cultural attachés and the information officers in every American embassy to offer the fullest cooperation.

An advisory council was then appointed that was comprised of academic and public figures with valuable experience in international exchange. It included David Henry, the director of the foreign student service at Harvard; Henry Kissinger, then on the Harvard faculty; Mrs. Karl Compton, wife of the late president of MIT; Leonard Bernstein; Benjamin V. Cohen, one of Franklin Roosevelt's first foreign policy advisers; and a number of other committed advocates of international cultural exchange. Several members of our faculty were included, not only because of their own experience, but also so they could interpret the program to their colleagues. There was a tendency among some of them to resist "service" programs, however attractive, so long as committed needs for faculty salaries and fringe benefits were still not fully protected, and I hoped that the expected criticism would be diluted if key faculty members were part of our committee. We also took precautions to dissipate possible resentment among our American students. If scholarship funds for their own needs proved inadequate, they might wonder why foreign students were being treated with such hospitality. Student government leaders were therefore carefully briefed so the message would get back to their classmates that the Wien funds represented a special grant, and that no general scholarship resources would be diverted for the program. The procedures that governed recruitment and selection and the methods of financing were also discussed in detail with the Educational Policy Committee of the faculty and at the student press conferences that I held at regular intervals.

From the outset the Wien program worked closely with the Institute for International Education (IIE). Its files were always at the disposal of the Wien staff and each year a number of promising applicants were channeled to the University. But the majority of the Wien students were recruited directly through the special committees that were set up in many of the foreign countries.

We had the advantage of easy access to faculty members who were living abroad, either on sabbatical or on leave, and they were only too glad to accept assignments to establish such committees for us. Thelma and I spent several weeks, every few years, in university centers in Europe, Asia, Latin America, and Africa. In one twenty-three-day period we circled the globe and left behind working committees in twelve countries. There was little problem in obtaining the cooperation of the

American ambassadors and their staffs, the heads of universities and their key officers, the ministries of education, the directors of binational commissions. The offices of the cultural attachés distributed the application forms; the committees screened and evaluated the returns, conducted personal interviews, and made their recommendations to the director of the Wien Program at Brandeis. Within a few years Wien agreed to add another $60,000 in annual income so that graduate students could be included. As the availability of the Wien scholarships became widely known, applications poured in and the pool for selection was large enough to ensure a steady stream of students of the highest caliber.

The counsel of the foreign committees was indispensable in coping with specialized problems. The representative of the Ministry of Education in East Pakistan (later Bangladesh) pointed out that the most brilliant applicants were not necessarily the ones who could be of most service when they returned. If they achieved their degrees with honors in biochemistry or physics or literary studies, there were neither facilities nor opportunities in their homeland to utilize their training fully. Would it not be better to learn from government officials what national services were most urgent and then select the students interested in these areas? General Carlos Romulo, then president of the University of the Philippines and later foreign minister, was deeply concerned that Filipino youngsters most often stayed on in the United States because career opportunities there were so overpoweringly alluring. He suggested that contracts be drawn that would assure return to the Philippines for at least a few years, with the additional inducement of guaranteed positions there.

Such counsel, and growing experience with the problems of the students themselves, brought considerable flexibility in structuring the programs. Orientation sessions were set up in advance of the opening of the school year that included the participation of already fully adjusted Wien scholars. The curriculum was modified for some of them so they could make fuller use of the precious limited time that they had at Brandeis.

Every attempt was made to introduce them to the realities of American life. Families in the environs of the University gladly offered frequent hospitality, and the foreign students enjoyed the informality of American home life. In the early years, when the Wien students were virtually the only foreign youngsters on campus, it was possible to send them on University-sponsored tours so that they could become acquainted with other centers of American life. During recess periods, they would visit Washington and have interviews with government officials under the guidance of faculty couples. In New York, they would tour newspaper plants, television and radio stations, universities, and meet with the most important media personalities and political and educational figures.

The operation of the program was not limited in its impact on the Wien students. Though their numbers were small and represented only a fraction of the total enrollment, they brought a delightfully exotic quality to the campus and to all extracurricular activities. They were not isolated as foreign students had been in the early years of the Rockefeller International Houses at the University of Chicago and at Columbia. They lived and ate with the American students, attended classes and social functions with them, and were frequent visitors in their homes. Brandeis fielded a soccer team quite early, and the formidable array of Finns and Swedes, Italians and Greeks, Israelis and Kenyans brought impressive victories and high standings in intercollegiate competition.

The program won the enthusiastic support of governmental and educational officials around the world. The University was eager to create ambassadors for the democratic ideals of American life, not through propaganda, but through education, and prepared the students for crucially needed service in their homelands. Within two years of its inauguration the application pool reached 1,000, of whom 350 were eminently qualified. Dr. Jean-Pierre Barricelli of our Romance Language Department, the first Wien program director, reported, after a long tour in 1959, "The countless talks I had with local government officers, university representatives, and cultural attachés, during my recent visit to ten Asian and African countries, provided ample support for the belief that cultural and educational exchanges are not just a matter of philanthropy, but rather of survival. . . . When the youngsters come back they are swamped with requests to tell of their experiences. They are called upon to interpret their experiences to many others, sometimes in as many as a hundred talks to ten thousand people, to be on the radio about fifteen times, and to write or to be the subject of fifty or sixty newspaper stories. . . . In the aggregate, it is evident that those who spend some time at an American institution can do a sturdy amount to foster an appreciation of our country, of its achievements, and of the democratic ideals it aspires to realize." One of the Kenyan legislators told Barricelli that the Wien program was "the most energetic and encouraging contribution made by an American university to the growth of my country."

Inevitably some proportion of the Wien students did not return to their homelands. The problem of the "brain drain" that troubled General Romulo was not limited to the Philippines. It occurred with students who came from many of the underdeveloped countries. In addition to the lack of opportunity in their homelands, some were undoubtedly glamorized by American life and its standard of living. Some could not return home because of changed political conditions. Some of the men married American girls; a larger number of women married American men. Three Turkish girls in successive years became Americans through marriage to American men, one of them the son of a trustee. At the ceremony I gave the bride away in place of her absent father. Wien was elated over a romance that was so happily consummated, but he too worried about the potential "brain drain." He wondered whether it would not be wise thereafter to bring over only ugly Turkish girls. At one of our Commencements, when an honorary degree was conferred upon Barbara Ward, editor of the *London Economist*, whose husband was Lord Jackson, a British government official in Ghana, I introduced her to one of our Ghanian Wiens and she expressed concern that such potentially valuable leaders for Ghana might be tempted to stay on in America. But the majority of the Wien scholarship students did return. In the first few years of the program, it was not to be expected that their impact would be significant, but there were gratifying results when they had adjusted to relocation and had taken advantage of their special opportunities.

Subghi Abu Gosh was an attractive young Arab who came from the village of Abu Gosh, on the outskirts of Jerusalem, whose inhabitants had opted to remain when Israel had been established. The little village had never emerged from its semiprimitive agricultural status. No one had reached out for advanced education. Subghi's family rejoiced that he was offered an opportunity at Brandeis through the Wien program. He studied at Brandeis for three years and was then assisted to continue with graduate studies at Princeton. During one of the summer recess periods, Thelma and I visited the village where Subghi's uncle was the mukhtar, and we were received with overwhelming hospitality. We did not meet the women of the family, who were still tied to the medieval tradition where mixed company was forbidden. But their culinary art, simple but overample, was a delight. When Subghi returned to Israel he joined the faculty of the University of Tel Aviv, teaching Arab subjects there, cherishing the ambition that someday he might sit in the Knesseth and serve as a link between the Arab and Israeli peoples for a future of reconciliation and peace.

Age Kristoffersen was a gifted young pianist from Norway who was named a Wien student in 1959. In his several years at Brandeis he supplemented his program in the liberal arts with special training that the University provided in its music course conducted in cooperation with members of the Boston Symphony Orchestra. When he returned to Norway he performed often as a solo pianist with Norwegian symphony orchestras and gave recitals not only in his native land but in Germany, Holland, Belgium, and in the United States. In 1973 he was appointed director of culture for one of the communities near Oslo and continued to direct opera for the Norwegian Broadcasting Company. Meantime, he had married Anna Borg, the prima ballerina and artistic director of the Norwegian National Ballet Company.

Adriano Arcelo came to us from the Philippines in 1960 and took advantage of every course in economics that he could crowbar into his schedule. He graduated with the Class of 1963 and a place was waiting for him in the Economics Department of the University of the Philippines. Three years later the president of the Philippines took him into his office as an assistant for economic affairs, and he continued to teach as professor of economics and environmental planning. Then, when the government established a fund for assistance to private education, Adriano was named project director. Meantime he was writing extensively on problems of school planning, and his series of monographs on institutional management and development became a key textbook for the educational system of the Philippines.

Elsa Valdes had chosen a career of social work in her native Panama. The little country, with only one school of social work, was in desperate need of personnel. When the Florence Heller School at Brandeis was launched, it met her needs for policymaking training, and she was one of the first Wien students chosen for graduate study. She received her doctorate with honors and returned to become the director of the School of Social Work at the University of Panama. And there were scores of others who brought distinction to the Wien program and their alma mater.

Meantime, we had become interested in what might properly be called a combined degree program. It was based on the principle that students could take a portion of their concentration in their own university and then supplement their studies with work in a university abroad where they might find more ample resources in their specialization. Upon satisfactory completion, they would receive full credit for their studies in both universities. In effect, it would be as if two universities, though oceans apart, had pooled their offerings in a field, permitting the student to choose the best from both, receiving the degree from either one or the other or, in some special instances, from both. I had broached the plan to Philip Coombs of the State Department several years earlier, and he was quite impressed.

We were able to work up such combined programs as pilot experiments with one of the new British universities, Sussex, whose president, Asa Briggs, was an adventurous maverick. We found that our Brandeis science departments were quite superior to those of Sussex, and that the offerings at Sussex in the humanities opened areas that were not adequately covered by our curriculum. We established similar relationships with the University of the Andes in Bogotá, Colombia, and for a number of years their students took science and social science courses at Brandeis and our students took Latin American history, economics, and anthropology at Bogotá. The exchange was mutually useful. But mainly, I believe, through the conservatism of our faculty and its Educational Policies Committee, we never really got beyond the negotiations for combined degree programs. Our faculty set up study groups, spent long periods of time on equating credits, and made their way through all the bureaucratic, statistical comparisons that kept delaying the formalization of the programs. If there had been genuine confidence in the usefulness of such exchange, the technical obstacles could have been overcome. Perhaps it was not so much lack of confidence as sheer inertia in effecting change that prevented implementation. Soon it no longer mattered. When my incumbency as president was over, the program was quietly dropped. I imagine I could have fought the issue through, especially since it was fully funded through the Wien program, and many of the foreign universities, especially in England, Germany, and in Latin America, were quite ready to cooperate. But there are always innumerable issues in dispute between faculty and administration in a lively university, so there must be an order of priority in what to battle about if one is not to be bogged down continuously in conflict. Curriculum theoretically belongs within the jurisdiction of the faculty and its Educational Policies Committee, and there were more crucial issues in the early 1960s that demanded considerable time and energy. I learned once more that however young a university may be, it is in the nature of the average faculty member to remain conservative and to give the benefit of the doubt to routine. It is easier to let sleeping courses lie. To this day I regret that a program so full of promise for international education and for bringing universities closer together across frontiers could not have been brought to life through sensible and patient negotiation.

Another venture involved us for several years with the training of Peace Corps volunteers who were to be posted to Bolivia and Colombia. In the fall of 1964, on a grant of $138,000 from the State Department, fifty volunteers for a Bolivian Peace Corps came to Brandeis for their three months of special training. They were required to submit to a grueling schedule of fifteen hours daily, living in conditions that simulated what they were expecting to find in Bolivia. Pierre Gonon, head of our career planning office, who was coordinating the project, wrote: "The Center will prepare volunteers in a health project to teach nutrition, install sanitary facilities and train citizens in their use, conduct inoculation campaigns, and treat diseases. In addition, the education project will train volunteers to become instructors and teaching assistants in Bolivian universities."

For this purpose, the Peace Corps curriculum at Brandeis included the study of Bolivian history, politics, and culture; technical studies for assigned jobs; American studies and world affairs; health and medical training; physical education and recreation typical of both the United States and the host country. After three months, sixteen of the volunteers left for Puerto Rico for a few final weeks, mainly for language practice; the others remained on campus and then joined their classmates in Bolivia. The grant was repeated in 1965 for similar training with a slightly larger group. The experience was even more effective, since a great deal had been learned in the initial year.

The third Peace Corps training program, in the summer of 1966, was organized for service in Colombia. It brought together sixty volunteers to prepare them for university teaching and secondary school teacher training in some of Colombia's urban areas. What the Colombian government most desired was specialized assistance in strengthening the competence of its primary and secondary school teachers in mathematics, biology, chemistry, physics, and elementary science. An important innovation in this mathematics-science component of the program was the institution of a laboratory school that was developed in cooperation with the nearby Lexington school system, which invited Peace Corps trainees to participate in planning, teaching, and evaluating a special mathematics-science curriculum.

Campus life was much enriched during the fall in the three years of Peace Corps training by the presence of the volunteers and the seriousness with which they went about their preparation. We were gratified that members of our staff and faculty later became important national leaders — Joseph Kauffman, our dean of students, as deputy to Sargent Shriver; Lawrence Fuchs of our American Civilization Department, heading up the largest Peace Corps unit in the Philippines; and Joseph Murphy of our Politics Department, as director of the unit in Ethiopia. Kauffman then became president of Rhode Island College, and Murphy, president of Queens College in New York. Fuchs returned to Brandeis as chairman of the American Civilization Department.

Because of my own concern for the international programs, it was natural that, when a tribute designation was offered me at the conclusion of my incumbency, I chose fellowship support for our most gifted students who wished to study abroad, and a center where such programs could be adequately housed. Later, in Chapter XXIII, I describe how the tribute fund was subscribed and how it climaxed my presidency with the establishment of the fellowship program and the erection of the International Center.

The site chosen was in one of the newer parts of the campus, looking out on the woods, and it lent itself to the most imaginative treatment. I was especially gratified with the chancellor's suite and its adjacent patio office, where, on lovely days, my work could go forward as if in the heart of the woods. On the façade of the building, metal plates with the flags of all the members of the United Nations were mounted. The roof, which became a colorful plaza for open-air gatherings, carried twelve flagpoles, and on special occasions selected flags were flown to welcome visiting foreign dignitaries. Apart from housing the administrative headquarters for all the international programs, the center could also serve as a lounge and study hall for our foreign students. They would live among their American fellows, their activities on campus would be completely interwoven with the routines of their classmates, but they would have an attractively appointed center for their leisure hours. The library lounge was underwritten by Jack and Helen Lazar, who made the Kimberly name a symbol for exquisitely styled women's clothes; it would contain volumes related to international affairs and magazines and newspapers from around the world.

A beautiful, intimate auditorium, seating about three hundred people, was included as the gift of Mrs. Harold Silver, in memory of her husband. An entire wing was set apart for the Economics Department, underwritten in full by Edward and Sayde Goldstein of Boston, who were responsible for much of our fund-raising success in Boston and Palm Beach.

Several years after the International Center was dedicated, Viola Addison, one of our closest personal friends and a most generous patron of the University, died. She left virtually all of a $700,000 estate to Brandeis, stipulating that she wanted a designation for the bequest that would serve both the library, which she helped found, and the International Center, which carried Thelma's name and mine. Half the bequest therefore went for a new level in the library. The plaza on the International Center roof was also designated in the names of Viola Addison and her late husband and parents. This portion of the bequest was turned into a trust fund, whose income would provide the maintenance costs of the center. I had always hoped that the day would come when our physical facilities would be protected with guaranteed funds for maintenance. In the earliest years the University could not insist upon such provisions when donors provided essential facilities. Therefore I felt special satisfaction that a start could be made toward this objective in a building that carried our family name.

After the International Center had been constructed there was still enough money left over for a handsome capital fund to provide income for what became known as the Sachar Foreign Fellowship Program. Each year a faculty committee screened the applications from students and faculty who hoped for the experience that the fellowships and grants-in-aid offered.

XVI

University Governance

BRANDEIS came into being and developed its precedents in the period immediately after World War II, before problems of university governance became as public and emotionally charged as they did in the sixties. The colleges were full of men, both faculty and students, who had survived Guadalcanal and Anzio and Omaha Beach, and to whom the petty squabbles of academe seemed trivial or amusing. They had sterile years to make up, work to do. The faculty at Columbia, which included such critics of American education as Henry Steele Commager, Jacques Barzun, and Lionel Trilling, made no overt protest when the board gave them Dwight Eisenhower as president, as academically undistinguished as he was amiable and well intentioned. The editors of the *Harvard Crimson* kept their peace during James Conant's long absences as high commissioner for Germany; a later generation of student editors would keep a running tally of the days Nathan Pusey spent out of town in fund-raising efforts (usually to make their scholarships possible). So at this stage the mechanics of internal university government, even the issue of participatory decision-making responsibility, seemed irrelevant.

The dominant fear was that political pressures from without would erode the hard-won right to teach and write freely. This was the time when the junior senator from Wisconsin and a cocksure congressman from California were, to paraphrase Alistair Cooke, placing a generation on trial. Both tax-supported institutions and those that were underwritten by private philanthropy were often subject to coercion, however subtle, to hedge on commitments to complete freedom since support could easily crumble if those with the power of the purse were offended. McCarthy used his demagogic powers unabashedly for blackmail and his witch-hunts were totally intimidating. Despite Nathan Pusey's forthright stand against McCarthy's proposed invasion of Harvard Yard, the deeply respected literary scholar F. O. Matthiessen plunged to his death in despair. Eminent Sinologists and long-honored political scientists were forced into resignation and obscurity. Robert Oppenheimer was put through experiences that made the next generation of public officials heartily ashamed of their cowardice. It was not an easy period to serve as the president of a university, to remain loyal to the principle of the campus as the citadel of conscience, while carrying the responsibility for winning support from easily swayed constituencies.

Through all this ordeal Brandeis came off well. Problems of freedom and independence were taken in stride. The Board of Trustees regarded faculty with what was close to awe, an attitude rooted in the traditional Jewish respect for the teacher and the learned. I had come to the presidency out of a long university experience and fully appreciated the dignity of the faculty and the importance of protecting their independence. But above all, the University was still a very small family. There was no faculty senate, not only because of the very limited size of the school, but because, to use scientific terminology, we still had no "critical mass" with a career commitment to Brandeis. Governance meant informed consensus. A small group of faculty and administrative officers met frequently with me at the President's House or in my office, or, most often, at lunch for casual off-the-record discussions with no motions and no resolutions and no minutes. The conversation ranged over the expansion of faculty as the classes grew, changing strategies of recruitment, problems of facilities, and, above all, the reforms that were everywhere under scrutiny in educational orientation. Ludwig Lewisohn pontificated, and probably no more outrageous or reactionary proposals in education were ever put forth in such magnificent literary style. Max Lerner would have just enough time between classes and planes to detail his experiences at Williams, or Sarah Lawrence, or the New School, so that we could profit from others' trial and error.

Our main planning, of course, came from some of the younger faculty who had decided that Brandeis was to be their career — Leonard Levy, Saul Cohen, Milton Hindus, and a few others who worked their students into a fury by impossible academic demands and were always thanked afterward for their coercive perfectionism. These younger men converted doctrinaire abstractions into practical formulas that became the organic curriculum. When visiting professors came for a season, they added yeast and ferment to our discussions. Since we were already seriously concerned about graduate studies, a library, and the labyrinthine diplomacy necessary to garner research funds from the great national agencies, it was fortunate that we had Henry Steele Commager's counsel. Our testing point, therefore, did not come in issues that involved freedom of expression. It came in recruitment of faculty, where it would have been easy to avoid trouble by steering clear of controversial appointments. Two episodes, both occurring in the McCarthy period, may point up the approach of the trustees and the administration.

In 1952, as the University was preparing for the first Commencement,

I addressed a fund-raising conference in Miami and appealed for help in the development of our physical plant. Joseph Morse, a partner in a major paperback firm and editor-in-chief of the *Funk and Wagnalls Encyclopedia*, indicated that he would be glad to underwrite the facilities for our undergraduate Department of Economics. "Would you tell me, however," he added, "whether it would be possible for me to know, in advance, of faculty appointments to the department — who the projected men would be, and something about their background." There was a hush in the room, for obviously this was more than a perfunctory question about the designation of a building. "Joe," I responded, "if we gave any donor even implied veto power over faculty appointments, I don't believe you could have sufficient respect for the school to want to offer it any support." Morse responded quickly, "I wanted to be sure about the spirit of this young school. Had you given any other kind of response, you would get no contribution from me or my firm." There was nothing heroic about my reply; any school of quality would be expected to stand by the principle of complete freedom in the choice of faculty. The test came for Brandeis because these were its founding years and the need for physical facilities compelled an almost desperate quest.

Another testing point came soon after, in 1956. At the recommendation of the Mathematics Department I had brought the name of Felix Browder to the board for routine confirmation. Browder was the son of the head of the Communist party in the United States. He had served with distinction in the military forces during World War II and was an excellent mathematician. Since the sinister shadow of McCarthy hung over every university, several of the most important ones had rejected Browder's application. I wondered if our trustees would feel a similar concern. The discussion recognized the public relations problem the appointment might pose. Mrs. Roosevelt was present and she spoke up at once. She noted that Brandeis had excited her because, established in a climate of great national tension when the forces of repression were striving for mastery in the political, business, and academic worlds, it had the opportunity to demonstrate its freedom from fear. There was indeed no obligation to bring in Browder: there were many other excellent candidates; but the appointment would be a litmus test of the University's courage in a time of trial. Her statement was quickly seconded by one of the most conservative members of the board, Joseph Proskauer, a former justice of the Supreme Court of New York, who indicated that exactly because Brandeis was so young it was important to announce to the academic world that there would be no buckling to threat or intimidation, real or fancied. The board, basically a conservative group, unanimously endorsed these sentiments. When the new faculty appointments were announced the next day, a *Christian Science Monitor* reporter, who had spotted the name in our routine release, called me for a statement. I indicated that Browder's father was not under consideration, any more than Benjamin Cardozo's father, a Tammany Hall hack, had any bearing on the choice of his gifted son for a vacancy on the Supreme Court. I added that the rationale for our action had already been voiced three thousand years earlier by Ezekiel, when he declared that each man must be judged on his own: "If the father hath eaten sour grapes shall the teeth of the children be set on edge?" Old Ezekiel and young Browder both made the front page.

The wholesale appointments of faculty went forward all through the early years. When graduate areas were opened, often two or three in one year, staffing was similarly recruited in multiples. There were inevitably strong differences of opinion as senior faculty members discussed candidates and recommendations. Disagreements usually involved academic considerations: teaching ability, research and writing productivity, concern for students, capacity for growth. Some of the individuals who were gladly welcomed revealed they had been unable to make headway in their applications elsewhere, so Brandeis was a haven as well as a professional career.

Early incumbents at Brandeis included Herbert Marcuse, the maverick in philosophy and politics who achieved national prominence as a radical guru. Marcuse's appreciation for the hospitality with which he was received at Brandeis deserves relating, since he became perhaps the most relevant symbol in my experience of the cynical radical who demands independence as a right for himself, but considers it "hypocrisy" when it is expected of him. Marcuse was appointed to the faculty in 1954, when the first graduate schools were established. His revolutionary views, highly critical of capitalism and moderate socialism, and his association with extreme radical movements had brought him into difficult confrontations with government agencies and with the institutes he served at Harvard and Columbia. But he was welcomed to Brandeis as a seminal thinker and there found complete freedom to teach, to write, to lecture.

He was a man who apparently equated effrontery with boldness, but he nevertheless worried continuously that his past associations might create problems of security for him. There was the instance when the spy Soblen was brought back to this country to stand trial for possible treason. Marcuse came to see me in great agitation. He noted that the government records would undoubtedly reveal his associations with Soblen, and he was fearful that, when this became public, the University might not be willing to stand by him. I asked him if any of his activity had been subversive, and he assured me that this was not so. He had indeed been an intellectual mentor in the movements Soblen had manipulated, but he had never participated in activity that could be legally judged subversive. I assured him that he had nothing to fear if he had indeed restricted his activity to the exposition of his views. Soblen committed suicide before his trial began, and his case became moot.

As Marcuse grew older, his corrosive style became more biting. He baited academia unmercifully, as he did national government and the economic and social system. He was contemptuous of the principle of free speech, which he called "repressive tolerance," treating it as a ploy by the power groups who exercised their control in more subtle ways. He became one of the rallying points in the offbeat youth movements, along with Ché Guevara and Mao Tse-tung. I was constantly placed on the defensive by our more conservative supporters, who wondered how the University could continue to tolerate Marcuse as an objective teacher. But in the twelve years of his stay at Brandeis, no attempt was ever made to silence or censor him.

In the spring of 1965, approaching his sixty-eighth year, Marcuse came in to see me to discuss the University's rules for retirement. The Faculty Handbook prescribed retirement at age sixty-eight, but there could be extensions to sixty-nine and seventy, if recommended by the president to the Board of Trustees. At seventy retirement was mandatory, a provision that the faculty itself had set to make way for the promotion of younger men and women. Marcuse said that he had been offered a three-year appointment at the newly created University of California branch at San Diego, and he asked if he could have a matching three-year extension at Brandeis, through his seventy-first year. I indicated that I would be glad to recommend his reappointment to age sixty-nine and then to age seventy, after a physical examination. But a three-year contract would not be possible. This was the practice at Harvard and at other elite colleges, and it was strictly enforced by the Brandeis faculty. He would, therefore, have to make his own decision; he could stay on with us for two more years, until seventy, or he could be assured of an extra year of active teaching at San Diego. Marcuse chose the longer contract of San Diego. After the interview and the announcement of his decision, the word went out through the Students for a Democratic Society (SDS) that Marcuse had been "fired" for his radical views. This distortion was uncritically repeated as student editors of *Justice* kept going back into its files, and it congealed into an anti-administration record known as the Marcuse case. Marcuse remained silent through the years that followed, making no effort to set the record straight. We had views that were poles apart; we had clashed often on political and philosophical issues; but no man at the University had been treated with such impeccable fairness through his long years at Brandeis, and Marcuse knew it.

There was only one case during my twenty-year tenure where the administration's record on the principle of faculty freedom of expression was challenged. It came in 1962 during the Cuban missile crisis. David Aberle and his wife, Katherine Gough, a British citizen, were members of the Anthropology Department, Aberle serving as chairman. The headlines were dominated by the problems that the Kennedy administration was having with Fidel Castro when the confrontation brought the world perilously close to a nuclear war. On the campus the climate was not unlike that in the last act of Bernard Shaw's *Heartbreak House,* where all the characters prepare to go out into the garden to watch for the bombers. The director of our international services was besieged with lines of foreign students inquiring anxiously whether or not they should go home. In this near-panic atmosphere, a public meeting was held in Ford Hall and several faculty speakers vigorously upheld the Khrushchev-Castro policy as a legitimate response to "American imperialism." Katherine Gough was on the program and, before a wildly excited audience of youngsters, she exclaimed that if she were back in London, where anti-American demonstrations were taking place at the American embassy, she would join the demonstrators in their cry: "Viva Fidel, Kennedy to Hell." She added the hope that, if war broke out, the United States would be defeated so that its imperialism would be repudiated before the world.

When the report of the meeting reached me, along with indignant protests from the community that Miss Gough had spoken with such irresponsibility, I called her in to learn at first hand what she had said. She repeated her statements and stood firmly by them. I made it clear that I did not quarrel with her right to denounce American foreign policy. Three other speakers, including Herbert Marcuse, had been as forthright in their denunciation. But they had spoken with the discipline and self-control that was to be expected on a university platform. I told Miss Gough that freedom of the platform gave her no warrant for a wild attack. Her husband, as head of the department, came to protest my reprimand. I asked him why he considered it perfectly legitimate for his wife to lash out, consigning the President of the United States to hell, but for my remonstrance to elicit immediate protest. "Apparently," I remarked, "freedom of speech means to you and Katherine that you can dish it out, but you cannot take it." Aberle responded that a faculty member has every right to speak without restraint, but when a president ventures a reprimand it becomes "intimidation." This incident gradually tapered off into casual campus conversation, but it was revived when budgets for the next school year were under consideration. Aberle had submitted a salary schedule for his department, listing his wife's name with the others who were recommended for merit increases. I put aside gaucherie, but strengthened my resolve to revise our nepotism procedures. I discussed the case itself with the dean of the graduate school, Leonard Levy, who had always staunchly defended faculty rights and standards. We agreed that Miss Gough's contract would be renewed and that there would be no salary freeze, but that there was no reason to reward her conduct with the increase recommended by her husband.

The Aberles had already been negotiating for other positions. Soon after the budgets had been approved, they announced that they had accepted posts at the University of Oregon. Inevitably the media got wind of the controversy. The Aberles allowed themselves to be photographed walking together through the snow-covered landscape, arm in arm. A picture that appeared on the front page of a Boston newspaper was captioned: "The last walk across campus." That their contractual obligations to the University ran through June was ignored. It was after this that the Aberles revealed their acceptance of the Oregon appointments. But before leaving the campus, Miss Gough brought her grievance of unfair treatment to the national American Association of University Professors (AAUP), the Brandeis faculty, and the Massachusetts American Civil Liberties Union (ACLU). The national AAUP declined jurisdiction, since the case had become moot with the Aberle resignations. The faculty debated whether academic freedom had been involved and concluded that, while there may have been mistaken judgment on the part of the president in the procedures of the reprimand and in the salary decision, his record in protecting academic freedom had been outstanding and his action warranted no rebuke.

I was rather bewildered a few weeks later when the ACLU's judgment was announced that I had "blemished the reputation of a highly respected institution" and a good record of protecting academic freedom by an unwarranted reprimand of Miss Gough and a discriminatory denial of an appropriate salary increase for her. My bewilderment came because the executive committee of the Massachusetts ACLU reached its decision in my absence abroad, without offering me any opportunity to present my interpretation of the circumstances or to defend my action. Further, I was the president of a university whose dedication to academic freedom had never been questioned, and I had played no small part in creating this climate of freedom. One of the projects that had brought me the greatest pride was the establishment of an institute, fully subsidized by the Lasker family, for a semester of updated study that would strengthen the background of carefully selected people whose careers were linked with the protection of civil rights and civil liberties. Miss Gough had been given a full hearing before the union officers, but I had not been given the courtesy of a personal call. Kermit Morrissey, assistant to the president, had been reached by phone and asked a few questions to which he replied, not knowing that what he said was to be "the evidence," after which the executive committee rendered its judgment.

Much later I learned that one of the members of the executive committee had once applied for a position in the Department of Economics. I had submitted her credentials to Dr. Sven Laursen, the chairman, who concluded that she did not meet the required standards. She had appealed for intercession to a number of University contributors, who were sensible enough to refuse. She had apparently nursed her resentment through the years and, when the Aberle case came up, she had pressed for an immediate judgment. It might have been reached anyway, but it would have been more seemly had she disqualified herself. Quite apart from her involvement, it was astonishing that an agency created to defend due process offered an example of arbitrariness it so quickly condemned in others.

When the ACLU at once publicized its statement, it brought a flood of protests and a number of resignations from the Massachusetts union's executive committee, which had not been consulted, including one from Henry Steele Commager. Mark Howe of the Harvard Law School wrote: "Too many of today's libertarians seem to me to be looking for a crusading fight and it sounds to me as if the local chapter had revealed this tendency on this occasion. . . . I don't suppose it's in the cards that either an apology or a retraction will be forthcoming. You may have succeeded, however, in giving the eager warriors a useful fright. I hope so." Dean Levy presented a personal reaction, but he spoke for many in the community who, quite apart from the judgment on Brandeis, resented the kangaroo procedures that had been followed. He wrote to the state chairman of the Civil Liberties Union:

> I would not have thought it possible that the Civil Liberties Union of Massachusetts on the basis of ex parte evidence would gratuitously chastise Dr. Sachar and Brandeis University without first affording a hearing or inquiry in which we might have the opportunity of defending ourselves, *before* you and your Executive Committee passed judgment. Due process or fair hearing, I should not have to remind you, as well as common courtesy, required that you at least give us notice of your interest in the case. By us I refer not only to the President, but to the faculty and its instrumentalities, principally the Faculty Senate. I should have thought too that you would have been keenly sensitive to the obligation of securing all the facts before forming an opinion. Your statement, which is improperly founded, turns out to be an irresponsible distortion interlaced with insulting and false innuendoes. . . .
>
> The President of this University — I note again — has been praised by this faculty for his *courageous* fifteen-year record in defense of academic freedom. There is no doubt whatever of this President's or this University's commitment to free inquiry and free speech, despite the misinformed judgment of your committee. Nor is there any doubt of the right of our students to assemble, select speakers, and discuss issues of their

choice. Gus Hall, Herbert Aptheker, and Malcolm X have been denied the right to speak on other campuses; all three, as well as other leaders of extremist groups, spoke to student organizations at this University during this academic year. There has never been any censorship at this University. . . .

The chairman of the ACLU fell back on legalities in his response and reminded Dean Levy that the union "never conducts hearings." He did not indicate that Katherine Gough was given her full say before the union officers who passed and publicized the judgment. Dean Levy rejected the chairman's explanation.

"You feel free," he wrote, "to condemn an honored and honorable institution and its President; you feel free to publish your condemnation; you feel free to do all this without at any time writing or calling the President himself or any of the several deans of this University or the Chairman of its Faculty Senate; and, yet, you can state, 'reference to academic "due process" in this matter is wholly beside the point.' "

As I look back upon the episode, I am inclined to agree with the faculty's decision. It was perhaps a mistake to take upon myself the full responsibility for the reprimand of Miss Gough. The issues of academic freedom are so sensitive that, though the times were tense and emotions ran high, I should have protected myself and the University by having the dean of faculty or a faculty committee undertake the responsibility.

Several useful consequences followed the tempest raised by the Aberle case. The faculty statement was the best refutation to the concern that independent faculty action, even in criticism of the president, had to be avoided because of fear of reprisal. And I was reassured that the leading liberal of the faculty community expressed himself so forthrightly throughout the controversy.

Except for the refusal to recommend the continued service of Marcuse into his seventy-first year, and the reprimand and bypassing of a merit bonus for Katherine Gough, there were no other major problems of freedom.

There were more frequent disagreements over the issue of shared decisions in the appointment of senior members of the faculty and of deans and administrative officers. By now, no president could be an unqualified, authoritarian figure. Gone were the days when he could follow the counsel of Jowett, the autocratic master of Balliol at Oxford, whose rule was simple: "Never retract, never explain, Get it done, and let them howl!" The pendulum had now swung to the other extreme. There were many faculty activists who regarded administrative officials as necessary evils who could serve best when they concentrated on fund-raising, public relations, and circuit-riding for speeches to alumni. They insisted that the welfare of academia belonged exclusively to the faculty.

I agreed that the substance of the curriculum, the standards of student admission, the rules of tenure and similar concerns should be left to the faculty for final judgment. But I could not agree that a president had to go along automatically with a senior faculty appointment that a department recommended. I respected the high motivation of most faculty, their devotion to their students and their deep commitment to their scholarly disciplines. But to me the profession was no saintly fellowship. It had its fair share of careerists, who were concerned about their own standing if scholars of greater stature were brought in. And it also included occasional opportunists, who were as much concerned with the pursuit of the dollar as their counterparts in other professions and in business. When the pursuit became too blatant and seemed to threaten the integrity of the University's commitments, I felt it necessary to exercise the presidential prerogative of the veto. Fortunately, such circumstances arose rarely.

In the spring of 1963 the head of the Economics Department brought up the appointment of a well-recommended candidate, who was then at a neighboring university. He had been carefully screened and had met all academic standards. I always made it a point to meet the applicants for senior positions, and he had therefore also been interviewed by me. I too was quite favorably impressed, and informed him that I would confirm the recommendation of the department chairman and submit it to the board for its technical approval. To my surprise, he hesitated and indicated that he was not quite ready for a decision. He wanted a written offer from the University, which he would consider carefully for several days. I already had had a number of experiences when bona fide offers were similarly delayed, after which the candidates had decided to remain where they were, but at increased salaries. Confronted now with what again seemed like a ploy to parlay a salary increase, I indicated that our oral offer had been given in good faith and it would have to be accepted or rejected, and that we had no interest in improving his bargaining position.

The applicant, as I later learned, went back to his provost, explained that he had an attractive offer, but that he would remain if the offer were met. The provost was apparently as repelled, and the applicant was advised that he was welcome to leave. Quite chagrined, he returned to the Brandeis chairman and expressed his willingness to transfer. It was then that I stopped the appointment, determined that we would not encourage the spreading practice of pitting universities against each other to hike up salaries. The senior members of the department argued that the action of the applicant was no disqualification, that our sole criterion for appointment had to be his professional competence. I stood my ground, making the further point that senior faculty could scarcely be counted on to give priority to the ongoing welfare of our young university if they were as tolerant as they seemed to be of such rip-offs by their colleagues. The chairman was quite unhappy with the decision, and he even expressed his unhappiness to the candidate, to whom he wrote to apologize for my arbitrary action!

There are, of course, occasions when the ablest faculty inevitably are sought out, and they must weigh what they have against what they may expect if they decide upon a change. There is then legitimate reason for negotiation, and the University too must consider how far it can afford to go to encourage an incumbent to remain. But the bargaining practice is much more dubious when the incumbent has no intention of leaving, but arranges for an induced bid that is spurious. Sometimes the stratagem comes off, but it has rarely been successful at Brandeis. We were not desperate for good people. We had many more outstanding applications than we could absorb. In the years that followed, the practice by faculty wheeler-dealers of pitting schools against each other grew until it became almost routine. But during my administration, when I knew that it was being practiced, I refused to condone it.

I also believed that, as president, it was my responsibility to prevent a faculty or administrative position from becoming a peg on which to hang a hat, with no basic responsibility for its routine duties. Unfortunately, Brandeis too had prima donnas who interpreted their relationship to the University as subsidized security so that they could go on with their own pursuits. There were several cases in which our men held down two college teaching jobs simultaneously, arranging to have their classes at Brandeis telescoped into two days so they would be free the rest of the week. They were usually the leaders in resisting the "heavy teaching load." A case of a different order developed at the Goldfarb Library. The director of library services was Louis Schreiber, a conscientious, hardworking, deeply committed technician. His training had been limited to library administration and it was considered important therefore to protect the academic role of the Library by the appointment of a distinguished man of letters, for his judgment on acquisitions, for representation at scholarly conferences, and for negotiations with patrons who might be persuaded to make major contributions to the Library. In 1961, the post was offered to a theater critic who had earned a national reputation as a perceptive essayist. From the very beginning he treated his tasks as a man-of-letters-in-residence. He could spend virtually all of his time and effort on his writing and travel, since the faithful Schreiber was there to carry all the more taxing administrative duties. When Schreiber was killed during the summer of 1965 and the Library was suddenly left without leadership, I cabled the librarian, who was vacationing in Europe, hoping that since the Library was in a crisis he would forgo the rest of his vacation, which could be made up at another time. His response was that a vacation was a vacation, and he could not change his plans. When he returned the following month he was informed that the University could not afford the luxury of a symbol to head its library and that the position would be phased out. He insisted that he was protected by tenure and threatened suit. He had no legal leg to stand on: the invitation for him to take the position at Brandeis carried no tenure guarantee. But his attorney was shrewd enough to know that we could not engage in a legal battle where ugly public relations repercussions were inevitable. A compromise was effected whereby he would relinquish the librarian's post and instead be given a three-year contract to teach several courses in one of the departments. In a volume that he wrote later he relieved some of his disappointment by castigating the president for his irritating habit of interference in matters of academic administration. But he omitted the episode of his assistant's death and the critical situation that had required a librarian's leadership.

Perhaps the closest that the administration came to a direct confrontation with the Faculty Senate was near the end of my leadership; it revolved about the issue of where the final authority was vested in the appointment of a dean. The incumbent had resigned as dean of the graduate school because of failing health, which led to his early death. I invited recommendations for succession, and included academicians among the Board of Trustees in my request for help. One of them, Milton Katz, head of the School of International Legal Studies at Harvard, had just completed a consultant's task that had merged Western Reserve University and Case Institute in Cleveland. His aide had been Lawrence Finkelstein, a brilliant student of institutional problems of organization, and Katz warmly recommended him. The appointment was challenged by the senior faculty leaders. The ostensible objection was that Finkelstein had no doctorate, but this was obviously a pretense, since some of our ablest faculty — Irving Howe, Philip Rahv, Howard Bay, Charles Schottland — also had no formal doctorate. The issue really came down to whether the faculty had veto power in the appointment of deans. I still followed the traditional line that, in the final decision, the appointment was for the president to make.

The confrontation lasted several weeks, drawn out primarily because Thelma and I were abroad in the interest of our foreign student exchange program. When we returned it was clear that some kind of compromise would have to be reached. I realized that a dean, however well qualified, forced upon the graduate faculty would find the going extremely rough; the faculty leaders understood that I could not yield without abandoning the principle that the final decision must still lie with the president. When I suggested that we name Finkelstein acting dean, the situation to be reviewed after a year, the faculty leadership eagerly accepted the compromise. The issue no longer mattered by then because I had resigned the presidency and had been named chancellor.

My successor had too many other problems to keep this issue alive. He yielded to the Faculty Senate, abruptly fired the graduate dean, and named the senate's choice. Finkelstein went on to Harvard, where he quickly completed his doctorate and became secretary of its Center for International Affairs and consultant to the State Department on defense analysis.

The issue did not disappear, however. It came to life several times in the incumbencies of my successors. I am still firmly convinced that the progress of the university depends on a cabinet form of government, where the deans, though necessarily sensitive to the needs and objectives of the Faculty Senate, must be presidential appointees. I cannot forget the paralysis that has overtaken the progress of the Hebrew University since a solid core of German refugee professors established the European system of governance there. The president was little more than a symbol and a traveling fund-raiser. The rector carried the entire academic responsibility and he was a spokesman for the faculty who elected him, for short terms, so that he would be sure to remain a temporary official with very little authority. I believed further, as I watched the developments in our own University world, that though it was wise to involve the faculty and students in limited decision-making, the shift in the fulcrum of responsibility for academic administration and the erosion of the authority of the president have seriously weakened the innovative opportunities of the University. Most of the service projects that I had proposed to expand the role of the University — the Wien Scholarship Exchange, the Florence Heller School of Social Welfare, the Center for the Study of Violence — had been invariably initially opposed by the faculty. Their virtual reflex response was that any new resources that the administration uncovered should go for faculty salaries and fringe benefits. And in many instances those who fought hardest for shifting control of academic policy to the faculty, as the appropriate arbiters of the destiny of the University, left for other positions that seemed to offer better personal opportunities.

None could blame them for such mobility. As noted in an AAUP address that I gave in 1963 in the lion's den itself, the primary loyalty of a faculty member is to his discipline rather than to the university that sponsors it. I noted that when Harlan Cleveland was dean of the Maxwell Graduate School at Syracuse, he wrote that the dynamics of a university are inevitably centrifugal rather than centripetal. This is simply because the career of the faculty member does not depend primarily on his position within the power structure of his own institution, but on his reputation in his own field of specialization. Pursuing this line of thought, I added: "My own view is that faculty should be given *every leeway* where the welfare of their own discipline is involved. And since they have both a personal and an academic stake in the institution which they serve, however temporarily, they should be called upon for counsel

in the planning and the development of the totality of the University.
. . ." Matthew Arnold's *Scholar Gypsy* calls up no heroic image for
today's faculty, here at Brandeis or elsewhere. Granted, the academician
is a pretty special sort of bird, but as a former member of the aviary I
would be embarrassed to regard the scholar as a peacock in a terraced
garden: "Look, but don't touch. Admire, but do not fraternize." Collaboration, with mutual respect and with mutual understanding, is a
primary condition in the pursuit of excellence.

"But where the total welfare of the University is concerned," I continued, "the faculty ought not to be the final decision makers. To begin
with, they have an innate conservatism, a natural dislike of change and
innovation. David Riesman refers to faculty as 'intellectual veto-groups.'
A university whose welfare can be influenced by faculty veto power
would thus not only soon resemble Chaucer's 'Parliament of Fowles,'
but would shortly cease to be a university, since dedicated scholars
would soon return to their own work and leave policies and committees
to others. . . ." I therefore appealed for a continuous exploration of
methods to widen the avenues of consultation. But because of the nature
of the University, its legal structure, and its many constituencies, the
"consent area" had to have specific limitations.

Of course, in determining such limitations, there must have been
times when my actions were considered paternalistic. I make no claim to
omniscience. Undoubtedly, especially in the early days, when decisions
had to be reached quickly, I did bypass procedures that later could be
judged a violation of normal handbook regulations. I may have lost patience when it would take faculty committees and subcommittees endless argument to reach a decision, and then — fortunately not often — I
would have to cut through the argument with action. This could be
condoned only because we were a young school in the process of tool-
ing up. When our country was being built, even our most sensitive
statesmen were not always models of procedural restraint. I take refuge
in remembering the protest of a very pious Israeli who complained that
the workers in the war-ravaged country often desecrated the Sabbath
during their military leaves. The wise old chief rabbi reminded him that,
when the Holy of Holies was being built in the ancient Temple of
Solomon, it was understood that, when completed, only the high priest
would be permitted to enter it, and then only on the Day of Atone-
ment. But during the building period it was necessary for the laborers to
use it as a workroom and to walk in and out to perform their appointed
duties. The procedures of emergency activities in a building period must
be judged differently in relation to regulations that are wise and valid
when times are normal.

Apparently, most of the faculty who had gone through the pioneering period with me agreed with this judgment. After I ended my
twenty-year incumbency, Abraham Maslow told a magazine inter-

viewer: "When we're all dead, when the personalities are forgotten, nobody will know whether Sachar was lovable or not lovable. All they'll see are the consequences, what happened here. All they'll see is a great university."

XVII

Policymaking Training in
Social Welfare

Since Brandeis was committed not only to teaching and research but also to communal service, it was inevitable that in time it would sponsor professional schools. But it was also early agreed that any such development must not simply duplicate other programs. If Brandeis were to decide upon a law school, it would be unwise to plan upon the models of Harvard or Yale or Columbia, or the scores of schools whose prestige would attract the best candidates and leave the neophyte institution with rejects from their first choice. Similar considerations had to be kept in mind if plans would be broached for a school of medicine,* education, diplomacy, or business and commerce. Priority, it was agreed, ought to be given to professional school expansion only if some national need could be filled or some original approach could be devised for which Brandeis was especially equipped.

These considerations gave not only validity but urgency to the planning for the School for Advanced Studies in Social Welfare. It was not to be a conventional training center for social workers. In the Greater Boston area alone there were three major schools of social work, which,

---

* It is interesting to remember that in 1963, Mount Sinai Hospital in New York offered Brandeis the opportunity to create a medical school in New York and to become its hospital affiliate. It was prepared to allocate an initial grant of $50 million to get started. The offer was carefully studied by a faculty committee headed by our dean of science, Dr. Louis Levin. Though it was strongly supported by most of our New York trustees, it was finally declined, primarily because Brandeis would simply be repeating a medical school objective that was no different from scores of others. Besides, the responsibilities of a first-class medical school nearly two hundred miles away from the University itself would inevitably channel most of the energies of the officials and the supporters to sustain the enormous requirements of the hospital's teaching and research responsibilities. Mount Sinai Hospital then proceeded to establish its own medical school, which quickly became one of the best in the country, but its cost mounted to hundreds of millions of dollars, and its maintenance became a tremendous drain on the energies and resources of its devoted leadership.

despite their prestige, were at that time having difficulty recruiting highly qualified candidates.

The overriding need was for training on the higher level of policy leadership in social welfare. The time was ripe. After World War II, every communal institution was confronted with new challenges that required a revaluation of objectives. There were calls for radical changes in techniques to meet burgeoning problems in community organization, Social Security, population planning, international service, gerontology, deviant behavior, mental health, ecology, and a disturbing drug culture. There were no schools of social work that specialized primarily in training for broad-gauged policy, either in these or in more traditional areas. Here was an unparalleled opportunity for Brandeis. At the end of its first decade it already had an excellent faculty in the social and the life sciences. They could work in tandem with a core faculty of specialists who had won distinction in the frontier fields of social welfare. There were hundreds of social workers, community and government officials, and academicians who were eager for advanced training to qualify them for tasks for which their conventional schooling in social work, even when supplemented by experience, had become outdated.

For a number of years, even as Brandeis strove to strengthen its liberal arts offerings, intense discussions went forward with men and women, prominent in community and government service, who encouraged the University to undertake a training center for policymakers and for advanced research in social welfare. One of the Fellows of the University, Mrs. Florence Heller of Chicago, a lay leader in the activities of the Jewish Welfare Board and later its first woman president, was especially eager for such a program to be mounted and indicated she would make substantial contributions to help underwrite it.

In the fall of 1957, after lengthy consultation with advisers, I brought to the Board of Trustees the outline of a program for a graduate school of social welfare. I was considerably surprised by the opposition it encountered, led by Dr. Isidore Lubin, who brought to our board the experience of a long and brilliant career in public service. He had taught economics in leading universities, had served President Roosevelt as head of the Bureau of Labor Statistics, and had been secretary of commerce in the cabinet of Governor Harriman of New York. He was supported in his opposition by two of the more recent members of the board, Dr. Merrill Thorpe, professor of economics at Amherst, and Mrs. Adele Rosenwald Levy, the daughter of Julius Rosenwald, one of the most generous philanthropists of the last generation. Their opposition was not based on concern that we could not succeed in creating such a program. But they had always hoped that Brandeis would remain a liberal arts and sciences university and would avoid professional schools of any kind. Merrill Thorpe added another caveat. How could a doctorate be offered in social welfare when there was really no body of knowledge that could be taught to earn such a degree? Social welfare had no standing in the university world as an academic discipline. Would it not be better to send candidates who wished to update and strengthen their skills into the recognized departments of the social sciences, perhaps augmenting them with a few appointments in the more specialized areas of social welfare? Then, argued Dr. Thorpe, the integrity of the doctoral degree would be fully protected.

These were all valid concerns and they were put forward with compelling eloquence and conviction. Our response was that there was a crying need for a training center for objective policymaking in social welfare, for its research, and for the evaluation of the complex and confusing data emerging from the changes and dislocations of the contemporary world. The pledge was added that the development of such an advanced professional school would in no way jeopardize the commitment to the preservation of highest standards in the liberal arts and sciences: indeed, the presence of distinguished authorities in this crucial professional area would enrich the continued dialogue that characterized the intellectual climate of Brandeis. As for Dr. Thorpe's misgivings, would it not be an exciting challenge for Brandeis to contribute its insights to develop this data, to formulate and evaluate it, to identify its research objectives, so that the advanced students would meet the standards that the doctorate demanded?

The discussions continued for nearly two years since they had to be wedged in between many other academic and financial concerns. In February 1958 the board authorized the convening of a high-level advisory group to explore both the theoretical and practical implications for the immediate present and for the long-range objectives of Brandeis if the School for Advanced Studies in Social Welfare were established.

The participating counselors were an impressive group. They included Charles Schottland, the federal commissioner for Social Security; Dr. Katherine Kendall, the associate director of the Council on Social Work Education; Wilbur Cohen, later secretary of health, education and welfare; Philip Bernstein, the executive director of the Council of Jewish Federations and Welfare Funds; Fedele F. Fauri, dean of the School of Social Work at the University of Michigan; and Donald Howard, dean of the University of California School of Social Welfare. Selected members of our own faculty and the Board of Trustees sat in with the advisers, and, in the interchange, the concept of the school was validated and the unanimous recommendation made that the School of Advanced Studies in Social Welfare should be undertaken. The conference also formulated suggestions for the parameters of the school and how they should be protected.

One of the auxiliary purposes of convening the advisory group was to spot possible leadership for the new program. Charles Schottland stood out both for his practical insights and for the prestige he commanded. Before being named by President Eisenhower to head the federal Social Security office, he had had a long administrative and military experience. Trained for the law, he had moved into social welfare and had been the executive director of the Jewish Federation in Los Angeles and had taught at the University of California in Los Angeles. During World War II he had been assistant director of UNRRA for Germany, supervising the relief and relocation programs for tens of thousands of survivors in the Displaced Persons' Camps. He was decorated by the governments of France, Czechoslovakia, Greece, Holland, and Poland. After he returned to California in 1950, Governor Earl Warren was sufficiently impressed with his record and experience to appoint him director of the Department of Social Welfare. When Warren was called to Washington as Chief Justice, he recommended Schottland to the President for the rapidly developing federal program of Social Security. Schottland had been serving in this post for more than four years when he joined our advisory council. After the first sessions, where he played a leading role, I began exploring with him the possibility of his assuming the post of dean if our plans were authorized by the board.

Schottland was very much intrigued by the challenges of the post: a new approach to social welfare problems, in a new university, in a new era. His wife, Edna, was initially not very enthusiastic about still another uprooting, and even less so about exchanging the fascination of the world's most exciting capital for the quiet tempo of a college campus in what she imagined were the dusty bowers of staid New England. But after several visits to Brandeis and the welcome that she and her husband received, her misgivings were allayed.

The board's formal decision to go ahead was made in February 1959, with the understanding that the school, under Schottland's direction, would be launched in the fall. My announcement called attention to the frontier fields that would become its major concerns: "The program recognizes the need for trained social policy workers in the newer, emerging fields of international social work, federal, state and municipal government, labor and industry, intergroup relations, the socioeconomic aspects of city planning, suburbia, and a host of new developments in our society."

Dean Schottland began at once to recruit faculty. Since the student body would be limited to less than twenty, only a few core faculty members were required initially. It was expected they would be supplemented by visiting specialists and by the Brandeis faculty itself. Fears that it might be difficult to persuade distinguished authorities to cast their professional destinies with a speculative concept proved groundless. The first faculty, which was to set the image of the school, was a most impressive group. It included Robert Morris, a widely respected authority in social planning who, like Dean Schottland, had served as a welfare officer for UNRRA in Germany and had been chief of social services for the Veterans' Administration in California. He had written extensively on the use of social science theory and research in social work. After he came to Brandeis he was joined by David French, then an editor of the *Social Work Journal,* who had taught and written on the use of social science theory in social work at the Chicago Theological Seminary and the University of Michigan. He was later called upon by the technical assistance program of the UN to direct the patterns of social work in Asia, mainly in India and Pakistan.

These men were soon reinforced by other specialists who represented the fields where the school determined to make its early contributions. Herbert Aptheker was a leading authority in social work; Peter Gutkind, an anthropologist, had headed research missions in East Africa and came to supervise the training for international social work; Howard Freeman had a solid grounding in the fields of sociology and mental health and was especially concerned with the patterns of social welfare research. In addition to his teaching, he was appointed the director of research in 1960, funded by grants from the Permanent Charity Fund of Boston. Roland L. Warren joined the faculty in 1964. He had been professor of sociology at Alfred University and was widely known both as a theorist in the sociology of the American community and as an expert in the application of social theory and research to social welfare programs. For two years before coming to us, he represented the American Friends Service Committee in a project that sought to establish communication between leaders in East and West Berlin. In his later career at Brandeis he became one of the most sought out scholars on problems of community planning. Gunnar Dybwad trained in the law in Geneva and later in social work in the United States; he served in both governmental and voluntary agencies as an authority in child development and child welfare. He was recruited for Brandeis in 1967 from the position of director of the Mental Retardation Service of the International Union of Child Welfare in Geneva. After coming to Brandeis he was called upon as a consultant to expand the opportunities for retarded people to achieve their maximum potential. He was also a major factor in the recent struggles to protect the legal rights of mental patients to health and education. David Gil was our expert in child welfare and conducted a pioneering study of child abuse; Norman Kurtz, teaching social theory and research methods, was a widely acclaimed specialist in problems of alcoholism and deviant behavior; Robert Binstock became a national authority in the field of gerontology, his distinction recognized when he was later elected the national president of the American Gerontological Society; Violet M. Sieder had been a full professor in the Columbia School of Social Work when she joined Brandeis's first student group; she later became one of the professors in administration and rehabilitation.

Above all, there was Arnold Gurin, who had obtained his academic and professional training at City College in New York, and at Chicago, Columbia, and Michigan. He had a long experience with various relief agencies and with the Council of Jewish Welfare Funds and Federations of New York, where he served variously as director of Budget Research and of Field Service. His writings in the professional journals, mainly on community organization, identified him as one of the best-informed men in the field. He was teaching in the School of Social Work at Michigan State University when Dean Schottland brought him to Brandeis in 1962 as associate professor of social administration. He was later tapped as the dean of the school when Schottland was named president of Brandeis in 1970.

The visiting professors demonstrated the prestige and the goodwill that the school had from the very beginning. They included Karl de Schweinitz, the noted social work historian and former dean of social work at the University of Pennsylvania, and Richard Titmuss, of the London School of Economics, another pioneer of British social welfare legislation.

The public announcement of the launching of the school and the description of its objectives brought more than one hundred applications for the seventeen available places. They included social workers, center directors, religious and civic leaders, authors, educators, and field-workers from throughout the United States and abroad. They were men and women, mainly in their thirties and forties, prepared to take leaves of absence from their professional duties to update their backgrounds and to become better equipped for more responsible policymaking positions. After careful screening, thirteen men and four women were enrolled. This hopeful venture was under way as the university was completing the decennial year of its launching.

The problem of seed money was considerably eased through the generosity of Mrs. Florence Heller, who by now had become a trustee. She agreed to underwrite the deficits of the school for the first years until a steady state budget could be ascertained and promised that thereafter she would provide endowment resources to assure realistic planning. Other families concerned with social welfare were appealed to, and their supplementary grants sustained our hope that the school would not have to rely on the general funds of the university.

Before the first year was completed, Dean Schottland was able to announce a grant from the Ford Foundation to demonstrate and evaluate experimental programs to improve community services for the aged. The charge was to offer technical and consultant assistance over a two- to four-year period to eight selected communities, where the Ford Foundation had made an investment of $300,000 in programs for the aged, and to help them test both traditional and experimental approaches. The reports would be evaluated by a research team headed by Robert Morris, and it was expected that the recommendations that emerged would set minimum standards for agencies that were attempting to cope with the problems of the aged.

Many more grants were to follow — some substantially larger, involving millions — but few carried the significance of this Ford grant. It came before the Florence Heller School had even graduated its first class. It involved a field of study whose importance for American welfare could not be overemphasized, for senior citizens had become a considerable part of the nation's population and programs for their social needs now compelled priority. Dean Schottland noted the startling statistic that every third American who reached the age of sixty had at least one living parent! The Ford Foundation had demonstrated enough confidence in Brandeis that it was ready to assign to a university research-based center the long-range study of key planning agencies. After the Ford grant was announced, the officers of the Young Men's Philanthropic League of New York, an influential funding agency, were persuaded to help underwrite the first chair in gerontology, which was held in the years ahead by Robert Morris. Many other research grants in gerontology were undoubtedly triggered by the resourcefulness and competence with which gerontological study and research were pursued by the Heller School team.

Soon there were other important research grants that involved both faculty and visiting specialists. A grant from the Russell Sage Foundation was received for a broad study of the voluntary financing of health and welfare projects in the United States. General Electric made funds available for a study of corporate philanthropy and the corporation as a concerned citizen. There were grants to study the welfare policies of private industry in relation to its employees; to analyze the competence of social welfare programs in selected Latin American countries; to evaluate the effects of urban renewal upon the displacement of families and the services needed to assist them during the transition period. Even as the projects were assigned and funded, our key faculty people were called upon for consultantships by federal, state, and local bureaus and by the agencies of the United Nations and foreign governments.

The school was invariably included in the visits of foreign government commissions for briefing on their programs and for counsel in specialized areas. In the fall of 1960 the State Department routed a delegation of visiting Japanese city planners to Brandeis to discuss the objectives of their social welfare programs. There were commissions that came from developing countries — Indonesia, Pakistan, the Philippines — from Britain and the Netherlands, and from many of the social welfare agencies of the United Nations. Within five years of its launching, twenty-two research grants totaling more than a million dollars had been assigned to the school. There were many satisfactions, therefore, as we began planning to award doctoral degrees to the first graduates. The record of placement for the class exceeded our expectations. Virtually all of them, even before Commencement, had confirmed posts in major communal, university, or government agencies, mostly in important policymaking roles. There was understandable gratification, too, over the complete conversion of most of those who had been ideologically opposed to the school. Dr. Lubin had become one of its most enthusiastic and influential interpreters. The long arguments that thrashed out the need for the school had never been personalized. Once the decision to proceed had been made, Dr. Lubin became a key member of the Board of Overseers and made himself available in the recruitment of students and faculty and visiting authorities, and his counsel was invaluable in developing approaches to foundations for research assignments.

By now the confidence of Florence Heller in the school had been fully validated and she was ready to make a major commitment. The negotiations with her and her attorney, Charles Aaron, a Fellow of the University, were conducted through the fall, and in December the announcement was made that she was adding a million dollars to her earlier gifts. She wrote that she hoped the endowment would cover the administrative costs of the school and such deficits as developed until enough chairs and fellowship support could be obtained to emulate the Harvard principle in its professional schools: "Every tub on its own bottom." In tribute, the board gladly named the school for Florence Heller, and decided to dedicate the 1961 Commencement to its progress.

Accordingly, invitations for honorary degrees were offered to a distinguished group of men and women who had given long years to public service and particularly to welfare projects and agencies. When all of the guests gathered for the traditional Sunday morning breakfast, the affair resembled a reunion of the stalwarts of the old Roosevelt New Deal, who had seen the country through the orderly revolution from the Hoover days of rugged individualism to the near–welfare state.

The roster was headed by Lord Beveridge, the father of modern Social Security and the author of the now-famous Beveridge report, which laid the groundwork for the British social insurance plan "from cradle to grave" and served as a model for the American system. Beveridge was joined by Thurgood Marshall, who had been chosen by the senior class to give the baccalaureate address. Marshall had earned a national reputation as the legal counsel for the National Association for the Advancement of Colored People (NAACP). It was he who had directed the great 1954 battle in *Brown* v. *Board of Education of Topeka*, which produced the unanimous decision of the Supreme Court to outlaw segregation in education "with all deliberate speed." Later he crowned his legal career when he became the first black elevated to the Supreme Court. The citation saluted both his achievement and his strategy: "The master tactician, using resourceful persistence rather than radical demagoguery, and dynamic nonviolence rather than force." The proposal to offer an honorary degree to Congressman John Fogarty of Rhode Island came from our own Dr. Sidney Farber of the Children's Cancer Foundation. He told our trustees that no one in Congress had done more than Fogarty to extend government participation in promoting medical research. As chairman of the House Subcommittee on Appropriations for HEW, he had been particularly effective in obtaining millions from the government to expand teaching facilities for retarded children and research resources to alleviate the lot of the impecunious aged.

Special prestige was added to the honorary-degree roster when we included Charles P. Taft of Cincinnati, the son of the twenty-seventh President of the United States. He had served as mayor of Cincinnati, and his record there was a model of progressive administration. *Fortune* magazine had cited him as one of the best mayors in the country, and Cincinnati, under him, as the best-governed city. He had become the first layman ever elected as president of the Federal Council of Churches. From Canada came the social welfare pioneer George Davidson. During his incumbency in the Canadian cabinet he profoundly influenced his country's policies in public welfare by shepherding to enactment an exemplary family allowance program. He represented Canada before many of the United Nations' committees responsible for health and welfare research. He offered invaluable counsel to the representatives of many underdeveloped countries that knew little of government's responsibilities for the poverty-stricken.

An old personal friend and colleague was also included among our guests of honor. Harold Case had been plucked from an active Methodist ministry for the presidency of Boston University. His vigor and imagination had not only vastly expanded the university's facilities but had reached out to serve many newly independent African countries. He and his wife, Phyllis, were virtually roving ambassadors on the African continent, and the African Research Center at Boston University, during his incumbency, won an international reputation for imaginative projects that trained leadership for the newly emerging African nations. We were glad to pay tribute also to Dr. Maurice Hexter, then in his ripe seventies, the dean of social welfare executives who later became chairman of the Florence Heller School Board of Overseers. He had been executive vice-president of the Federation of Jewish Philanthropies in New York, the world's largest and most diversified welfare fund. He was both its practical statesman and its theoretician. He had such unique ways of opening the sluices of generosity that he was a legend in his lifetime.

At a Commencement dedicated to social welfare progress we were especially pleased that we could bring in Frances Perkins, who had been the first woman cabinet member in American history, and who had served with Franklin Roosevelt while he was still governor of New York. She was at his side when he was using his state as the testing ground for the great reforms of the New Deal. She served several terms in the cabinet, right into the early years of the Truman incumbency. In her eighties, a witty, vivacious little lady, she was the perfect symbol of the progress America had made since the antediluvian days before the New Deal. At the Sunday breakfast she summarized the austere work ethic of her Yankee ancestry by telling of her ninety-five-year-old father's trip to the village cobbler to have his shoes repaired. He returned a few days later, outraged by the cobbler's workmanship, storming that he could not believe that the repaired shoes would last another ten years.

Abraham Feinberg, having served as chairman of our Board of Trustees for seven years in the period of the university's greatest physical and academic expansion, was stepping down after Commencement and thoroughly deserved the honor that was now to be extended. His business career had been one of meteoric success. His primary devotion had been to Israel, and in its wars for liberation and survival he had used his considerable influence to obtain credits and arms for the embattled country. For many years he served as chairman of the board of the Weizmann Institute and led it to its preeminence as a respected science research center.

Our Commencement speaker was Hubert Humphrey, senior senator from Minnesota, who was then serving as assistant Senate majority leader. He had long been the voice of the liberal wing of the Democratic party and had led the fight for progressive civil rights legislation in the party councils. He was a devoted friend of the University and one of its most valued and honored trustees.

During the first few years of operation, while the school was small and intimate, it was possible to operate out of the old President's House that had been inherited from the Middlesex Medical School and modestly renovated. But as the faculty expanded and research grants multiplied, it was quickly outgrown. My search for more adequate facilities began, as usual, with Forence Heller. Very little persuasion was needed. She was quite proud of the program and the reputation it had so quickly achieved, and she shared our desire to provide dignified facilities for its housing.

Meantime, a warm friendship had been developed with Stephen Mugar, an Armenian immigrant who became one of the most successful food-chain magnates of New England. He fled as a boy from the Turkish atrocities that decimated his people, and he worked his way up from a poor grocery errand boy to build the Star Market chain. He never forgot the miraculous circumstances of his escape or the role that American opportunity played in his success. On the fiftieth anniversary of his American citizenship, he climaxed his many years of exemplary philanthropy by making major gifts to eight of the less fortunately endowed colleges and universities in Greater Boston. I discussed with him our need for a home for our school of social welfare and indicated that Florence Heller was prepared to add half a million dollars to her previous gifts to help us. Mugar, too, needed little persuasion. He readily agreed to match Florence Heller's grant. But he insisted that the name of his Jewish comptroller, Benjamin Brown, who had shared the largest part of his upward struggles, be chosen for identification. The building therefore was planned in two sections, at the crest of one of the highest areas of the campus. One wing, for teaching and administration, would bear the name of Florence Heller; the other, to house the research center, was named for Benjamin Brown.

With an enlarged faculty, more adequate facilities, and the professional standing that had been achieved, the Florence Heller School accelerated its pace of service after its first Commencement. Ever more research grants were obtained. In May 1962 a new grant was assigned by the National Institutes of Mental Health, under the supervision of Herbert Aptheker, for training workers in the area of mental health. This grant enabled the school to bring in five social workers for each of two years, fully subsidized, to receive advanced graduate training in policy planning, administration, and research as applied to deviant behavior and mental illness. Aptheker had a background of fifteen years in mental health clinics on Long Island, had taught at the University of California, and had recently returned from an eighteen-month assignment in India, where he was engaged in similar problems. He left the Florence Heller School in 1969 to become dean of the School of Social Work at the University of Hawaii. It was a tragic loss for the whole social work field when he died suddenly in 1974.

In May 1963 a three-year grant from the United States Public Health Service was received to broaden still further the research program in problems of the aged. This study, under Howard Freeman, was intended to learn more about what happened to the aged who were discharged from hospitals to enter nursing homes, and it was undertaken in cooperation with the Boston College School of Nursing. The research pattern involved a thousand aged men and women who were transferred from hospitals to nursing homes in Greater Boston, and contrasted their welfare with five hundred similar individuals who returned to private homes. It was hoped that the study would not only offer valuable information on the experience in Greater Boston but would provide guidelines for more effective ways to use nursing homes within a medical care system.

A year later, in May 1964, Robert Morris joined twenty-one civic and professional leaders in a three-year study, sponsored by the American Foundation for the Blind, to devise means of improving the service programs for the 400,000 blind in the United States and to develop adequate national standards for the accreditation of the voluntary agencies.

In the same year the Department of Health, Education and Welfare assigned a grant for a two-year study, in collaboration with Harvard Medical School, to appraise the educational experience of the hospital intern. Internship had been identified as "a central time span." It marked the intern's first experience as a functioning physician, with responsibility for the care of patients. Yet this crucial experience had never been adequately evaluated. The study was placed under the direction of Howard Freeman, in association with Everett Hughes of our Sociology Department and Dr. Stephen Miller of Kansas City. Dr. Miller went to great lengths to fulfill his assignment. He donned a white medical coat and lived at the Boston City Hospital with the interns on the Harvard Teaching Service. All aspects of their training were observed and recorded: their work hours, their diagnostic ability, their therapeutic skill and managerial competence. It was hoped that the recommendations of the study would set guidelines for other professional groups that were concerned with the training of apprentices. In March 1967, within seven or eight years of the launching of the school, its reputation for research leadership in the area of aging was again recognized by a federal grant for a six-day institute on the campus to bring together the leaders and the executives in the field. It was organized and directed by Robert Binstock, who had become one of the outstanding authorities on aging. Twenty-eight state officials were invited to explore the views of ten experts, who prepared the position papers and led in their discussion. The U.S. commissioner on aging, William D. Bechill, who participated throughout, pointed up the significance of the institute. "It will help," he said, "to develop greater skill in policy analysis, translate research findings into concrete policy proposals, and deal with the complexities of local, regional, state and national organizations."

Meantime, the Florence Heller School had developed a gratifying reputation for training and research in vocational rehabilitation. In this case not only was the outstanding faculty responsible. It was also the endless cooperation of one of the overseers of the school, Mary Switzer, who had gladly joined the inner family because of her friendship with Dean Schottland. She also recognized that the school was an ideal training center for personnel in a position to take over high-level policymaking administrative positions in vocational rehabilitation. Miss Switzer was one of the most influential officials in Washington. She had been commissioner of vocational rehabilitation in the Department of HEW and supervised the expenditure of hundreds of millions of dollars. When many of the welfare programs were combined — public assistance, social services, and vocational rehabilitation — Miss Switzer became head of the overall agency. Stimulated by her interest, the school developed a training program and related research in rehabilitation. Soon there were graduates who had fully vindicated her confidence. Violet Sieder wrote a definitive handbook, and Edward Newman, who received his doctorate in 1968, later became commissioner of vocational rehabilitation services of the United States, the position created by Mary Switzer.

In the first week of January 1966, Florence Heller died. She had been fighting gallantly against cancer for many months, and near the end was prepared to meet death not as an enemy but as a friend. She had many satisfactions to review in her long career of communal service. She was especially proud of the school that now bore her name. Only six years had passed since it had been launched, and already Dean Schottland had been elected president of the International Conference of Social Welfare. Graduates were serving in major policy positions in this country and abroad and on the faculties of leading universities. And the publications of the faculty and graduates had begun to influence important areas of community life worldwide.

XVIII

Honoris Causa:
Earned and Unearned Increment

I T is a coveted distinction in American life to be honored by a university. The citations and plaques and Man or Woman of the Year awards of philanthropic and community service organizations are gratifying salutes, but they rarely carry exceptional prestige. But the honorary degree of a highly ranked university is a tribute greatly cherished in a country that has no titled nobility. Thomas Jefferson helped to set the evaluation pattern by preparing his own epitaph. He did not list the fact that he had been President of the United States, or secretary of state, or ambassador to France. He included no political or diplomatic achievements. He limited himself to but three identifications: he had written the Declaration of Independence, he was the author of the statute of religious liberty for the State of Virginia, and he had founded the University of Virginia. To have been thus identified as the founder of the university was, to him, more important than having been the President of the United States.

Unfortunately the practice of awarding honorary degrees has been too often abused. Under the pressure of overwhelming financial need, many universities have succumbed to the temptation of dangling the degree as an incentive to a wealthy patron, with the implication that some large gift will be offered in return. Some institutions have allowed their overenthusiastic public relations departments to lead them into absurd gaucheries. The University of Idaho bestowed an honorary doctorate on a New York restaurateur for "promoting better health in the world with the genuine Idaho baked potato." Charlie McCarthy, Edgar Bergen's brash and flippant dummy, was given an honorary master's degree for "the finesse that he used in the art of innuendo and snappy comeback," eliciting the comment that this was not the first time that a blockhead had received a university honor. Because the honor was often blemished by misjudgment, it was an easy butt of satire. When Mark

Twain was offered an honorary degree by Oxford, he hesitated because he had vowed that in his advancing years he would make no more transatlantic trips. But since the degree was unearned he decided that he could take as much joy in it as an Indian would in an unexpected scalp, or as anyone would who found coins that were not his. He now had three honorary degrees, all unearned: two from Yale and one from the University of Missouri. "It pleased me beyond measure," he wrote,

> when Yale made me a Master of Arts because I didn't know anything about art. I had another convulsion of pleasure when Yale made me a Doctor of Literature because I was not competent to doctor anybody's literature but my own, and I couldn't even keep my own in a healthy condition without my wife's help. I rejoiced again when Missouri University made me a Doctor of Laws, because it was all clear profit, I not knowing anything about laws except how to evade them and not get caught.

Brandeis tried from the outset to emulate the impeccable standards of its elite neighbors. The screening of recommendations for honorary degrees always called for long and careful consideration. It did not, of course, exclude men and women whose munificence helped to fulfill the University's long-range objectives, but, to qualify, such service to the University had to be part of more generalized philanthropy or public service in the tradition of highest citizenship. Lawrence Wien, chairman of the Board of Trustees, contributed many millions to Brandeis, but, beyond Brandeis, he headed the Jewish Federation of Philanthropies of New York; he led the Columbia Alumni Association to its most productive year of university support; he was in the forefront of the campaigns for Lincoln Center and the Institute for International Education. A national magazine listed him as one of the three men who had most influenced the economic life of New York City. His honorary degree from Brandeis was followed by similar honors from his own alma mater.

Robert Benjamin, vice-chairman of the Board of Trustees, was exemplary in his philanthropic contributions to Brandeis, but his career in public service matched his professional success, both as a distinguished lawyer and as chairman of the board of United Artists. He served successively as senior adviser to the United States Mission to the United Nations and as ambassador-designate to the Twenty-second United Nations General Assembly. He succeeded Eleanor Roosevelt as chairman of the American Association for the United Nations, Chief Justice Earl Warren as chairman of the United Nations Association, and Adlai Stevenson as chairman of the Eleanor Roosevelt Memorial Foundation.

So it was clear from the outset that while our young university, with no influential alumni and with virtually no endowment, very appropriately expressed appreciation to donors who made its academic reputation possible, the honorary degree itself was a tribute that had to be reserved for more than simply a major financial gift to Brandeis. Therefore the roster of the first generation is a proud one, and the meticulousness with which the degrees were assigned induced acceptance by the elect. It included two presidents, Harry S Truman and John F. Kennedy; such notable judicial figures as Chief Justice Earl Warren, Justices Felix Frankfurter, Thurgood Marshall, and Arthur Goldberg; foreign statesmen Pierre Mendès-France, David Ben-Gurion, Golda Meir, General Yitzhak Rabin, Lord Beveridge, and Madame Pandit; and some of the world's most distinguished scientists, scholars, and creative artists: Marian Anderson, Leonard Bernstein, Jacques Lipschitz, Marc Chagall, Helen Hayes, Louis Ginsberg, Harry A. Wolfson, Theodore Hesburgh, Alfred A. Knopf, Gunnar Myrdal, Edward R. Murrow, Jean Piaget, and Leo Szilard.

Quite early the procedure was established of linking the honorary degrees of Commencement with a theme. Also, when singular programs were inaugurated or valuable facilities were dedicated, the occasions were dramatized further by awarding honorary degrees to illustrious representatives of these fields.

Nineteen fifty-six marked the hundredth anniversary of the birth of Justice Brandeis, and commemorative exercises were planned in many parts of the country and in Israel. It was natural for the University bearing his name to provide leadership in the tribute offerings. Surely no one would consider it presumptuous to celebrate a centennial in the eighth year of the University, for a rather impressive achievement had been telescoped into less than a decade. So the University offered honorary degrees to leaders in American life who were associated in some meaningful way with the career of the justice: federal Judge Calvert Magruder, his first law clerk; Dean Acheson, former secretary of state and another of Brandeis's law clerks; Felix Frankfurter of the Supreme Court, who cooperated with Brandeis in drafting and obtaining Woodrow Wilson's support for the Balfour Declaration; Erwin Griswold, dean of Harvard Law School, where Brandeis had compiled his superlative academic record; Judge Charles E. Wyzanski, Jr., chairman of the Board of Overseers of Harvard; Robert Szold, president of the Palestine Economic Corporation, which had been created by Justice Brandeis to help place Palestine on a firm economic base; Irving Dilliard, editor of the *St. Louis Post-Dispatch* and the interpreter of Justice Brandeis's liberal tradition.

It was at this birthday weekend that we began a tradition of informality that made it possible for our honorary degree recipients to be seen and heard away from the more stylized protocol of Commencement. Since the exercises initially were held on Sunday afternoons, we usually preceded them with an informal brunch at the President's House. The large grounds permitted our inviting the inner family of trustees and Fellows and several hundred friends of the University. Just before we sat down, Thelma whispered to me that it might be a refreshing experience to call on each of the honored guests to speak, not too seriously, for a few minutes. Men of the caliber of Dean Acheson, Felix Frankfurter, and Charles Wyzanski, who were justly noted as brilliant conversationalists, assuredly needed no preparation. Their display of wit, each taking his cue from what the others had said, was offered with gay spontaneity and proved sheer delight. The practice was followed during the next few years; it was continued even when the number of guests outgrew the facilities of the President's House and the brunch had to be transferred to the campus, where it was held under a huge tent. In time even the tent on the campus could no longer accommodate all who clamored for invitations, and regretfully the affair was shifted to Saturday night, into the banquet halls of Boston hotels. After my incumbency, the change in locale and the more structured program ultimately transformed the character of the function. But in the dozen and more years when it was unplanned, it was remembered as "a keen encounter of our wits." At one of the later functions Pierre Mendès-France said, in mock terror, "*Mon Dieu,* bantering can be a very serious business!"

The centennial events continued into the fall and were climaxed by a convocation on Justice Brandeis's natal day itself, in mid-November. To signal the centennial, Congress approved the striking of a medallion by the United States Mint. Lawrence Wien had offered to commission a statue of the justice, which would be mounted on a knoll in the very heart of the campus. He had been very much impressed with the work of a young sculptor, Robert Berks, who was given the commission. Within the year he created a statue that symbolized the courageous dissenter defying the forces of precedent and tradition. In the summer of 1956 I flew down to Washington to invite Chief Justice Earl Warren to come to the campus for the special convocation at which the statue would be dedicated. Justice Warren was the soul of courtesy and cooperation and he readily agreed. Warren ranked Brandeis with Oliver Wendell Holmes as the two most creative members of the twentieth-century Court. During our interview he provided a fascinating footnote. He recalled that when he was named Chief Justice in 1953 by President Eisenhower, he learned, to his surprised dismay, that Oliver Wendell Holmes's bequest of his estate to the government of the United States had been transferred to the treasury and it was on deposit there, apparently unremembered and unused. Justice Holmes had not been a very wealthy man, as wealth was judged in his generation, but the bequest came to about $300,000, which represented his lifetime savings and investments. The Holmeses were a childless couple, and the justice willed the entire estate to his country as a tribute for the opportunities it opened to all free men. Eighteen years had now passed and the bequest had still not been designated for service.

As Warren recalled the unconcern of the officials in charge, all of his original indignation welled up. He had set up an immediate appointment with President Eisenhower, to whom he expressed his chagrin and disappointment that the memory of one of America's titanic legal figures, who had willed his estate to his countrymen, had been so abominably neglected. Eisenhower, too, had not known about the bequest and he acted at once. An advisory committee, including Justice Warren, determined to convert the Holmes bequest into a memorial trust fund that would sponsor a history of the Supreme Court. Paul Freund of Harvard Law School was named as editor-in-chief and, under his scholarly guidance, the multivolume history was launched. Warren concluded by referring sadly to the resigned judgment of Francis Bacon: "Fame is like a river that beareth up things light and swollen, and drowns things weighty and solid." He added, "We so often have short memories when we deal with nonpolitical figures who shun the limelight. But *your* people never forget. Brandeis has been gone only a few years and there are creative remembrances of him in this country, in Israel, and in many other parts of the world. And you already have a great university named for him."

The convocation was held on November 8, 1956. We had no facility large enough to accommodate the huge assemblage that gathered, and decided to risk an open-air ceremony. It turned out to be so cold that it was necessary to distribute several thousand blankets for the crowd that shivered on the hill where the statue stood. But the presence of the Chief Justice, his moving address, the spirit of the occasion itself — all provided the warmth that the inhospitable weather denied. No one present would forget the testament of faith that Chief Justice Warren uttered at a time when nuclear threat had created a paralyzing mood of despair: "If he were alive today Brandeis would act according to the belief that over the long haul, universities such as this would have more power than the H bomb, and that disciplined minds will eventually have more penetrating effect than guided missiles."

When we invited President Truman to participate in our Commencement of 1957, we were delighted that he decided to attend an informal tribute dinner the night before, although, since he was to deliver the Commencement address, he asked to be excused from also speaking at the dinner. I had been scheduled to summarize the University's progress, but I hoped the President would take my place on the program and would join the other honorary degree recipients in the traditional off-the-cuff remarks. I drew upon a Talmudic legend to explain our presumption. I noted that Adam had been allotted a thousand years of life, but he had prophetic foresight and knew that in later generations David would be stillborn. He therefore pleaded with God to assign seventy of his years to David so that the historic work needed to establish the first Jewish state could be fulfilled. After all, he would still have nine hundred and thirty years in reserve! In the same spirit I suggested that throughout the school year I had endless opportunities to exaggerate our achievements before Brandeis audiences. Hence there was no sacrifice in assigning my part in the program to President Truman for what I was sure would be a memorable addition to the evening.

It was. Truman was at his homespun best. He confided that his daughter, Margaret, had reminded him that she had spent long, taxing years to earn her college degree, and here was her father, without even a college education, being awarded a doctorate. How could she go on believing in the American principle of hard work and fair play! Turning serious, he paid a glowing tribute to one of the most faithful aides of his first administration, our own trustee, the late David Niles. Noting that Brandeis was a very young school, functioning in the midst of some of the world's most distinguished universities, he counseled ambitious planning, prosecuted with confidence and self-reliance. "Don't get bogged down," he asserted, "by petty objectives. They have a way of muffling and stifling major achievement." It was stirring advice for a nine-year-old university where every venture was a battle between audacity and prudence.

After Commencement we sent several Brandeis T-shirts to Truman's grandsons. A few years later, on a mission in Israel, Thelma and I spent an evening with Margaret's husband, Clifton Daniel, who was covering some assignments in the Middle East for the *New York Times*, where he headed the Washington Bureau. He told us that the shirts had been worn to tatters by the children until they had outgrown them. We took delight in conjuring up the spectacle of the grandchildren of a former President, cavorting about in well-used Brandeis T-shirts.

Another special guest of honor at the 1957 Commencement was Arthur Compton, a Nobel laureate in physics at the age of thirty-five, whose scientific genius had helped win the race against the Nazis in developing the atomic bomb. There was a sentimental satisfaction in his participation, for when I was inducted as president nine years before, he had been chancellor of Washington University, my alma mater. Compton had had a commitment in St. Louis the night before, but he had flown through the night so that he could be the speaker at the inaugural ceremonies the next morning at Symphony Hall in Boston. At the Commencement brunch Thelma commented on what seemed to have become a family tradition: two of Compton's brothers were also college presidents, one of Massachusetts Institute of Technology, the other of the University of Washington. She wondered whether there were enough satisfactions to compensate for the inevitable frustrations. Dr.

Compton chuckled and noted also that his sister was married to the president of Berea College in Kentucky. So all four of the Compton children had gone the route! He left Thelma's question unanswered, but noted that he went back to scientific research much before the retirement age of college presidents.

The Commencement weekend of 1959 brought as impressive a roster of distinction as any university could muster: Leonard Bernstein; Pierre Mendès-France; Fritz Lipmann, the Nobel laureate in biochemistry; General Yigael Yadin of Israel; Ernest Gruening, governor of the territory of Alaska and its undeterred advocate for admission as a state, then its first senator; General Alfred Gruenther, chief of staff in World War II, commander in chief of the North Atlantic Treaty Organization (NATO), and president of the American Red Cross; Jacques Lipschitz, the sculptor; Julius Stratton, president of MIT, who prepared engineers for unprecedented tasks in World War II with his pioneering volumes on electromagnetic radiation and electronics; and Edward R. Murrow, whose broadcasts from besieged Britain during the darkest days of World War II bound the democratic people together in a communion of faith.

During the weekend Lipschitz, enamored with the intellectual ferment of the campus, offered to transfer the models of all of his sculpture to Brandeis if we could house them permanently, as the Rodin masterpieces were housed in Paris. Unfortunately the University, at this stage, could not command the resources to undertake a commitment that would overwhelm even the best-endowed institutions. But it was a touching and flattering offer. At the Commencement breakfast Murrow revealed that, blessed with such a resonant voice, he had been initially destined by his parents for the clergy, but he was certain that, with his views, he would quickly have been unfrocked. I comforted him by commenting that he had really been in no danger, since he was obviously unsuited.

Our most gratifying achievement was the complete conquest of Mendès-France. He was sufficiently impressed with the University to accept our invitation to return in the next school year for a series of lectures on contemporary Europe. He also agreed to accompany me to some of the major U.S. cities to serve as guest of honor at our interpretive functions. His lectures attracted both a popular audience and leading academic and government figures throughout the area. It was a measure of the deep interest in him and his views that McGeorge Bundy, later a defense policy adviser for Presidents Kennedy and Johnson, sat in the seminar, taking notes.

During one of our flights Mendès-France detailed an experience that pointed up how difficult it was for Jews to shake off the onus of alienism, no matter where they lived, even in the advanced countries of the western world. In 1954, as premier of France, he had succeeded in extricating his country from the quagmire of blood in Indochina and, afterward, in Tunis and Morocco. He would have carried out similar settlements in Algeria, where the costly colonial wars had begun to threaten the social fabric of France itself, but he was thwarted by the opposition of De Gaulle, who later, as premier, went far beyond the concessions that Mendès-France had been willing to make in the interest of peace. One of his closest friends in the Chamber of Deputies said to him, after the settlements in Asia and Africa, "It was fortunate for France, Pierre, that *you* were the premier when the amputation of French territory had become inevitable! A *real* Frenchman could never have gone through with it." Apparently the comment was meant kindly. Mendès-France's family had lived in France for more than six centuries; it had produced personalities of great capacity in every generation; but it was neither peasant in ancestral stock, nor Gallic, nor Catholic, and it was difficult, therefore, for it to be accepted as "genuinely" French.

Another of his experiences touched a lighter note. When France fell to the Nazis in 1940, Mendès-France fled with other Resistance leaders to North Africa, where he was captured and imprisoned by the Vichy leadership. He managed a dramatic hacksaw-bedsheet escape, dropping from his window to a ledge about ten feet from the ground. However, he had to remain hidden on the ledge because, on the grass below, a young couple was going through the preliminaries of a romantic consummation. But the girl kept resisting the final stage and the persuading process dragged out for what seemed an eternity. Mendès-France said that he had never prayed as hard for a girl to lose her virtue. At last the girl succeeded in giving the boy his triumph, the couple departed, and Mendès-France made his escape to England, where he joined De Gaulle and flew bombing missions in the Free French air force until the Nazis were driven out of France. When I published *The Course of Our Times*, I omitted this episode, believing that it was meant as a confidence. I was delighted when Mendès-France later told the full story in a documentary film, *The Sorrow and the Pity*.

Nineteen sixty represented the fifteenth anniversary of the founding of the United Nations, and the Commencement weekend was planned as an appraisal of efforts to achieve broader international understanding. The honorary degree guests were mainly men and women whose careers had been identified with the search for peace. One of them, Marian Anderson, stayed on for the sessions of the National Women's Committee. It had not been too many years since the Daughters of the American Revolution had denied her access to a concert in Constitution Hall in Washington because she was a black. Her address, given in a rich gentle voice without a note of rancor or resentment for all the tribulations she had suffered, made this one of the most moving experiences for the delegates.

I felt a strong kinship with another guest, Joseph Schwartz, who had launched upon a promising career as a scholar and educator and then, in Israel's recurrent crises, became the fund-raising strategist for the Joint Distribution Committee, the United Jewish Appeal, and Bonds for Israel. He could not accept the offer to become president of the Hebrew University when he was persuaded that the overwhelming financial needs of Israel had more urgent claims upon his talents. The scholar had proved he could also be a superb administrator and a most effective interpreter of causes that called for sacrificial compassion. But as we renewed our old friendship, I sensed the wistful note of regret that he could not have stayed with scholarship and its more serene life-style. He should only have known!

Ralph Bunche was also one of our guests, and his presence recalled our frustration when he came for our first convocation in 1949. We then went through a whole series of embarrassments in reserving hotel accommodations for him. Those were days when a southern governor stood in a school doorway to prevent the entrance of black children. Bunche had just been awarded the Nobel Peace Prize, but when the reservation was sought for a suite in one of Boston's hotels, the assistant manager, horrified by the prospect of a black in his elite establishment, reluctantly agreed to make the reservation on condition that Bunche take his meals in his room. Bunche was to be widely entertained, so there was no problem about his meals. It was with satisfaction that our public affairs officer told the assistant manager to go to hell. A little more than a decade had passed, and Bunche could speak with restrained satisfaction of the interracial progress that had been made. But in his luncheon remarks, his banter was still interlaced with more than a touch of melancholy. He related some early experiences of discrimination when he was a student at the University of California. He became much more acceptable there when he demonstrated expertise on the football field. As he ran toward the goal with the ball, the cheering was almost as deafening as if he had been white, "and the faster I ran, the whiter I got."

It was especially gratifying to welcome Marc Chagall, who came with his wife, Vava, and remained for nearly a week. They apparently loved their stay, identifying with the students, with whom they spent a great deal of time. I have very vivid memories of the scene where Chagall, sitting on the floor with his young admirers, answered their eager questions, his reminiscences and observations flowing with uninhibited enthusiasm. He hit it off well when he told them, "When I was young I wanted to learn from older men. Now I only want to learn from the young." At an informal dinner party at the President's House, we showed him one of his own early sketches of his father's grave. Nearly seventy years had passed since it was done and he had not remembered it. When he saw it he wept, and then added that the sketch represented the only peace his father had ever known in his wretched surroundings.

Chagall was intrigued by our plans for the Goldfarb Library and the magnificent wall that was to be a part of it. What a perfect setting, he said, for an all-encompassing mural! Then, with impetuous enthusiasm, he promised that as a gift he would come back to do such a mural, a study of the Creation itself! We were exultant. But when Chagall returned to France and other substantial commissions arrived, his business-minded wife kept postponing the fulfillment of the promise until it faded as a reality. I remember one of Vava's letters, which began with the gloomy announcement that her husband had slipped on some ice and therefore could not proceed just then with his design. I was genuinely concerned, of course, and not for some weeks did I wonder where Chagall had found the ice to slip on in the South of France in spring! However, we had no claim on Chagall and were grateful for the heart-warming experiences that were ours, shared so fully by the student body. But a mural of the Creation on the main library wall by Chagall — ah!

In the fall of 1963 we celebrated the fifteenth anniversary of the founding of Brandeis with a special convocation. It was one of the last public affairs for more than a decade that was planned with little or no anxiety about turbulence and disruption. Kennedy was still in the White House, dreaming his dreams of Camelot. Pope John XXIII was in the Vatican, astonishing the world by a refreshing ecumenism. Colonialism was being challenged ever more successfully, and peoples in Africa and Asia who had suffered for centuries were now tasting the first fruits of independence. It was a period, all too brief as it turned out, when young people could get off the mourner's bench and believe again that they had some control over their fate.

Hence, it was appropriate at such a time to link the theme of our convocation to the prophetic injunction "to seek peace and to pursue it." This brought us an impressive group of honorary degree recipients, including the president of the United Nations, Madame Pandit, and Dr. Hastings Banda, prime minister of newly liberated Nyasaland. We were privileged to receive Dr. George Beadle, the recently named president of the University of Chicago who had won a Nobel Prize for his trail-blazing research in biomedical genetics, and another distinguished Chi-cagoan, Newton Minow, the youthful chairman of the Federal Com-munications Commission. Minow had early recognized the power of the sleeping giant that was television. As chairman of the commission, he challenged the "wasteland" that he had found, and he labored endlessly to improve its standards. There was Ralph McGill, the fighting editor of the *Atlanta Constitution;* John Kenneth Galbraith, the iconoclastic Har-vard economist, just back from his service as ambassador to India; and Father Michael Walsh, president of Boston College, the vigorous and courageous promoter of Pope John's ecumenical policies in this country. We also welcomed the opportunity to salute the memory of Justice

Brandeis through his daughter, Susan, who had always been one of the University's most enthusiastic emissaries, and Jack Goldfarb, one of our own trustees whose generosity had made our library possible.

The preconvocation banquet was a fascinating evening. Banda described how, as a boy, full of ambition that could never be fulfilled in his homeland, he had walked a thousand miles from Nyasaland to South Africa to earn an education. Afterward he confided to me, with what I can only term a kind of pleasant malice, that the story was sheer fiction and was told to dramatize what obstacles had to be overcome in his early days because of the tyranny of the white overlords! His confession was offered so artlessly that I could not be upset that he had tarnished our record for accuracy in our citations. For it was now too late to change the reference to that long trek, whose description we had dug out of his autobiography and incorporated in the printed citation.

Galbraith, whose wit was always sharp, was at his best and, for our audience at least, he swept away Carlyle's canard that economics was "the dismal science." Father Walsh, deadpan, took the audience into his confidence by telling of the problems that the iconoclasm of Pope John XXIII was creating. He related the dilemma of the village priest who received a present from one of his parishioners, six towels designated "His" and six more designated "Hers." What was the poor priest to do with them? He was advised to hold onto them: "With this Pope in the Vatican you can never tell what he is likely to decree next." Susan Brandeis told some stories about her father's consideration and sensitivity. What she did not know as she spoke, but what revalidated how consideration ran in the family, was that this very weekend had originally been chosen by her daughter Alice and her fiancé for their wedding. The young couple agreed in camera that the marriage date must be postponed so that the convocation day could be Alice's mother's own.

Sunday morning dawned bright and clear but, for October, it was unusually warm. We were concerned about the comfort of the audience, outdoors in the Ullman Amphitheater. Banda and Madame Pandit were the featured speakers. Banda used the occasion to discuss the overwhelming problems that came with freedom after a people had been obliged to live, for centuries, shackled by ignorance and disease and poverty. He, to be sure, had been personally fortunate, having won scholarship support to study medicine in the United States and to practice in Britain among the African émigrés in Glasgow before returning to his homeland. But there were less than ten college graduates in his entire country when its colonial status had ended. He hoped that the friends of independence for the African peoples would not be discouraged by the travail, often violent and disruptive, through which Africans would have to pass before they could learn how to use their freedom with dignity and discipline. It was easy to forgive Banda for going beyond his allotted ten minutes; his was a difficult theme to compress. But as the ten minutes grew to twenty, and then to thirty and more in the mounting heat of the morning, two clearly marked lines of indignation deepened on the beautiful brow of Madame Pandit, who was usually the essence of personal charm and grace.

Her felicitously phrased speech had been carefully prepared, but it now had to be severely abbreviated, and when she was finally called upon, the gauzy end of her sari snapped like a starched cat's tail. But once she began speaking she calmed down, and her plea for a better understanding of India's determination to remain a liberal democracy left a deep impression, not least on Kenneth Galbraith. Later, as I walked back with her to our luncheon, I asked her how India, which she had described as very close in spirit to the United States, permitted Krishna Menon, as foreign minister, to show so openly his violent anti-American bias. By now Madame Pandit was smiling again, and she replied mischievously that Krishna Menon was the Indian John Foster Dulles. When I recalled the sanctimonious pontification of the late secretary of state, who had earned the reputation of a "card-carrying Christian," I had to admire Madame Pandit's apt Roland for an Oliver.

The hooding went smoothly until we called Galbraith to the lectern. I had considerable trouble getting the hood over his shoulders, for he towered nearly seven feet tall. He recognized my problem and his bow to me, to bring his shoulders down to my level, must have been deeper than the one he offered when he presented his ambassador's credentials in New Delhi.

We had special citations for the two college presidents, who were men of rare scholarly distinction as well as highly successful educational administrators. Beadle had spent a lifetime probing the mysteries of life and their infinite mutability. Our citation wondered whether from such research as his might not come the answer to the question of Emerson: "How shall a man escape from his ancestors?" Father Walsh had also come to the presidency of his college from the biology laboratories. The night before he had bantered about Pope John's religious flexibility. The citation stressed the serious side of his contribution and noted that "he dissects enigmas of heredity as skillfully as he synthesizes the humanist heritage of his faith, thus wedding Loyola's zeal to Lacordiare's heart of fire for charity."

While all the degree recipients were enthusiastically received, perhaps the most heartwarming ovation was reserved for Jacob Goldfarb. He had demonstrated in his own experience how wealth could be used to make a career of enlightened philanthropy. The library that he gave to Brandeis was only one of his endless gifts to causes that touched his heart. His citation read: "Himself deprived of formal education, his school is equated with his breadth of heart, his college with his open hand." When he stood to be hooded I was reading the citation, and therefore could not see the tears trickling down his face. But the audience could, and they not only offered tremendous applause but cheered without restraint. After the ceremonies, a new member of the economics faculty, as brash as she was brilliant — and by no means reticent in her acidulous appraisal of administrations as the vassals of big business — stupified a member of the staff by remarking, "Mr. Goldfarb is wonderful. You tell the administration to give honorary degrees to more people like him."

The Commencement of 1964 was intended as a tribute to international leaders in education, religion, the arts, and medicine. We approached it with a measure of dread, for the national climate was beginning to heat up for the great confrontations that demoralized almost every aspect of American life and, above all, the universities. We could hardly expect that our Saturday night session would sparkle with its usual gaiety. But halfway through the evening the mood changed, due to the arrival of the irrepressible Cardinal Cushing.

The cardinal was an extraordinary character, and I use the noun advisedly. He had already undergone treatment for cancer, and emphysema was beginning to make inroads on that longshoreman's voice of his. He was very much outside the pattern of the prelates who had been assigned to New England. Indeed, he fitted no one's preconception of a Catholic prelate. As Phyllis McGinley wrote of Simon Stylites, "I think he puzzled the good Lord, rather." He prided himself on coming up from the poorest neighborhood: "I am not lace-curtain Irish," he would say, "and I am not comfortable with them." He was easily accessible, with a wry sense of humor, and his public-speaking style was a startling melange of primitive English filtered through an accent that carried no connotation of a prince of the church. He took delight in baiting the families that had painfully mastered the New England Brahmin vocabulary. He was close in spirit to Pope John XXIII and shared his iconoclasm. With a twinkle in his eye he used to say that "Pope John is the only pope who really understands me." He was a genius at fund-raising for Catholic education and welfare projects. Who could forget Cardinal Cushing's contribution at the ecumenical council, Vatican II, during the debate to remove the ancient canard of Jewish guilt for the Crucifixion. No scholar, which he freedly admitted, his prepared remarks had been translated into Latin, but in the midst of his plea he abandoned the formal statement and lapsed into his own South Boston Irish-English. The "bishops near the door," which is to say the younger prelates present, burst into spontaneous and prolonged applause. I remembered also how he used to twit me about our bizarre adventures in the tasks of philanthropic mendicancy. "Dr. Abe," he teased, "why don't you turn Catholic and then the two of us can conquer the world."

When he was invited for the Commencement tribute affair, he alerted us that he could stay only for a moment. A long evening had been prohibited by his physician: "I must be home by ten." We told him that he could come after the dinner, that he would be called upon early, and that it was our tradition for the speakers to limit themselves to five or ten minutes. He arrived when the program was under way and, when called upon, launched on a lively biographical odyssey, with comments about his sister who had married a "wonderful, considerate Jewish businessman who, like all Jews, knew how to cherish a wife." It was a tragedy, he said, that Lou had died so early, and he only hoped that his sister would be fortunate enough to marry another Jew! He mocked the Catholic establishment and its sonorous ecclesiastical rhetoric. He wandered all over Jewish history and showed remarkable knowledge of Jewish problems. He spoke for an hour and a quarter and had the audience howling with laughter throughout. When he concluded, fresher than when he had started, he looked at his watch and exclaimed in mock horror: "I thought you had promised me a short evening."

We worried a good deal about what would happen at the exercises the next morning, not only because the weather had been threatening, but because scores of recent commencements had been quickly taken over by militants who turned the exercises into pandemonium. We were greatly relieved that, though the student speaker outdid himself in vituperative indignation, the graduates, many of them restless and sullen, stayed well within the limits of civility. Perhaps it was the choice of honorary-degree recipients, whose statesmanship and compassion could not be questioned by even the most rebellious, that turned what might have been mutinous bedlam into an impressive occasion. Even Clark Kerr was received with respect, though as president of the "multiversity" in California he later received some of the roughest treatment that any college head had endured.

The honorary-degree list included Dr. George Packer Berry, the retiring dean of Harvard Medical School. When I came into the robing room for the processional lineup, he was looking about almost distractedly, intent above all to meet Helen Hayes. "My daughter," he said, to explain his search, "went to school with her." I marveled at the agility of the man who had recently undergone a drastic spinal operation; as a young medical researcher he had worked with psittacosis, parrot fever, and his dangerous research had ultimately affected the tissues of his spinal column. He had come to accept our degree trussed up in a painful steel brace. But he insisted upon marching with the others.

Then there was General Yaacov Dori, president of Technion in Israel, who was rapidly converting the young, unendowed school into a world-famous technological center. The versatility of the man, diminutive in size, shy, and quiet-spoken, was demonstrated during the blitz Suez War of 1956, when the schoolmaster carried out his duties as chief of staff for the Israeli forces and won the war that astounded the military world.

And I rejoiced in the opportunity to convey the University's tribute to one of my oldest friends, Maurice Samuel. In an astonishing succession of more than twenty volumes he had literally resurrected the old European Jewish world, now virtually extinct after the obscene horror of the Holocaust.

Then there was lovely Helen Hayes, who already had had her enchanting reunion with Dean Berry. In her citation I alluded to the very first remark ever made to her by her adoring Charles MacArthur, when he passed her a handful of peanuts, saying, "I wish they were emeralds." Miss Hayes's eyes were suspiciously moist at that stage in the reading. After the hooding, I had just finished congratulating her when, to the surprise of everyone, Miss Hayes, who was by no means an ingenue, turned and gracefully knelt to kiss Cardinal Cushing's ring. She had, however, to wait a moment or two for the completely dumbfounded cardinal to extricate his hand out of his voluminous robes. It was an old-fashioned reverence, and undoubtedly a memorable moment for the cardinal and the actress.

Our list also included Leo Sharfman, the Michigan economist and a longtime Brandeis trustee, chairman of its academic policy committee. In his late years, rarely well, he not only flew in for trustees' meetings but undertook the thankless task of reasoning with dissident student leaders. I will risk the cliché to say that it was an education to watch Leo Sharfman dealing graciously but trenchantly with youngsters who could well have been his grandchildren.

There was a special sentimental gratification for me because the Commencement speaker was James "Scotty" Reston, perhaps the ablest of my students at Illinois, who had now risen to the highest editorial position at the New York Times. None of us realized to what lengths Reston had gone to join us on that June Sunday. One of his sons had been graduated from college in the Washington area only the day before, and our public relations people had the curious experience of watching a world-famous newsman finishing his Commencement address in one of their offices, using the only manual typewriter to be found in the building. Because his wife wished to stay on in Washington for the remainder of their son's festivities, Scotty brought his mother, a lively little lady who must have been in her eighties, whose Scots burr was a joy to hear. In drawing on material for the Reston citation, I was struck by the frequency of his allusions to the Scottish Presbyterian catechism, especially on the "chief end of man." We included the quotation, and to my delight Reston began his own address with the very words. He made no attempt to evade, with the platitudes of conventional Commencement oratory, the problems that sorely troubled young people. He told the graduates bluntly that he had no intention of suggesting that they, in their wisdom, take over the world. His generation, with all its mistakes, had not managed badly. By and large, the American democratic system had proved itself; it had managed two world wars and a major depression and the evils of McCarthyism without sacrificing its heritage of freedom. He urged the students to stop feeling sorry for themselves, to get off their buttocks (it was not yet fashionable to refer more familiarly to such parts of the anatomy), and to do their part to change what they found to be wrong.

A final scene remains etched in my memory of that extraordinary day. Ralph Norman, the Brandeis school photographer, noticed a very tired Cardinal Cushing leaning against a fence at the edge of the Commencement platform. His cardinal's robe outshone everything else in splendor, but with his usual informality, the stunning red watered-silk cape was wrapped around his arm like a dish towel. Norman had an assistant, Shusheela, a Brandeis Wien student, a tiny slip of a girl whose father was minister of education in one of the larger Indian provinces. Norman came up to the cardinal with Shusheela and said, "Your Eminence, this young lady is scheduled to return home to India, and may she take a picture with you so she can have a precious souvenir of this day?" The Cardinal acquiesced, but, looking down at Shusheela, whose long black hair had blown all out of place, remarked, "My mother said I should never go out without a comb," and reaching into some mysterious pocket in his robes, he produced a comb and proceeded gently to rearrange Shusheela's windblown locks. Norman sneaked in a picture of the scene. I have always believed that Shusheela treasured it more than the formal one that was published in her hometown newspaper.

The summer of 1964 also brought us to the twentieth anniversary of one of the most moving experiences in modern history, the secret removal to Sweden of the approximately 7,000 Danish Jews through the intercession of King Christian of Denmark. They were marked as certain victims of Hitler's extermination camps after the Nazi occupation of Denmark. The dangerous evacuation, with the cooperation of the Norwegian underground, and the compassionate spirit behind it, was one of the few heartening episodes of the Holocaust.

We had long dreamed of paying tribute to the royal family and people of Denmark, who, almost alone of the European nations, acted in unison to save their Jewish communities from the Nazis. Before our 1964 Commencement we approached, through proper diplomatic channels, the reigning monarch, King Frederick IX, the son of Christian X. The appreciative reply of the Danish embassy indicated a quandary. In general, royalty do not accept honorary degrees. In this case the king may have been persuaded to make an exception, although he believed the tribute belonged to his people. But his younger daughter had been betrothed to Prince Constantine of Greece, and the wedding date fell during the weekend of the Brandeis Commencement. However, an alternative was tentatively proposed. A national society of Danes and

Danish-Americans held an annual festival in Rebild, in the northern province of Jutland, every Fourth of July. The American Independence Day had assumed the status of a Danish national holiday, and the royal family often attended the ceremonies in Jutland. Word came to us that, were it convenient, the king would be pleased to accept the Brandeis tribute on that day on the hillside where the celebration was always held. We were elated.

Obviously we could not "hood" King Frederick. This would have been difficult in any case, even on a Brandeis platform, for the king was one of the tallest of his subjects, an authentic Viking! We wrestled with the problem of how to express our tribute. Fortunately, we had on hand a few of the gold medals struck by the United States Mint on the occasion of Justice Brandeis's centennial. One of these, along with the University's citation, in an artistically designed presentation case, went along with Thelma's and my luggage on the mission to Denmark.

July 4, 1964, was a beautiful day. Denmark itself looked as if it had been delivered, at great expense, straight from F. A. O. Schwartz's toy emporium, although we well understood that the lush countryside belied the toughness of its inhabitants. There were tens of thousands of celebrants on the hillside in Rebild, when King Frederick received and acknowledged the University's tribute. Later the king directed that the medal and the citation be prominently displayed in the window of an elegant Copenhagen shop. I always hoped that a good many of the nurses and doctors, postmen and policemen, clergymen, booksellers, and taxi drivers would stop for a moment to read the salute to a gallant people:

> Ours is a young university, named for Louis Dembitz Brandeis, distinguished American jurist, himself the son of refugees. We humbly claim kinship with a people whose tradition of sovereignty is 900 years old, whose respect for individual liberty was codified in 1814, whose cities have never known the shadow of a ghetto, and whose bright islands and pleasant pastures are truly "the land of the free and the home of the brave!"

By 1966 the universities of the country — and, for that matter, of most European countries — were in the throes of disruption. The militants among the students, abetted by many of the faculty, were apparently determined to effect radical changes in university governance or to bring down the institutions themselves. Brandeis was comparatively quiet in comparison to the physical and administrative havoc that other schools suffered. All the same, a Commencement program was an ideal opportunity to obtain visibility for protest. As we planned the 1966 Commencement, therefore, we knew there would be attempts at disruption, but we hoped that the bizarre dress of the dissidents, to show their contempt for all such proceedings, the language of the posters, the displays themselves, could be kept to reasonable limits. We had established the tradition that the Commencement program would include a student speaker, chosen by the seniors themselves. We made no attempt to censor what the student would say, but in discussing procedures we made the point that the occasion was not a political rally, that parents and other relatives had waited many anxious years to see their children graduate, and that to upset the dignity of Commencement to protest conditions over which the University as such had no control would be very much like carrying on a political rally at a wedding ceremony. Perhaps this reasoning had some slight influence in holding the exercises within bounds. But it did not prevent the student speaker from berating the older generation, the officials in Washington— indeed, all administration officials, including those at Brandeis — for him they were all part of the recreant establishment. It was fortunate that the honorary-degree recipients on this occasion were all unaffiliated with these controversial issues.

The one possibly vulnerable figure was Arthur Goldberg, the Commencement speaker. His rise in American life had been spectacular: from a poor boy in Chicago to the head of the legal staff for the United Steel Workers, secretary of labor for President Kennedy, and a justice of the Supreme Court of the United States. He was now the head of the American delegation at the United Nations. There was the rub. It would not have mattered what his political or governmental affiliation had been. The fact that he represented the United States and was a spokesman for American foreign policy in Vietnam made him a natural target, and the militants had planned carefully to put the bead on him. To take some of the danger of disruption out of the exercises, I suggested to the leaders among the graduates that it might be useful to invite Goldberg to meet with the senior class at an early breakfast, just before the ceremonies. There they would have the opportunity to question him fully, instead of being obliged to sit as a captive audience, as most Commencement audiences do. The young people were impressed, and I at once called Justice Goldberg to give him the background of our dilemma. He needed little persuading. He knew that he was not the most persuasive of platform speakers, but he was in his element in the give-and-take of discussion. The breakfast was arranged and virtually all the seniors rose at the crack of dawn — no mean sacrifice — to come out for it.

It was an experience that few would forget. Goldberg reminded the students that he was himself the father of the sit-down strike. He had planned it when he represented the United Steel Workers, and he had justified it only because he could not get management to listen; "all other alternatives failed." But here was a university that not only gave students every opportunity to voice their points of view, but in most instances shared them. Whom were they fighting? Disruption at their own Commencement would be meaningless and would undoubtedly be counterproductive. The questions, though not disrespectful, were blunt and forthright. Goldberg treated every inquiry or argument as if it came from the representative of a major national power. He was considerate, patient, and completely aboveboard. At the conclusion of the breakfast dialogue, the young people gave him a standing ovation. When he was called upon to speak at Commencement, about three-quarters of the graduating class, wearing special armbands, rose in their seats and stood throughout the address to express their protest against the American policy. But there was no heckling, and when Goldberg finished (and he was wise enough not to speak too long), the dissidents sat down quickly and then rose with the rest of the huge audience to applaud heartily. It was a superb personal tribute to Goldberg's persuasiveness, and also to the good sense of a mature student body.

There were other dramatic moments during the weekend. One that stood out for members of the Brandeis inner family was the return, for a degree, of a beloved native son. Benjamin Swig, one of our trustees, had left Boston many years before, his family resources not only strained but his father's ill-fated business ventures having left a mountain of debt. Swig had vowed that the family name would not rely on legalities to evade its responsibilities. He paid every creditor down to the last penny, and in California he became its leading philanthropist. It was an enormous personal tribute when the Catholic-founded Santa Clara College elected him as the chairman of its board of trustees, and he soon taught the trustees how to keep the ever impecunious college out of debt.

The 1967 Commencement was planned as the demonstrations on college campuses reached their noisy and disruptive climax. There was naturally much concern about student behavior at Brandeis, but since the theme that linked the degree recipients was the quest for international peace and understanding, only the extreme militants remained surly, and even they created no disturbance.

We were glad to welcome Kenneth Holland, the president of the Institute for International Education. Holland had been mainly responsible for translating the concept of Fulbright fellowships into the practical reality that opened opportunities for exchange to thousands of gifted students and faculty. After the abortive uprising of the Hungarians in 1956 to shake off the incubus of Soviet control, he had found places for hundreds of young freedom fighters in American universities, saving them from the terror that followed the crushing of the uprising.

One of the most interesting and stimulating of our guests was the erudite Sir Isaiah Berlin, who came to us from All Souls College at Oxford. He combined profundity in analysis with lucidity in expression.

During World War II, with assignments in both the United States and the Soviet Union, his dispatches were models of style and wisdom. They won an accolade from Winston Churchill, himself a master of prose and eloquence. His citation read: "Whether philosophically debating free will, examining Tolstoy's view of history, or proving concepts of liberty and political theory, his gaiety is as irrepressible as his erudition is austere. The least superficial of men, he cannot swim with the tide without being drawn irresistibly beneath the surface to investigate the darker depths below."

We had invited Ambassador Averell Harriman months before to give the Commencement address and he accepted, warning us, however, that there was always the possibility that President Johnson might send him out of the country on an emergency mission. We therefore decided to be prepared with a second speaker, and we invited the former ambassador to Japan Edwin O. Reischauer, who had returned to his teaching duties at Harvard. Harriman spoke first. He was not a dynamic speaker, but he had never relied upon oratory or dramatics for the quiet, commonsense diplomacy that had made him a beloved symbol of integrity in American life. He was enthusiastically received, especially by the students, since he had been a consistent opponent of the foreign policy that had involved ever larger legions of young Americans in the jungles of Indochina, where he forthrightly declared we did not belong.

Dr. Reischauer turned to what he believed was responsible for the blunders of our Asian policies. He deplored the parochialism of American teaching, which centered so completely on the western world, with little attention paid to the Far East. He believed that the failures of American foreign policy in postwar China, Japan, and Southeast Asia were largely the failures of ignorance. He emphasized the imperative need for revision of the curriculum in American schools in order to create a better understanding of the Far Eastern world and its cultural and social institutions. I was gratified that, during the telecasts that I did after my retirement as president, I could return to his home in Belmont, exquisitely appointed by his Japanese wife, and use it as the setting for the interview in which, again, he emphasized his lifelong concern for a broadened concept of education in our schools that would eliminate the barriers of ignorance that separated great peoples.

For the immediate University family the Commencement program was highlighted by the tribute of an honorary degree for Samuel Lemberg, one of their most beloved colleagues. Lemberg was that rare phenomenon in communal philanthropy whose sole motivation was the appeal of a great cause. He was embarrassed by compliments and eschewed all honors. Often he was besieged to accept a tribute dinner, offered partly because of the respect he commanded and partly because we knew that any affair that was built around him would be unusually productive in gifts for the University. He steadfastly refused, and then made up for what might have been contributed by princely gifts of his own. His widely diversified relationships in the real estate world eased the task of finding leaders for our major functions. For who could say no to this man who so completely fulfilled Solomon's evaluation of the greatest of all human virtues: "a listening heart." The citation brought an ovation and the students led in the spontaneous salute: "Neither the poverty of his childhood within the pale of settlement, nor his decades in the marketplace of American business, have coarsened the fiber of his humanity or quenched the flame of his compassion."

I cannot close this review of our honorary degrees without referring to an ambitious plan for a reunion of all the recipients. The unique occasion was scheduled for early December 1963, to coincide with the fifteenth year of the University. There were now more than a hundred recipients of our hood. Within a few weeks, acceptances had been received from the great majority of them. Tragically, only a month before the affair would have taken place, President Kennedy was assassinated, and of course the gathering had to be canceled. We did not, however, give up the concept of such a reunion, although eight years passed before it could be held. By then, a new harvest of greatness had been added, although the reconstituted affair was interlaced with sadness because we had by then also lost, through death, some of our most cherished foster alumni.

The reunion was held in 1971, during the administration of my successor Morris Abram, and few evenings could have surpassed the fascination of the occasion. It recalled the White House dinner to which President Kennedy had invited all the Nobel Prize winners who could arrange their schedules to be in the United States at that time and the President's matchless toast that "no more brilliance had ever been gathered at one time under the roof of the White House since the evening Thomas Jefferson had dined there alone." For us at Brandeis, the reunion, apart from the sentimental journey that it made possible, spelled out an important message about the sense of values of the University, and I referred to it during the program.

I recalled a long debate in Israel when, soon after the War of Liberation in 1948, recommendations came to the prime minister, David Ben-Gurion, to authorize awards for outstanding courage and valor. Ben-Gurion at first resisted. He saw no reason for special honors to those who were fulfilling the obligations of service to their country, even when the service was rendered far beyond the call of duty. But he was overruled; and the main thrust of the rebuttal was that the medals and awards were not primarily meant to honor the recipients. They were intended as a message to the nation and to the world about the values most deeply cherished in Israel. The choices for the awards answered the question that lies at the heart of national life: Who are your heroes?

Our honorary degrees were tributes to outstanding men and women who enriched the life of their generation. Undoubtedly the awards were personally appreciated for the honor that was involved and for the fact that they came from Brandeis. But in the final analysis, the choice of recipients was an alert to the academic world that, by the quality of those who were honored, the University was committed to the highest traditions of integrity.

XIX

The Jewish Component

THE deep concern of Brandeis for Jewish life and values was demonstrated by the many special projects it undertook and, of course, by its emphasis on a strong Judaic curriculum. Yet it may well be that the Jewish component of Brandeis was an intangible — its unique atmosphere, an atmosphere that had been developed by the nature of its sponsorship and the students and faculty that it attracted. One thinks of cities in this country with a special personality that distinguishes them from the hundreds of others so much like each other. But New Orleans or Boston is *sui generis,* and so are St. Louis or Miami Beach, San Francisco or New York or Chicago. There are colleges as well whose history and sponsorship give them a unique character. They have a special personality, perhaps undefinable but pervasive and intellectually and socially osmotic. They defy a catalogue description because they do not depend exclusively on the courses that are listed. They are vitally influenced by the life-style or the subculture of the students and the faculty, the subjects that engage their interest, the causes they espouse, even the adversaries with whom they contend.

Chemistry is chemistry, or at least its basic matter is the same wherever it is taught, as is mathematics, or physics, or anthropology, or modern languages. The academic difference from one school to another comes through only in the quality of the teaching and the reaction of those taught. But no one will mistake Harvard for Swarthmore or Fordham or several other equally singular universities whose lineaments are as distinctive as their history had made them. I do not refer to the old wheeze: "You can always tell a Harvard man — but you can't tell him much." Perhaps it would be fairer to quote John Marquand's rueful amendment: "If you've ever gone to Harvard, you can be sure of one thing. You will never be allowed to forget it." Behind Marquand's self-deprecating irony, however, lurks a somewhat larger truth. Too many Harvard men have been absorbed in the public service of our country for there not to be some mysterious stamp put on its sons by the university. Harvard today is rarely thought of as a Congregationalist strong-hold: it long ago shed its Puritan ethos. Yet one cannot dismiss the impression that the civic commitments of the Congregationalists, who brought Harvard into being and kept it going against many odds, con-tinuously surface. Walking quietly in its beautiful Yard, studying in tradition-packed buildings, the portraits on every public wall of those who molded the patterns of American life, must leave its summons, regardless of one's ultimate calling, to communal service. When one reads Van Wyck Brooks's *The Flowering of New England*, one begins to understand the compelling impact of this unspoken pledge of *noblesse oblige*. And for all of Henry Adams's slighting remarks in his *Education* about his alma mater in the nineteenth century, the Harvard stamp was left on him, and on later generations of Adamses and Roosevelts and Herters and Kennedys.

Then there is the phenomenal impact of the Quakers on higher educa-tion. In a sense this is a kind of miracle, for the entire Quaker group today is little more than 120,000 adherents, one of the smallest in the roster of denominations. Yet this group has made the building of small, quality colleges one of its major corporate objectives, and schools like Haverford, Swarthmore, and Bryn Mawr are a crowning glory. No one can mistake their special character. It reveals itself in more than their high academic standards as attested by the fact that every responsible survey of schools their size invariably places them close to the top of the list. It goes beyond such academic pioneering as the honors system, which was the brainchild of the distinguished Swarthmore president Frank Aydelotte, who lived to see this tradition established in most of the major colleges of the land. Over and above the passion for excel-lence — although in roguish off-moments they refer to themselves as Swarthmorons — is a climate of simplicity and modesty, often ap-proaching austerity, in action and thought, a search for what Quakers call "the inner light." There is nothing ornate, neither in its instructional buildings, its residence halls, nor its unpretentious chapel. In the same vein, I remember a quiet aside made by a former member of our mu-seum staff who was a graduate of Haverford: "We were called 'Mister' on the first day we arrived, seventeen and foolish. It had an effect."

When we turn to Brandeis, founded little more than a quarter of a century ago, we may ask whether there has been time, in just one generation, to develop a special character. I believe there has been. I would say that it is a sensitive social consciousness, a concern for the underdog, resistance to any kind of discrimination. Some of it comes from the prophetic tradition, which has woven the passion for social justice into the warp and woof of Jewish life. Some of it comes from the economic stratum out of which most first- or second-generation immi-grant groups emerge. Whatever the historical matrix, the result is plain to see. The student body is unusually activist and is very much concerned with rights. The faculty, brought together for its special skills in diverse academic areas and with no thought of personal temperament or outlook, have somehow quickly shown a more than average concern for the protection and advancement of progressive social values. Indeed, many of them may have been attracted to Brandeis because it afforded a hospitable climate for such concern. I cannot believe it is altogether accidental that the main writing and research going forward so early at Brandeis had to do with the attack on restraints on freedom, restraints that threaten the fullness of life. This would be the reason for the unusual succession of articles and books that stream from faculty who are so often involved in the attack on privilege or the abuse of power. There must be some subtle relationship with the orientation of research in the laboratories that seeks to sustain and enrich life and primarily interests such agencies as the National Institutes of Health and the American Cancer Society. There is a similar relationship in the fervent concern of the young people with racial integration and Hungarian freedom fighters and Vietnam. As one of the yearbook editors put it: "At Brandeis the status is certainly not quo."

Of course Brandeis is not alone in such concern. Fortunately many other universities are in the forefront of the battle to link truth with justice, and Brandeis gravitated naturally to this doughty band. It was not always comfortable for the administration to function in such a climate. We could become very impatient with a student newspaper that probed into every area, far beyond normal student jurisdiction, that scolded, preached, and attacked. It would be much more comfortable to deal with a conforming student leadership, quietly deferential. But these were youngsters who had cut the umbilical cord of filial obedience, and they continued to question and oppose when they reached a college where the environment was favorable for challenging all credentials and sanctions. I imagine that Hosea and Jeremiah and Ezekiel were not easy to live with either, but in the long run they were a lot more creative and valuable than the custodians of the establishment who preceded and followed them. At any rate, the educational process is expected to inflict pain, to cavil and demur and defy. The trustees have asked only that the spirit of criticism be constructive and respectful, even during the most trenchant reappraisal. All of this is in the spirit of the reforming justice for whom the University is named. "Brandeis and Holmes dissenting" was appended to hundreds of majority decisions reached in the Supreme Court. The seal of the University reads *Emeth* (Truth), and its motto comes from the psalmist, who demanded "the search for truth, even unto its innermost parts."

What I have called the special personality of Brandeis, though intangible, was a pervading presence. Every care, however, was taken to make sure that it did not affect our academic objectivity. This undoubtedly disappointed many who, because Brandeis was Jewish-founded, identified it as a Jewish parochial school on a university level. Indeed, preparatory and high school counselors, in offering advice to their graduates, often steered non-Jewish students away from Brandeis, or encouraged intensely Jewish-oriented youngsters to apply there, because it was a "Jewish university." Actually, there was no intention to develop Brandeis as such a parochial school. Its support, indeed, was to be the responsibility of its Jewish sponsors, but it was planned to serve in the tradition of the great schools, from Harvard to the present, which were the nonsectarian gifts of the religious denominations to American higher education.

Nevertheless, by virtue of its sponsorship, it was properly expected that there would be unique strength in the Judaic components (which belonged in the academic structure of any good university), particularly in the Department of Judaic Studies, the library, and in foreign studies, where Israel would be a natural magnet. In developing Judaic studies, we assigned high priority to the classical aspects of Bible, Jewish philosophy and literature, and Jewish history and archaeology. Three outstanding scholars helped to give distinction to this area: Nahum Glatzer, Simon Rawidowicz, and Alexander Altmann.

The first major appointment went to Nahum Glatzer in 1951. He was an Austro-German émigré who had come to the United States in 1938, having taught at both Frankfort and Haifa. His fields were Jewish philosophy, history, and Hebrew literature, and he wrote authoritatively on the life and thought of the German theologian Franz Rosenzweig. He had held a number of fill-in positions at the College of Jewish Studies in Chicago, at the Hebrew Teachers College in Boston, and at the Yeshiva in New York. But he had been mainly engaged as editor-in-chief for Schocken Books, publishers of Hebrew and German classics in English translation. He was a quiet, modest, low-keyed man, deeply respected by his colleagues and students. Meeting and working with him, one thought immediately of old-world dignity, and yet the impression never connoted pomposity. His dry humor always surprised because it usually emerged from such a serious façade. He had the knack of transmitting the excitement of Jewish history and literature, and was proud of the many students whom he sent into the field of Judaic studies. As chairman of the department during its formative period, he was determined to give it preeminent standing in the world of Jewish studies, and he was personally involved in recruiting outstanding undergraduates and a distinguished faculty. It was significant that upon retirement, after more than twenty years, he was the first faculty member to receive the University's honorary degree, recommended for it by his own peers; his most devoted students presented him with a *Festschrift*.

One of Glatzer's first coups was to bring to Brandeis Simon Rawidowicz, a Russian émigré. His erudition and the profundity of his philosophical thinking had earned him full honors among Jewish scholars. But when he came to this country, positions worthy of his background were very difficult to find. When Glatzer called him to Brandeis, he was filling a modest post in the College of Jewish Studies in Chicago, then still a third-rate institution with no standing in the Jewish scholarly world. Typical of his influence was the long ideological discussion that he carried on with the prime minister of Israel, David Ben-Gurion, who believed that there could be no wholesome, creative Jewish life outside of Israel, and who therefore regarded the Diaspora as vestigial. Rawidowicz was devoted to Israel, but he passionately defended the affirmative role of the Jewish communities in the lands where they had been rooted and where, despite the assaults of fate, they continued to function. It was the deep respect in which he was held by the scholarly world and by the highest echelons of the new Israel that bespoke the influence he created for the Department of Judaic Studies. I remember a reception at the White House in honor of the president of Israel, the late Zalman Shazar. When Thelma and I were presented to him, he exclaimed, "Brandeis — that's where Rawidowicz is," and he then held up the receiving line to explain to President Johnson what a magnificent scholar Rawidowicz was! Tragically, he was lost to the University and the world of scholarship by an early death. He was barely sixty when he died in 1957.

Alexander Altmann was also a German-born scholar. Ordained as a rabbi, he had held one of the most distinguished pulpits in Berlin until the country was engulfed by the Nazis. He found a welcome refuge in England, where he became the chief rabbi of Manchester. When he was recruited for Brandeis, he brought with him a superb reputation for his writings in Judaeo-Arabic philosophy, rabbinical literature, Jewish mysticism, and the eighteenth-century enlightenment. As a "supplement" to his Brandeis classes, he began editing classical texts in a scholarly series, and climaxed his incumbency with a definitive two-volume work on Moses Mendelssohn. His value to the University went far beyond his teaching. In 1963, on a special grant, he made a tour of important Italian libraries and brought back duplicates of ten thousand items, including biblical commentaries, philosophical treatises, Kabbalistic texts, and other documents of priceless historic value. He had them microfilmed and they were deposited in the Goldfarb Library.

Even as the department grew in numbers and distinction, pressure mounted to supplement classical studies and research with training for contemporary Jewish affairs. There was genuine compulsion behind this pressure. It was of no small significance that it had been necessary to build our Judaic faculty almost exclusively with scholars from abroad. The American Jewish community had not yet produced many native-born specialists. Until midcentury there had been little call for them; only a few universities offered courses related to contemporary Jewish life. The upsurge of interest began, undoubtedly stimulated by the Holocaust, the role of Jews in the political and economic life of the United States and Western Europe, their changing fate in the Soviet Union, and, above all, by the emergence of a sovereign Israel. Scholars with this specialization were now very much in demand. Each year there were many offers from institutions where newly established positions now promised dignity and security. But the posts went unfilled except where rabbis were tempted away from their pulpits; they were virtually the only reservoir of competence.

The time was therefore ripe to expand the curriculum in classical studies with offerings in contemporary affairs to help meet the overwhelming need for qualified faculty. It was also important to provide a training center for service in Jewish communal life, welfare funds, philanthropic institutions, and cultural undertakings. The fulfillment came in 1965 through the generosity of a New England shoe merchant, Philip Lown, whose basic communal interest had always been the training for Jewish leadership. He had played a large role in the development of the Boston Hebrew Teachers College and had served as its president for many years. Early in the life of Brandeis he had established the chair in Jewish philosophy that was held by Altmann. Now Lown provided the endowment to launch the School for Contemporary Jewish Affairs. A whole new component was thereby added to the service the University could render. Additional faculty were brought in for contemporary Jewish history, the problems of Israel and its relation to the Diaspora, and American Jewish history. A close relationship was established with the Florence Heller School, which looked to the Philip Lown School to offer Jewish background for those who sought careers at the executive level in areas of Jewish communal service. The enrollment escalated, and within a few years Brandeis had become the most important center for the training of Jewish communal leaders.

The honorary degree that was conferred upon Lown in his eightieth year was well earned for his role in this achievement. He, however, was not so sure that a humble shoe merchant deserved such an accolade and, at the dinner where the recipients spoke informally, he professed concern about his inclusion among the elect who were to be honored the next day. "In 1952," he revealed, "Dr. Sachar hinted that I should sponsor the first chair in Judaica at Brandeis. Who could resist his hypnotic charm? Thus my tale of woe commenced. Before committing myself, I should have remembered the story told of Mrs. Chauncey Depew III, who was a wealthy society matron, and anxious to have a family tree and history prepared. She went to an outstanding genealogist to have this done, but told him that there was one stumbling block — her family, like most, had an ancestor who had blemished a proud tradition.

Indeed, his final crime was punished by the electric chair at Sing Sing. Said the genealogist, 'Don't worry, Mrs. Depew, I'll take care of Uncle Charles,' and he came up with a masterpiece of equivocal ambiguity. 'Charles Depew occupied a chair of applied electricity in one of the government's great institutions. He died in harness, and his death came as an extreme shock.' "

When the American Jewish Historical Society decided in 1966 to establish its national headquarters on the Brandeis campus, it further validated the symbolic central position the University had achieved in the Jewish community. It was following the precedent of the Virginia Historical Society and many other similar cultural agencies that had linked up with college campuses. There were natural, mutual advantages. The Brandeis and society libraries functioned virtually side by side, each amplifying the other's resources. In addition, the University's dining facilities, lectures, and colloquia were all happily merged in an advantageous partnership with people of similar academic interests. It should be added that while the headquarters was on the campus — or, technically, contiguous to it — the society itself was completely autonomous.

Yet the action did not come easily. The headquarters of the society had bounced around in rented or donated quarters for many decades in New York City, the officers reluctant to consider other locations both because there were no funds available and because there was no agreement on which city would best serve the interests of the society. Philadelphia disputed the claim of New York, and New York disputed the claim of any other community. Suddenly the funds for adequate headquarters became available in a multimillion-dollar bequest to the society from Lee M. Friedman, a well-known Boston lawyer whose devotion to the society went back half a century and who had served as its president for a number of terms. Brandeis offered a place on its campus after the proponents of New York and Philadelphia had canceled out each other's polemics. The Brandeis advantages were acceptable to a majority of the membership in a referendum that was taken, especially when Friedman's law partner, Frank Kozol, closest to him in friendship and professional association, became the strongest advocate for the move to Massachusetts. The case for the advantages to the scholarly world was strongly presented by Oscar Handlin, the Harvard Pulitzer Prize historian, who journeyed to the 1966 Charleston, South Carolina, annual meeting where the final decision was made. The officers of the society — including Leon Obermayer, of one of the major law firms of Philadelphia, and Dr. Abram Kanof, president of the society, a New York physician and bibliophile — all joined in the advocacy for a Brandeis connection.

The vote was close because many of the New York delegation were convinced that the center of Jewish historical scholarship should remain in the largest Jewish-populated city in the world, where there was easy access to the basic leadership in American and world Jewish life. But the decision to establish the headquarters at Brandeis prevailed and was confirmed in a court action brought by some of the unreconciled dissidents, and a beautiful structure bearing the name of Lee Friedman was constructed.

The move brought new life to the society, whose membership rolls increased rapidly and whose scholarly acquisitions soared. Indeed, much of the archival material on American Jewish history that had been contributed to the Brandeis library was transferred, for easy access and specialized procedures, to the headquarters of the American Jewish Historical Society. The arrangement was permanently validated after a seven-year trial experience.

It was inevitable that close relationships should be established with the universities of Israel and that every encouragement be offered to student and faculty exchanges. The precedent of study and research relationships by American universities with their foreign counterparts was of long standing. Already at the beginning of the twentieth century Yale had sponsored what was a university branch in China — Yale in China — and it brought active exchange of faculty and students. Many American universities had junior-year-abroad programs linked with specially selected foreign institutions. It was following a well-established pattern, therefore, for Brandeis to have many of its students leave the campus for a year abroad, and it was natural for large numbers to choose Israel. Brandeis was in a very literal sense one of the products of the reawakened pride in Jewish dignity and creativity; it came into being in May 1948, in the same month as Israel's Declaration of Independence. At the inaugural convocation in October, Israel was represented by its delegate to the United Nations, Eliahu Elath, who, though not yet a fully accredited ambassador, brought greetings from the newly established state of Israel. At virtually every convocation or Commencement, Israeli statesmen and scholars were welcomed as special guests or as recipients of honorary degrees.

Many of the visiting Israelis could not resist the temptation to chide the students for not emigrating to Israel. At an early convocation, in June 1951, when thousands of students converged on the Brandeis campus from more than twenty-five New England colleges, Ben-Gurion scolded them affectionately for not being in Israel. "What are you doing here," he exclaimed, "when there is a *Maase B'reshet*, a work of creation, with so much exhilaration and pioneering adventure, waiting for you in a land that you can help build and fashion!" Some of the Israelis wondered why millions of dollars should be channeled to Brandeis when the American Jewish community was likely to be only a temporary doubtful refuge; surely the day would come when Jewish life in America would suffer the fate of other great Jewish settlements of the Diaspora! But these were only occasional voices, doubtless the reaction to the disappointment that the dreams of equality in the Diaspora had been so tragically betrayed by the Holocaust and so callously accepted by the Christian establishment. There was sober understanding that Israel needed a strong American Jewish life, and that American Jews could profit from a healthy continuing relationship with Israel. Dr. Rawidowicz had expressed the relationship graphically by the geometric symbol of the ellipse with two foci.

Cooperative projects, eagerly promoted by Israeli institutions and by Brandeis, were therefore established early. There was generous scholarship support available for Israeli students who came to Brandeis, and encouragement was given to our students to spend some time in Israeli universities, with full credit assigned for satisfactory work done there. Indeed, the American Friends of the Hebrew University, who raised funds in the United States to provide scholarships for American students who wished to study there, noted that the largest number from any one college always came from Brandeis.

In 1961 a special approach was worked out for the relationship with Israel by my son, Howard, who had earned his doctorate at Harvard in Middle Eastern studies. He began annual visits to Israel and concentrated most of his writing on the development of Israel and its relationship to the Middle East and the Diaspora. His proposal to Brandeis was to establish a traveling university, with its base in Jerusalem, where the teaching and study would be coordinated. This was to be no junket; the courses would be subjected to the usual standards that the Brandeis faculty maintained at home. They would relate to the social, economic, and political structure of Israel and to the history and politics of the Middle East. These would be supplemented by visits to the Knesseth, the law courts, and to local and rural councils. Observation sessions would also be arranged, by special permission, at military training centers. Students would visit cooperative farm settlements, agricultural research stations, newly created industrial areas, irrigation and desalinization projects, and mineral drilling outposts in the Negev Desert. Under the guidance of the late Dr. Johanan Aharoni, of the Hebrew University, the study of biblical history would be climaxed by watching the digs in the Byzantine ruins of Ramat Rachel. In an almost literal sense, all Israel would become the classroom.

To acquire at least a working proficiency in the Hebrew language, it was planned that the students arrive early in the summer for an intensive eight-week *ulpan* training before the regular school term. By then it was expected that the enrollees would acquire at least tolerable conversational ability in order to communicate with the Israelis and to read the

Israeli press. The enrollees were not to be limited to Brandeis students but would be drawn from universities across the country, with credit to be transferred for all work certified by the Brandeis Institute.

The complete funding for this ambitious program came from Jacob Hiatt of Worcester, Massachusetts, then a member of the Board of Trustees and later its chairman. Hiatt was a native of Lithuania who had completed his studies there at the national university and who had become an assistant district attorney and a circuit court judge. He immigrated to the United States in 1936 and quickly achieved industrial success as a paper box manufacturer, sharing his good fortune by complete involvement in Jewish and community causes. He became a generous patron of Clark University, where he received a master's degree in history, Holy Cross, Assumption, and the Hebrew Union College, and he was one of the earliest supporters of Brandeis.

The early days were not all milk and honey, and the students needed courage to cope with the problems of pioneering. My son recalls that in the first year, 1961, on a drive to Sodom, six students were jammed into the director's tiny Ford Falcon and the rest in a beat-up Peugeot driven by an honorary member of the group, a Canadian who had settled with his family in Israel and whom the Jewish Agency had assigned to the Hiatt program because of the excellent orientation it would give him to the land and its problems. Pounding along the miserable, rutted road back from Sodom, the Ford suddenly coughed to a stop. The gas tank had been punctured by a boulder. The party was miles from nowhere. The Canadian was able to siphon some of his gas into the Ford, but how could he plug the leak in the tank? The problem was solved by one of the girls, an inveterate gum chewer. Her gum went into the hole, the gas went into the tank, the caravan drove off with a prayer. Miraculously, the gum held until the car reached Beersheba and a garage.

There were other adventures that were not foreseen in the original prospectus. Typical was a visit to the great Bedouin camel market in Beersheba. Two of the Hiatt girls, clad in shorts, made the rounds, oohing and ahing in fascination as they watched the Arab sheikhs bidding and counterbidding. Only belatedly did they realize, to their horror, that the leading sheikh of the district was bidding with Howard — for them!

But such episodes soon faded into table conversation. Jacob Hiatt kept augmenting his support, steadily refining the program so that, while there were no luxuries, food, living quarters, and travel became tolerable. Howard obtained support from the State Department, which assigned annual grants of $25,000 for several years. The turning point came when Hiatt purchased a lovely home in Jerusalem that became the institute's headquarters. It was remodeled and enlarged every few years as the program expanded and, by 1970, it had become a respected and aesthetic symbol of the Brandeis presence in Israel. At a special dedication ceremony Hiatt outlined his hopes for the institute in limpid Hebrew. Israel was represented by the deputy prime minister, Yigal Allon, who jested that he would not dare to compete with Hiatt by speaking in Hebrew. He hailed the institute for its original approach and for its ambassadorial service.

Howard directed the institute for three years, and then, with the program safely launched, resumed his teaching career as a professor of history at George Washington University. He was succeeded as director by Ernest Stock, who had earned his doctorate at Princeton and then settled in Israel. The popularity of the Hiatt Program grew steadily and the colleges that adopted the courses for credit included Yale, Princeton, Stanford, Wellesley, Vassar, Swarthmore, Clark, Cornell, Holy Cross, Oberlin, New York University, Rutgers, Boston University, Barnard, Pennsylvania, and many others.

The Hiatt students' experience in Israel was, of course, not confined to the Jewish population; every effort was made to bring the group into contact with Israel's Arab citizens, too. A three-day visit to Nazareth became part of the curriculum; this time was used to explore the special problems encountered by the Arab minority in the Jewish state. Hiatt students were the guests of Arab host families, and warm relationships often developed and were maintained. One prominent Arab citizen of Nazareth heaved a sigh when he commented to the Hiatt director: "If only the Jews of Israel were like these American Jews, there wouldn't be any problems!" What he forgot, of course, was that the American students who came to Israel for a relatively short period were not party to the intense political quarrels of the area, and that, once these political issues were solved, there would probably be few obstacles in the way for the same warm relationships between Israel's Arabs and Jews.

Fifteen years later, there were over five hundred alumni of the institute experience, many of whom indicated that the direction of their lives had been changed as a result of their exposure to Israel. Several entered the rabbinate or returned to settle in Israel, and there were at least a half-dozen marriages of fellow participants. In time, the institute was expanded into a two-semester program that included the humanities as well as the social sciences. It has become one of the strongest cultural exchange programs between Israel and Brandeis.

Meantime, there were other special responsibilities that Brandeis could assume because of its special position. In 1956 I was approached by Erwin Griswold, dean of Harvard Law School, who informed me that the State of Israel was eager to launch a major project for the codification of Israeli law, for the newly created state was plagued by the mixture of legal systems and practices that were hopelessly snarled. There was Talmudic law, British law, Arabic law, Turkish law, and the laws that had evolved in an ad hoc way in the successive occupations of the land and the influx of immigrants from nations around the world.

A commission was appointed to study the enormous social and cultural changes that had taken place in recent centuries and to evolve a modern system that could then be submitted for enactment to the Israeli legal authorities and to the Knesseth. The project was as sweeping in its scope as the Justinian Code of ancient days and the Napoleonic Code of the last century. Harvard Law School was quite willing to cooperate with the State of Israel and to place its faculty resources at the disposal of the commission. What was needed was the seed money, an initial grant of $100,000, and Dean Griswold hoped that Brandeis, with its access to imaginative and generous supporters, could approach some of them in the interest of a Harvard-Brandeis-Israel legal codification project. It would become a significant contribution not only for the development of a consistent and efficient legal code for Israel; it could become the model for many of the developing countries.

I responded cordially to Dean Griswold's proposal, for it seemed especially appropriate for Brandeis to cooperate. The University was named for the justice who was a son of Harvard, one of the two or three most outstanding students ever produced by its law school, and whose Zionism had been rooted in reason and order and efficiency; therefore, the project was sentimentally as appealing as it was practical. I promised to approach some of our donors and then to remain in a consultant's role with whomever was appointed by the State of Israel to direct the research.

Within the next few months I obtained the ready cooperation of Judge Joseph Proskauer, one of our board members, who had been chief justice of the Supreme Court of New York, and James Rosenberg, who had had a long and successful career as a New York lawyer and was deeply interested in the University. They in turn brought into the project a number of their friends. The funding assured, a research director was appointed, Joseph Leifer, an Israeli with an excellent background in corporation law. By the end of three years, draft codes were ready in several areas. The data was sent on to the authorities in Israel, who assumed responsibility for its further use. The venture was a gratifying example of the special service to Israel that the University could perform.

Another instance of useful intercession came in 1960, after several years of strained relations between Israel and the U.S. State Department that grew out of the Suez War of 1956. It was deemed critical for Prime Minister Ben-Gurion to meet with President Eisenhower on a man-to-man basis to seek better understanding. But there was no initiative from the White House. The Israeli ambassador, Avraham Harman, approached me in the hope of using a ceremonial occasion at Brandeis to provide Ben-Gurion with an opportunity to visit the United States. Courtesy would then dictate that, as a visiting prime minister, he be received by the President. Using University occasions as the instrument for accomplishing diplomatic missions was not unprecedented; the Marshall Plan had been announced at a Harvard Commencement in 1947. Brandeis was a natural intermediary for Ben-Gurion's purpose, and its good offices were quickly made available. In March 1960 a special convocation was planned; the invitation from the White House was extended to Ben-Gurion as soon as it was announced that he was to receive an honorary degree. The meeting between Ben-Gurion and Eisenhower was cordial and effective.

Apparently Ben-Gurion also had confidence in the ability of the University to offer guidance in educational projects that were close to his heart. After he had completed his incumbency as prime minister, he became deeply interested in establishing a university in the Negev, building upon the nucleus that already existed in Beersheba. Early in 1967, he asked me to set up a conference with academicians and administrators to discuss some of the problems that a desert university would have to face and ways of coping with them. I welcomed the opportunity to have him return to the campus and suggested we might use the occasion to tape a television interview in which he could relate some of the dramatic turning points in his long career. We were then sponsoring a program called *Living Biography*, in which we recorded the remembrances of selected contemporaries. Ben-Gurion readily consented and the two purposes were happily combined.

During his stay on campus, in mid-March 1967, I asked some of the most knowledgeable men in the area to join the prime minister for lunch at the Faculty Center. There was our own trustee Milton Katz, head of international legal studies at Harvard, Jerome Wiesner, provost and later president of MIT, and senior members of our faculty and administrative staff. It was fascinating to watch Ben-Gurion as he interpreted his dream of a university that would not only convert the Negev Desert into what the Bible had termed "a place of springs" but would also help to fructify the arid wastes of the world. Ben-Gurion hoped that when imaginative scientists applied themselves to such problems as the desalinization and purification of brackish water, the whole world would profit. The university would have access to nuclear power, since there was already a fully equipped reactor nearby at Dimona.

As the dreamer talked on, all practical problems seemed trivial. Milton Katz, one of the behind-the-scenes architects of the Marshall Plan, broke the spell. Gently he asked what table of organization Ben-Gurion had in mind, the scope of the university's faculty and research personnel, the necessary facilities, the source of funds — all practical questions. Ben-Gurion looked startled. What table of organization? What funds? What blueprint? "Do you think," he asked, "that there would have been an Israel if we had worried about such matters before moving into action!"

Yet miraculously, the University of the Negev came into being, although, it must be added, it required some hard-nosed administrators to give it shape and form. They were sensible enough, however, in their procedures, never to allow the dream to be eclipsed. They remembered that dreams often produce substantive support, but that support alone is never enough to sustain a dream. And they remembered, too, that when Ben-Gurion moved into the desert and settled with his Paula in the village of S'de Boker, his farewell speech was just one word: "Follow." It was such a spirit that vindicated Ben-Gurion's working principle: Anyone who does not believe in miracles is not a realist. Thelma and I visited the university in 1969. Though the facilities for study and research were almost primitive, the esprit de corps of the pioneering faculty and the grim determination of the students were clear evidence that Ben-Gurion's spirit had enveloped the project. It was appropriate that, after Ben-Gurion's death in 1973, the university was renamed for him.

Sometimes, because of the symbolic respect that Brandeis evoked in the political as well as in the academic world, much more was expected of it than could possibly be delivered. Thus, in 1965, I was approached by Avraham Harman, still ambassador of Israel, who expressed grave concern at the increasing unfriendliness of the government of India toward Israel. India had never recognized the sovereignty of Israel and there were no diplomatic relations between the two countries. There was widespread admiration for Israel's democratic institutions, its service to the underdeveloped countries of Africa and Asia, but with eighty million Moslems in its population India's diplomatic dilemma was inevitable. In Nehru's last years and during the incumbency of his successor, Shastri, the diplomatic coolness had turned into outright hostility. Israelis were now continuously denied visas to attend international scientific and cultural conferences in India, even when they were specifically invited by their Indian colleagues.

Harman knew that Brandeis's contacts with Indian academic and political figures had been cordial. At the 1963 Commencement, Nehru's sister, Madame Pandit, had been the featured speaker. There had been a good opportunity to review with her not only the frustrating relations between Israel and India but also the growing anti-American influence there. When Nehru died in the fall of 1964, the memorial to him, in cooperation with the Indian Students' Association of Greater Boston, was planned at Brandeis, and Ambassador B. K. Gandhi of India flew in for it. With such excellent rapport, strengthened further by the continuous stream of Wien students from India, it seemed practical to explore ways in which the University could mitigate the alienation of India and Israel. I consulted with John Kenneth Galbraith, who had returned to Harvard after his post as American ambassador to India. He indicated that one of India's most influential diplomats, M. J. Desai, who had directed the Foreign Office under Nehru, had now retired and was eager to write a volume on the foreign policy of India during the first decades of Indian independence. He could do much of his research and writing if he were attached to a university, and Galbraith offered to be the intermediary if Brandeis invited Desai to accept a visiting professorship. This seemed like an excellent approach, and the invitation for a Ziskind Visiting Professorship was extended and promptly accepted.

Desai spent the 1965–1966 school year on the Brandeis campus, teaching several advanced courses in the history and politics of contemporary India and the Southeast Pacific and pursuing his own research. When Israeli officials visited the campus they conferred with Desai, who offered confidential advice. Unfortunately the times were not propitious for any diplomatic progress. The continued exacerbation of relations between Israel and the Arab states led to the Six-Day War in 1967 and ranged the entire Arab and Moslem world against Israel. Though the intellectual community of India and many of its leaders remained personally friendly, there was no diplomatic improvement with Israel.

But of course it was primarily in promoting academic exchange with Israeli institutions that Brandeis was most influential. A special fund was created by Joseph Foster of Leominster, a plastics manufacturer, who early in the history of the University established an endowed chair in Mediterranean studies, held by Cyrus Gordon. Upon urging by one of his dearest friends, Jack Hiatt, Foster agreed to set up a million-dollar trust whose income would provide an exchange so that our students and faculty could go to Israel to fulfill educational objectives, and their students and faculty could come to us. He died before the program was fully under way, but his wife, Esther, saw that his objectives were fulfilled and the program became one of the strongest links in the relationship between the University and Israel.

The strong emotional tie with Israel was demonstrated dramatically in 1967, when scores of Brandeis students volunteered for service in the war. This outpouring of concern was repeated in the Yom Kippur War of 1973. This response was in keeping with what happened in many colleges where there was a substantial Jewish enrollment. Those who were not accepted or who could not go made financial contributions from their earnings or their allowances, and they organized teams that spent long hours in solicitation of funds. Brandeis, too, demonstrated its concern. It was the first institution in the country to declare a moratorium on fund-raising, during the Israeli crisis, for new capital gifts and endowments and, when sorely pressed to meet its ongoing budget, it weathered its own crisis by concentrating on the collection of older pledges. Wherever possible Brandeis urged its supporters to make their contributions in the form of bonds of the State of Israel, expanding its long-established policy of placing substantial portions of its endowment funds in loans to Israel and in investments in its major industrial and commercial enterprises.

The pledge was given at the inaugural exercises in 1948 that Brandeis would always remain a school of opportunity, that there would never be any restrictions on the basis of creed or color or ethnic origin. This was meant as more than a commitment to avoid quotas in enrollment or employment. It was meant to emphasize that Brandeis was created for learning and scholarship, not for indoctrination. In reviewing the special emphasis and activities that gave the University its "Jewish character," I hope it is fair to conclude that the pledge was not in jeopardy. The Jewishness of Brandeis was in its climate, not its orientation. In the classrooms and laboratories it functioned in the highest tradition of other denominationally supported universities, which protected and encouraged the components that linked them with ancestral traditions without impinging on the completely nonsectarian quality of their academic contribution. It was by meticulously maintaining this sensitive balance that it was possible for Brandeis to earn a reputation for excellence in its studies and research while it also was sought out as an influential center of Jewish learning and communal responsibility.

XX

The Lemberg Center
for the Study of Violence

WITHIN a few weeks of the issuance of the Warren Commission *Report* on the assassination of President Kennedy, I was called by a New York manufacturer, Frank Cohen, head of the Biflex Corporation, who indicated that a group of his business associates, deeply concerned about the escalation of violence in our country, wondered whether the University would be willing to undertake a scientific study of the causes of such violence. His colleagues were prepared to provide the seed money for a preliminary exploration that might lead to useful recommendations. I met with him and his associates in New York and found that they were thoughtful citizens, seriously motivated. They realized that such research, if pursued under controlled conditions, would require a major investment. But they were hopeful that, if a series of preliminary conferences was held under the auspices of Brandeis, support for the research itself might then be secured through some of the major foundations or private philanthropy.

There was no doubt that the whole area of social violence required earnest study. The country was threatened by extremely dangerous corrosive forces spawned by racial tensions, deplorable conditions in the black urban ghettos, the mounting opposition to American involvement in Southeast Asia, and the campus disorders that were linked to such opposition and to dissatisfaction with university governance. Remedial action in communities and on the national level was piecemeal and hopelessly involved in self-serving politics and demagoguery.

Brandeis was in an excellent position to undertake such studies. It had a core of faculty in sociology, psychology, politics, and social welfare who could bring helpful insights to the problem. It was located in an area where the faculties of some of the best universities in the country offered further resources. And the University had earned a commendable research reputation and could command the cooperation of some of the ablest specialists. The offer of Frank Cohen and his colleagues was therefore accepted, and a series of three national conferences on the campus was held under the direction of Louis Cowan, the director of our Morse Communications Center, and Dr. Norton Long, professor of politics.

The first conference was convened in December 1964; it attempted to define the problem. The participants, along with our faculty representatives, were drawn from many of the professions, especially psychiatry, medicine, government, and law. They included J. Lee Rankin, chief counsel to the Warren Commission and solicitor general of the United States during the Eisenhower administration; Judge David Bazelon, chief justice of the U.S. Court of Appeals in Washington, who had pioneered the relationship between psychiatry and the law; Milton Katz, head of the International Legal Studies program at Harvard Law School and one of our own trustees; Frank Freidel, chairman of the American Civilization Committee at Harvard; Karl Menninger, president of the famed clinic and mental center in Kansas; and Gresham Sykes, executive director of the American Sociological Society. There was a wide-ranging discussion that covered "senseless" individual action by loners and "wierdos" as well as the conspiratorial violence of large groups who planned the disruptions and explosions that shook our society in the 1960s. Ralph McGill, editor of the *Atlanta Constitution*, hailed the discussions of the conference, commenting, "Brandeis has moved; now imitators and followers are needed."

A second conference was convened in April 1965, and it concentrated on the economic problems whose frustrations and disappointments often triggered violence and riot. Many labor leaders and corporation executives attended, and they presented their opposing views with utmost candor. Problems of housing, mass unemployment, inadequate educational opportunities, the intransigent power of labor unions, the overwhelming compulsion of giant industrial and commercial enterprises to create profits — all came under review. A third conference was held in July of that same year and brought together leaders in the communications field. Attention was focused on the reporting of violence and the influence of such reports as a factor in its escalation. Many thoughtful observations were made on the dilemma posed by the need for complete and uninhibited reporting to illumine the problems that stimulate the response of violence. But, it was asked, are not difficult situations exacerbated when the reporting focuses on sensationalism, when it takes episodes and reactions completely out of context, when it gives visibility to unrepresentative and irresponsible elements? It was obvious that there was an urgent need for the refinement of guidelines. All the conferences encouraged the establishment of an institute for continuing discussions and research so that the recommendations of the Brandeis sessions would not trail off into ineffectual rhetoric.

Within a few months, the problem of adequate funding had been solved. As so often before, it was the generosity of one of our own trustees, Sam Lemberg, that was responsible. Lemberg was a self-made success, an authentic genius in real estate and its intricacies. But his greatest talent lay in winning support for communal causes. He had already underwritten the psychology center and the nursery school. Through a contribution of a million dollars, he had launched the campaign to give the growing student body one of the most impressive student union buildings in New England. Every time a special academic need was announced at a trustees' meeting, Lemberg's name was part of the initial list who responded. He now became a fellow conspirator with me in the task of finding a donor for the violence center. A very likely prospect was one of his oldest friends, a New York manufacturer and philanthropic leader who had recently contributed half a million dollars to Brandeis for a dormitory complex. I was standing with them at a university reception when Lemberg began his low-keyed persuasion, outlining the beneficent effect if the violence center were properly funded. "We need a million dollars to do all that has to be done," he said amiably, as if he were asking for some modest membership dues. His friend replied that he was already vastly overcommitted to other philanthropies. Lemberg gently warned him that he was missing a one-shot opportunity. He added, "If you do not take it, I will!" The reply was, with a chuckle, "So take it, Sam, and you'll have my blessing." Lemberg turned to me and said, "All right, you are a witness that I offered it to him first. Now, go ahead with the center, and I'll pledge the million-dollar trust fund whose income you will need to set it up." With such trustees, it was not difficult to ride the legend current in the land that the University was built on miracles.

It was expected that the center would function autonomously and might need seven years to fulfill its tasks. We hoped its recommendations would be used by communities in trouble, and perhaps then government agencies would take over the responsibilities. The trust would then be diverted for other pressing University needs.

The appointment to head the center went to Dr. John Spiegel, associate clinical professor of psychiatry at Harvard Medical School and lecturer in the Department of Social Relations at Harvard. He had been chief of psychiatric service at the Army Air Force Convalescent Hospital in Spokane, Washington, during World War II and had later served as director of the psychiatric clinic of the Michael Reese Hospital in Chicago. He had been engaged in numerous research enterprises, among them the response of various populations to acute disaster. Dr. Spiegel added teaching duties to the directorship of the center when he was named professor of social psychiatry in the Florence Heller School. He quickly organized a national board of overseers under the chairmanship of Philip Klutznick, who had been housing commissioner for

President Truman and a former U.S. representative to the United Nations. Simultaneously recruitment went forward to build a research staff for the center, and by the spring of 1967 its activities were well under way.

The first research assignment was virtually dictated by circumstances. The incidence of urban ghetto violence had risen alarmingly in many parts of the country: in 1964 there had been fourteen serious disturbances in major cities; in 1965 the pattern was repeated, including the seven-day riot in Watts. By 1966 the whole country was engulfed and there were more than fifty riots with heartbreaking loss of life and property. Dr. Spiegel and his staff, supported by a major grant from the Ford Foundation, undertook a study in depth of six major cities, three that had been torn by riot — Cleveland, Dayton and San Francisco — and three that had thus far escaped such disturbance — Pittsburgh, Akron and Boston. The Roper Associates was given the contract to interview 500 blacks and 500 whites in each of the cities, black interviewers for the blacks, white interviewers for the whites. There were long and detailed interviews with the city officials, police officers, school authorities, church and labor leaders, militants, moderates — as many segments of the community profile as could be reached. The social and economic structure of each community was thoroughly studied. Political and educational officials and business and labor leaders were closely questioned on the methods of accomplishing social change. All the material was not only fed into computers for statistical analysis, but was discussed with authorities in carefully structured seminars to ascertain the grievance levels, how they were reached, and how they were met or not met. The technique was as thorough as the most sophisticated research could make it. It was significant that it was later followed in detail by the President's Commission on Civil Rights when it undertook an expanded study of fifteen cities where major disruptions had occurred.

The center's Six-City Study covered the period through 1966. It brought out some obvious results: the deep grievances rooted in the high levels of black unemployment, the maldistribution of educational opportunities, the housing restrictions that condemned tens of thousands to the degradation of the slums. But the major grievance that emerged with startling clarity was that "no one listens." The report noted that hardship can be endured, but when there is complete indifference on the part of those who should be concerned, the detonation level is dangerously close. The most trivial incident can set it off with consequences to life and limb and property that make a mockery of fancy rhetoric and the platitudes of Christian compassion. In Cleveland the hatreds, fed by humiliation and hopelessness, had been festering for years, but no one listened. There were reassuring phrases uttered, only for action to be put off. Apparently it was always "business as usual." Hence, when a black youth was refused a drink of water by a white man in a Cleveland bar, the arson and pillage and killing that exploded had little relation to the incident that set it off.

Through 1967 the rioting escalated and in many cities raged out of control. The studies at Brandeis were not considered esoteric research. A substantial grant was now assigned by the National Institutes of Mental Health so that the Six-City Study could be expanded to ten cities. The same kind of exhaustive data was now sought in four additional key communities — Birmingham, Nashville, Atlanta, and New Orleans. Out of the data that was gathered the center developed "early alert guidelines," spotting symptoms that could be more readily interpreted as a warning to community leaders that a crisis was dangerously close to catastrophe. The early alert became a community fever thermometer.

Among the most serious problems that contributed to lack of communication was a misreading of the hold the black militants had on their people. Because of their angry, unbridled language and their disruptive action, they were labeled subversives, thugs, terrorists, outlaws. Not only were the white liberals repelled by them, they were also repudiated by the white-oriented black moderates. The Ten-City Study made it clear that they were not to be so easily dismissed. They were folk heroes to their people, who had given up hope that conventional negotiating tactics would ever accomplish anything more than cosmetic changes. Dr. Spiegel and his associates spotted early the ominous significance of their "gladiator response," their determination to make their needs felt and to fight for their solution even if it meant perishing in the attempt. "We are not afraid to die" was their defiant message, and Speigel warned that this was not to be interpreted as grandiloquent rhetoric.

It was therefore considered useful to convene a major conference in May 1967 to which representative militants would be invited, where the issues could be considered candidly, with no preconditions. It was cosponsored by the National Conference on Community Values and Conflict and by the New York Commission on Human Rights. It had the full cooperation of the Department of Justice and it was held in Brotherhood House in New York City. Three hundred participants came from forty cities and they included mayors, white and ghetto civic leaders, social workers, law enforcement officials, and above all, advocates of black nationalism and the proponents of root and branch radicalism.

It was a stormy conference, with confrontations, strident voices, and bitter words. The civil war within groups often surfaced: white liberals assailed by white extremists; black moderates representing the traditional social welfare organizations — the Urban League, the NAACP — denounced by the black militants as obsequious, ineffective Uncle Toms. The issues cut too deeply for any consensus, and the recommendations that were formulated at the end of the conference were excoriated by the militants as the usual liberal phony gobbledygook. One New

Jersey observer remarked cynically that the only thing that resulted from all the luncheons and dinners that dealt with disorders was obesity. Yet the conference was not altogether futile. The impassioned confrontations must have shaken the men and women who commanded a measure of influence. They must have been sufficiently sobered by the experience to realize that new approaches, cutting into new territory in law and education and social welfare, would have to be ventured. Only three or four years had passed since President Johnson had hammered through the landmark Civil Rights bill, but in the light of the volcanic changes that had occurred it now seemed as obsolete as the Emancipation Proclamation. Lawrence Landry, president of ACT of Chicago, warned bluntly that "ghettos are jails and the blacks are determined to break out, with or without the law." In a New Brunswick conference in 1968, Robert Curvin said, "To be black and powerless in American society is to live in a state of rage. . . . And tragically the decisions are being made by neocolonial masters who hide in the suburbs or luxury mainstreet apartments in the city." Ernest Chambers of Omaha flung the challenge directly upon the white establishment: "You are the problem. You have to find out and figure out what you can do to help solve this."

Publicizing the confrontations of the conference was not left to the official report. It was decided to turn them into a documentary film directed by John Marshall, who had already established a reputation for imaginative craftsmanship. He developed a film based on the gut issues of the conference, "You Are Our Problem," jointly sponsored by the Lemberg Center and National Educational Television, which received extensive network coverage.

Meantime, as tensions mounted and disruptions multiplied in many parts of the country through 1967 and well into 1968, there were calls for counsel from harassed and beleaguered officials. Dr. Spiegel and his staff spent a great deal of time away from the campus. They met with the governors of Michigan and Massachusetts and Pennsylvania while cities in these states seethed with violence. They testified at length before Senator Ribicoff's committee on the crisis in the cities and the Senate Judiciary Committee as it considered legislation to cope with the escalating disorders. They were called in by Robert Kennedy and Ramsey Clark as the problems of racial tension reached the offices of the attorney general. They were advisers to the federal Civil Rights Commission and participated in innumerable television and radio panels on violence and crime. The *Riot Data Review*, published by the Lemberg Center, and the special articles analyzing the data on violence commanded the widest distribution.

By 1970 the main work of the center had been incorporated into other national programs. The government had established a series of similar commissions to study violence and to offer recommendations that might cope with it. Some of the foundations were allocating major grants for specific undertakings in cities that had been victims of disruption. Hence the center was gradually phased out. Dr. Spiegel gave more and more of his effort to the Florence Heller School as professor of social psychiatry. He turned to the completion of a number of volumes that had been shunted aside during the years of intense pressure. His time at Brandeis had given him a reputation for scholarship and statesmanship, and soon he was elected president of the American Psychiatric Society.

The six-year operation of the center became a major contribution in a critical period in American life. The problems of racial tension and the militancy they spawned had been studied by well-qualified specialists with laboratory objectivity. Scores of troubled cities had used the resources of the center in their periods of deepest trouble. The University had become a respected clearinghouse for data that was indispensable in order to deal rationally and practically with the problems of urban disruption. Above all, the Lemberg Center served as a model for the utilization of the expertise of a university in rendering service to the country in a time of grave crisis. And since virtually all of the research activities had been funded by foundation or federal grants, the trust that Sam Lemberg had established was still virtually intact. It could now be assigned elsewhere.

XXI

Communications
and Educational Television

WHEN Brandeis came into being in 1948, educational television was still in its infancy, and its impact on the cultural life of American communities was still minimal. There were only a few functioning stations, precariously financed, regarded with suspicion or outright hostility by the commercial networks. But their progress, though slow, could not be retarded. The expansion of interest in adult education, the need for programming above the level decreed by the major networks as acceptable to Main Street America, the enthusiastic cooperation of colleges and universities, museums, symphony orchestras, and other cultural agencies stimulated support. The educational channels began to increase in numbers even as their programming won ever more viewers.

Brandeis was in an ideal position to join in the broader use of educational television. It was young, untrammeled by tradition. It already had a number of eloquent faculty members who were at ease before microphone and camera and eager to be there. From the outset, Brandeis also brought distinguished personalities to the campus, whose messages usually had considerable public interest. Moreover, a near neighbor in Cambridge was WGBH, then and now one of the most imaginative of the educational TV channels. Its support and programming were participated in by most of the universities and cultural agencies of the area, whose representatives sat on the station's advisory council. The founding father of WGBH was Ralph Lowell, scion of one of the oldest New England families, and he early attracted the interest and support of the Ford Foundation, the State Department, and other government agencies. Many of them readily provided seed money for television projects to the universities that were part of the Lowell Broadcasting Council. In addition, there was interest and enthusiasm from such leaders as Edward

R. Murrow and Fred Friendly of CBS and Newton Minow, head of the FCC.

Brandeis therefore gave every encouragement to faculty members who were interested in television as a teaching medium. Max Lerner, whose course *America as a Civilization* had been edited for a volume that became a best-seller, taped his lectures for the educational channels. Equally popular was his *Age of Overkill*. The courses of Robert Koff, who had come to the Music Department of Brandeis from Juilliard, and of Edwin Pettet, who headed the Department of Theater Arts, were widely sought. Pettet's series, *Laughter Is a Funny Business*, in which he collaborated with another member of the Theater Department, John Sommers, won high awards. By 1959, three of the twelve programs adopted by WGBH for national distribution were the work of Brandeis faculty — those of Lerner and Pettet, and an extraordinary series presided over by Eleanor Roosevelt, by then a Brandeis visiting faculty member.

It was an impressive achievement for Brandeis and for educational television to have Mrs. Roosevelt agree to moderate a monthly television program, *Prospects of Mankind*. It was underwritten by a Ford Foundation grant whose managers were well aware of its built-in success factor. The format was that of a colloquium, based on crucial national and international issues, between Mrs. Roosevelt and her guests in the presence of interested Brandeis students. The program was directed by Henry Morgenthau III on behalf of WGBH. The advisory group, which planned the sessions and made recommendations for the participants, included Henry Kissinger of Harvard, who was already serving as the foreign policy adviser for Governor Nelson Rockefeller of New York.

For the next three years, many of the newsmakers of the world were welcomed to Brandeis. Mrs. Roosevelt was meticulous in fulfilling her assignment and she never missed a session. Her "guests," as we regarded them, included Nelson Rockefeller; Ralph Bunche; Adlai Stevenson; Luis Muñoz Marin, governor of Puerto Rico; Krishna Menon, foreign policy adviser for Prime Minister Nehru; Barbara Ward (Lady Jackson), editor of the *London Economist;* John Kenneth Galbraith of Harvard; Julius Nyerere, a young African nationalist, soon the first prime minister of Tanganyika; Erwin D. Canham, editor of the *Christian Science Monitor;* and John Kennedy, senator from Massachusetts. Since even the most unyielding of Kennedy's posthumous detractors admit his political and public relations acumen, it said something for both Mrs. Roosevelt and the *Prospects of Mankind* that Kennedy saw fit to hold a news conference in conjunction with his appearance at Brandeis to announce his availability for the Democratic nomination for President. Another program of 1960 that excited interest discussed the theme of the survival of democracy; the participants were Adlai Stevenson, Henry Kissinger, and the Yugoslav dissident Dedijer, who had just broken with Tito and had fled his homeland. The three years of *Prospects of Mankind*, 1960–1963, represented one of the early high points in national educational television programming, and they enabled the University to render a major service to millions of families. Such programs made it clear that an institute, related to a university, and relying upon its faculty and research techniques, could offer influential guidance to the fast-developing worldwide communications field.

Beginning in 1959, a series of seminars was held to decide what areas such an institute could best undertake and the structure it would require for effective service. Participants included R. Gordon Arneson, director of the U.S. Office of Cultural Exchange; Henry Morgenthau III; Louis Lyons, curator of the Neiman Fellows at Harvard; Henry Kissinger; and Louis Cowan, who had been president of the CBS television network and was on the faculty of the Columbia University School of Journalism.

One of the seminars was built around Edward R. Murrow, the dean of commentators. His immensely popular program *Person to Person* proved that Americans wanted more from the "boob tube" than escapist entertainment. He strongly advised that the projected institute avoid emphasis on broadcasting technology. "Leave techniques to the practitioners," he said. "The objective must be the target and not the missile." It was sound counsel, and when two leaders in New England philanthropy, Alfred and Lester Morse, offered seed money, it was decided to establish the institute, which would concentrate on the programming aspects of educational radio and television. It could make its most significant contribution by sponsoring special research projects and by counseling the directors of communications, especially in the developing countries. Louis Cowan, who had been outstanding in the preliminary exploratory sessions, was now invited to take over the directorship of the institute. During the war he had been a senior official in the Office of War Information, and in 1959 he had been in charge of the communications section of the famed Salzburg Seminars in Austria. As president of CBS, he not only had been exposed to all the reefs and shoals of commercial broadcasting, but he had also established important relationships with government agencies and foundations concerned with communications, so he knew his way around Washington and its complex bureaucracies. He at once brought over Henry Morgenthau from WGBH to serve as his associate.

Within weeks of Cowan's assumption of responsibility, he had negotiated a $130,000 grant from the State Department to conduct a 120-day multinational communications specialists' seminar. The plan was to invite those who were in charge of communications in Asia, Africa, Latin America, and even in the main centers of Europe to spend about four months in the United States, mainly on the Brandeis campus, to familiarize themselves with the uses of radio, television, and other media for policymaking purposes in government and education.

Morgenthau spent many months through 1961 and early 1962 traveling to clarify for governments and broadcasting officials what the institute hoped to provide and to screen the participants. Fourteen countries agreed to send delegates and, in June 1962, thirty-five men and women assembled at Brandeis. They came from Britain, Sweden, Cyprus, and Italy in democratic Europe, and from Poland and Yugoslavia in the Communist bloc. The Africans came from Ghana, Nigeria, Kenya, and Southern Rhodesia; the Asians, from India, Japan, and Singapore.

The only Middle Eastern country represented was Israel. Television had held no charm for Prime Minister Ben-Gurion and his government. Ben-Gurion had, as always, expressed himself with colorful vigor: "We need no idiotic stories on cowboys and Indians while we are surrounded by one hundred million Arabs!" Now more sober evaluation of the problems of administration and cultural integration in a land that drew its Jews from seventy countries and that had more than a million Arabs brought changes in its thinking. The government concluded that Israel had better take fullest advantage of the powerful new medium. So the Israeli officials were among the most eager participants.

Their stay on campus was made extremely comfortable. A magnificent seven-acre estate that included a Tudor-style mansion had recently been donated to the University by the family of Mrs. Babette Gross, a longtime resident of nearby Weston, who was planning to move to California. Themis House, as it was called (after the Greek goddess of law and justice), was set amid beautiful woodland with a small lake. It had eighteen bedrooms, spacious reception and living rooms, a library, two kitchens, two dining halls, and many small studios. The University had accepted the gift to use in the tradition of MIT's Endicott House and Columbia's Arden House, which had been contributed by Averell Harriman. The communications institute was its first large-scale event and it bore out our hope of providing a gracious atmosphere to promote friendliness and encourage compatability.

For the first six weeks participants attended classes, visited neighboring colleges and universities, interviewed specialists and wrestled with required reading. A strong battery of Brandeis faculty gave lectures and led discussions. They included John Roche, chairman of political science; Leonard Levy, dean of the graduate school and constitutional historian; Max Lerner, who not only explored problems of democracy but was able to bring in his own considerable experience with media; and American historian Merrill Peterson. They concentrated on the American experience, its history and politics, social complexities and diplomatic policies. They were reinforced by Henry Kissinger and David McClelland of Harvard, Ithiel de Sola Pool of MIT, James Hagerty, former press aide to President Eisenhower and then vice-president of the National Educational Television and Radio Center, and Theodore Conant of the Ford Foundation. Several sessions of *Prospects of Mankind* were being taped while the institute was in session, which gave the delegates opportunities to confer with Mrs. Roosevelt and her guests. And Commencement, which was scheduled during this time, allowed them to meet the people receiving honorary degrees.

After the sessions at Brandeis, the participants fanned out over the country for two months of observation and study, visiting the main radio and broadcasting stations, newspaper plants, book and magazine offices, public relations firms, colleges, and universities. The participants were given access to whomever and whatever they wished to see and the policies they wished to probe. In all instances the way for the interviews was cleared by State Department officials, who made it clear that the visitors were under the sponsorship of the American government and were guests of Brandeis University.

In scheduling a final fortnight at Brandeis, Cowan and Morgenthau were sensitive to several factors that, when neglected, had vitiated the usefulness of other exchange programs. Not least of these was the need for a "decompression chamber" for easily offended visitors who had become involved in an unusually sensitive program and who required a period of reflection and mature analysis before returning to their homelands. It was realized that at least some of the Africans and Asians would have encountered experiences of prejudice that could poison all the good results that had been achieved. These debriefing sessions were found indispensable for the purposes of both the institute and the sponsoring State Department. Then, as a climax, the participants were routed to Washington for a long, productive session with Newton Minow and his staff at the Federal Communications Commission.

When the program had been completed, perhaps the highest tribute to its effectiveness was the urgent request from the State Department for Brandeis to plan a similar program for the next year, in the fall of 1963. Though the time was shortened to three months, the base of sponsorship was broadened: seventeen of the participants came under the auspices of the State Department, seven came through the Agency for International Development (AID), and two each through the Asia Foundation and the Ford Foundation. This second round involved twenty-eight new participants from twenty-eight countries, some of which had not been previously represented.

There were instances of almost immediate impact in foreign lands. The Japanese were apparently particularly impressed. Television and radio had been expanding sensationally in postwar Japan and had become virtually a way of life. It was therefore arranged, again through the good offices of the State Department and its generous subvention, to have twenty of the leading communications specialists of Japan come to the Brandeis campus for an institute program similar to earlier ones for the more diversified groups. Similarly, the Nigerians carried glowing reports of their experiences to their homeland. They brought back a much deepened respect for the power of radio and television and the determination to make it available for their countrymen. Soon after their return, the University of Ife in West Nigeria, in conjunction with the African American Institute, moved to set up a national school of communications. Staff members from our Morse Communications Center were invited to serve as consultants, and they cooperated fully as West Nigeria launched its program. Television in Israel, too, now received major impetus as the earlier objections were dispelled, and the Brandeis consultants proved invaluable in the planning. Meantime, the United States Information Agency commissioned the institute to make a study of the publications issued by AID that influenced the methodology of the Voice of America. These results of the institute could be documented. There must have been many others, less tangible, but equally decisive, in the development of the new media in education and government.

The State Department also sponsored a special two-week seminar on American politics and economics in the fall of 1964. Fourteen student leaders, from this country and abroad, came for intensive discussions at Brandeis and followed them with visits to the campaign headquarters of political candidates, union meetings, settlement houses, and urban and suburban communities. The second week was spent in New York during one of its hard-fought election campaigns, and on the night of the election, the students visited network and wire service headquarters to watch the American experts tabulating the returns. While at Brandeis, the participants were housed in campus dormitories, each with a student host, and they were invited to observe regular undergraduate extracurricular activities.

One of the most important projects that grew out of the seminars was the conference, subsidized by a $44,000 grant from the Department of Health, Education and Welfare, to appraise the economics of educational television. It was sponsored jointly with the American Academy of Arts and Sciences and the United States Office of Education. A distinguished panel was brought together on campus and at Themis House for a long May weekend in 1963. It was ten years since the first educational television station had gone on the air; now there were eighty, and new ones were being launched almost weekly. There was significant growth also in Britain and Canada, and their representatives joined the seminars, whose sixty participants included broadcast specialists, teachers, business and labor leaders, scientists, government officials, lawyers and foundation heads. There was little time for entertainment; the discussions proceeded all day and evening. Prior to the conference, sixteen background papers had been prepared. Financial data had also been gathered so the participants would be able to deal with practical realities. Among the resource people who gave authoritative guidance were Jerome Bruner, director of the Center for Cognitive Studies at Harvard; Kenneth Cox and Frederick Ford of the FCC; Ralph Burhoe, executive officer of the Academy of Arts and Sciences; Irby Carruth, president of the American Association of School Administrators; Bruce Chalmers of Harvard; Philip Coombs of the Brookings Institution and former assistant secretary of state; Hartford Gunn, director of WGBH; Gerald Holton and Edward Purcell of Harvard; Leonard Levy and Henry Morgenthau of Brandeis; Jerrold Zacharias of MIT; Seth Spaulding, director of research, New Educational Media Branch of the U.S. Office of Education; and John White, president of National Educational Television.

The object was to explore the social objectives of and the community stake in educational television and how high standards and imaginative use would affect costs. There was agreement that educational television had now become a major force in the entire English-speaking world, and that it would inevitably play an increasing role in government and education. The dangers of irresponsible censorship and political manipulation were clear, and the sessions devoted considerable time and thought to these problems. Bruner warned against cramming too much material into instructional programs. Cox and Ford discussed the need for subventions of tax money to sustain and expand the progress of educational TV. Segal reminded the group that "the nonprofit or cultural aspects of ETV programming will not long permit it to set substandard conditions for the personnel." One of the most timely recommendations was that every priority must be given to assure enough channels for educational television. The conference also made clear the urgent need for further exploration and stimulated at least two more national conferences that were held in Washington by the National Education Association. Following the conference, several of the participants met at the Federal Communications Commission in Washington to respond to FCC-proposed criteria for ultrahigh-frequency channel allocations. A volume based on the conference proceedings and recommendations, with updated financial material, was published by the U.S. Office of Education.

Meantime, other significant research projects had been undertaken. In conjunction with the American Academy of Arts and Sciences, a study was made of a typical week of educational television. Such a study was deemed necessary because educational television meant different things to different people. It was controlled locally and its purpose and content varied widely from station to station. About the only thing the eighty-odd stations had in common was the fact that they were noncommercial. It seemed logical, then, in studying them, to bring together in one place information that would detail what all these loosely connected stations were broadcasting. No agency had yet undertaken such a survey.

Every public broadcasting station was monitored in the week of May 21–27, 1961, and the tabulated results indicated that science and technology had now become the most important program material, comprising more than 21 percent. There was a sharp drop to 1.377 percent in programs dealing with religious topics. The news programs, which had been steady fare in the early days of television and had provided sophisticated analysis, had apparently been taken over completely by the well-informed, perceptive commentators on the major commercial networks, for such programs now comprised only .61 percent on educational television.

When the report was published, the demand for it exceeded the Morse Communications Center's expectations. Since the service that it rendered was clearly important, a study of another typical week, this time March 18–24, 1962, was monitored. Requests for the studies continued for many years from educators, broadcasters, government offices, libraries, critics, foundations, businesses, and advertising institutions. Impressed with the studies, National Educational Television asked to cooperate with the Morse Center for a third survey and took the responsibility for the monitoring procedures of the much-increased number of educational stations. A third report, with additional information on station ownership and program sources, was prepared in 1964 to include all the programs that had been monitored in the week of April 19–26.

Still another valuable project was initiated in November 1964 to study crisis decision-making. The actions of the broadcasters in the dramatic hours and days that followed the assassination of President Kennedy the year before were considered indispensable data for such a study. It became clear at the end of one day of coverage that the broadcasters had been undergoing one of the severest tests they had ever faced. The problems were manifold and the decisions were of extreme importance. There seemed to be little question that television and radio were the prime source of news; that the broadcasters were being placed in a series of familiar but new roles, roles that kept shifting during the four days covered, and it was thought that important data could be secured that might have multiple uses in years to come. To be effective, it was essential that no time be lost. The Morse Center worked with Paul Lazarsfeld, Robert Merton, and Herta Herzog of Columbia University in structuring the question guides, the periods to be analyzed, and the methodology. A phalanx of the best-trained sociologist-interviewers was assembled and put into the field to select the taped material that related to the four broadcast days during and after the assassination coverage. The center ultimately gathered nearly half a million words of raw interview material from thirty states and related broadcast materials from England and France. This was made available to the Warren Commission and to scholars from many disciplines. Almost everything in the archives was obtained without cost from the three networks, many stations, and political candidates. A small grant of $5,000 from the Hearst Foundation was all that was needed to cover the supplementary costs for the creation of an archive, now housed in the Brandeis library.

By the end of 1965 the number of educational channels had risen well beyond one hundred; every large city was actively involved. Such progress inevitably stimulated immense interest in developing their most effective use. There was now a government-sponsored Committee on Economic Development, whose research agenda gave high priority to communications problems. It was felt therefore that our own research program in communications had fulfilled its purpose, and the Morse Fund was transferred to become the base for an endowed chair in urban studies.

The four-year record had been gratifying, especially for its service to many of the developing countries. Quite apart from the research results, the cooperation of the State Department, the Department of Health, Education and Welfare, the American Academy of Arts and Sciences, the Ford Foundation, and the participation of national and international celebrities had gained new and influential friendships for the University.

It was during the seminars of the Morse Institute that references were made to the techniques of oral history, then being developed by the distinguished American historian Allen Nevins of Columbia. Under his supervision, interviews had been taped with personalities who had deeply influenced their times. In a twenty-year period, more than three hundred people had participated, discussing their areas of interest, the turning points in their lives, their appraisals of the events and the men and women whom they had come to know. The conversations, especially when guided by skillful interviewers, developed considerable original data to supplement the conventional documentation used in writing history and biography. Some of the interviews had been excerpted to become valuable volumes. One such book, *Frankfurter Speaks,* summarized many hours of interviews with one of the most fascinating members of the Supreme Court, whose long tenure stretched through many presidencies.

But why, it occurred to some of us, could not such a program be amplified by adding a visual dimension, the camera? Then all the lineaments of personality would come into focus more convincingly and significantly, without losing any of the vitality of the conversation; indeed, it would enrich it by the magic of the camera's unerring eye. If only such a technique had been perfected and available for interviews with Woodrow Wilson or Lloyd George or Mahatma Gandhi or Chaim Weizmann, or Justice Brandeis, how much clearer our insights would be in appraising and understanding temperament and motivation. Such considerations sent us into the project we labeled Living Biography. And fortunately a donor was secured to give it full support without encroaching upon the general funds of the University.

The donor was Samuel Dretzin, the head of the World Wide Automobile Corporation. He had participated in many of the major philanthropies of Greater New York and had become deeply interested in educational television and its potential for broader adult education. In 1965 he had given a substantial contribution to the University to experiment with closed-circuit television. This project turned out to be not very practical at Brandeis, so that all the acquired equipment was eventually contributed to the educational station, Channel 56, in Springfield, Massachusetts, in return for which the Filene Foundation assigned special funds for the audiovisual aids in the teaching programs of the University. Dretzin was intrigued by the possibility of improving on the Nevins oral history project and, after several conferences, he agreed to contribute $36,000 annually, for a twenty-year period, to underwrite what became known as the Dretzin Living Biography Program.

At first it was centered at Brandeis itself. Half a dozen audiovisual programs were taped. David Ben-Gurion, past eighty but as vital and ebullient as ever, readily submitted to many hours of interviewing on the Brandeis campus, as he ranged over the great turning points of his dramatic career. The last living disciple of Sigmund Freud, Dr. Grete Bibring, associated with the mental health service of Harvard, discussed Freud as an influence on his students and the significance of the differences that resulted in conflicting schools of thought in psychiatry. General Carlos Romulo, president of the University of the Philippines and later foreign secretary, covered the earlier period of his life, carrying the story through World War II. Dr. David Seegal, an almost forgotten pioneer in the problems of chronic illness and one of the best-loved teachers at Columbia, discussed the obstacles that had to be overcome in coping with the conservatism of the medical profession. These interviews were all deposited in the Brandeis archives for future research. Some have already become invaluable.

During our negotiations for interviewees in the Living Biography series, we sustained one most regrettable disappointment. We had planned to include the president of the Irish Free State, Eamon de Valera. His interview was to be taped in Dublin, and I journeyed there to arrange for it. The old rebel who had led the Irish uprising, now nearly ninety, had never yielded to such requests. But educational television, as a medium to tell his story to the young people of the new world and of the future, apparently intrigued him and he consented. Our preliminary conversations with the almost legendary figure, sharp as ever, brimming with memories of the long struggle for independence and sovereignty, made the discussion an unforgettable experience. Unfortunately, at the last moment, as the taping was to begin, a dangerous attack of bronchitis compelled De Valera's physician to cancel the commitment. It was too risky to place the gallant nonagenarian for many hours under powerful lights. Among our memories was De Valera's wistful envy of his much-admired friend, David Ben-Gurion, "who knew so much about philosophy, including the wisdom of the Orient." I suggested that Ben-Gurion probably envied the extraordinary mathematical genius of De Valera, who would have been a distinguished scientist if the Irish cause had not called him to leadership.

Many other interviews were planned, but it had now become clear that if they were to be more than research data and were to be widely distributed they needed a relationship with a well-established television station to take such responsibility. When the project, fully underwritten, was suggested to WGBH, a partnership was quickly established.

The scope and format of the interviews were immediately transformed. With the consent of the Dretzins, we decided that the University would annually offer an award to an outstanding public figure whose career had beneficently affected our times. The recipient, to be chosen by a distinguished national jury, would also be invited to take part in an extensive interview on television, during which the turning points of a decisive career could be discussed and evaluated.

There was little difficulty in reaching a consensus for the first recipient. The jury, which included educators as well as the program directors of the best in educational television, unanimously agreed it should be offered to Earl Warren, whose sixteen-year incumbency as Chief Justice of the United States decisively altered the course of American life. Justice Warren had never granted a television interview. For that matter, he had never wished to discuss his Court experiences, since what he had to say might become political static during a Nixon presidency. Apparently, however, Warren was satisfied by the pledge of meticulous respect for his position, and he therefore consented to return to campus. I was privileged to conduct the interview.

Justice Warren, then eighty-one, was astonishing in his vitality. He sat under the harsh television lights for hours, relaxed, poised, incisive in his responses, now teasing and bantering, again serious and reflective. I began by asking him about the psychological demands made on him when he was called by President Eisenhower to shift suddenly from the world of politics to that of judicial objectivity. He confessed that his first day on the Court was the loneliest and most difficult of his life. Eisenhower's sudden summons had left him with little time to wind up his eleven-year governorship of California, and none to prepare for the huge backlog of controversial cases waiting for final disposition by the Court. He added that life in the Court compelled immense restraint, for "a justice cannot respond to criticism, he cannot explain anything he does . . . and that's the reason why the courts are so much traduced in this country; they can be so easily used as the whipping boy." I remarked that this must have been hard on Mrs. Warren. He chuckled and revealed that she could not for years abide the signboards on the highways that caterwauled "Impeach Earl Warren," but that she had ultimately learned to smile resignedly.

Soon the discussion turned to the 1954 landmark court decision in *Brown* v. *Board of Education of Topeka.* I asked how he was able to persuade a Court made up of such rugged individualists to reach a unanimous decision. In the Chief Justice's opinion this was no personal accomplishment, and he refused to take credit for it. The arguments in the case had begun in November 1953, and in the justices' weekly review, the members of the Court were encouraged to bring up debatable points. He let the discussion go on informally so that no polarization would take place that would prevent a unanimous judgment. Not until the following February did Warren ask if the justices were ready to vote. He seemed to be saying that the months of reflection had brought each man to his own decision. From this deliberately uncolored assessment, he went on to speak compassionately of several of the justices, who, in their action, refuted Mr. Dooley's famous remark: "The Soopreem Court don't vote, but they follows the Ilection returns." He noted that Hugo Black was not welcomed in his home state of Alabama for many years, that Tom Clark was rejected by East Texans, "and Stanley Reed, the Kentuckian, gentle soul that he is, I know that it was a great strain on him to determine the case as he did. . . ."

I asked, too, for the sake of the historical record, if the phrase "all deliberate speed" had been the creation of the Warren Court and if it had been hard to come by. He explained that the term was a centuries-old term from British Admiralty law, that it had been used by Justice Holmes in *Virginia* v. *West Virginia,* and that it was ideally appropriate here since the Court was looking for "a progression of action. A progression, I may say, with which we still live. . . ."

The visceral conviction of Justice Warren that the American people could be trusted to decide their destiny by basic democratic procedures emerged in his evaluation of *Baker* v. *Carr.* He considered this case, unequivocally, the most important to be decided during his sixteen years on the Court. He called it "the parent case of the one man–one vote doctrine, which guarantees to every American citizen participating in government, an equal value of his vote to that of any other vote that is cast. . . ." The situation had been murky for years, and there had been no way for people to obtain justice in a state that was malapportioned. The Court finally cut the Gordian knot and separated what was political from what was *sub judice.*

Inevitably we came to the presidentially appointed Warren Commission, which examined the circumstances of President Kennedy's assassination. Warren affirmed his resistance to the President's request that he assume the chairmanship of the commission or even join it. He had cited the unfortunate consequences of the involvement of earlier justices in such matters as the Tilden-Hayes election, the Pearl Harbor investigation, and the Nuremburg trials. President Johnson had brushed aside Warren's reluctance. He was oppressed by the fear of a possible nuclear war, since there were ugly rumors afloat that there might have been complicity by Castro and Khrushchev. Warren, scrupulous to a fault, pointed out that there was also a strong group of conspiracy believers who attributed a plot to extreme right-wing Texas oilmen. When Johnson asked him to remember that the request to serve came from the commander in chief, Warren yielded.

The commission, he said, found no evidence to support any conspiratorial theory. He cautioned the television audience to remember that the commission published not only a one-volume condensed report but twenty-six volumes of testimony, which recorded the words of hundreds of witnesses and tracked down every shred of purported evidence. The Justice Department at that time was presided over by Robert Kennedy. The commission had had the fullest cooperation of the CIA, the FBI, and the Secret Service and its resources. Every shade of political opinion was represented on the commission, which also employed fifteen independent lawyers, some of the highest in the profession, including Lee Rankin, former solicitor general. He had, the former Chief Justice averred, kept up with all material published in the intervening years, and not one iota of proven evidence had appeared to challenge the conclusion of the *Report* that Oswald was acting alone. Warren characterized him as a loner, a Dostoevsky nobody, looking for a place in history. In this aberration, he concluded sadly, Oswald was in the tradition of the assassins of Garfield and McKinley and the psychopath who had killed Mayor Cermak of Chicago in the attempt to shoot Franklin Roosevelt.

It so happened that the interview took place on the very day that a volume by the Chief Justice had been published, and I had his copy at hand for the interview. The title, *A Republic, If You Can Keep It*, was based on a riposte of Benjamin Franklin to an elderly lady who waylaid him as he left a meeting of the Continental Congress in 1787: "What kind of a government are we to have?" asked the woman. "A Republic — if you can keep it," replied Franklin. Warren believed the admonition to be even more apposite in our own time, with all the complexities of our society. He noted, "A Republic is not an easy kind of government to keep, because it depends upon the continuous concern of all the people. It is because I believe the responsibility to keep it must be equated with the rights it bestows, that I used Benjamin Franklin's phrase."

On the day after the interview, we held an informal ceremony in the Brandeis three chapels area, where Warren was asked to plant what we hoped would be the first of many maple trees that succeeding Dretzin

Prize winners would plant. The ceremony took place near the Protestant Harlan Chapel. The beaming Chief Justice, his extraordinary record, the chapel site, the remembrance of the elder John Marshall Harlan — all became part of the significance of this first Dretzin award. The Chief Justice further lightened the proceedings by expressing his gratitude for the availability of a left-handed shovel, the only kind he could handle. Privately, he returned the cash award to the University, which was promptly used to purchase several hundred copies of *A Republic, If You Can Keep It* for distribution to the inner family of the University and close friends and associates of the Chief Justice.

Not only was this first Dretzin program aired as a special throughout the public television network; it was often rerun. There was editorial comment by the *New York Times* and other influential newspapers, and the entire transcript was reprinted in the *Law Review Journal*. On the night of Warren's death two years later, it was shown again on network prime time. Once the tradition of the Dretzin Prize had been set with the award to Justice Warren, it was not difficult to persuade other men and women of international stature to follow. The next interview was arranged with Averell Harriman, and negotiations for others were well under way.

Meantime, I had become integrally involved in educational television with a program of my own, and it was to become one of my chief activities when I had completed my incumbency. I had been teaching the course in contemporary affairs, History 36, and Hartford Gunn, Jr., the director of WGBH, suggested that the "classroom" would be substantially extended if the course were put on the air. The temptation to reach an impressively diverse viewing audience was irresistible. I agreed to experiment with a series that would begin chronologically with the period immediately after World War I, and we could then evaluate the reaction. It turned out surprisingly well, and the telecasts grew into five series of thirteen half-hour lectures that involved an ever-increasing number of channels, until the telecasts were being viewed, at different times, on different days, in scores of cities. Often, when the series had been completed, it was scheduled for reruns. I attribute the rapid achievement of such national coverage to a generous three-column review by the *New York Times* television critic Jack Gould, who noted that the series, covering twentieth-century history, "has been one of the past summer's bright spots on Channel 13." Publishers also expressed interest in the telecasts and I agreed to expand them and update them for a volume that was subsequently published by Alfred A. Knopf. It quickly went into three printings, and a paperback edition.

The series were all underwritten either by the stations themselves or by sponsors in the different communities. I would not permit the use of any of the Dretzin funds, or other University funds, for this purpose.

Nor would I permit it to be a professional assignment. My only condition was that it be noted in the credits that I was the chancellor of Brandeis University. My largest and most permanent satisfaction came when colleges in many parts of the country began to use, for classroom credit, the kines and the cassettes that had been created from the master tapes. For example, in a consortium of six San Diego community colleges, *The Course of Our Times* and Bronowski's *Ascent of Man* became the two pilot courses to test the use of television lectures, with faculty surveillance, a paperback text, and a syllabus as a means of bringing exceptional teaching to colleges that could not afford high-salaried, permanent faculty in more than a few of their major courses.

The mail load for me, both from communities where the series was publicly aired and from the colleges where students often took issue with an interpretation, especially after controversial subjects had been raised, hurtled me into an almost full-time correspondence responsibility. But since the substance of the correspondence related to historical problems, I felt that I was back in my teaching days, but to a vastly augmented classroom. I needed little further validation that the University was rendering still another academic service after a handwritten note arrived from Fred Friendly of the National Broadcasting Company to say, "I hear that the series is the best thing on serious television since the days of Ed Murrow."

XXII

Athletics

THE legendary president of a midwestern university who appealed in frustration to the state legislature, "Give us a library worthy of our football team," was not very successful. He did not get a new library: the university got a new president. The apocryphal episode was set in the jaunty days before World War II, when intercollegiate athletics in mammoth stadia drew fifty, sixty, and seventy thousand spectators and dominated university life. Red Grange of Illinois and Benny Friedman of Michigan were better known than any Nobel laureate. The Four Horsemen of the Fighting Irish of Notre Dame were national heroes. In recruiting student athletes every blandishment was held out to build gridiron strength, and the rules that governed amateur athletics were interpreted with such subterfuge that a Philadelphia lawyer would have been immensely impressed. I had Red Grange in my history course and he was a competent student: he probably would have done better than the qualifying C if so much of his waking time had not been spent in football practice. But Frosty Peters, who mistakenly registered for my course, sat like a zombie and, on the insistence of Coach Zuppke, transferred to some more compatible course when the word got through to him that Sachar was a tough grader.

By the time Brandeis was launched, after World War II, the great era of intercollegiate football was beginning to yield to the highly professional competition. The national leagues recruited their best players from the colleges, but their choices were now narrowed to major universities that could afford to field impressive teams. We knew at Brandeis that, while physical education was indispensable, we would have to be quite conservative about the competitive sports we sanctioned for recruitment. Most reluctantly we included football; the decision was based on some very special problems that Brandeis encountered in creating a representative student body. If the University were ultimately to become diversified in its regional, ethnic, and economic character, it could not concentrate exclusively on hard-driving intellectuals who remained encysted among their books and in their laboratories. Persuasive also was the yearning of many of our most generous supporters to make sure that Brandeis, in addition to its intellectual standards and its national service, also projected the traditional American image of college as a center for wholesome physical fitness. To them, modestly organized athletic squads, whose schedules were limited to the smaller schools where intercollegiate athletics did not dominate, could provide not only the intangible asset of "school spirit," but could also give visibility to the pattern Brandeis was anxious to achieve.

A great deal depended on the resourcefulness of the director of athletics. I approached Benny Friedman, the Michigan All-American, whom I remembered with respect from the days when he was the rival of Red Grange. He had since opened a summer camp for boys, had lectured widely on physical fitness, and, since he had avid admirers in every community, he could be a most useful drawing card in our interpretive affairs throughout the country. Our interview took place in the early part of the University's second year, when our student body was still limited to two classes, freshmen and sophomores, numbering approximately 250. Benny was intrigued by the challenge that Brandeis offered as an institution of learning; he was not so sure about its ability to promote a viable program of intercollegiate sports. "How large is the student body?" he asked. "Over two hundred and fifty," I replied bravely. "Does that include girls?" "Of course!" (This with a touch of defiance.) "Do you have an adequate playing field?" "Not yet," I said, but moved quickly into the realm of hope. "I am quite sure that we will acquire one fairly soon after we announce our sports program and can say that Benny Friedman is its director." His look seemed to be equally bewildered and amused. "Do you have a football?" Anyway, he joined the Brandeis family with the understanding that his summers would be as free as those of any of the faculty, so that he could still manage his camp. Fortunately, we had constructed the Shapiro Athletic Center, where Friedman could get under way. It was easy enough for him to organize the program of physical education, despite some trouble with a small group of doctrinaire libertarians who were opposed to compulsory nonacademic activity. Benny got around that hurdle with surprising dialectic skill by reminding his critics that the ancient classical authors had always advocated sound minds in sound bodies. "*Mens sana in corpore sano.*" This was probably all the Latin that Benny knew, but he had it down so pat that the defenders of individual choice beat a hasty retreat.

To create even a freshman football squad in the beginning of our third year challenged all of Benny's resourcefulness. He was given access to the application pool, but the pickings there seemed bleak. He called upon his coaching friends in high school athletics and asked them to cooperate. He traveled widely, especially in the middle western regions he knew best, and interviewed scores of youngsters who had never heard of Brandeis. All the while he kept doggedly after colleges in the area to make room in their freshman schedules for a Brandeis engagement. The goodwill of many of our neighbors was heartwarming. Even Harvard made room, and the schedule that emerged was quite impressive. It was now necessary to meet my promise to acquire a playing field. The land, thirty-six acres just across from the original campus, was available for purchase. In those early days, before the proximity of Brandeis had sent costs through the stratosphere, we could acquire land at $1,000 an acre. We gave the assignment of raising the money to a group of supporters in Memphis. At the interpretive affair there it was understood that whatever was contributed would underwrite the land acquisition. The sum was quickly pledged and the first major acreage augmenting the original campus was designated the Memphis Tract.

Meantime, I was actively seeking friends of the University who might be attracted by our sports program. The donor who was sought was in our own backyard: Frank Gordon, a successful Boston industrialist who was an avid outdoors enthusiast and very much interested in competitive sports. There were two or three Sunday morning breakfasts at his home and the deal was completed for a combination football field and encircling track. The underwriting included the preparation of the field, stands for 7,500 spectators, and even an elevated press box for our budding journalists, our enthusiastic radio broadcasters, and perhaps some of the metropolitan sportswriters who might find occasional human-interest stories in the challenge that the Brandeis Davids offered the widely touted Goliaths.

The season of 1950 opened on one of the Harvard playing fields, and our brave stalwarts faced the Harvard freshmen. We were prepared, down to the pretty cheerleaders, decked out in new blue and white costumes. Thelma and I had been joined by Adolph and Mary Ullman. Ullman was a German immigrant whose major interest was in art and music; he knew nothing about football, but had come because the game represented a first in Brandeis history. He wondered who the little blue and white moppets were who shouted and gesticulated in curious rhythm. I told him that they were there to alert the crowd when to get enthusiastic. Our total student body was now about 400, and apparently most of them had turned out to cheer our warriors on. The older Sachar boys attended the game, too, and since they were both at Harvard — Howard as a graduate student, Edward as a freshman — there was a hard decision to make. Ultimately, they decided to give their support to the underdog. Benny had coached the team with all the intricacies of his Hall of Fame days, and one of the early Brandeis miracles came to pass. Brandeis beat Harvard, 3-0. If a Pulitzer Prize for literature or history had been announced in the next morning's press, it could not have made the impact on our constituency that the Brandeis victory did.

At no time during the next few years could the thrill of the opening game be duplicated, even when the University fielded full-fledged football teams and played against rather formidable rivals. But under Benny's skillful coaching the teams did well, and though no championships were won, the Judges, as the teams were inevitably labeled, gave good accounts of themselves. A basic purpose was also fulfilled as the team lineups were detailed in newspaper summaries. There were Goldfaders and Steins and Shapiros, but there were also Baldaccis and Hemingways and Napolis. The message reached the student bodies of the country and their counselors that, though Brandeis was Jewish-founded, it was not a parochial school.

One ambition that Benny had could not be fulfilled. He tried to make a golfer out of me. He loved the game and played with the power and poise of a champion. He insisted that I could do my work much better if I spent at least two afternoons on the beautiful course of the Pinebrook Country Club, which had given us honorary memberships. Benny spent patient hours to teach me the proper stance, rhythm in my swing, follow-through without taking eyes off the ball, and scores of other techniques that separated the natural golfer from the duffer. Either I did not concentrate on Benny's pointers or my coordination just did not measure up. When I played with some of our trustees, I did not mind my own frustration as the ball invariably landed in the rough or in the traps, but I was disgracing Benny, and I began to look for an excuse to seek other sports outlets. One day when I hit the ball a full 200 yards, but onto the wrong fairway, Benny muttered something that sounded like *Shema Yisroel*, and then added ruefully: "Doctor, maybe you had better stick to education." After that, for exercise, I went back to the long walks from the President's House to the campus, and I took out of my *Vita* that one of my favorite hobbies was golf.

The golden age of Brandeis intercollegiate football lasted only six years. But when it was suspended, the reasons were not those that caused similar actions in hundreds of colleges. It was not the exorbitant cost of recruitment, for Brandeis never bought its players. The furthest it went in recruitment competition was to offer scholarship assistance to those who needed it to afford a college career. The problem for Brandeis arose when applications far exceeded the capacity of a small University to offer enrollment. In the first years, virtually all qualified applicants could be accepted. But after the University received accreditation and its graduates were quickly accepted in professional schools across the country, applications poured in. There was some expansion in the size of freshman classes, but there was a strong determination that Brandeis would not become a mass enrollment school. When only one out of seven or eight fully qualified applicants could be taken, those who were recruited so that they could participate in the intercollegiate football program were at a grave disadvantage academically. They may have been qualified to survive the rigorous standards that Brandeis had set, but it would have been grossly unfair to give them the precious few places and reject better qualified applicants, who were well above them in their testing scores and their high school records. The difficult decision to drop intercollegiate football had to be made and, though it was strenuously resisted by Benny Friedman, by outstanding alumni, and by many loyal supporters of the University, the decision stood.

The suspension of football did not mean the elimination of all intercollegiate sports. There were many outlets for those who had other athletic talents and for the stimulation of school spirit. Brandeis was especially well equipped to sponsor soccer, still too much regarded as basically European to have achieved popularity in American colleges, but growing fast in interest and participation. Many of the Wien students, particularly those from the Scandinavian countries, Greece, Italy, Spain, and many parts of Africa, turned out for soccer and played with surprising power and skill. Even Notre Dame could not boast of such diversity of polysyllabic, tongue-twisting names on its teams. Brandeis was soon regarded as a major soccer center and its games were reported even more frequently than football had been. The 1960 team, trained by a brilliant British coach, Glenn Howells, went through its season as undefeated champions against formidable opponents. The sportswriters of 1961 found it newsworthy to report the Brandeis games when the teams included Dinos Sinioris, Dimitri Procos, and Evangelos Djimopoulos of Greece, James Chen of Jamaica, Anthony Lorraine of Scotland, Faruk Logolu of Turkey, Reno Schiavo-Compo of Italy, Sylvester Awuye of Ghana, Peter Nagy of Hungary, Daniel Obasum of Nigeria, Saha Amanasingham of Ceylon, and Ernest Van der Boogaart of Holland.

Brandeis's surprising supremacy in fencing was basically a tribute to its resourceful coach, Lisel Judge, an Olympic fencing star who brought her skill and her teaching magnetism to the University early in its history. She stimulated interest in fencing's grace and precision and had scores of our men and women consider it their favorite sport. Her squads kept winning regional honors and, in some years, went on to the highest national competition. When I attributed her success to her teaching talent, she modestly demurred and offered an interesting rationale for the University's record. "Fencing," she said, "more so than most other sports, seems to have a special appeal to the intellectually oriented Brandeis student. Not only does it bring to the physical education curriculum a background which is rich and fascinating in historical significance, but it also is a sport of skill and dexterity, demanding the keenest of intellectual acumen for those who master its techniques. It is not a game of brute force — for 'jocks' only." There may have been some validity in her analysis; but that her finesse and her extraordinary patience counted most of all was demonstrated one year when she took charge of a totally blind girl and, by skillfully evoking all the sensory potentials beyond sight, interested her in fencing, and helped to train her for teaching in a school for the blind. No one was more happily surprised than the girl's mother, who remarked with jesting affection, "How could this be? She was such a klotz!"

Basketball was the game where Brandeis could create the largest interest and do extremely well in competition. Many of the high schools in New York with a large Jewish enrollment had won preeminence in the sport. We brought one of their coaches, Harry Stein, to take charge, and his own competence, as well as his influence with former colleagues who were glad to recommend their best prospects to him, gave Brandeis an advantage that it maintained steadily. In 1953 minuscule Brandeis, with a very small pool to draw upon, found a star in Rudy Finderson, an honors student, who racked up 1,700 points in intercollegiate competition and won a place on the New England all-star basketball team. Stein died in early middle age, one of the most deeply loved of all the faculty at Brandeis. The character of the man was beautifully set forth in the memorial tribute by Dean Joseph Kauffman: "He was tolerant of imperfection in skills, but detested mediocrity in character or motivation."

Then, in 1966, Brandeis again reached to the top and recruited K. C. Jones, one of the stars of the Boston Celtics who had helped bring them continuous national professional basketball championships. There was a special significance in his appointment, for it made Brandeis the first college in the country to name a black as the coach of a major sport. Jones's reputation became an important recruiting asset. Both his extraordinary ability and the youngsters whom he persuaded to enroll at Brandeis gave the University a new golden age for a leading intercollegiate sport. Jones remained as head coach for three years; then the call from the University of California could not be denied, and it led directly to a similar appointment at Harvard. K.C. never lost his devotion to Brandeis and the affection was heartily reciprocated.

Though intercollegiate activities had to be continuously deemphasized, there was always an outlet in intramural sports — competition between dormitories, or classes, or specially organized teams. And such sports included not only baseball, basketball, and soccer, but swimming, tennis, track, golf, bowling, and wrestling. There were endless opportunities for the women, too, who took early to most of the regular sports and added others, such as volleyball and archery. A major expansion of opportunity for women's participation came when Mrs. Charles Revson, emulating her husband, the Revlon cosmetics magnate who contributed a million dollars for graduate fellowships in science, set up a special fund to encourage sports for women, not only at Brandeis, but at other colleges in the area.

Brandeis also discovered in the 1960s that it could field superb track teams. The sports world was incredulously agog as records fell right and left. For several years a versatile youngster, Ed Gastonguay, a Dean's List scholar and president of the Catholic Newman Club, headed the track teams, which competed with the best New England colleges. In 1963, he flashed the 880-yard dash in 1:50, won the track meet, and was listed as one of New England's most formidable middle-distance runners.

In 1967, following the appointment of K. C. Jones, the University was fortunate to recruit another stellar head coach, Nick Rodis, a Harvard man who had made athletics his professional career. He had demonstrated his versatility in the major positions he had held in a number of New England universities. Then, for five years he was identified with the Bureau of Educational and Cultural Affairs of the State Department and developed its international athletic programs around the world. From this highly successful post he came to Brandeis, and it was simultaneously announced that he had become president of the United States Collegiate Sports Council. It was comforting, in the last year of my incumbency, to know that a wholesome, sensibly proportioned program in athletics was in good hands.

The major sports patron of Brandeis was the highly popular liquor magnate and racetrack proprietor Joseph Linsey, who had come up the hard way to become one of the major philanthropic leaders of Greater Boston. He led two of the campaigns for the Combined Jewish Philanthropies in one of the blackest and most dangerous periods of the Israeli struggle for survival. He took over the presidency of the Jewish Memorial Hospital, when it had little standing and its financial woes threatened its continuance, and led it to security and a coveted relationship as one of the teaching hospitals of Boston University. His dog track interests brought him into advantageous personal relations with leading figures in the sports world, and they readily consented, when he asked for their cooperation for public programs, to intercede in approaching donors and in placing stories in the press and other media.

Linsey accepted the chairmanship of the Brandeis Athletic Association and joined the Board of Trustees. He quickly demonstrated that, while he interpreted it as his responsibility to encourage and protect the sports activities of the University, its general financial welfare was an even greater concern. He launched the national and regional dinners that interpreted the University to special trade and industry groups, eliciting annual support. He began with liquor, and soon the technique was expanded to food products, shoes and rubber goods, jewelry, cosmetics, discount houses, soft goods, real estate, and banking. At the liquor dinners, held usually in New York, Linsey could produce the most sought-after public figures to serve as guests of honor. Senator John Kennedy, in the year before he won the presidency, greeted the huge audience as old family friends. After all, he bantered, his father belonged to this group, and he was glad to be welcomed back into its fold.

Meantime, Linsey was publicizing the needs of the athletic program and made a major conquest in reaching his friend and colleague Louis Smith, the enterprising owner of the Rockingham Race Track. By the time Linsey had drawn up the bill of particulars for his Brandeis sports ambitions, Smith felt that he had come off fairly cheaply with his gift of more than $300,000. It was most appropriate, in the light of Linsey's undeviating concern for Brandeis, and particularly for its sports program, that when it became impossible to postpone the construction of a swimming pool and its corollary facilities any longer, the campaign should be structured as a tribute to him. We knew that he had many friends in the sports world and in the liquor industry, but we were gratified and astonished by the response to the appeal to help us underwrite the facility that would be known as the Joseph Linsey Sports Center. The effort could scarcely be called a campaign. To begin with, Linsey himself insisted upon contributing more than half the cost. The committees in Boston, New York, and in other areas where Linsey's contacts were most numerous and influential went about their tasks with more determination than they would have in promoting some personal enterprise. The architects and the construction firm were subjected to special prodding, and within less than a year the center was completed, with an Olympic-size pool, saunas, squash courts, lockers, and administrative offices. Students, faculty, and staff would no longer need to journey to the ends of Waltham and rely on the goodwill of the Boys' Club and the other agencies that had offered hospitality during the long wait.

The dedication brought out many colleagues from the industries in which Linsey was a key figure as well as representatives from the philanthropies he had served so well. Lewis Rosenstiel, though in frail health, flew in to pay his tribute. When the announcement was made that unforeseen costs had sent the construction bill about $165,000 beyond the estimate, Rosenstiel's brief speech consisted in asking the various committees to stop their penny-ante appeals; "I shall pick up the tab."

There were animated reunions at the end of each college year when awards were presented to those who had excelled in particular sports. Alumni who had been part of the past battles on the field or the diamond or the court often traveled long distances to recall their younger days and to salute the new generation who were upholding the tradition that they had zealously supported against the "intellectuals" who regularly derogated college athletics or even physical education. They need not have been defensive. Brandeis never aspired to preeminence in sports, but it encouraged participation in them as a wholesome complement to the heavy demands of the curriculum.

XXIII

Valedictory

In November 1967, soon after the beginning of my twentieth year as president, I notified several close friends on our Board of Trustees that I wished to relinquish my office and asked the chairman to begin the procedures that would lead to the selection of a successor. I made it clear that I was at the peak of health and vitality but that, approaching my sixty-ninth year, I believed it was time to assign leadership to a younger man, one who would be a more integral part of the postwar world and its very much changed conceptions about our society and its problems. "New eras," I wrote to the board chairman, "especially in education, call for new techniques; new challenges demand new solutions. The University should now have the reappraisal that new leadership can provide." I hoped that the "changing of the guard" could be effected by the end of the school year, and offered to be of continued service in any way that would not affect the authority of my successor.

I felt that transition in leadership at this stage carried no danger: the ship was safely in port. Its new adventures and destinations could be undertaken with infinitely more confidence than when it was launched nearly twenty years before. Virtually the entire physical plant of eighty buildings — supplied and furnished with the most sophisticated equipment, representing a fully paid or pledged investment of $70 million — had been completed, so that the new president could give much more of his time and energy to the substantive problems of education. An endowment fund had not been stressed, since immediate needs were much more important than the quest for future guaranteed safety. Hence it was not large by the standards of the major universities. But, at $40 million, it was still larger than many very much older institutions. We had no way of knowing what sums had been reserved for us in wills that would mature in later years; smaller bequests were usually not discussed with us by their donors. But when the amounts were substantial, there were often conferences to make sure that what was planned would serve the University to best advantage. In twenty years there had been frequent such conferences, and at the completion of my incumbency we could guess with a measure of realism that about $50 million, intended for diverse purposes, had been written into wills. Indeed, by 1968, 14 percent of the University's income was accounted for by bequests that were already becoming increasingly frequent.

The unique method by which supporting funds were raised by the University offered an additional cushion of safety for the future. Generous donors made pledges that could be paid over a period of time, usually averaging about five years. By 1968, such pledges on our books totaled $63 million, and even if there were an inevitable falloff because of unforeseen contingencies, there must have been at least $50 million that could be counted on as a guarantee. These pledges later became a vital factor in tiding the University over recession and war periods, when the cash flow tapered off, and they were acceptable collateral for even conservative banks when application was made for emergency assistance. The long-term government loans that subsidized the construction of dormitories were payable over a forty-year period, at about 3 percent, and since both interest and amortization were structured to come from student room rentals, this was less a debt than a self-liquidating investment. In summary, the pledges that had been raised over the years for every purpose totaled about $200 million, of which $40 million had gone into endowment, $70 million into plant, and $63 million remained in pledges. About $27 million had been used up to cover the excess of assured income over expenditures over the twenty-year period. We therefore were able not only to end every year in the black, but the pledge balance kept growing steadily. We were a very long way from those early days when Ruggles Smith had to invent the most ingenious excuses to keep persistent creditors at bay.

On the academic side, the reputation of the University no longer was lined with the patronizing sentimentality accorded the prodigy, running breathlessly to keep up with bigger and older brothers. It was now solidly anchored in achievement: accreditation that included twenty-four graduate departments, many of them included among the top twenty in special categories in the American Council on Education evaluations, a Phi Beta Kappa chapter authorized in record time, and admissions of our students in astonishingly disproportionate numbers by the best professional and graduate schools, many with highly coveted fellowships and awards. This record elicited applications for enrollment in such numbers that only a fraction of the qualified who applied could be accepted.

My friends among the trustees were not surprised by my request. I had been discussing such an action, off and on, for several years. They knew how eager I had become to enjoy with Thelma the leisure of travel and to complete several volumes that I had wistfully kept postponing because of the heavy burdens of academic administration and fund-raising. But the trustees were all successful business and professional men, and they urged some kind of continuing relationship that could preserve the "leverage" they insisted was far from exhausted in winning friendships and support for the University. Surely a service formula could be devised that would still, for such creative years as were destined for us, permit whatever travel Thelma and I were planning and make room for the writing that would be my major objective. The new president, inheriting a magnificent legacy, would be completely responsible for the administration of the University. Would I remain on the active list in a specially created post, as chancellor? I would be freed from the tyranny of clock and calendar. My only obligation would be to offer counsel when it was sought and to interpret the University's needs to selected families where I had the advantage of lifetime relationships.

The inducements were irresistible, and when I consented to the arrangement, the chairman formalized it with the prelude that its acceptance by the board represented "the most painful decision in its history. . . . Recognizing fully President Sachar's role in leading Brandeis to its esteemed position in the academic world, and knowing how valuable are the services that he can continue to provide to the University, the Board has voted to elect him as chancellor when his successor is appointed and installed."

The search committee included representatives from every element of the University. Recommendations poured in and there were many interviews, a few in depth. But the choice gravitated very quickly to one of the most gifted men in American Jewish life, Morris Abram, a New York attorney, born and reared in the South, who had been actively identified with many civic and Jewish causes, including the presidency of the American Jewish Committee. He was just turning fifty and was handsome, eloquent, and extremely personable. The decision was not long and drawn out: indeed, it was accelerated because of a deadline that Abram set if he was to be considered. By the end of March 1968, all names for nomination for a vacant United States Senate seat from New York had to be filed, and Abram had expressed interest in the possibility.

When our committee's recommendations had been informally circulated and approved, Abram withdrew from the political race in New York and was invited to meet all of the trustees. There was only one misgiving, but it was vague and at the time seemed quite irrelevant. When it was voiced at the trustees' get-acquainted session by Jack Hiatt (who later became board chairman), it was more for the record than for assurance. Addressing Abram, Hiatt said, "You have a major senior position with one of the best law firms in the country. In every respect — prestige, influence, emoluments, creative service — your opportunities are virtually limitless. Why would you be willing to change all of this for a college presidency where, despite all that has been accomplished, there is still so much to do that represents tough slogging?" Abram's reply was reassuring. "The Brandeis post," he said, "is not just another college presidency. For years it has been my ambition that I might some day deserve consideration for it. When I come in, only one call would offer the temptation to leave, a seat on the Supreme Court, and this is so remote as to be fantasy. I have indeed toyed with the idea of making myself available for the Democratic nomination for a Senate seat, representing New York. But there are one hundred senators. There is only one president of Brandeis, and I pledge that my commitment to its service is basic and permanent."

The trustees were deeply impressed and Abram's formal election to the presidency, to take effect at the opening of the next college year, was enthusiastically unanimous. He was to begin working by my side during the final months of the school year, and I would use the summer to clear up unfinished business and to offer such transitional briefing as would be requested.

I was not to be let off easily, however. All my sins in having urged others to lend themselves to fund-raising testimonials now came back to demand expiation. Two years before, a vicennial campaign had been undertaken for $20 million, and it was now well past the halfway mark. Why not now wind up that effort by offering a salute to the retiring president, fulfilling objectives that had always been a priority for him? Five million dollars raised as a tribute fund would permit the acquisition of expanded acreage to protect the future expansion of the University; it would make possible the construction of a center to house all the international programs; and it would establish a special fellowship fund to supplement the Wien program. It was an ambitious package, but the committee insisted that probably no project could more successfully climax the vicennial than one that linked it with a tribute fund to the retiring president.

As it happened, just about the time I had asked to be relieved, we had learned that twenty-seven acres directly opposite the entrance to the campus were available for purchase. Only seven acres were occupied by the plant of Judson Thompson, a manufacturing firm that had suffered severe reverses and had sold out to the Rockefeller interests. Larry Wien enjoyed an intimate friendship with David Rockefeller, and was informed by him that the purchasing combine, IBEC, planned to close the plant and transfer its operations elsewhere. Wien began negotiations for the University to take over the IBEC investment, plant and acreage, at a purchase price of $2.32 million. We realized the catastrophic impact on the Waltham community if the plant, which had more than two hundred employees, were closed. Our proposal was to sublease the plant so that its operations could continue: we would still have available twenty unencumbered acres for future needs. The land would probably not be used for centuries, but it would be comforting to know that the front of the campus, down to the Charles River, would not be hemmed in by future industrial or commercial developments. All the negotiations were successfully completed, and we were given about a year to raise the necessary funds.

Our 1968 annual Palm Beach affair was only a few months away. Wien suggested that there could be no more productive way to begin our testimonial than by raising the money for the purchase in Palm Beach and to name it the Sachar part of the campus. I was eager to cooperate in the fund-raising venture, but I would have none of the suggestion for a personal designation for the newly acquired acreage. There was but one campus; there must always be but one. I closed this part of the discussion before it went any further.

Wien then prepared to approach the Palm Beach group with an ingenious adaptation of his syndication technique. He divided up the goal into one hundred units of $23,000 each, with the understanding that a pledge could be paid out over a period of years. There would be no restriction on the number of units that a benefactor could take. And, for those to whom a unit was beyond philanthropic capacity at the moment, parts of a unit would also be available. How better demonstrate to the president that his virtual obsession with land to protect the future of the University was fully understood and respected?

There were about two hundred men and women at the Palm Beach luncheon in February 1968. Larry Wien explained his program quietly and with affectionate references to my role as the first president. Probably few who were there had ever had the experience that followed his presentation. He himself subscribed ten units, and his example triggered other pledges for multiple units. Half the goal was reached in the first few minutes; the other part of the objective took nearly fifteen minutes longer. At one point there were more than thirty hands waving at the chairman, signaling the desire to get in on the commitment to units before they were all gone. Some of the purchasers must have thought that they were at an art auction at Parke-Bernet or Sotheby's. At the end, one had the feeling that bargains had been gobbled up!

All through the rest of 1968, the campaign for the other parts of the tribute program was continued and fulfilled. There had been some thought to try to underwrite an auditorium, but the idea was quickly abandoned when objections were raised that such a facility, while useful on great public occasions, would probably be used infrequently. An international center in daily use, administratively and academically, had infinitely greater functional appeal. I should add that the proposal for an international center was not made only in deference to my request. I was proud that it was to be a tribute gift that would carry Thelma's name and mine, but it had been an integral part of our physical master plan for many years. In my file was a memorandum of January 1958, sent to me by the dean of students, Joseph Kauffman, who later became president of Rhode Island College, and by Lawrence Fuchs, of the Department of American Civilization, strongly urging that we interest a donor in such a center. "Our suggestion," the memorandum read, "is that we create an International Center rather than an International House — a center for browsing, music, lectures, some classrooms, art, and the like. The International Center would be a functional symbol of the international idea without its major role being one of housing." I heartily supported the concept then and had looked forward to the day when it could be established. Now the fulfillment was to come, considerably modified, to be sure, but in essence embodying the functions we had hoped for it.

The tribute campaign was sufficiently successful also to establish the planned fellowship fund, with a pledged capital of approximately three-quarters of a million dollars. I suggested that its income be supplemented each year by invasions of the capital so that more fellowships and travel support could be available. The total fund would therefore probably be exhausted in about fifteen years, but by then there would surely be other resources to carry out the objectives that would then warrant priority. A faculty committee administered the fund, and in the first years that followed my retirement, scores of students and faculty were enabled to include periods of study and research abroad.

Despite the many manifestations of respect and affection, I approached with some trepidation the 1968 Commencement weekend, which was dedicated to the transition in leadership. By the late spring, campus protests against American foreign policies in Southeast Asia and the ongoing struggle for civil rights, culminating in the assassinations of Martin Luther King and Robert Kennedy, had spread from Berkeley and San Francisco State to many other universities, including such Ivy League citadels as Columbia. The anger and frustration that were at first directed against the government swept on to threaten all visible symbols of authority.

Brandeis had been largely spared the uglier incidents, but not because our students were less concerned or involved in what Justice Holmes had called "the actions and passions" of our times. Rather it was because the majority believed in following the tradition of free discussion and free access to all points of view, and they had always received full cooperation from the administration in their efforts to make their views felt. But the climate of student life was changing at Brandeis, too, during my last year, and the summer of 1968 was an emotionally combustible period in which no one could predict what would happen.

My misgivings began to dissipate when the president of the Student Council came to my office at the opening of the weekend, bringing with him a generously inscribed silver platter, which he presented on behalf of the student body, conveying their respect and high regard for a long and productive incumbency. I was cautious enough not to inquire by what kind of vote the gift had been authorized or how the contributions toward its cost had been achieved. I remembered the experience of a trade union leader who was going through a long illness and who received a telegram which indicated that the union executive council wished him a speedy recovery and that this sentiment had been passed by a vote of 71 to 69. We cherished, too, the farewell statement in the yearbook. Under the photograph of my welcome to my successor, the senior editors wrote: "Despite unavoidable growing pains, the meteoric growth of Brandeis is unrivaled in American education. . . . As the Senior Class leaves Brandeis for places unknown, we are happy to know that Abram Sachar is staying." On Commencement Day itself, the student speaker, though he followed the tradition that had become routine by blasting our social system, announced that the senior class had gathered a tribute fund that would be set up for scholarships in Thelma's name and mine. Apparently I need not have worried about the spirit of the class which welcomed me into the ranks of the alumni.

The degree list for the Commencement would have done honor to any great university. This time there was no special theme to link it to some aspect of public affairs, since it was intended as a windup for my own presidency. I was graduating with the seniors, so I was to give the valedictory address.

The roster included two of our most distinguished trustees and deeply cherished personal friends, Senator William Benton, the nemesis of Senator McCarthy, and Jack Poses, a trusted adviser throughout my incumbency, who had built a great cosmetics empire and then used its proceeds to make significant contributions to art and education. We included Dr. Grete Bibring, who, having fled to America from Hitler's Austria, had organized a nationally famous psychiatric workshop and had crowned her career as the first woman clinical professor at the Harvard Medical School. She sat on the Commencement platform with Wilbur Cohen, secretary of HEW, who had served under five presidents of the United States and, as father of Medicare and Medicaid, had led the country from its days of rugged individualism to government responsibility for the social welfare of its needy millions. It was also most appropriate to invite Judge Henry Friendly, one of Justice Brandeis's law clerks, whose record in Harvard Law School had surpassed that of his mentor, a record that had stood unchallenged since the law school was founded.

There were also tributes to four educators who were, in their separate ways, attempting to structure their institutional programs to cope with the alienation of the new generation of restless youngsters. There was Asa Knowles, the pragmatic president of Northeastern University in Boston; William Saltonstall, president of the Massachusetts Board of

Education and former principal of Exeter Academy; and Sister Jacqueline Grennan, the vivacious young president of Webster College in Webster Grove, Missouri, who was later released from her canonical vows as a nun to go on to a brilliant career as president of Hunter College in New York.

When our fourth college president, Edward Levi, came to the lectern to receive his degree, the tribute was going to one of the ablest educators in the country. As the longtime provost of the University of Chicago, he had been virtually the administrator of the university in all but title. Now, in the fall of the year, he was to become president officially. Jews had occasionally been chosen as college presidents during the past generation, but such choices were limited to small and comparatively insignificant schools, none of them with the standing of Chicago.

The Commencement was to have been made even more illustrious by the presence of Walter Lippmann, who, for more than half a century, had been commenting on world affairs with such wisdom and prescience that he helped influence American global policies as if he had been holding highest office. Unfortunately, he was now ailing and his physician, fearful of any new risks, forbade him to make the trip to our campus. For only the second time in our history the degree was conferred in absentia (the first exception having been made when the saintly Rabbi Leo Baeck died on the eve of the Commencement that was to honor his defiance of the Nazis).

We welcomed the Israeli ambassador to the United States, Yitzchak Rabin, who was later to succeed Golda Meir as prime minister. Rabin was the son of Americans who had settled in Palestine when it was still under British control. Essentially a man of peace, trained for diplomacy, he had won decisive military victories in each of Israel's wars and, in 1967, had been the chief of staff who planned the campaign that won him the rare accolade Architect of Victory. The citation was both tribute and hope as it read: "Eschewing the soldier's role, preferring to seek peace and pursue it, he suggested that the lightning triumph be named the Six-Day War, paralleling the span of Creation, hopeful that the Sabbath of reconciliation would follow."

After I conferred the degrees on our guests and returned to my seat, the chairman of the board came forward to bring me back to the lectern to receive my honorary degree. When the entire audience rose I was quite moved, for I knew full well that on that very day scores of college presidents were being hounded from their positions in what appeared to be virtually a national revolt against the university establishment. James Reston had gibed that the boys were no longer chasing girls: they were chasing college presidents.

Yet I had to begin my valedictory address in sorrow. I was talking to a class that came to us out of the raw wound left by the assassination of President Kennedy, a class that had tried to carry on its studies during the violent explosions and revolutions on every continent, that had witnessed the civil rights battles in their own country, with the wanton murder of many of its leaders and participants. The spirit of hatred, vengeance, and frustration was abroad in the land. It recalled Horace Walpole's judgment on another turbulent age: "The world is a comedy to those who think, a tragedy to those who feel." This was no time to use a valedictory as a review of the founding years of our university. I spoke instead of the travail of this generation, "children of the dusk," as the Hebrew poet Bialik had designated those who had to live their lives in interregnums, between a world that was passing and a world that was a-borning. I expressed the hope that the understandable mood of disillusionment and defeatism would not harden into a permanent philosophy of repudiation and despair, calling for a root-and-branch destruction of what was all too glibly called a sick society.

"I am honestly convinced," I said,

> that the crises which dislocate and disrupt the world are not the crises of disintegration. This is no Spenglerian apocalypse. The crises come because we are in the midst of the greatest and most promising revolution in human history. They come from the release of hope in once darkened continents, so long chained by the old slaveries of ignorance, poverty and desperation. They come because hundreds of millions of people are reaching for the sun at last. They come because in every part of the world colonialism is being routed and, in our own country, the millions who had for so long been submerged and humiliated, are on their way up to dignity and opportunity. . . .
>
> How can we expect such cataclysmic changes as are now going on all over the world to occur without disturbance? An old order does not quietly fold its tent and steal away. When revolutions come they inevitably tear into the valuable, the precious, and the sanctified, as well as into the obsolete. What is astonishing then is not that there is so much violence, but that there is so *little*. . . . On what is my valedictory Commencement, I would emphasize that however deep the sense of frustration in this sorrowful hour, you must get off the mourner's bench, you must not cloak yourself in the mantle of a wailing Cassandra. You are participants in a great revolution — indeed you are at the very heart of it — and the pains of birth must not be confused with the agonies of death.

The end of August fell on one of the most beautiful days of the New England summer. All my books and personal papers had been transferred either to my home or to the small suite in the Faculty Center that

I would occupy as an office until the international center had been completed and the chancellor's wing had become available. I had not gone through formal good-byes with anyone because I was not really leaving Brandeis. I expected to be seeing and occasionally conferring with the personnel that remained in the administration center. The working day was over and the hum in all the offices had died out. I stood at the window of the president's office in the Irving Enclave, which had been the center of all the planning and the action of the last decade. The copper beech on the far side of South Street overlooking the playing fields had grown, I thought fancifully, into a noble tree in all too short a time.

So much came back — in a jumble to be sure — of our days of festival: the summer morning that our usually elegantly groomed director of special events spent, in hip boots, looking in the campus dump for the two-by-four card on which the aged Lord Beveridge had written his remarks — and finding it; Kermit Morrissey, as University marshal, striding around the corridors reciting the more complicated names of graduating students; the baccalaureate processions winding ahead of me over the green field to the chapels' area, where the iris stood sentinel and a young family of mallards always quacked garrulously through the ceremonies; the time the students declared Gentle Thursday and tied balloons to the hand of Justice Brandeis's statue — and the morning I requested someone to remove the pumpkin sitting on his head; the Nobel laureate who dozed off during someone's very long speech and was propped up discreetly on either side by equally distinguished colleagues; Adlai Stevenson's name being called and the appearance on the platform of Cholmondley, a badly overstuffed sausage of a dog belonging to Ralph Norman, our school photographer, Cholmondley amiably walking across the stage and positioning himself gravely beside Stevenson; Mordecai Kaplan, eighty years old at one of our later Commencements, processing companionably solemn with the other honorees, having declined use of the golf cart; back through other great days to the first graduation in 1952, held during the frustrations of the Korean War, when Eleanor Roosevelt, the Commencement speaker, gently heard out graduate Gus Ranis's gloomy valedictory, put aside her written speech, and spoke with youthful determination of the unsinewing effects of playing it safe.

Other vivid remembrances: Marianne Moore in her tricornered hat, coming to read poetry of a spring evening; the philodendron or aspidistra or whatever it was in my secretaries' precincts, which could not be discouraged from growing along the ceiling even after it was festooned with toy monkeys; and the day Jim Armsey came on a site visit for the Ford Foundation when all the administration center staff, including the youngsters in the basement purchasing office, wore their very best clothes; the Arab Israeli Sughi, in the first Wien class, presenting me with an elaborately headed cane that had been in his Abu-Gosh family for generations and that I hung in my office under a portrait of Ben-Gurion; the night at Education S when Norman Thomas prophesied that if international action to contain the nuclear bomb were not soon achieved, no one in his youthful audience would live out a normal life span; the affectionately barbed salute in one of our student yearbooks to the college dining hall menu: "The fire of Norman's culinary concoctions will burn in our hearts forever"; the ever-faithful Ted Conrad, our custodian for so many years, who always came early on Commencement Sundays to predict the weather for me, Ted who had fished the Grand Banks in his Maritime Province boyhood; the alumnus who had been an especially angry malcontent in his student days returning for a fifteenth reunion, after many chastening experiences in a world where action supersedes rhetoric, moving up to the dais shyly after the dinner, shaking hands quickly, saying only "Thank you," and fleeing; and all the colored hoods that represented more than twenty honorary degrees from colleges around the country, and the three that meant most to me — from Washington University, where I had spent my undergraduate days, from Illinois, where I had taught in my middle years, and from Brandeis, where I had garnered a third harvest; and some of our alumni and staff members who were now in college presidential positions, some of whom as students or faculty had been pretty thorny problems, causing me to wonder how they felt and acted when they sat on the other side of the table.

Winter, and my reliance on the snowplow and its driver, Walter Mahoney, who doubled as groundsman and baseball coach; and Abraham Goodman, merchant, driving and trudging through a vicious storm to keep an appointment to tell me that he and Etta had decided to endow a chair in full; the morning when Joanna and David presented Thelma and me with our first grandson and no work got done because everyone had a favorite name to suggest; the Japanese landscape in motion of students wending uphill through the snow, and the mysterious girl on the unicycle who never fell off; the squirrels and wild rabbits in the president's office garden, who got handouts against all advice; the faculty and winter "revue" — "We wish you a Merry Gryzmish, we wish you a Merry Gryzmish . . ." and the arresting note on the Goldfarb Library bulletin board: "God is dead" — Nietzsche, footnoted by "Nietzsche is dead" — God; and further back, when we all walked webfooted on treacherous duckboards between the Scylla of the snowbank and the Charybdis of muddy ditch to get from one half-finished facility to the other, and hardly anyone really grumbled.

Above all, the autumns, when year after year the change of season flung a Joseph's coat over the campus; the annual wonder of the freshman class lining up to board the buses to go to the President's House for the get-acquainted tea; the faculty receptions at our home beginning with the thirteen in the first year, the entire group and their wives greeted in the living room, winding up with hundreds after twenty years, under the huge, gaily decorated tent on the two-acre lawn, and the children of our neighbors, lined up outside until Thelma beckoned them to come in to dispose of the delicacies that the diet-conscious guests had reluctantly waived; the beautiful weather that fell for Rosh Hashonah and Yom Kippur, and the yearly elaborate booth the more traditional Jewish students built for Succoth; all the autumns back to that first October morning of my inauguration in Symphony Hall, when my father, once a poor immigrant from Lithuania who had made possible everything good that came to his family in this country, was unable to attend the greatest triumph of his courage and perseverance because he lay dying in a St. Louis hospital, waiting only for word that his son was now officially inducted as president of the university that made the American Jewish community a host at last.

Index